MANAGEMENT EFFECTIVENESS:

DEVELOPING LEADERSHIP SKILLS

Robert N. Lussier, Ph.D. and Christopher F. Achua, D.B.A.

THOMSON
LEARNING™

Australia • Canada • Mexico • Singapore • Spain • United Kingdom • United States

Management Effectiveness: Developing Leadership Skills by Robert N. Lussier, Ph.D. and Christopher F. Achua, D.B.A.

First trade edition, 2001

Printed in the United States of America
1 2 3 4 03 02 01 00

For more information contact South-Western College Publishing, 5101 Madison Road, Cincinnati, Ohio, 45227. Or you can visit our Internet site at http://www.swcollege.com

For permission to use material from this text or product contact us by:
• telephone: 1-800-730-2214
• fax: 1-800-730-2215
• web: http://www.thomsonrights.com

Library of Congress Cataloging-in-Publication Data
Lussier, Robert N.
   Leadership: theory, application, skill building / Robert N. Lussier, Christopher F. Achua
      p. cm.
   Includes bibliographical references and index.
   ISBN 0-324-07474-3
      1. Leadership. 2. Teams in the workplace. I. Title.

HD57.7 .L87 2000
658.4'092—dc21

This book is printed on acid-free paper.

Dedication

To my wife Marie and our six children: Jesse, Justin, Danielle, Nicole, Brian, and Renee

Robert N. Lussier

To my mother, Theresia Sirri Achua, for whom I am eternally grateful; and to my children—Justin, Brooke, Jordan, Cullen, and Valery—to whom I owe so much. I love you all and treasure the blessings of being your father and friend.

Christopher F. Achua

Contents

Preface

GOALS AND OVERVIEW OF COMPETITIVE ADVANTAGES

The overarching goal of this book is reflected in its subtitle: developing the theory, application and skills of leadership. We wrote this book to teach leadership theory and concepts, to improve the reader's ability to apply the theory through critical thinking, and to develop leadership skills. Following are our related goals in writing this book:

- To be the only traditional leadership book to incorporate the three-pronged approach. We make a clear distinction between coverage of theory concepts, their application, and the development of skills based on the concepts.

- To make it the most "how-to" leadership book on the market. We offer behavior models with step-by-step guidelines to handling various leadership functions, such as how to set objectives, give praise and instructions, coach followers, resolve conflicts, and negotiate.

- To offer the best coverage of traditional leadership theories, by presenting the theories and research findings without getting bogged down in too much detail.

- To create a variety of high-quality application material using the concepts to develop critical thinking skills; there are six different types of applications.

- To offer behavior-modeling leadership skills training.

- To suggest self-assessment materials that are well integrated and illustrate the important concepts discussed in the text. Readers begin by determining their personality profile in Chapter 2 and then assess how their personality affects their leadership potential in the remaining chapters.

SPECIFIC COMPETITIVE ADVANTAGE—

Three-Pronged Approach

As the title of this book implies, we provide a balanced, three-pronged approach:

- A clear understanding of the traditional theories and concepts of leadership as well as of the most recently developed leadership philosophies

- Application of leadership concepts through critical thinking
- Development of leadership skills

Theory

Leadership Theories, Research and References, and Writing Style. The book has been written to provide the best coverage of the traditional leadership theories, presenting the theories and research findings clearly without being bogged down in too much detail. The book is very heavily referenced with classic and current citations, and all appear at the end of the book as endnotes. Unlike the books of some competitors, this book does not use in-text citations, to avoid distracting the reader and adding unnecessary length to the text chapters. Readers can refer to the endnotes for the complete citation of any sources they want to learn more about. Thus, the book includes all the traditional leadership topics, yet we believe it is written in a livelier, more conversational manner than that of our competitors.

The following is provided to support the first step in the three-pronged approach—theory.

Step-by-Step Behavior Models. In addition to traditional theories of leadership, the text includes behavior models: how-to-steps for handling day-to-day leadership functions, such as how to set objectives, give praise, coach, resolve conflicts, delegate, and negotiate. There are also models to determine the appropriate leadership style in a given situation based on the capability level of the followers (contingency leadership), the development stage of the group (contingency group leadership), and the level of participation to use in decision making (contingency leadership decision making).

Application

The second prong of our book is to have readers apply the leadership theories and concepts to develop critical thinking skills. Readers can develop their application skills by using the following features.

Opening Case. Each chapter begins by introducing a manager and the organization he or she leads. Our unique feature is that we discuss the case as it applies to the leader and organization throughout the chapter, so that readers can follow how a specific leader and organization use the text theories and concepts on the job. Organizational websites are provided so that readers can get updated information about firms with Internet addresses.

Applying the Concept. Every chapter contains a series of "Applying the Concept" boxes that require readers—in a specific, short example—to determine the leadership concept being illustrated. Answers appear in the Appendix.

Skill Development

The difference between learning about leadership and learning to be a leader is the acquisition of skills, our third prong. This text focuses on skill development so readers can use the leadership theories and concepts they learn to improve their personal and professional lives.

Self-Assessment Exercises. Included within each chapter, and as part of several Skill-Building Exercises, are Self-Assessment Exercises. Readers will use these exercises to gain personal knowledge about themselves. All information for completing and scoring the assessments is contained within the text. Readers determine their personality profile in Chapter 2 and then assess how their personality affects their leadership in the remaining chapters. Self-knowledge leads readers to an understanding of how they can and will operate as leaders. Although they do not develop a specific skill, self-assessment exercises serve as a foundation for skill development.

SUMMARY OF KEY INNOVATIONS

- The three-pronged approach (theory, application, skill development) in the text.
- Unique skill-building materials that develop leadership skills for use in personal and professional lives
- Use of the Internet to provide additional cutting edge leadership information
- Flexibility—use any or all of the features that work for you

---

Applying the Concept 1-1

Leadership Managerial Roles

Identify each of the 15 behaviors by its leadership role. Write the appropriate letter in the blank before each item.

Interpersonal roles
a. figurehead
b. leader
c. liaison

Informational roles
d. monitor
e. disseminator
f. spokesperson

Decisional roles
f. entrepreneur
h. disturbance-handler
i. resource-allocator
j. negotiator

_____ **1.** The leader is talking with two employees who were verbally fighting and refuse to work together.

_____ **2.** The leader is holding a meeting with his followers to discuss a new company policy.

_____ **3.** The production leader is talking to a maintenance person about fixing a machine.

_____ **4.** The leader is conducting a job interview.

_____ **5.** The sales leader is signing an expense reimbursement form for a sales representative.

_____ **6.** The leader is holding a press conference with a local newspaper reporter.

_____ **7.** The leader is assigning followers to various accounts and giving them the files.

_____ **8.** A follower is asking the leader for a raise.

_____ **9.** The leader is presenting organizational pins to

employees for five years of service during a special meeting of all organizational unit members.

_____ **10.** The leader is reading the daily e-mail.

_____ **11.** The leader and his manager, who must authorize the funding of the project, are discussing having new customized software developed for the leader's department.

_____ **12.** The leader is disciplining a follower for being late again.

_____ **13.** The leader is visiting another organizational unit to watch how it processes work orders.

_____ **14.** The leader of a stock brokerage branch is trying to get the telephones turned back on so brokers can use the phone.

_____ **15.** The leader is having new customized software developed for the organizational unit.

ACKNOWLEDGMENTS

I dedicate my first acknowledgment for this book to Judi Neal, University of New Haven, because of her influence on my work and this leadership book. Judi indirectly influenced my use of the three-pronged approach by making me aware of an article in the *Journal of Management Education*[1] comparing my *Human Relations in Organizations: Applications and Skill Building*[2] to other skills books. Author John Bigelow gave it a top rating for a general OB course in "Managerial Skills Texts: How Do They Stack Up." I got the three-prong idea by reading John's article suggestions for improving skills training books (thanks, John). The three-pronged approach has been used successfully in the new fourth edition, and in my current book, *Management Fundamentals: Concepts, Applications, and Skill Development*, also with South-Western, copyright 2000. The three levels of analysis framework for this book was Judi's idea. Judi introduced me to using the MG website as a supplement to the book, and I thank her for introducing me to Tom Brown, its editor (who gets his own thanks). I'm deeply honored that she wrote Appendix A, "Spirituality in the Workplace."

I thank Tom Brown for reviewing and giving his input about using the MG website in Appendix B, and for creating a seamless integration between the book and website. I'm amazed at how he continues to add cutting-edge leadership material from the leaders in the field month after month. My students, who use the MG website, also thank him.

Justin Lussier also desires credit for reviewing Appendix B, "Basic Information about the Internet and Its Software."

I also want to thank my mentor and co-author of many publications, Joel Corman, for his advice and encouragement during and after my graduate education at Suffolk University.

I hope everyone who uses this text enjoys teaching from these materials as I do.

Robert N. Lussier
Springfield College

My very first acknowledgment is to my co-author, Bob Lussier. His friendship and mentoring have been a blessing and a heartwarming experience. He is my inspiration; I am forever indebted to him for giving me the opportunity to work together in writing this book. Second, I would like to thank my professor in graduate school, Dr. H. Igor Ansoff, for his masterful skills at imparting his pioneering theories in strategic management and leadership during the three years I spent with him. His multidisciplinary approach both to theory and to the practical tools that help organizations succeed in turbulent environments is evident in the three-pronged approach we have taken in writing this book.

Deep gratitude is expressed to Linda Meade for her ability to focus on the typing and revision of chapters on a timely basis and for work beyond the call of duty. Recognition and thanks also go to my colleagues here at the University of Virginia's College at Wise, and to friends and family members who have always been there for me.

Finally, Bob and I would like to acknowledge the superb assistance we received from our editorial team. The guidance, support, and professionalism of John Szilagyi (executive editor), Deanna Quinn (production editor), Christianne Thillen (copy editor), and last but most important, Theresa Curtis (developmental editor) were invaluable to the completion of this project. We sincerely acknowledge the reviewers who provided feedback that greatly improved the quality of this book in many areas.

Christopher F. Achua
The University of Virginia's College at Wise

REVIEWERS

Max E. Douglas	Indiana State University, Terre Haute
Charles N. Toftoy	George Washington University
Ethlyn A. Williams	University of Colorado, Colorado Springs
Christine Nelson	University of Phoenix
Kenneth A. Bates	Houghton College
Nell Hartley	Robert Morris College
Ron Stone	Keller Graduate School of Management
Avis Johnson	University of Akron

I

Individuals as Leaders

1 Who Is a Leader?

Jack Welch, Chief Executive Officer (CEO) of General Electric (GE) since 1981, has been consistently rated by his peers as the most respected CEO. A major reason others say they admire Jack is for his commitment and ability to develop leaders. He is acknowledged around the world for his innovative management ideas. As Jack has said, "We have made leadership development the most important element in our work. We focus on some aspect of it every day. My most important job is to choose and develop business leaders." Steve Kerr, VP for Corporate Leadership, says, "Jack loves being around people. He loves to stretch them and make them grow." Proof of Jack's ability to develop leaders is based on the fact that more ex-GE executives have gone on to become CEO's of other major companies than from any other company. Jack Welch has been given much of the credit for GE's success.[1] Through Jack's leadership, GE has achieved one earnings record after another. GE has consistently been ranked among the most admired companies by *Fortune Magazine*—it took first place back-to-back in 1998 and 1999—and by *Financial Times*, *Forbes,* and *Business Week*. The company has also won other awards.

GE traces its beginnings to Thomas A. Edison. Today, GE is a diversified service, technology, and manufacturing company with a commitment to achieving worldwide leadership in each of its businesses. Its major lines of businesses include multiple business units in the following divisions: Aircraft Engines, Appliances, Capital Services, Industrial Systems, Information Services, Lighting, Medical Systems, NBC, Plastics, Power Systems, and Transportation. GE is one of the largest companies in the world: It has operations in more than 100 countries, employs more than 293,000 people, and earns annual revenues of over $100.5 billion.[2] You are either a customer of GE or have indirectly been exposed to its products and services without realizing it.

Jack Welch is just one example among thousands of great leaders who understand the importance of leadership development. The focus of this chapter is on helping you understand what leadership is and what this book is all about. We begin by defining leadership and the ten roles that leaders perform. Then we explain the three levels of leadership analysis, which provides the framework for the book. After explaining the four major leadership paradigms that have developed historically over the years, we end this chapter by stating the objectives of the book and presenting its organization.

LEADERSHIP IS EVERYONE'S BUSINESS

In this section, you will learn our definition of leadership, discover why leadership skills are important, and find out if leaders are made or born.

Defining Leadership

The topic of leadership has generated excitement and interest since ancient times. When people think about leadership, images of powerful dynamic individuals who command victorious armies, shape the events of nations, develop religions, or direct corporate empires come to mind. How did certain leaders build such great armies, countries, religions, and companies? Why do certain leaders have dedicated followers while others do not? How did Adolf Hitler rise to a position of great power? It wasn't until the twentieth century that researchers attempted to scientifically answer such questions. More than 30,000 journal and magazine articles and books have been written about leadership,[3] using many different definitions. Today, we better understand the answers to some of these research questions; but much of the research generates more questions, and many questions surrounding the mystery of leadership remain unanswered. In this book, you will learn the major leadership theories and research findings regarding leadership effectiveness.

There is no universal definition of leadership because leadership is complex, and because leadership is studied in different ways that require different definitions. As in leadership research studies, we will use a single definition that meets our purpose in writing this book. Before you read our definition of leadership, complete Self-Assessment Exercise 1-1 to get a better idea of your leadership potential. In the following section we will discuss each question as it relates to the elements of our leadership definition, and to your leadership potential.

Self-Assessment Exercise 1-1

Leadership Potential

As with all the self-assessment exercises in this book, there are no right or wrong answers, so don't try to pick what you think is the right answer. Be honest in answering the questions, so that you can better understand yourself and your behavior as it relates to leadership.

For each pair of statements distribute 5 points, based on how characteristic each statement is of you. If the first statement is totally like you and the second is not like you at all, give 5 points to the first and 0 to the second. If it is the opposite, use 0 and 5. If the statement is usually like you, then distribution can be 4 and 1, or 1 and 4. If both statements tend to be like you, the distribution should be 3 and 2, or 2 and 3. Again, the combined score for each pair of statements must equal 5.

Here are the scoring distributions for each pair of statements:

0–5 or 5–0   One of the statements is totally like you, the other not like you at all.

1–4 or 4–1   One statement is usually like you, the other not.

2–3 or 3–2   Both statements are like you, although one is slightly more like you.

1. _____ I'm interested in and willing to take charge of a group of people.

   _____ I want someone else to be in charge of the group.

2. _____ When I'm not in charge, I'm willing to give input to the leader to improve performance.

   _____ When I'm not in charge, I do things the leader's way, rather than offer my suggestions.

3. _____ I'm interested in and willing to get people to listen to my suggestions and to implement them.

_____ I'm not interested in influencing other people.

4. _____ When I'm in charge, I want to share the management responsibilities with group members.

   _____ When I'm in charge, I want to perform the management functions for the group.

5. _____ I want to have clear goals and to develop and implement plans to achieve them.

   _____ I like to have very general goals and take things as they come.

6. _____ I like to change the way my job is done, and to learn and do new things.

   _____ I like stability, or to do my job the same way; I don't like learning and doing new things.

7. _____ I enjoy working with people and helping them succeed.

   _____ I don't really like working with people and helping them succeed.

To determine your leadership potential score, add up the numbers (0–5) for the first statement in each pair; don't bother adding the numbers for the second statement. The total should be between 0 and 35. Place your score on the continuum in the right column. Generally, the higher your score, the greater your potential to be an effective leader. However, the key to success is not simply potential, but persistence and hard work. You can develop your leadership ability through this course by applying the principles and theories to your personal and professional lives.

0——5——10——15——20——25——30——35
Low leadership potential   *High leadership potential*

leadership: the process of influencing leaders and followers to achieve organizational objectives through change.

Leadership is the influencing process of leaders and followers to achieve organizational objectives through change. Let's discuss the key elements of our definition; see Figure 1-1 for a list.

Leaders-Followers. Question 1 of Self-Assessment Exercise 1-1 is meant to get you thinking about whether you want to be a leader or follower. If you are not interested and willing to be in charge, you are better suited to be a follower. However, as you will learn in this section, good followers also perform leadership roles when needed. And followers influence leaders. Thus in our definition of leadership the influencing process is *between* leaders and followers, not just a leader influencing followers; it's a two-way street. Knowing how to lead and developing leadership skills will make you a better leader and follower. So whether you want to be a leader or follower, you will benefit from this book.

Throughout this book, leadership is referred to in the context of formal organizational settings in business corporations (GE, IBM), government agencies (Department of Motor Vehicles, the Police Department), and nonprofit organizations (Red Cross, Springfield College). Organizations have two major classifications of employees: managers, who have subordinates and formal authority to tell them what to do; and employees, who do not. All managers perform four major functions: planning, organizing, leading, and controlling. Leadership is thus a part of the manager's job. However, there are managers—you may know some—who are not effective leaders. There are also non-managers who have great influence on managers and peers. Thus, in this book we do not use the terms *manager* and *leader* interchangeably. When we use the word *manager*, we mean a person who has a formal title and authority. When we use the term *leader*, we mean a person who may be either a manager or a non-manager. A leader always has the ability to influence others; a manager may not. Thus, a leader is not necessarily a person who holds some formal position such as manager.[4]

A *follower* is a person who is being influenced by a leader. A follower can be a manager or a non-manager. Good followers are not "yes people" who simply follow the leader without giving input that influences the leader. In short, effective leaders influence followers, and their followers influence them. The qualities needed for effective leadership are the same as those needed to be an effective follower.[5] Throughout this book, we use the term *behavior* in referring to the activities of people or the things they do and say as they are influenced. You will learn more about followership in Chapter 6.

As implied in question 2 of Self-Assessment Exercise 1-1, good followers give input and influence leaders. If you want to be an effective follower, you need to share your ideas. Also, as a leader you need to listen to others and implement their ideas to be effective.

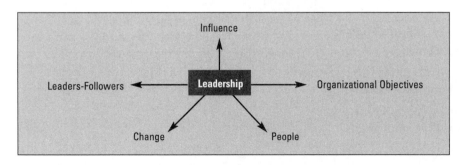

Figure 1-1 *Leadership definition key elements.*

Influence.　*Influencing* is the process of a leader communicating ideas, gaining acceptance of them, and motivating followers to support and implement the ideas through change. Influence is the essence of leadership. Question 3 of Self-Assessment Exercise 1-1 asked if you were interested in and willing to influence others, as a leader or follower. When you have a management position, you have more power to influence others. But, effective followers also influence others. Your ability to influence others (to get what you want) can be developed. Influencing includes power, politics, and negotiating; you will learn more about these concepts in Chapter 9.

Influencing is also about the relationship between leaders and followers. Managers may coerce subordinates to influence their behavior, but leaders do not. Leaders gain the commitment and enthusiasm of followers who are willing to be influenced. Most of the leadership research is concerned with the relationship between leaders and followers.[6] Effective leaders know when to lead and when to follow. Thus leaders and followers often change roles through the influencing process. Question 4 of Self-Assessment Exercise 1-1 asked if you want to share management responsibility as a leader. Effective leaders do; the two types of shared responsibility are described below.

Peer-leadership is the term used when different group members carry out various leadership functions. Thus, multiple group members influence the group behavior.[7] The manager usually sets the example of appropriate peer leader behavior. When given all the credit for GE's success, Jack Welch is quick to say that GE is not a one-man show. Peer-leadership was found to be associated with a high level of organizational performance.[8]

Co-leadership is the term used when power and credit are freely dispersed throughout the organization. You have probably heard of Sherlock Holmes, who is widely recognized as a great detective. His co-leader Dr. Watson is not as well known. You most likely have heard of Bill Gates, CEO of Microsoft. Who is his co-leader? Few people know that it is Steve Ballmer. Despite the hurrahs given to the headline-stealing leaders of the world, such heroes are often incomplete, and perhaps even ineffective as leaders, without the proactive co-leadership of others throughout the organization.[9] In other words, effective leaders have one or more close associates who influence them.

Effective leaders teach leadership skills to their staff.[10] Recall that Jack Welch clearly believes in giving power and credit to the managers at GE, stating that his most important job is to develop leaders. As the GE managers run their business units, Jack works with them to develop their leadership skills through a positive mentor relationship.

Organizational Objectives.　Effective leaders influence followers to think not only of their own interests but the interest of the organization. Leadership occurs when followers are influenced to do what is ethical and beneficial for the organization and themselves. Taking advantage of followers for personal gain is not part of leadership. Members of the organization need to work together toward an outcome that the leader and followers both want, a desired future or shared purpose that motivates them toward

influencing: the process of a leader communicating ideas, gaining acceptance of them, and motivating followers to support and implement the ideas through change.

this more preferable outcome. Leaders need to provide direction; with the input of followers, they set challenging objectives and lead the charge ahead to achieve them.[11] Jack Welch has clearly stated that the overarching value of GE is that it leads with integrity. Setting specific, difficult objectives leads to higher levels of performance.[12] As implied in Question 5 of Self-Assessment Exercise 1-1, effective leaders set clear goals. You will learn how to set objectives in Chapter 3.

Change. Influencing and setting objectives is about change. Organizations need to continually change, in adapting to the rapidly changing global environment. At its website, GE says it's the only company listed in the Dow Jones Industrial Index today that was also included in the original index in 1896. The other companies may have become too comfortable with doing business the same old way, perhaps causing these former business stars to fade. Effective leaders realize the need for continual change to improve performance. Jack Welch has continually reshaped GE by purchasing more than 600 companies (acquisitions).

Statements like these are not in a successful leader's vocabulary: we've always done it this way; we've never done it that way before; it can't be done; has anyone else done it; and it's not in the budget. Leadership involves influencing followers to bring about change toward a desired future for the organization. Jack Welch asks his managers for every idea they have to improve the performance of their work unit. For ideas that he likes, Welch asks, "What resources do you need to make it happen?" And he gives them the resources.

As implied in question 6 of Self-Assessment Exercise 1-1, and the information in this section, to be an effective leader and follower you must be open to change. The people who advance in organizations are those who are willing to take a risk and try new things. Every promotion requires change. When was the last time you did something new and different? You will learn more about leading change in Chapter 10.

People. Although the term *people* is not specifically mentioned in our definition of leadership, after reading about the other elements, you should realize that leadership is about leading people. As implied in question 7 of Self-Assessment Exercise 1-1, to be effective at almost every job today, you must be able to get along with people. Effective leaders and followers enjoy working with people and helping them succeed. You will learn how to develop your people skills throughout this book.

Research, experience, and common sense all point to a direct relationship between a company's financial success and its commitment to leadership practices that treat people as assets. There is little evidence that being a mean, tough manager is associated with leadership success.[13]

Why Leadership Is Important

Like Jack Welch, Gary Henson (VP of Chrysler Corporation Division) also recognizes the importance of leadership.[14] Here are other examples of what people are saying about leadership:

- Managers must realize that motivation and leadership are the key to developing effective managers. Leadership skill is an important part of managing a growing business. The companies that will survive in the new global competitive environment are those that can attract and maintain leaders. Global leadership skill is the key intangible resource that will leverage sustainable competitive advantage in the twenty-first century. Financial analysts credit companies' success to various factors, including strong leadership. If you want to be successful, you need to develop your leadership skills.[15]

- Jack Welch says that if you don't get recognition and you have the wrong manager, it can be awful. Researchers agree with Jack, saying there is a strong relationship between human-oriented leadership and job satisfaction. Leadership skill of supervisors is the most important factor in retaining employees. Your boss's leadership skill will directly affect how happy you are on the job and whether you stay or leave.[16]

- Productivity growth has slowed, despite increases in technology, because organizations are focusing on technology-skills training rather than people-skills training. Neglecting people-skills training impairs leadership. People are the key to economic development. We must always remember that it's people who invent and use technology; without people, we have no technology.[17]

Are Leaders Born or Made?

You may think this is a trick question, because the answer is neither and both. Effective leaders are not simply born or made, they are born with some leadership ability and develop it. Researchers indicate that many cognitive abilities and personality traits are at least partly innate.[18] So certain natural ability may offer certain advantages or disadvantages to a leader. You will learn more about leadership traits in Chapter 2.

Legendary football coach Vince Lombardi once said, "Contrary to the opinion of many people, leaders are not born, leaders are made, and they are made by effort and hard work."[19] We are all leaders, and all people have potential leadership skills.[20] Whatever your natural leadership ability is now, you can invest in developing your leadership skills, or you can allow them to remain as they are now. You may never become the CEO of a large business like GE, but you can improve your leadership ability through this course. We'll talk more about this in the last section of this chapter.

The global marketplace rewards companies that invest heavily in developing their employees.[21] If top managers did not believe that leadership skills could be developed, their companies would not be spending millions of dollars annually to do so. At its website, GE says it spends $500 million dollars a year on training and developing its employees. Leadership is a hot topic today; it influences all types of training and development programs.[22] Jack Welch doesn't just say that selecting and developing leaders is his most important job. In addition to coaching leaders on a daily basis, he teaches leadership at the GE leadership-development facility. Jack speaks of the ethics, the responsibility, and the morality of being a leader.[23] GE and other organizations are seeing the benefits of leadership training. For example, Kraft Foods reduced its employee turnover rate by training its staff in technical and leadership skills.[24]

LEADERSHIP MANAGERIAL ROLES

In this section, you will learn more about what leaders do on the job—the leadership managerial roles. Henry Mintzberg identified ten managerial roles that leaders perform to accomplish organizational objectives.[25] The roles represent the dominant classes of behavioral activities that managers or their followers perform. Mintzberg defined a *role* as a set of expectations of how a person will behave to perform a job. He grouped these roles into three categories. *The **managerial role categories** are interpersonal, informational, and decisional.* Mintzberg's management role theory has been supported by research studies.[26] Figure 1-2 shows the ten managerial roles, based on the three categories.

managerial role categories: interpersonal, informational, and decisional.

Interpersonal Roles

*The **interpersonal leadership roles** include figurehead, leader, and liaison.*

interpersonal leadership roles: figurehead, leader, and liaison.

Figurehead Role. Leaders perform the *figurehead role* when they represent the organization or department in legal, social, ceremonial, and symbolic activities. Top-level managers are usually viewed as figureheads for their organization. However, leaders throughout the organization perform the following behavior, as well as other related activities:

- Signing official documents (expense authorization, checks, vouchers, contracts, and so on)
- Entertaining clients or customers as official representatives and receiving/escorting official visitors
- Informally talking to people and attending outside meetings as an organizational representative
- Presiding at certain meetings and ceremonial events (awards ceremonies, retirement dinners, and so on)

Leader Role. According to Mintzberg, the *leader role* is that of performing the management functions to effectively operate the managers' organization unit. Therefore, the leader role pervades all managerial behav-

INTERPERSONAL ROLES	INFORMATIONAL ROLES	DECISIONAL ROLES
Figurehead Leader Liaison	Monitor Disseminator Spokesperson	Entrepreneur Disturbance-handler Resource-allocator Negotiator

Figure 1-2 *Managerial roles.*

ior. In other words, the leader role influences how the leader performs other roles. You will learn more about the leadership role throughout this book. Here are some of the many leader behaviors that can be performed by the manager or followers:

- Hiring and training
- Giving instructions and coaching
- Evaluating performance

Liaison Role.   Leaders perform the *liaison role* when they interact with people outside their organizational unit. Liaison behavior includes networking to develop relationships and gain information and favors. Organizational politics is an important part of the liaison role, and you will learn more about how to conduct politics in Chapter 9. Here are a few of the liaison role behaviors:

- Serving on committees with members from outside the organizational unit
- Attending professional/trade association meetings
- Calling and meeting with people to keep in touch

Informational Roles

*The **informational leadership roles** include monitor, disseminator, and spokesperson.* You will learn more about informational roles in Chapter 4.

Monitor Role.   Leaders perform the *monitor role* when they gather information. Most of the information is analyzed to discover problems and opportunities, and to understand events outside the organizational unit. Some of the information is passed on to other people in the organizational unit (disseminator role), or to people outside the unit (spokesperson role). Information is gathered by behavior, including:

- Reading memos, reports, professional/trade publications, newspapers, and so forth
- Talking to others, attending meetings inside and outside the organization, and so forth
- Observing (visiting a competitor's store to compare products, prices, and business processes)

Disseminator Role.   Leaders perform the *disseminator role* when they send information to others in the organizational unit. Managers have access to information that is not available to employees. Some of the information that comes from higher levels of management must be passed on to employees, either in its original form or paraphrased. Information is passed on in one or both forms:

- Orally through voice mail, one-on-one discussions, and group meetings. You will learn how to conduct meetings in Chapter 7.
- Written through e-mail and snail mail (U.S. mail)

informational leadership roles: monitor, disseminator, and spokesperson.

Spokesperson Role. Leaders perform the *spokesperson role* when they provide information to people outside the organizational unit. People must report information to their boss (board of directors, owner, managers) and people outside the organizational unit (other departments, customers, suppliers). Leaders lobby and serve as public relations representatives for their organizational unit. Here are some examples of when the spokesperson role is performed:

- Meeting with the boss to discuss performance, and with the budget officer to discuss the unit budget
- Answering letters
- Reporting information to the government (the IRS, OSHA)

Decisional Roles

decisional leadership roles: entrepreneur, disturbance handler, resource allocator, and negotiator.

*The **decisional leadership roles** include entrepreneur, disturbance handler, resource allocator, and negotiator.*

Entrepreneur Role. Leaders perform the *entrepreneur role* when they innovate and initiate improvements. Leaders often get ideas for improvements through the monitor role. Here are some examples of entrepreneur behavior:

- Developing new or improved products and services
- Developing new ways to process products and services
- Purchasing new equipment

Disturbance-handler Role. Leaders perform the *disturbance-handler role* when they take corrective action during crisis or conflict situations. You will learn more about how to handle conflicts in Chapter 4. Unlike the planned action of the entrepreneur role to take advantage of an opportunity, the disturbance is a reaction to an unexpected event that creates a problem. Leaders typically give this role priority over all other roles. Here are some examples of emergencies leaders may have to solve:

- A union strike
- The breakdown of important machines/equipment
- Needed material arrives late, or a tight schedule has to be met

Resource-allocator Role. Leaders perform the *resource-allocator role* when they schedule, request authorization, and perform budgeting activities. Here are some examples of resource allocation:

- Deciding what is done now, done later, and not done (time management; priorities)
- Determining who gets overtime, or a merit raise (budgeting)
- Scheduling when employees will use material and equipment

Negotiator Role. Leaders perform the *negotiator role* when they represent their organizational unit during routine and nonroutine transactions that do not include set boundaries, such as only one price and term of a sale/purchase for a product/service or pay of an employee. When there are no set prices or pay and conditions, leaders can try to negotiate a good deal to get the resources they need. You will learn how to negotiate in Chapter 9. Here are some examples of negotiations:

- Pay and benefit package for a new professional employee or manager
- Labor union contract
- Contract with a customer (sale) or supplier (purchase)

Although managers are responsible for all ten roles, which roles are more important—and which roles the manager performs and which are performed by other leaders—will vary based on the manager's job. The relative emphasis placed on these roles will vary as a function of organizational technology, the day-to-day problems faced by leaders, and the task environment of their organizations.[27] Like all managers who are good leaders, Jack Welch of GE performs the ten roles, and he delegates these roles to his followers. After answering Work Applications 1-7 through 1-9, you should realize that you and others perform the leadership roles.

Applying the Concept 1-1

Leadership Managerial Roles

Identify each of the 15 behaviors by its leadership role. Write the appropriate letter in the blank before each item.

Interpersonal roles	Informational roles	Decisional roles
a. figurehead	d. monitor	f. entrepreneur
b. leader	e. disseminator	h. disturbance-handler
c. liaison	f. spokesperson	i. resource-allocator
		j. negotiator

____ 1. The leader is talking with two employees who were verbally fighting and refuse to work together.

____ 2. The leader is holding a meeting with his followers to discuss a new company policy.

____ 3. The production leader is talking to a maintenance person about fixing a machine.

____ 4. The leader is conducting a job interview.

____ 5. The sales leader is signing an expense reimbursement form for a sales representative.

____ 6. The leader is holding a press conference with a local newspaper reporter.

____ 7. The leader is assigning followers to various accounts and giving them the files.

____ 8. A follower is asking the leader for a raise.

____ 9. The leader is presenting organizational pins to employees for five years of service during a special meeting of all organizational unit members.

____ 10. The leader is reading the daily e-mail.

____ 11. The leader and his manager, who must authorize the funding of the project, are discussing having new customized software developed for the leader's department.

____ 12. The leader is disciplining a follower for being late again.

____ 13. The leader is visiting another organizational unit to watch how it processes work orders.

____ 14. The leader of a stock brokerage branch is trying to get the telephones turned back on so brokers can use the phone.

____ 15. The leader is having new customized software developed for the organizational unit.

LEVELS OF ANALYSIS OF LEADERSHIP THEORY

levels of analysis of leadership theory: individual, group, and organizational.

One useful way to classify leadership theory and research is by the levels of analysis. *The three **levels of analysis of leadership theory** are individual, group, and organizational.* Most leadership theories are formulated in terms of processes at only one of these three levels.[28] You will briefly learn about each level in this section, and the details of each in Parts One through Three of this book.

Individual Level of Analysis

The individual level of analysis of leadership theory focuses on the individual leader and the relationship with individual followers. The individual level is also called the *dyadic process*. Dyadic theories view leadership as a reciprocal influencing process between the leader and the follower; there is an implicit assumption that leadership effectiveness cannot be understood without examining how a leader and follower influence each other over time.[29] Recall that influencing is also about the relationships between leaders and followers. As a leader and as a follower, you will influence other individuals and they will influence your behavior at work. You will also have multiple dyadic relationships at work. In Part One, "Individuals as Leaders" (Chapters 1–4), the focus is on the individual level of analysis. As a manager, you will be held responsible for providing the most effective leadership to each person in the workforce.[30]

Group Level of Analysis

The second level of analysis of leadership theory focuses on the relationship between the leader and the collective group of followers. This level is also called *group process*. Group process theories focus on how a leader contributes to group effectiveness. Extensive research on small groups has identified important determinants of group effectiveness.[31] You will learn about determinants of group effectiveness in Part Two, "Team Leadership" (Chapters 5–8). An important part of group process is meetings. In Chapter 7, you will learn how to conduct productive meetings.

Most of the prevailing theories of leadership are distinctly American. Although current research recognizes the importance of groups, the literature comprises individualistic approaches to leadership. Thus, it is questionable if leadership theories based on U.S. research on the group level can be applied to cultures that have a collectivist or group approach, such as Japan.[32] We will discuss the applicability of specific leadership theories throughout the book.

Organizational Level of Analysis

The third level of analysis of leadership theory focuses on the organization. This level is also called *organizational process*. Organizational performance in the long run depends on effectively adapting to the environment and acquiring the necessary resources to survive, and on whether the organization uses an effective transformation process to produce its products and services.

Much of the current research at the organizational level focuses on how top-level managers can influence organizational performance. Successful leaders, like Jack Welch of GE, have had a positive impact on organizational performance. Charismatic leadership by CEOs can create positive effects across the organization through effective strategic leadership.[33] You will learn more about determinants of organizational performance in Part Three, "Organizational Leadership" (Chapters 9–11).

Interrelationships among the Levels of Analysis

Figure 1-3 illustrates the interrelationships among the levels of analysis of leadership theory. Note that the individual is placed at the bottom of the triangle, because group and organizational performance are based on individual performance. It has been said that an organization is the sum of all of its individual transactions.[34] Depending on the size of the group and organization you work for, your individual performance may influence the performance of the group and organization positively or negatively. If individual performance is low throughout the organization, the triangle will fall because it will not have a firm foundation, or performance will be low.

The group-level approach provides a better understanding of leadership effectiveness than the individual, but groups function in a larger social system, and group effectiveness cannot be understood if the focus of research is limited to a group's internal process level of analysis.[35] Thus, the group part of the triangle supports the organizational side. If the groups are not effective, the triangle will fall, or organizational performance will be low.

Both group and organizational performance also affect the performance of the individual. If both the group members and the group are highly motivated and productive (or not productive), chances are the individual will be productive as well. Success tends to be contagious. Working for a winning organization tends to motivate individuals to perform at their best to stay on top. GE does not stay in any line of business unless it has the potential to become first or second in global success; business units that cannot attain that level are sold. However, an organization and its performance are more than the simple sum of its individuals and groups.[36]

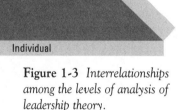

Figure 1-3 *Interrelationships among the levels of analysis of leadership theory.*

LEADERSHIP THEORY PARADIGMS

The first thing we need to do is define the important concepts of this section. A ***leadership theory*** *is an explanation of some aspect of leadership; theories have practical value because they are used to better understand, predict, and control successful leadership.* There are four major classifications of leadership theory,[37] also called *research approaches*, to explaining leadership.

leadership theory: an explanation of some aspect of leadership; theories have practical value because they are used to better understand, predict, and control successful leadership.

leadership theory classifications: trait, behavioral, contingency, and integrative.

leadership paradigm: a shared mindset that represents a fundamental way of thinking about, perceiving, studying, researching, and understanding leadership.

Leadership theory classifications include *trait, behavioral, contingency, and integrative*. In this section, you will learn about each classification, and where it is covered in more detail later in this book.

A *leadership paradigm is a shared mindset that represents a fundamental way of thinking about, perceiving, studying, researching, and understanding leadership*. The leadership paradigm has changed during the past 60 years that it has been studied. The four major classifications of leadership theory all represent a change in leadership paradigm. You will also learn about the change in paradigm from management to leadership in this section.

The Trait Theory Paradigm

The early leadership studies were based on the assumption that leaders are born, not made. Researchers wanted to identify a set of characteristics or traits that distinguished leaders from followers, or effective from ineffective leaders. *Leadership trait theories attempt to explain distinctive characteristics accounting for leadership effectiveness*. Researchers analyzed physical and psychological traits, or qualities, such as high energy level, appearance, aggressiveness, self-reliance, persuasiveness, and dominance in an effort to identify a set of traits that all successful leaders possessed.

leadership trait theories: theories that attempt to explain distinctive characteristics accounting for leadership effectiveness.

The list of traits was to be used as a prerequisite for promoting candidates to leadership positions. Only candidates possessing all the identified traits would be given leadership positions. Hundreds of trait studies were conducted during the 1930s and 1940s to discover a list of qualities. However, no one has come up with a universal list of traits that all successful leaders possess, or traits that will guarantee leadership success. On the positive side, although there is no list of traits that guarantees leadership success, traits that are related to leadership success have been identified.[38] You will learn more about trait theory in the next chapter.

The Behavioral Leadership Theory Paradigm

By the 1950s, most of the leadership research had changed its paradigm, going from trait theory to focusing on what the leader actually did on the job (behavior). In the continuing quest to find the one best leadership style in all situations, researchers attempted to identify differences in the behavior of effective leaders versus ineffective leaders. Another subcategory of behavioral leadership focuses on the nature of management work. Thus, *behavioral leadership theories attempt to explain distinctive styles used by effective leaders, or to define the nature of their work*. Mintzberg's ten managerial roles are an example of behavioral leadership theory. Behavioral research focuses on finding ways to classify behavior that will facilitate our understanding of leadership. Hundreds of studies examined the relationship between leadership behavior and measures of leadership effectiveness. However, there was no agreement on one best leadership style for all management situations. On the positive side, Mintzberg's leadership theory is widely used to train leaders. And other researchers did identify two

behavioral leadership theories: theories that attempt to explain distinctive styles used by effective leaders, or to define the nature of their work.

generic dimensions of leader behavior: task- and people-oriented leadership, which has importance in accounting for leadership effectiveness.[39] You will learn about some of the most popular behavioral leadership theories in Chapter 3.

The Contingency Leadership Theory Paradigm

Both the trait and behavioral leadership theories were attempts to find the one best leadership style in all situations; thus they are called *universal theories*. In the 1960s, it became apparent that there is no one best leadership style in all situations. Thus, the leadership paradigm shifted to contingency theory. **Contingency leadership theories** *attempt to explain the appropriate leadership style based on the leader, followers, and situation.* In other words, which traits and/or behaviors will result in leadership success given the situational variables? The contingency theory paradigm emphasizes the importance of situational factors, including the nature of the work performed, the external environment, and the characteristics of followers. One aspect of this research is to discover the extent to which managerial work is the same or different across different types of organizations, levels of management, and cultures. You will learn about the major contingency leadership theories in Chapter 5.

contingency leadership theories: theories that attempt to explain the appropriate leadership style based on the leader, followers, and situation.

The Integrative Leadership Theory Paradigm

In the mid-to-late 1970s, the paradigm began to shift to the integrative, or neo-charismatic theory.[40] As the name implies, **integrative leadership theories** *attempt to combine the trait, behavioral, and contingency theories to explain successful, influencing leader-follower relationships.* Researchers try to explain why the followers of some leaders are willing to work so hard and make personal sacrifices to achieve the group and organizational objectives, or how effective leaders influence the behavior of their followers. Theories identify behaviors and traits that facilitate the leader's effectiveness, and explore why the same behavior by the leader may have a different effect on followers depending on the situation. You will learn about the major integrative theories in Chapter 10. However, the integrative leadership theory paradigm is emphasized in our definition of leadership and thus influences this entire book.

integrative leadership theories: theories that attempt to combine the trait, behavioral, and contingency theories to explain successful, influencing leader-follower relationships.

From the Management to the Leadership Theory Paradigm

There are differences between managers and leaders.[41] In the first section we talked about some of the differences between a manager and a leader, because the paradigm has shifted from management to leadership. Today's managers have an evolving role: Successful managers use a truly democratic form of leadership as they share the responsibility of management with employees.[42] Today, managers must be able to lead as well as manage. Thus, they must continue to manage and focus on leading to be successful. In general, women make good leaders because they focus on people and relation-ships.[43] You will learn about these differences in Figure 1-4.

MANAGEMENT	LEADERSHIP
• Is viewed as implementation of the leader's vision and changes introduced by leaders, and the maintenance and administration of organizational infrastructures.	• Is viewed as involving the articulation of an organizational vision and the introduction of major organizational change; provides inspiration and deals with highly stressful and troublesome aspects of the external environments of organizations.[1]
• Focuses on the tasks (things) when performing the management func-tions of planning, organization, and controlling.	• Focuses on the interpersonal (people) leadership management function.
• Planning. Establishes detailed objec-tives and plans for achieving them.	• Establishes directions; develops a vision and the strategies needed for its achievement.
• Organizing and staffing. Sets up structure for employees as they do the job the way the manager wants it done.	• Innovates and allows employees to do the job any way they want, so long as they get results that relate to the vision.
• Controlling. Monitors results against plans and takes corrective action.	• Motivates and inspires employees to accomplish the vision in creative ways.
• Predictable. Plans, organizes, and controls with consistent behavior. Prefers stability.	• Makes innovative, quick changes that are not very predictable. Prefers change.[2]
• Managers do things right.	• Leaders do the right things.[3]
• The focus is on stability, control, competition, work, and uniformity.	• The focus is on change, empower-ment, collaboration, people, and diversity.[4]
• The focus is on a short-term view, avoiding risks, maintaining, and imitating.	• The focus is on a long-term view, taking risks, innovating, and originating.[5]

[1] R.J. House and R.N. Aditya, "The Social Scientific Study of Leadership: Quo Vadis," *Journal of Management 23* (May-June 1997): 409–474.
[2] Some of the five items above are adapted from J.P. Kotter, *A Force for Change: How Leadership Differs from Management* (New York: Free Press, 1990).
[3] W. Bennis and B. Nanus, *Leaders: The Strategies for Taking Charge* (New York: Harper & Row, 1985).
[4] R.L. Daft, *Leadership: Theory and Practice* (Fort Worth, TX: The Dryden Press, 1999).
[5] R. L. Hughes, R.C. Ginnett, and G.J. Curphy, *Leadership: Enhancing the Lessons of Experience* (Burr Ridge, IL: 1999).

Figure 1-4 *Management and leadership differences.*

Although we have made a comparison between managers and leaders, you should realize that successful leaders are also good at managing, and successful managers are good leaders. There is overlap between the two paradigms. To simplistically stereotype people as either managers or leaders does little to advance our understanding of leadership. Also, because the term *manager* is an occupational title, to foster an inaccurate, negative stereotype of managers may do more harm than good.[44]

Applying the Concept 1-2

Leadership Theories

Identify each research approach by its leadership theory paradigm. Write the appropriate letter in the blank before each item.

a. trait
b. behavioral
c. contingency

d. integrative
e. management to leadership

_____ 1. The researcher is investigating the specific company work, environment, and followers to determine which leadership style is most appropriate.

_____ 2. The organization's human resources director is training its managers to be more effective in their interpersonal relationship with their followers, so that managers can better influence their followers to work to accomplish the organization's vision.

_____ 3. The researcher is observing managers to determine how much time they spend giving employees praise for doing a good job and criticism for poor performance.

_____ 4. The researcher is attempting to understand how leaders who are charismatic influence followers to achieve such high levels of performance.

_____ 5. The researcher is attempting to determine if there is a relationship between how a manager dresses and leadership effectiveness.

2

Leadership Traits and Ethics

K ay Koplovitz founded USA Networks in 1977. USA was the first service to distribute live sports and entertainment programming via satellite to cable systems. Until then cable television was nothing but an antenna service, but USA changed the way cable operated. Under Koplovitz's leadership, USA distribution grew to cover three continents, reporting annual revenues of over $500 million and a company value worth $3 billion. USA Networks are beamed to 70 percent of U.S. households every day. What's more, Koplovitz broke the glass ceiling in an industry that was all men. She is also dedicated to helping others: in 1996, President Clinton named her chair of the National Women's Business council, an influential advisory board for women-owned businesses.

Kay Koplovitz attributes much of her success to her leadership ability to influence others. As she puts it, "Nobody says no to me. I'm just terrible when I have an idea. Actually people have said no to me a million times; I just don't hear them." A good example of her influencing skill goes back to her ability to convince the major advertisers to pay USA to run advertisements on cable. USA was the first cable to run paid ads, so it was not easy to convince the advertisers to take a risk with an untried source. She also negotiated cable rights to major league sports (baseball, basketball, and hockey).

Koplovitz has the following advice based on three important lessons she learned in school: (1) Get involved in a leadership position in school. Doing so provides the opportunity to develop leadership skills that you can use on the job. (2) Develop your communication skills so you can get your message across. Take opportunities to speak in front of groups. (3) Encourage people to do their best and work together as a team.

Koplovitz's leadership theory includes hiring the best people, and those who are highly motivated. These leaders have vision, clearly express their vision, are capable of understanding the business, and hire the right people and motivate them.

Kay Koplovitz handed over the CEO leadership position at USA Networks in 1998, after winning numerous honors, titles, and awards. Here are just a few of her awards: Emmy and Ace Awards, Anti-Defamation League Champion of Liberty award, Cable Ace Governor's award, Chairman's Award from the NATP. Koplovitz was named to the *Broadcasting Magazine* Hall of Fame for her contributions, accomplishments, and service to the media industry.[1]

■ *Go to the Internet:* For more information on Kay Koplovitz and USA Networks and to update the information provided in this case, do a name search on the Internet and visit USA's website at **http://www.usa-network.com.**

Kay Koplovitz is a strong, entrepreneurial leader. The focus of this chapter is on leadership traits, which includes ethics. We begin by learning about personality traits of leaders and the personality profile of effective leaders. Next we learn how attitudes affect leadership. We end with a discussion of ethics in leadership.

PERSONALITY TRAITS AND LEADERSHIP

Recall that trait theory of leadership was the foundation for the field of leadership studies. Trait theory is still being studied.[2] The original study of trait theory was called the *Great Man (Person) Approach,* which sought to identify the traits effective leaders possessed. Trait researchers examined personality, physical abilities, and social and work-related characteristics. Substantial progress in the development of personality theory and traits has been made since the early 1980s.[3] In this section you will learn about traits and personality, the Big Five Model of Personality, reasons why executives fail, and the traits of effective leaders.

Before you learn about personality traits, complete Self-Assessment Exercise 2-1 to determine your personality profile. Throughout this chapter, you will gain a better understanding of your personality traits, which help explain why people do the things they do (behavior).

Self-Assessment Exercise 2-1

Personality Profile

There are no right or wrong answers, so be honest and you will really increase your self-awareness. We suggest doing this exercise in pencil, or making a copy before you write on it. We will explain why later.

Using the scale below, rate each of the 25 statements according to how accurately it describes you. Place a number from 1 to 7 on the line before each statement.

Like me		Somewhat like me			Not like me	
7	6	5	4	3	2	1

_____ 1. I step forward and take charge in leaderless situations.

_____ 2. I am concerned about getting along well with others.

_____ 3. I have good self-control; I don't get emotional and get angry and yell.

_____ 4. I'm dependable; when I say I will do something, it's done well and on time.

_____ 5. I try to do things differently to improve my performance.

_____ 6. I enjoy competing and winning; losing bothers me.

_____ 7. I enjoy having lots of friends and going to parties.

_____ 8. I perform well under pressure.

_____ 9. I work hard to be successful.

_____ 10. I go to new places and enjoy traveling.

_____ 11. I am outgoing and willing to confront people when in conflict.

_____ 12. I try to see things from other people's point of view.

_____ 13. I am an optimistic person who sees the positive side of situations (the cup is half full).

_____ 14. I am a well-organized person.

_____ 15. When I go to a new restaurant, I order foods I haven't tried.

_____ 16. I want to climb the corporate ladder to as high a level of management as I can.

_____ 17. I want other people to like me and to be viewed as very friendly.

_____ 18. I give people lots of praise and encouragement; I don't put people down and criticize.

_____ 19. I conform by following the rules of an organization.

_____ 20. I volunteer to be the first to learn and do new tasks at work.

_____ 21. I try to influence other people to get my way.

_____ 22. I enjoy working with others more than working alone.

_____ 23. I view myself as being relaxed and secure, rather than nervous and insecure.

_____ 24. I am considered to be credible because I do a good job and come through for people.

_____ 25. When people suggest doing things differently, I support them and help bring it about; I don't make statements like these: it won't work, we never did it before, who else did it, or we can't do it.

To determine your personality profile on the next page: (1) In the blanks, place the number from 1 to 7 that represents your score for each statement. (2) Add up each column—your total should be a number from 5 to 35. (3) On the number scale on the following page, circle the number that is closest to your total score. Each column in the chart represents a specific personality dimension.

Surgency		Agreeableness		Adjustment		Conscientiousness		Openness to Experience	
	35		35		35		35		35
	30		30		30		30		30
_____	1. 25	_____	2. 25	_____	3. 25	_____	4. 25	_____	5. 25
_____	6. 20	_____	7. 20	_____	8. 20	_____	9. 20	_____	10. 20
_____	11. 15	_____	12. 15	_____	13. 15	_____	14. 15	_____	15. 15
_____	16. 10	_____	17. 10	_____	18. 10	_____	19. 10	_____	20. 10
_____	21. 5	_____	22. 5	_____	23. 5	_____	24. 5	_____	25. 5
_____	Total Bar	_____	Total Bar	_____	Total Bar	_____	Total Bar	_____	Total Bar

The higher the total number, the stronger is the personality dimension that describes your personality. What is your strongest and weakest dimension?

Continue reading the chapter for specifics about your personality in each of the five dimensions.

Personality and Traits

traits: distinguishing personal characteristics.

personality: a combination of traits that classifies an individual's behavior.

Why are some people outgoing and others shy, loud and quiet, warm and cold, aggressive and passive? This list of behaviors is made up of individual traits. *Traits are distinguishing personal characteristics. Personality is a combination of traits that classifies an individual's behavior.* Understanding people's personalities is important because personality affects behavior, as well as perceptions and attitudes. Knowing personalities helps you to explain and predict others' behavior and job performance.[4] For a simple example, if you know a person is very shy, you can better understand why they are quiet when meeting new people. You can also predict that the person will be quiet when you go places and meet new people. You can also better understand why the person would not seek a job as a salesperson; and if he or she did, you could predict that the person might not be very successful.

Personality is developed based on genetics and environmental factors. The genes you received before you were born influence your personality traits.[5] Your family, friends, school, and work also influence your personality. There are many personality classification methods. One model developed for leadership identifies 16 leadership personality types.[6] However, the Big Five Model of Personality traits is the most widely accepted way to classify personalities because of its strong research support.[7]

The Big Five Model of Personality

Big Five Model of Personality: categorizes traits into dimensions of surgency, agreeableness, adjustment, conscientiousness, and openness to experience.

The purpose of the Big Five is to reliably categorize, into one of five dimensions, most if not all of the traits you would use to describe someone else. Thus, each dimension includes multiple traits. *The Big Five Model of Personality categorizes traits into the dimensions of surgency, agreeableness, adjustment, conscientiousness, and openness to experience.* The dimensions are listed in Figure 2-1 and described below. As noted in descriptions, however, some researchers have slightly different names for the five dimensions.[8]

surgency personality dimension: leadership and extraversion traits.

Surgency. *The surgency personality dimension includes leadership and extraversion traits.* (1) People strong in surgency—more commonly called *dominance*—personality traits want to be in charge. Their dominant behavior ranges from interest in getting ahead and leading through competing and influencing. People weak in surgency want to be followers, and don't want to compete or influence. (2) Extraversion is on a continuum between extravert and introvert. Extraverts are outgoing, like to meet new people, and are willing to confront others, whereas introverts are shy. Review Self-Assessment Exercise 2-1 statements 1, 6, 11, 16, and 21 for examples of surgency traits. How strong is your desire to be a leader?

agreeableness personality dimension: traits related to getting along with people.

Agreeableness. Unlike surgency behavior to get ahead of others, the *agreeableness personality dimension includes traits related to getting along with people.* Agreeable personality behavior is strong when a person is called warm, easygoing, compassionate, friendly, and sociable; it is weak when a person is called cold, difficult, uncompassionate, unfriendly, and unsociable. Strong agreeable personality types are sociable, spend most of their time with people, and have lots of friends. Review Self-Assessment Exercise 2-1 statements 2, 7, 12, 17, and 22 for examples of agreeableness traits. How important is having good relationships to you?

Adjustment. The **adjustment personality dimension** *includes traits related to emotional stability.* Adjustment is on a continuum between being emotionally stable and unstable. *Stable* refers to self-control, being calm—good under pressure, relaxed, secure, and positive—praising others; *unstable* is out of control— poor under pressure, nervous, insecure, and negative— criticizing others. Review Self-Assessment Exercise 2-1 statements 3, 8, 13, 18, and 23 for examples of adjustment traits. How emotionally stable are you?

Conscientiousness. The **conscientiousness personality dimension** *includes traits related to achievement.* Conscientiousness is also on a continuum between responsible/dependable to irresponsible/undependable. Other traits of high conscientiousness include credibility, conformity, and organization. People with this trait are characterized as willing to work hard and put in extra time and effort to accomplish goals to achieve success. Review Self-Assessment Exercise 2-1 statements 4, 9, 14, 19, and 24 for examples of conscientiousness. How strong is your desire to be successful?

Openness to experience. The **openness-to-experience personality dimension** *includes traits related to being willing to change and try new things.* People strong in openness to experience seek change and trying new things, while those with a weak openness dimension avoid change and new things. Review Self-Assessment Exercise 2-1 statements 5, 10, 15, 20, and 25 for examples of openness-to-experience traits. How willing are you to try change and new things?

Figure 2-1 *Big Five dimensions of traits.*

adjustment personality dimension: traits related to emotional stability.
conscientiousness personality dimension: traits related to achievement.
openness-to-experience personality dimension: traits related to being willing to change and try new things.

Personality Profiles

Personality profiles identify individual stronger and weaker traits. Readers completing Self-Assessment Exercise 2-1 tend to have a range of scores for the five dimensions. Review your personality profile. Do you have higher scores (stronger traits) on some dimensions and lower scores (weaker traits) on others?

Personality profiles are used to categorize people as a means of predicting job success. Many organizations (such as the National Football League teams, including the Giants, 49ers, and Dolphins) give personality tests to ensure a proper match between the worker and the job.[9] For example, a study revealed that personality profiles of engineers and accountants tended to be lower in the trait of surgency but higher in the trait of dependability. Marketing and sales people were lower in dependability but higher in

personality profiles: identify individual stronger and weaker traits.

surgency.[10] Organizations frequently give personality tests to determine if a person has the personality profile that can predict job success.

The Big Five model has universal application across cultures. Studies have shown that people from Asian, Western European, Middle Eastern, Eastern European, and North and South American cultures seem to use the same five personality dimensions. However, some cultures do place varying importance on different personality dimensions. Overall, the best predictor of job success on a global basis is the conscientiousness dimension.[11]

Derailed Leadership Traits

Before we go on to the next section and discuss the traits of effective leaders, let's identify traits that led to leadership failure. A study was conducted that compared 21 derailed executives with 20 executives who had successfully climbed the corporate ladder to the top.[12] The derailed executives had prior success and were expected to go far, but they were passed over for promotion again, were fired, or were forced to retire early. See Figure 2-2 for a list of the six major reasons for derailment.

None of the derailed executives had all six weaknesses. Overall, their problem was the lack of poor human skills; they did not treat people as valuable assets. Derailed executives failed to make the paradigm shift from management to leadership.

Successful leaders have a range of stronger and weaker dimensions in the Big Five. However, as our definition of leadership indicates, they are relatively strong on all five dimensions and avoid derailment. To a large extent, Kay Koplovitz was a successful founder and leader of USA Networks because of her strong personality in the Big Five: She has a strong need for surgency while being agreeable and well adjusted, yet she is conscientious and open to new experience. You'll learn about the more specific personality profile of successful leaders in the "Motives of Effective Leaders" section of this chapter. But first, let's identify specific traits of effective leaders.

Applying the Concept 2-1

Personality Dimensions

Identify each of these 7 traits/behaviors by its personality dimension. Write the appropriate letter in the blank before each item.

a. surgency
b. agreeableness
c. adjustment
d. conscientiousness
e. openness to experience

____ 1. The manager is influencing the follower to do the job the way the leader wants it done.

____ 2. The sales representative submitted the monthly expense report on time as usual.

____ 3. The leader is saying a warm, friendly good morning to followers as they arrive at work.

____ 4. The leader is seeking ideas from followers on how to speed up the flow of work.

____ 5. As a follower is yelling a complaint, the leader calmly explains what went wrong.

____ 6. The leader is being very quiet when meeting some unexpected visitors in the work unit.

____ 7. The leader is giving in to a follower to avoid a conflict.

TRAITS OF EFFECTIVE LEADERS

Researchers who were not concerned with personality or a system of categorizing traits wanted to identify a list of traits that effective leaders have. There appear to be some traits that consistently differentiate leaders from others, so trait theory does have some claim to universality.[13] For the theory to be truly universal, all leaders would have to have all the same traits. However, again you should realize that there is no one list of traits accepted by all researchers, and that

- They used a bullying style viewed as intimidating, insensitive, and abrasive.
- They were viewed as being cold, aloof, and arrogant.
- They betrayed personal trust.
- They were self-centered and viewed as overly ambitious and thinking of the next job.
- They had specific performance problems with the business.
- They overmanaged, being unable to delegate or build a team.

Figure 2-2 *Why executives are derailed.*

not all effective leaders have all these traits. In this chapter you will learn which traits have strong research support. So if you are not strong on every one, it doesn't mean that you can't be a successful leader. Furthermore, you can develop these traits with some effort.

See Figure 2-3 for a list of the nine traits. In the following paragraphs, we will categorize each trait using the Big Five. The footnote given for each of the traits in Figure 2-3 is an empirical study supporting the effectiveness of the leadership trait; you can read these studies for more detailed information.

Dominance

Dominance, which we called leadership, is one of the two major traits of the *surgency* Big Five section. Successful leaders want to be managers and to take charge. However, they are not overly bossy, nor do they use a bullying style. If a person does not want to be a leader, chances are they will not be an effective manager. Thus, the dominance trait affects all the other traits related to effective leaders. For example, if you push people into management positions, there is a high probability that they will lack self-confidence and not have much energy for the job. Due to the pressure of the job they don't want, they may also not be stable in the position or sensitive to others, and the trait of intelligence may be questioned. If you are thinking, who would pressure someone into being a manager when they don't want to be, the answer is owners of small family businesses who want their children to work in the business and take over when they retire. This is one reason why some successful businesses taken over by the owners' children go out of business. To reach full leadership potential, you've got to want to be a leader, work to develop your skills, and enjoy it.

High Energy

Leaders have drive and work hard to achieve goals. They have stamina and tolerate stress well. Leaders have enthusiasm and don't give up. They deal with but don't accept setbacks. However, they are not viewed as pushy and obnoxious. They have a high tolerance for frustration as they strive to overcome obstacles through preparation. Leaders take initiative to bring about

Figure 2-3 *Traits of effective leaders.*

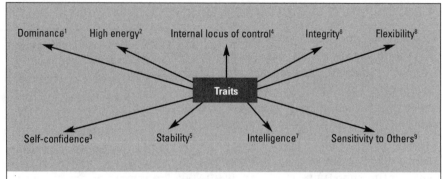

[1]R.G. Lord, C.L. DeVader, and G.M. Alliger, "A Meta-analysis of the Relation between Personality Traits and Leadership Perception: An Application of Validity Generalizations Procedures," *Journal of Applied Psychology* 71 (1986): 402–410.
[2]B.M. Bass, *Handbook of Leadership: A Survey of Theory and Research* (New York: Free Press, 1990).
[3]R.J. House and M.L. Baetz, "Leadership: Some Empirical Generalizations and New Research Directions," In B. Staw (ed.), *Research In Organizational Behavior,* vol. 1 (Greenwich, CT: JAI Press, 1979).
[4]B.J. Avotio and J.M. Howell, "The Impact of Leadership Behavior and Leader Follower Personality Match on Satisfaction and Unit Performance." In K. Clark (ed.), *Impact of Leadership* (Greensboro, NC: Center for Creative Leadership, 1992) 225–235.
[5]See note 2 above.
[6]C.J. Cox and C.L. Cooper, *High Flyers: An Anatomy of Managerial Success* (Oxford: Basil Blackwell), 1989.
[7]See note 1.
[8]S.J. Zaccaro, R.J. Foti, and D.A. Kenny, "Self-monitor and Trait-based Variance in Leadership: An Investigation of Leader Flexibility across Multiple Group Situations," *Journal of Applied Psychology* 76 (1991): 308–315.
[9]See note 8.

improvements rather than ask permission; they don't have to be told what to do. High energy is best categorized as the *conscientious* dimension of the Big Five. Do you have a high energy level?[14]

Self-confidence

Self-confidence, on a continuum from strong to weak, indicates whether you are self-assured in your judgments, decision making, ideas, and capabilities. Leaders display self-assurance about their abilities and foster confidence among followers. As leaders gain their followers' respect, they also influence them.

Self-confidence influences individual goals, efforts, and task persistence. Without strong self-confidence, leaders are less likely to attempt to influence followers, to take on difficult tasks, and to set challenging objectives for themselves and followers. Self-confidence is positively related to effectiveness and is a predictor of advancement to higher levels of management.[15]

Leaders are, however, realistically self-confident; they are not viewed as arrogant "know it alls" who alienate people. Kay Koplovitz, USA Networks, displays lots of self-confidence when she states, "I am not always right, but I'm never in doubt."[16] Self-confidence is best categorized as the *conscientiousness* Big Five dimension, because people who are dependable often have high self-confidence and high energy. Even though most people with a high surgency dimension have self-confidence, not all people with self-confidence want to be managers. People with strong self-confidence also often, but not always, have strong *adjustment* traits. Are you self-confident?

Locus of Control

Locus of control is on a continuum between external and internal belief in control over one's destiny. Externalizers believe that they have no control over their fate, that their behavior has little to do with their performance; and they generally have lower levels of performance. Internalizers (leaders) believe that they control their fate, that their behavior directly affects their performance. Leaders take responsibility for who they are, for their behavior and performance, and for the performance of their organizational unit. Internalizers tend to be future oriented, setting objectives and developing plans to accomplish them. They are usually self-confident and learn from their mistakes, rather than blaming others or just bad luck. The Big Five category is the *openness-to-experience* dimension. Externalizers (followers) are generally reluctant to change. Are you more of an internalizer or an externalizer?[17]

Stability

Stability, the *adjustment* Big Five dimension, is associated with managerial effectiveness and advancement. Stable leaders are emotionally in control of themselves, secure, and positive. Unfortunately, there are some unstable leaders—such as Adolph Hitler—who misuse power. There is an important part of stability that you should be aware of. Research has shown that people with good self-awareness and a desire to improve have higher advancement than those who don't. It has also been shown that effective leaders have a good understanding of their own strengths and weaknesses, and they are oriented toward self-improvement rather than being defensive.[18] This relates to effective leaders knowing when to lead and when to follow; they compensate for weaknesses by letting others with the strength lead in those areas. If you are an internalizer, you will tend to believe this; and if you are conscientious, you will work to improve yourself and advance.

Integrity

Integrity refers to behavior that is honest and ethical, making a person trustworthy. Ethics will be discussed later in this chapter. Honesty refers to truthfulness rather than deception. Honesty is nearly always the best policy; many believe that integrity is the most important asset you can possess. Trustworthiness is an important part of business success; trusting relationships are at the heart of profit making and sustainability in the global knowledge-based economy. Honesty and trust are so important at CompUSA that any employee caught telling a lie is fired immediately; according to the CEO, "We all trust each other."[19]

The ability to influence is based on integrity. Followers must trust the leader. Unless you are perceived to be trustworthy, it is difficult to retain the loyalty of followers or to obtain cooperation and support from peers and superiors. To be viewed as trustworthy, leaders need to be honest, support their followers, and keep confidences (don't tell secrets, or you will not hear them). If followers find out their leader has lied or in some way manipulated them for personal gain, changed his or her mind after making a decision, blamed others for a poor decision, taken credit for followers' work or given blame that is unjust, or betrayed confidences, then the leader will lose the followers' trust. Recall that these negative types of behaviors lead to executive derailment. Integrity is the number one trait that managers want in a leader. Integrity is so important at GE that it is its core value. At GE's website (**www.ge.com**), CEO Jack Welch tells employees to do everything with integrity. Integrity is categorized as the Big Five dimension of *conscientiousness*. Do you have integrity?[20]

Intelligence

Leaders generally have above-average intelligence. *Intelligence* refers to cognitive ability to think critically, to solve problems and make decisions. Organizations are investing heavily in developing their intellectual capital, as they train people to think critically and creatively. However, intuition, also called *hidden intelligence*, is important to leadership success.[21]

Contemporary research on intelligence offers renewed potential for leadership trait research. The notion of multiple intelligence has implications for managerial roles, meaning that differences in cognitive abilities between leaders and nonleaders may well go beyond conventional intelligence quotient (IQ) measures. Simply, multiple intelligence means that people are better at some things than others. This point is related to effective managers knowing when to lead or follow, based on their strengths and weaknesses. Intelligence has been categorized with the Big Five *openness-to-experience* dimension. Being in college implies that you most likely have above-average intelligence. This is one reason why most college graduates get better jobs and are paid more than those who do not go to (or finish) college.

Flexibility

Flexibility refers to the ability to adjust to different situations. Recall that leadership influencing and setting objectives is about change. Leaders need to stay ahead of the immense changes in the world, and the pace of change will continue to increase. Without flexibility, leaders would be successful only in the limited situations that fit their style of leadership. Thus effective leaders are flexible and adapt to the situation. Cynthia Danaher, general manager of the Hewlett-Packard Medical Products Group, says, "Change is painful, and someone may have to be the bad guy. You need to charge ahead, accepting that not everyone will follow and that some won't survive." Flexibility is categorized with the Big Five *openness-to-experience* dimension. Are you flexible?[22]

Sensitivity to Others

Sensitivity to others refers to understanding group members as individuals, what their position on issues is, and how best to communicate with and influence them. To be sensitive to others requires empathy, the ability to place yourself in another person's shoes—to see things from others' point of view. In today's global economy, companies need people-centered leaders, because financial success is increasingly being based on the commitment to management practices that treat people as valuable assets.[23]

Lack of sensitivity is part of the reason for executive derailment. You need to have and convey an interest in other people. Sensitivity means not focusing on putting yourself first, and remembering that often the more you give away, the more you have. Sensitivity is critical when playing the negotiator leadership role, since the goal is to influence the other party. If you are concerned only about yourself and don't understand what the other party wants, you probably will not be very successful. You will learn how to negotiate in Chapter 9. Sensitivity to others is categorized as the Big Five dimension of *agreeableness*. Are you sensitive to others?[24]

Applying the Concept 2-2

Personality Traits of Effective Leaders

Identify each of the following eight behaviors by its trait. The leader may be behaving effectively, or the behavior may be the opposite of the effective trait behavior. Write the appropriate letter in the blank before each item.

a. dominance
b. high energy
c. self-confidence

d. internal locus of control
e. stability
f. integrity

g. intelligence
h. flexibility
i. sensitivity to others

_____ 1. The leader is engaged in getting the production line working.

_____ 2. The leader is acting very nervous while she is disciplining an employee.

_____ 3. The leader tells a follower that he can have Tuesday off next week. But the next day, the leader tells the follower that he has changed his mind.

_____ 4. The leader very attentively listens to the follower complain, then paraphrases the complaint back to the follower.

_____ 5. The leader in situation 1 is still working to solve the problem, it's her fifth attempt.

_____ 6. The leader is telling her manager that her unit's poor performance is not her fault; she says that the employees are lazy and there's nothing she can do to improve performance.

_____ 7. The leader is telling his manager that his department is right on schedule to meet the deadline, hoping that he can catch up before the boss finds out.

_____ 8. The leader assigns a task to one follower, giving him very specific instructions. Then the leader gives another assignment to a different follower, telling her to complete the task any way she wants to.

THE PERSONALITY PROFILE OF EFFECTIVE LEADERS

McClelland's trait theories of Achievement Motivation Theory and Leader Motive Profile Theory have strong research support and a great deal of relevance to the practice of leadership.[25] Achievement Motivation Theory identifies three major traits, which McClelland calls *needs*. Leader Motive Profile Theory identifies the personality profile of effective leaders. You will learn about both of these theories in this section.

Achievement Motivation Theory

Achievement Motivation Theory:
attempts to explain and predict behavior and performance based on a person's need for achievement, power, and affiliation.

Achievement Motivation Theory attempts to explain and predict behavior and performance based on a person's need for achievement, power, and affiliation. David McClelland originally developed Achievement Motivation Theory in the 1940s.[26] He believes that we have needs, and that our needs motivate us to satisfy them. Our behavior is thus motivated by our needs. However, McClelland says this is an unconscious process. He further states that needs are based on personality and are developed as we interact with the environment. All people possess the need for achievement, power, and affiliation, but to varying degrees. One of the three needs tends to be dominant in each one of us and motivates our behavior.

The Need for Achievement (n Ach). The *need for achievement* is the unconscious concern for excellence in accomplishments through individual efforts. People with strong n Ach tend to have an internal locus of control, self-confidence, and high energy traits. High n Ach is categorized as the Big Five dimension of *conscientiousness*. People with high n Ach tend to be characterized as wanting to take personal responsibility for solving problems. They are goal oriented and set moderate, realistic, attainable goals. They seek a challenge, excellence, and individuality; take calculated, moderate risk; desire concrete feedback on their performance, and work hard. People with high n Ach think about ways to do a better job, how to accomplish something unusual or important, and career progression. They perform well in nonroutine, challenging, and competitive situations, while people low in n Ach do not.

McClelland's research showed that only about 10 percent of the U.S. population has a strong dominant need for achievement. There is evidence of a correlation between high achievement need and high performance in the general population, but not necessarily for leader effectiveness.[27] People with high n Ach tend to enjoy entrepreneurial-type positions.

The Need for Power (n Pow). The *need for power* is the unconscious concern for influencing others and seeking positions of authority. People with strong n Pow have the dominance trait, and tend to be self-confident with high energy. High n Pow is categorized as the Big Five dimension of *surgency*. People with a high need for power tend to be characterized as wanting to control the situation, wanting influence or control over others, enjoying competition in which they can win (they don't like to lose), being willing to confront others, and seeking positions of authority and status. People with high n Pow tend to be ambitious and have a lower need for affiliation. They are more concerned about getting their own way (influencing others) than about what others think of them.[28] They are attuned to power and politics as essential for successful leadership.

The Need for Affiliation (n Aff). The *need for affiliation* is the unconscious concern for developing, maintaining, and restoring close personal relationships. People with strong n Aff have the trait of sensitivity to others. High n Aff is categorized as the Big Five dimension of *agreeableness*. People with high n Aff tend to be characterized as seeking close relationships with others, wanting to be liked by others, enjoying lots of social activities, and seeking to belong; so they join groups and organizations. People with high n Aff think about friends and relationships. They tend to enjoy developing, helping, and teaching others. They seek jobs as teachers, in human resource management, and in other helping professions. People with high n Aff are more concerned about what others think of them than about getting their own way (influencing others). They tend to have a low n Pow; they tend to avoid management because they like to be one of the group rather than its leader.

Your Motive Profile. Note that McClelland does not have a classification for the *adjustment* and *openness-to-experience* Big Five personality dimensions; they are not needs. A person can have a high or low need for achievement, power, and affiliation and be either well adjusted or not, and either open or closed to new experiences. So these two dimensions of personality are ignored in determining the Achievement Motivation Theory personality profile. Complete Self-Assessment Exercise 2-2 to determine your motive profile now.

Self-Assessment Exercise 2-2

Motive Profile

Return to Self-Assessment Exercise 2-1 and place the scores from your Big Five personality profile in the following blanks, next to their corresponding needs. On the number scale, circle your total score for each need.

Need for Achievement (conscientiousness)	Need for Power (surgency)	Need for Affiliation (agreeableness)
35	35	35
30	30	30
25	25	25
20	20	20
15	15	15
10	10	10
5 Total Score _____	5 Total Score _____	5 Total Score _____

There is no right or wrong score for this profile. To interpret your score, check to see if there is much difference between the three need scores. If all three are about the same, one need is no stronger than the others are. If scores vary, one need is higher than the others and is called the stronger or dominant need, and the lower score is the weaker need. You can also have other combinations, such as two stronger and one weaker, or vice versa. Do you have stronger and weaker needs?

Knowing a motive profile is useful, because it can explain and predict behavior and performance. For example, if you know people have a high need for affiliation, you can understand why they tend to have friends and get along well with people. You can predict that if they are assigned a job as a mentor, they will enjoy the tasks and display helpful, supportive behavior toward the mentoree, and that they will do a good job. Complete Work Application 2-5, then read on to determine if you have the motive profile of effective leaders.

Leader Motive Profile Theory

Leader Motive Profile Theory:
attempts to explain and predict leadership success based on a person's need for achievement, power, and affiliation.

Leader Motive Profile (LMP): includes a high need for power, which is socialized; that is, greater than the need for affiliation and with a moderate need for achievement.

Leader Motive Profile Theory attempts to explain and predict leadership success based on a person's need for achievement, power, and affiliation motive profile. McClelland found that effective leaders consistently have the same motive profile, and that Leader Motive Profile (LMP) has been found to be a reliable predictor of leader effectiveness.[29] Let's first define the profile of effective leaders and then discuss why it results in success. *The Leader Motive Profile includes a high need for power, which is socialized; that is, greater than the need for affiliation and with a moderate need for achievement.* The achievement score is usually somewhere between the power and affiliation score, and the reason is described below.

Power. Power is essential to leaders because it is a means of influencing followers. Without power, there is no leadership. To be successful, leaders need to want to be in charge and enjoy the leadership role. You will need power to influence your followers, peers, and higher-level managers. You will learn more about how to gain power and be successful in organizational politics in Chapter 9.

Socialized Power. McClelland further identified power as neither good nor bad. It can be used for personal gain at the expense of others (personalized power), or it can be used to help oneself and others (socialized power).[30] Social power is discussed later, with ethics. Effective leaders use socialized power, which includes the traits of sensitivity to others and stability, and is the Big Five *adjustment* dimension. Thus a person with a low need for affiliation can have a high sensitivity to others. McClelland's research supports the reasons for executive derailment, because these negative traits are personalized power. Socialized power is not included in the motive profile, so complete Self-Assessment Exercise 2-3 to determine your motive profile with socialized power.

Applying the Concept 2-3

Achievement Motivation Theory

Identify each of the five behaviors below by its need, writing the appropriate letter in the blank before each item. The person may be behaving based on a strong need, or the behavior may be the opposite, indicating a weak need. Also state how the behavior meets the need and predict the performance.

a. achievement   b. power   c. affiliation

_____ **1.** The person is refusing to be the spokesperson for the group.

_____ **2.** The person is going to talk to a fellow employee, with whom she had a disagreement earlier in the day, to peacefully resolve the conflict.

_____ **3.** The person is working hard to meet a difficult deadline.

_____ **4.** An accounting major has volunteered to calculate the financial analysis for the group's case, and to make the presentation to the class.

_____ **5.** The fellow employee in situation 2 has made up his mind that he will not be the first one to make a move to resolve the conflict with the other person; but when the other party comes to him, he will be receptive.

Self-Assessment Exercise 2-3

Motive Profile with Socialized Power

Return to Self-Assessment Exercise 2-1 and place the scores from Self-Assessment Exercise 2-2 (your motive profile) in the following blanks. On the number scale, circle your total score.

Need for Achievement (conscientiousness)	Need for Power (surgency)	Socialized Power (adjustment)	Need for Affiliation (agreeableness)
35	35	35	35
30	30	30	30
25	25	25	25
20	20	20	20
15	15	15	15
10	10	10	10
5 Total Score _____	5 Total Score _____	5 Total Score _____	5 Total Score _____

Again, there is no right or wrong score. The adjustment score will give you an idea if your power is more social or personal. Also realize that the questions in Self-Assessment Exercise 2-1 (3, 8, 13, 18, and 23) are not totally focused on social power. Thus, if you believe you have higher sensitivity to others, your score on McClelland's LMP could be higher.

Achievement. To be effective, leaders generally need to have a moderate need for achievement. They have high energy, self-confidence, and openness-to-experience traits, and they are *conscientious* (Big Five dimension). The reason for a moderate rather than high need for achievement, which would include a lower need for power, is the danger of personalized power. People with a high need for achievement tend to seek individual achievement, and when they are not interested in being a leader, there is the chance for personalized power and derailment.

Affiliation. Effective leaders have a lower need for affiliation than power, so that relationships don't get in the way of influencing followers. If the achievement score is lower than that for affiliation, the probability of the following problems occurring may be increased. Leaders with high n Aff tend to have a lower need for power and are thus reluctant to play the bad-guy role, such as when disciplining and influencing followers to do things they would rather not do—like change. They have been found to show favoritism behavior toward their friends. However, recall that effective leaders do have concern for followers—socialized power.

The Leader Motive Profile is included in the definition of leadership. Our definition of leadership includes the five key elements of leadership (Figure 1-1) in the LMP. Our definition of leadership includes *influencing* and *leaders-followers* (power) and getting along with *people* (social power). It also includes *organizational objectives* (which achievers set and accomplish well) and *change* (which achievers are open to). Kay Koplovitz, USA Networks, has an LMP. Do you? Complete Self-Assessment Exercise 2-4 now.

Self-Assessment Exercise 2-4

Leadership Interest

Select the option that best describes your interest in leadership now.

_____ 1. I am, or want to become, a manager and leader.

_____ 2. I am, or want to become, a leader without being a manager.

_____ 3. I am not interested in being a leader; I want to be a follower.

If you want to be a leader, recall that research has shown that you can develop your leadership skills.

If you selected option 1, do you have an LMP? If you answered yes, it does not guarantee that you will climb the corporate ladder. However, having an LMP does increase your chances, because it is a predictor of leadership success. On the other hand, an LMP is not enough; you need leadership skills to be successful. If your Self-Assessment Exercise 2-3 score doesn't indicate that you have an LMP, go back to Self-Assessment Exercise 2-1 and review questions 1, 6, 11, 16, and 21. Did you score them accurately? The most important question is 16. If you believe you have an LMP, be aware that your profile could be different using McClelland's LMP questionnaire. Also recall that not all successful leaders have an LMP, so you can still be successful. Developing your leadership skills, through effort, will increase your chances of leadership success.

If you selected option 2, don't be concerned about your LMP. Focus on developing your leadership skills. However, your personality profile can help you to better understand your strengths and weaknesses to identify areas to improve on. This also holds true for people who selected option 1.

If you selected option 3, that's fine. Most people in the general population probably would select this option. Many professionals who have great jobs and incomes are followers, and they have no interest in becoming managers. However, recall that research has shown that leaders and followers need the same skills, that organizations are looking for employees with leadership skills, and that organizations conduct skills training with employees at all levels. To increase your chances of having a successful and satisfying career, you may want to develop your leadership skills. You may someday change your mind about becoming a leader and manager.

Your need for power and LMP can change over time, along with your interest in leadership and management and your skill level, regardless of which option you selected.

Before we go on and discuss leadership attitudes, let's review what we've covered so far in Figure 2-4 by putting together the Big Five Model of Personality, the nine traits of effective leaders, and Achievement Motivation Theory and LMP.

LEADERSHIP ATTITUDES

Attitudes are positive or negative feelings about people, things, and issues. There has been considerable interest in how attitudes affect performance, and companies are recruiting workers with positive attitudes. We all have favorable or positive attitudes, and unfavorable or negative attitudes about life, leadership, work, school, and everything else. Attitudes are not quick judgments we can change easily.[31]

attitudes: positive or negative feelings about people, things, and issues.

W. Marriott, Jr., president of Marriott Corporation, stated that the company's success depends more upon employee attitudes than any other single factor. Larry King, host of CNN's "Larry King Live," says that the right attitude is basic to success. Legendary football coach Lou Holtz says that attitude is the most important thing in this world, and that we each choose the attitude we have. So being a positive or negative person is your choice.[32] People with positive, optimistic attitudes generally have a well-adjusted personality profile, and successful leaders have positive, optimistic attitudes. Kay Koplovitz could never have gotten USA Networks off the ground if she had a negative, pessimistic attitude about her business.

Like personality traits, attitudes have an important influence on behavior and performance. For

THE BIG FIVE MODEL OF PERSONALITY	NINE TRAITS OF EFFECTIVE LEADERS	ACHIEVEMENT MOTIVATION THEORY AND LMP
Surgency	Dominance	Need for power
Agreeableness	Sensitivity to others	Need for affiliation
Adjustment	Stability	Socialized power (LMP)
Conscientiousness	High energy Self-confidence Integrity	Need for achievement
Openness to experience	Internal locus of control Intelligence Flexibility	No separate need; included within other needs

Figure 2-4 *Combined traits and needs.*

example, attitude toward a class or job can be positive or negative. Generally, if you like a class or job, you will attend more often and work harder; but not necessarily. Even if you have a negative attitude toward a class or job, you may still attend and work hard due to other factors, such as your personality traits and motives. If you have a high need for affiliation, and you like the instructor and/or students, you may try hard. If you have a high need for achievement, you may work hard to succeed even with a negative attitude toward the class or job.

In this section, we'll discuss how leadership attitudes relate to Theory X and Theory Y, and how the Pygmalion effect influences followers' behavior and performance. Then we will discuss self-concept and how it affects the leader's behavior and performance. Lastly, we will consider how the leader's attitudes about followers, and about his or her self-concept, affect the leadership style of the leader.

Theory X and Theory Y

Theory X and Theory Y: attempt to explain and predict leadership behavior and performance based on the leader's attitude about followers.

Today, *Theory X and Theory Y attempt to explain and predict leadership behavior and performance based on the leader's attitude about followers.* Before you read about Theory X and Y, complete Self-Assessment Exercise 2-5.

Self-Assessment Exercise 2-5

Theory X and Theory Y Attitudes

For each pair of statements distribute 5 points, based on how characteristic each statement is of your attitude or belief system. If the first statement totally reflects your attitude and the second does not, give 5 points to the first and 0 to the second. If it's the opposite, use 0 and 5. If the statement is usually your attitude, then distribution can be 4 and 1, or 1 and 4. If both statements reflect your attitude, the distribution should be 3 and 2, or 2 and 3. Again, the combined score for each pair of statements must equal 5.

Here are the scoring distributions for each pair of statements:

0–5 or 5–0   One of the statements is totally like you, the other not like you at all.

1–4 or 4–1   One statement is usually like you, the other not.

2–3 or 3–2   Both statements are like you, although one is slightly more like you.

1. _____ People enjoy working.
   _____ People do not like to work.

2. _____ Employees don't have to be closely supervised to do their job well.
   _____ Employees will not do a good job unless you closely supervise them.

3. _____ Employees will do a task well for you if you ask them to.
   _____ If you want something done right, you need to do it yourself.

4. _____ Employees want to be involved in making decisions.
   _____ Employees want the managers to make the decisions.

5. _____ Employees will do their best work if you allow them to do the job their own way.
   _____ Employees will do their best work if they are taught how to do it the one best way.

6. _____ Managers should let employees have full access to information that is not confidential.

_____ Managers should give employees only the information they need to know to do their job.

7. _____ If the manager is not around, the employees will work just as hard.

_____ If the manager is not around, the employees will take it easier than when being watched.

8. _____ Managers should share the management responsibilities with group members.

_____ Managers should perform the management functions for the group.

To determine your attitude or belief system about people at work, add up the numbers (0–5) for the first statement in each pair; don't bother adding the numbers for the second statements. The total should be between 0 and 40. Place your score on the continuum below.

Theory X 0—5—10—15—20—25—30—35—40 *Theory* Y

Generally, the higher your score, the greater are your Theory Y beliefs, and the lower the score, the greater your Theory X.

Douglas McGregor classified attitudes or belief system, which he called assumptions, as *Theory* X and *Theory* Y.[33] People with Theory X attitudes hold that employees dislike work and must be closely supervised in order to do their work. Theory Y attitudes hold that employees like to work and do not need to be closely supervised in order to do their work. In each of the eight pairs of statements in Self-Assessment Exercise 2-5, the first lines are Theory Y attitudes and the second lines are Theory X attitudes.

Managers with Theory X attitudes tend to have a negative, pessimistic view of employees and display more coercive, autocratic leadership styles using external means of controls, such as threats and punishment. Managers with Theory Y attitudes tend to have a positive, optimistic view of employees and display more participative leadership styles using internal motivation and rewards. In 1966 when McGregor published his Theory X and Theory Y, most managers had Theory X attitudes, and he was calling for a change to Theory Y attitudes. More recently, the paradigm shift from management to leadership also reflects this change in attitudes, as more managers use participative leadership styles.

Managers should acknowledge the influence of attitudes on behavior and performance.[34] A study of over 12,000 managers explored the relationship between managerial achievement and attitudes toward subordinates.[35] The managers with Theory Y attitudes were better at accomplishing organizational objectives and better at tapping the potential of subordinates. The managers with strong Theory X attitudes were far more likely to be in the low-achieving group. Your attitudes are important, because your leadership style will spring from your core attitudes about your followers. If you scored higher in Theory X for Self-Assessment Exercise 2-5, it does not mean that you cannot be an effective leader. As with personality traits, you can change your attitudes, with effort. You don't have to be an autocratic leader.

Pygmalion effect: leaders' attitudes toward and expectations of followers, and their treatment of them, explain and predict followers' behavior and performance.

The Pygmalion Effect

The **Pygmalion effect** *proposes that leaders' attitudes toward and expectations of followers, and their treatment of them, explain and predict followers' behavior and performance.* Research by J. Sterling Livingston popularized this theory, and others have supported it as discussed here.[36] We have already talked about attitudes and how they affect behavior (how to treat others) and performance, so let's add expectations. In business, expectations are stated as objectives and standards. Effective leaders set clear standards and expect the best from their followers.

In a study of welding students, the foreman who was training the group was given the names of students who were quite intelligent and would do well. Actually, the students were selected at random. The only difference was the foreman's expectations. The so-called intelligent students did significantly outperform the other group members. Why this happened is what this theory is all about: The foreman's expectations influenced the behavior and performance of the followers.

Lou Holtz advises setting a higher standard; the worst disservice you can do as a coach, teacher, parent, or leader is to say to your followers, "I don't think you are capable of doing very much—so I'm going to lower the standard," or just to do it without saying anything. Lou says there are two kinds of leaders: those who are optimists and lift others up, and those who pull everybody down. If you are in a leadership role, don't worry about being popular (need for affiliation); worry about raising the self-image and productivity of your followers. Having two different teams win the national college football championship within a couple of years after he took the job as head coach shows Lou's ability to set a higher standard.[37]

Marva Collins, recognized as one of the nation's most determined and successful teachers, opened her own inner-city school, which sets very high standards for students of all abilities. In grade school, these minority students read Shakespeare and do hours of homework each night. By contrast, many of the area's public schoolchildren cannot read and do no homework. Many of her students have gone on to successful careers, rather than being recipients of welfare, because of Ms. Collins' Pygmalion effect. To be an effective leader, like Lou and Marva, set a higher standard and treat people like winners—and they usually will be.

Self-Concept

self-concept: the positive or negative attitudes people have about themselves.

So far, we have discussed the leaders' attitudes about followers. Now we will examine leaders' attitudes about themselves. *Self-concept refers to the positive or negative attitudes people have about themselves.* If you have a positive view of yourself as being a capable person, you will tend to have the positive self-confidence trait. A related concept, *self-efficacy*, is the belief in your own capability to perform in a specific situation. Self-efficacy is based on self-concept and is closely related to the self-confidence trait, because if you believe you can be successful, you will often have self-confidence.

There is a lot of truth in the saying, "if you think you can you can, if you think you can't you can't." Recall times when you had positive self-efficacy and were successful, or negative self-efficacy and failed. Think of sports: sinking a basket, getting a goal or a hit, running a certain distance or time, or lifting a weight. Think of school: passing a test, getting a good grade on an assignment, or getting a certain final grade. Think of work: completing a task, meeting a deadline, making a sale, or solving a problem. Successful leaders have positive attitudes with strong self-concepts, are optimistic, and believe they can make a positive difference.[38] If Kay Koplovitz did not believe she could successfully start and run USA Networks, it would not exist today. If you don't believe you can be a successful leader, you probably won't be.

Developing a More Positive Attitude and Self-Concept. Your behavior and performance will be consistent with the way you see yourself. You cannot be an effective leader, or follower, if you don't have a positive self-concept. The environment around us influences our attitudes. Usually we cannot control our environment, but we can control our attitudes. Think and act like a winner, and you may become one.[39] Following are some ideas to help you change your attitudes and develop a more positive self-concept:

1. *Consciously try to have and maintain a positive, optimistic attitude.* If you don't have a positive attitude, it may be caused by your unconscious thoughts and behavior. Only with conscious effort can you improve your self-concept.

2. *Realize that there are few, if any, benefits to negative, pessimistic attitudes about others and yourself.* Do holding a grudge, worrying, and being afraid of failure help you to succeed?

3. *Cultivate optimistic thoughts.* Scientific evidence suggests that your thoughts affect every cell in your body. Every time you think positive thoughts, your body, mind, and spirit respond. You will likely feel more motivated and energetic.[40] Use positive self-talk—I will do a good job; it will be done on time; etc. Also use mental imagery—picture yourself achieving your goal.

4. *If you catch yourself complaining or being negative in any way, stop and change to a positive attitude.* With time, you will catch yourself less often as you become more positive about yourself.

5. *Avoid negative people, especially any that make you feel negative about yourself.* Associate with people who have a positive self-concept, and use their positive behavior.

6. *Set and achieve goals.* Set short-term goals (daily, weekly, monthly) that you can achieve. Achieving specific goals will improve your self-concept, helping you to view yourself as successful.

7. *Focus on your success; don't dwell on failure.* If you achieve five of six goals, dwell on the five and forget the one you missed. We are all going to make mistakes and experience failure. The difference between effective leaders and less-effective leaders is that the successful ones learn from their mistakes. They bounce back from disappointment and don't let it affect them negatively in the future. Happiness is nothing more than a poor memory for the bad things that happen to you.[41]

8. *Accept compliments.* When someone compliments you, say thank you; it builds self-concept. Don't say things like it was nothing, or anyone could have done it, because you lose the opportunity for a buildup.

9. *Don't belittle accomplishments or compare yourself to others.* If you meet a goal and say it was easy anyway, you are being negative. If you compare yourself to someone else and say they are better, you are being negative. No matter how good you are, there is almost always someone better. So focus on being the best that you can be, rather than putting yourself down for not being the best.

10. *Think for yourself.* Develop your own attitudes based on others' input; don't simply copy others' attitudes.

11. *Be a positive role model.* If the leader has a positive attitude, the followers usually do too.

We can choose to be optimistic or pessimistic—and we usually find what we are looking for. If you look for the positive, you are likely to be happier and get more out of life; why look for the negative and be unhappy? Even when the worst in life happens to you, you have the choice of being positive or negative. Christopher Reeve was a successful film star, best known as Superman, until he fell off a horse and was paralyzed. Rather than being bitter and negative toward life, and sitting at home feeling sorry for himself, Reeve started a foundation (The Christopher Reeve Foundation) to raise money to develop a cure for spinal cord injuries. Reeve raises millions of dollars by getting out and asking for donations. He also starred in a TV movie and is a director. During an interview, he said, "I'm actually busier now than I was before the accident. I find work more fulfilling than ever." When asked how he maintains a positive attitude that keeps him going, he said, "I believe you have two choices in life. One is to look forward and the other is to look backwards. To look backwards gets you nowhere. Backwards thinking leads to a place of negativity. That's not where I want to dwell."[42] Hopefully, your disappointments in life will not be so dramatic. But we all have disappointments in life, and we have the choice of going on with a positive or negative attitude. Here's one final tip:

12. *When things go wrong and you're feeling down, do something to help someone who is worse off than you.* You will realize that you don't have it so bad, and you will realize that the more you give, the more you get. Volunteering at a jail, hospital, soup kitchen, or homeless shelter can help change your attitude.

How Attitudes Develop Leadership Styles

We now put together the leader's attitudes toward others, using Theory X and Theory Y, and the leader's attitude toward self, using self-concept, to illustrate how these two sets of attitudes develop into four leadership styles. Combining attitudes with the Leader Motive Profile (LMP), an effective leader tends to have Theory Y attitudes with a positive self-concept. See Figure 2-5 to understand how attitudes toward self and others affect leadership styles.[43]

	THEORY Y ATTITUDES	THEORY X ATTITUDES
Positive self-concept	The leader typically gives and accepts positive feedback, expects others to succeed, and lets others do the job their way.	The leader typically is bossy, pushy, and impatient, does much criticizing with little praising, and is very autocratic.
Negative self-concept	The leader typically is afraid to make decisions, is unassertive, and self-blaming when things go wrong.	The leader typically blames others when things go wrong, is pessimistic about resolving personal or organizational problems, and promotes a feeling of hopelessness among followers.

Figure 2-5 *Leadership styles based on attitudes.*

ETHICAL LEADERSHIP

Before we discuss ethical behavior, complete Self-Assessment Exercise 2-6 to find out how ethical your behavior is.

Self-Assessment Exercise 2-6

How Ethical Is Your Behavior?

For this exercise, you will be using the same set of statements twice. The first time you answer each question, focus on your own behavior and how often you use it. On the line before the question, place the number from 1 to 5 that represents how often you did, do, or would do the behavior if you had the chance. These numbers will allow you to determine your level of ethics. You can be honest without fear of having to tell others your score in class. Sharing ethics scores is not part of the exercise.

Frequently   Never
1   2   3   4   5

The second time you answer each question, focus on other people in an organization where you have worked, or are now working. Place an O on the line after the number if you observed someone doing this behavior. Also place a W on the line if you reported (whistle blowing) this behavior within the organization or externally.

O—observed   W—whistle blowing

College

____ 1. ____ Cheating on homework assignments.

____ 2. ____ Passing in papers that were completed by someone else, presenting them as your own work.

____ 3. ____ Cheating on exams.

Job

____ 1. ____ Coming to work late and getting paid for it.

____ 2. ____ Leaving work early and getting paid for it.

____ 3. ____ Taking long breaks or lunches and getting paid for it.

____ 4. ____ Calling in sick to get a day off, when not sick.

___ 5. ___ Socializing or goofing off rather than doing the work that should be done.

___ 6. ___ Using the company phone to make personal calls.

___ 7. ___ Doing personal work while on company time.

___ 8. ___ Using the company copier for personal use.

___ 9. ___ Mailing personal things through the company mail.

___ 10. ___ Taking home company supplies or merchandise and keeping it.

___ 11. ___ Taking home company tools or equipment without permission for personal use and returning it.

___ 12. ___ Giving company supplies or merchandise to friends, or allowing them to take it without saying anything.

___ 13. ___ Putting in for reimbursement for meals and travel or other expenses that weren't actually eaten or taken.

___ 14. ___ Using the company car for personal business.

___ 15. ___ Taking spouse or friend out to eat and charging it to the company expense account.

___ 16. ___ Taking spouse or friend on business trips and charging the expense to the company.

___ 17. ___ Accepting gifts from customers or suppliers in exchange for giving them business.

To determine your ethics score, add up the numbers 1–5. Your total will be between 20 and 100. Place the number here ____ and indicate your score on the continuum below.

20—30—40—50—60—70—80—90—100

Unethical   *Ethical*

The higher your score, the more ethical is your behavior, and vice versa for lower scores.

Business graduates have been called ethically naive. Ethics is an especially hot topic, because it is a major concern to both managers and employees. It is so important that some large organizations have ethics officers who are responsible for developing and implementing ethics codes. Business ethics, and ethics codes, should provide assistance in making ethical decisions. However, you cannot go too many days without hearing or reading, in the mass media, some scandal related to unethical and/or unlawful behavior. **Ethics** *are the standards of right and wrong that influence behavior.* Right behavior is considered ethical, and wrong behavior is considered unethical.[44]

ethics: the standards of right and wrong that influence behavior.

Government laws and regulations are designed to govern business behavior. However, ethics goes beyond legal requirements. The difference between ethical and unethical behavior is not always clear. What is considered unethical in some countries is considered ethical in others. For example, in the United States, it is ethical to give a gift but unethical to give a bribe (a gift as a condition of acquiring business). However, the difference between a gift and a bribe is not always clear-cut. In some countries giving bribes is the standard business practice. In this section you will learn that ethical behavior does pay, and you will find some simple guides to ethical behavior.

Does Ethical Behavior Pay?

Generally, the answer to whether it pays to be ethical is yes. From the organizational level of analysis, good business and good ethics are synonymous. Ethics is at the heart of business, and profits and ethics are intrinsically related. Ben and Jerry claim that the success of their ice cream business is based on their ethics and social responsibility. However, organizations are not ethical or unethical; only people are. Organizational codes of ethics are helpful, but leadership by example has a greater influence on followers' behavior.[45]

From an individual level of analysis, recall that integrity is an important trait of effective leaders. Using ethical behavior is part of integrity. Though at first, you might be richly rewarded for knifing people in the back, eventually retaliation follows, trust is lost, and productivity declines. Many employees are fired for unethical behavior. More than just understanding what ethics is, you need to act ethically.[46]

Simple Guides to Ethical Behavior

Every day in your personal and professional life, you face situations in which you can make ethical or unethical choices. You make these choices based on your integrity trait as well as on influences by others.

Following are some guides that can help you make the right decisions.

Golden Rule. Following the golden rule will help you to use ethical behavior. The golden rule is:

"Do unto others as you want them to do unto you." Or, put another way,

"Don't do anything to other people that you would not want them to do to you."

Four-Way Test. Rotary International developed the four-way test of the things we think and do to guide business transactions. The four questions are (1) Is it the truth? (2) Is it fair to all concerned? (3) Will it build good will and better friendship? (4) Will it be beneficial to all concerned? When making your decision, if you can answer yes to these four questions it is probably ethical.

Stakeholder Approach to Ethics

*Under the **stakeholder approach to ethics,** one creates a win-win situation for relevant parties affected by the decision.* A win-win situation meets the needs of the organization and employees as well as those of other stakeholders, so that everyone benefits from the decision. The effective leader uses the moral exercise of power—socialized power, rather than personalized. Stakeholders include everyone affected by the decision, which may include followers, governments, customers, suppliers, society, stockholders, and so on. The higher up in management you go, the more stakeholders you have to deal with.[47] You can ask yourself one simple question to help you determine if your decision is ethical from a stakeholder approach:

"Am I proud to tell relevant stakeholders my decision?"

stakeholder approach to ethics: creates a win-win situation for relevant parties affected by the decision.

If you are proud to tell relevant stakeholders your decision, it is probably ethical. If you are not proud to tell others your decision, or you keep rationalizing it, the decision may not be ethical. Rationalizing by saying everybody else does it is usually a copout.[48] Everybody does *not* do it, and even if many other employees do it, that doesn't make it right. If you are not sure whether a decision is ethical, talk to your manager, higher-level managers, ethics committee members, and other people with high ethical standards. If you are reluctant to talk to others for advice on an ethical decision because you think you may not like their answers, the decision may not be ethical.

3

Leadership Behavior and Motivation

William Bratton, Police Commissioner of the New York City Police Department (NYPD), took the job with one major goal for the entire police department—to reduce the crime rate. Bratton asked for an immediate 10 percent cut in crime. He raised the goal to 15 percent for the next year, and the department achieved a 17 percent reduction in crime. During Bratton's two-year tenure, the crime rate dropped by 27 percent.

To determine if the goals were being accomplished, Bratton developed statistical techniques to measure the crime rate. He made the 76 precinct commanders and 38,000 police workers accountable for New York City's crime rate. To help fight crime, Bratton introduced other technology, including a computer local area network (LAN) system and cellular phones in squad cars. He put more police on the streets as part of his aggressive push for community policing to reduce street crime.

Commanders were held accountable for the crime rates in their precincts. They had to keep track of their statistical crime rates and develop crime-reduction strategies to further cut their rates. Bratton held Comstat (an abbreviation for *computer statistics*) meetings. At these meetings, commanders shared their statistics to show progress (or lack of progress) in cutting crime in their precincts, and presented crime-cutting strategies. Commanders who did not have well-prepared statistical reports and strategy plans were severely reprimanded by Bratton.[1]

William Bratton is not without his critics. Citizens have complained that the police are too aggressive and harass innocent people on the streets, and legal issues of police brutality have been raised. However, few can argue that Bratton's leadership has been successful; a 27 percent cut in crime in two years speaks for itself. New York has become the safest large city in America. Bratton's behavior and ability to motivate the police force affected his leadership success. These are the topics that you will learn about in this chapter.

■ *Go to the Internet:* For more information about William Bratton and the New York City Police Department, do a name search on the Internet and visit the NYPD website at **http://www.ci.nyc.ny.html/nypd/home.html.**

William Bratton was clearly an effective leader in getting the NYPD to lower the crime rate. This chapter focuses on behavioral leadership styles and motivation, the keys to Bratton's success. We will discuss four leadership models and seven motivation theories.

LEADERSHIP BEHAVIOR AND STYLES

Leadership Behavior

By the late 1940s, most of the leadership research had shifted from the trait theory paradigm to the behavioral theory paradigm, which focuses on what the leader says and does. In the continuing quest to find the one best leadership style in all situations, researchers attempted to identify the differences in the behavior of effective leaders versus ineffective leaders. Although the behavioral leadership theory made major contributions to leadership research, which we will discuss more fully later, it never achieved its goal of finding one best style. Unfortunately, no leadership behaviors were found to be consistently associated with leadership effectiveness.[2] The leadership behavior theory paradigm lasted nearly 30 years. Today research continues to seek a better understanding of behavior, its complexity, and its effects on employee performance.[3]

Leadership Behavior Is Based on Traits. Although the behavioral theorists focus on behavior, it's important to realize that leaders' behavior is based on their traits and skills. The best predictor of employee retention is the relationship between manager and employee. Employees who have a poor relationship with their manager are more likely to quit. The relationship is based on the manager's leadership personality traits and attitudes, which directly affect his or her behavior with the employee. Recall that the Pygmalion effect is based on traits, attitude expectations, and the manager's treatment (behavior) of employees, which in turn determines the followers' behavior and performance. Recent empirical research has confirmed that the leader's behavior has a causal effect on employee performance.[4]

Leading by example is important to managers.[5] In fact, as Albert Einstein said, "Setting an example is not the main means of influencing another, it is the only means." Leading by example takes place as followers observe the leader's behavior and copy it. And the leader's behavior is based on his or her traits. Thus, traits and behavior go hand-in-hand, or trait leadership theory influences behavioral leadership theory. However, behavior is easier to learn and change than traits.

Leadership Styles and the Iowa State University Research

Leadership style *is the combination of traits, skills, and behaviors leaders use as they interact with followers.* Although a leadership style is based on traits and

leadership style: the combination of traits, skills, and behaviors leaders use as they interact with followers.

skills, the important component is the behavior, because it is a relatively consistent pattern of behavior that characterizes a leader. A precursor to the behavior approach recognized autocratic and democratic leadership styles.

Iowa State University Leadership Styles. In the 1930s, before behavioral theory became popular, Kurt Lewin and associates conducted studies at Iowa State University that concentrated on the leadership style of the manager.[6] Their studies identified two basic leadership styles:

- *Autocratic leadership style.* The autocratic leader makes the decisions, tells employees what to do, and closely supervises workers.

- *Democratic leadership style.* The democratic leader encourages participation in decisions, works with employees to determine what to do, and does not closely supervise employees. The autocratic and democratic leadership styles are often placed at opposite ends of a continuum, as shown in Figure 3-1; thus a leader's style usually falls somewhere between the two styles.

The Iowa studies contributed to the behavioral movement and led to an era of behavioral rather than trait research. With the

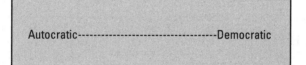

Figure 3-1 *Iowa State University leadership styles.*

shift in paradigm from management to leadership, the leadership style of effective managers is no longer autocratic, but more democratic and laissez-faire.[7] William Bratton, New York City Police Commissioner, uses a democratic leadership style. Although he sets goals for crime reduction and requires statistical analysis to measure results, the 76 individual precinct commanders develop their own strategies to reduce crime. They must have goals, but how they achieve their goals is left up to them.

UNIVERSITY OF MICHIGAN AND OHIO STATE UNIVERSITY STUDIES

Leadership research was conducted at Ohio State and the University of Michigan at about the same time during the mid-1940s to mid-1950s. These studies were not based on prior autocratic and democratic leadership styles, but rather sought to determine the behavior of effective leaders. Although these two studies used the term *leadership behavior* rather than *leadership styles*, the behaviors identified are actually more commonly called leadership styles today. In this section we discuss leadership styles identified by these two universities. Before reading about these studies, complete Self-Assessment Exercise 3-1 to determine your leadership style.

Self-Assessment Exercise 3-1

Your Leadership Style

For each of the following statements, select either a 0, "I **would** tend to do this," or a 1, "I **would not** tend to do this" as a manager of a work unit. There are no right or wrong answers, so don't try to select correctly.

____ 1. I (would or would not) let my employees know that they should not be doing things during work hours that are not directly related to getting their job done.

____ 2. I (would or would not) spend time talking to my employees to get to know them personally during work hours.

____ 3. I (would or would not) have a clearly written agenda of things to accomplish during department meetings.

____ 4. I (would or would not) allow employees to come in late or leave early to take care of personal issues.

____ 5. I (would or would not) set clear goals so employees know what needs to be done.

____ 6. I (would or would not) get involved with employee conflicts to help resolve them.

____ 7. I (would or would not) spend much of my time directing employees to ensure that they meet department goals.

____ 8. I (would or would not) encourage employees to solve problems related to their work without having to get my permission to do so.

____ 9. I (would or would not) make sure that employees do their work according to the standard method to be sure it is done correctly.

____ 10. I (would or would not) seek the advice of my employees when making decisions.

____ 11. I (would or would not) keep good, frequent records of my department's productivity and let employees know how they are doing.

____ 12. I (would or would not) work to develop trust between my employees and me, and among the department members.

____ 13. I (would or would not) be quick to take corrective action with employees who are not meeting the standards or goals.

____ 14. I (would or would not) personally thank employees for doing their job to standard and meeting goals.

____ 15. I (would or would not) continue to set higher standards and goals and challenge my employees to meet them.

____ 16. I (would or would not) be open to employees to discuss personal issues during work time.

____ 17. I (would or would not) schedule my employees' work hours and tasks to be completed.

____ 18. I (would or would not) encourage my employees to cooperate with rather than compete against each other.

____ 19. I (would or would not) focus on continually trying to improve the productivity of my department with activities like cutting costs.

____ 20. I (would or would not) defend good employees of mine if my manager or peers criticized their work, rather than agree or say nothing.

Add up the number of **would do** this for all *odd*-numbered items and place it here _____ and on the continuum below.

High Task 10   9   8   7   6   5   4   3   2   1 *Low Task*
Leadership Style   *Leadership Style*

Add up the number of **would do** this for all *even-numbered* items and place it here _____ and on the continuum below.

High People 10 9 8 7 6 5 4 3 2 1 *Low People*
Leadership Style   *Leadership Style*

The higher your score for task leadership, the stronger is your tendency to focus on getting the job done. The higher your score for people leadership, the stronger is your tendency to focus on meeting people's needs and developing supportive relationships. Read on to better understand these leadership styles.

University of Michigan: Job-Centered and Employee-Centered Behavior

The University of Michigan's Survey Research Center, under the principal direction of Rensis Likert, conducted studies to determine leadership effectiveness. Researchers created a questionnaire called the "Survey of Organizations" and conducted interviews to gather data on leadership styles. Their goals were to (1) classify the leaders as effective and ineffective by comparing the behavior of leaders from high-producing units and low-producing units; and (2) determine reasons for effective leadership.[8] The researchers identified two styles of leadership behavior, which they called *job-centered* and *employee-centered*. The U of Michigan model stated that a leader is either more job-centered or more employee-centered. *The University of Michigan Leadership Model thus identifies two leadership styles: job-centered and employee-centered.* See Figure 3-2 for the University of Michigan Leadership Model: a one-dimensional continuum between two leadership styles.

Job-Centered Leadership Style. The job-centered style has scales measuring two job-oriented behaviors of goal emphasis and work facilitation. Job-centered behavior refers to the extent to which the leader takes charge to get the job done. The leader closely directs subordinates with clear roles and goals, while the manager tells them what to do and how to do it as they work toward goal achievement. Enforcing standards is an important function. Review the odd-numbered items in Self-Assessment Exercise 3-1 for examples of job (task) oriented leadership behavior.

Employee-Centered Leadership Style. The employee-centered style has scales measuring two employee-oriented behaviors of supportive leadership and interaction facilitation. Employee-centered behavior refers to the extent to which the leader focuses on meeting the human needs of employ-

University of Michigan Leadership Model: identifies two leadership styles—(1) job-centered and (2) employee-centered.

Figure 3-2 *The University of Michigan Leadership Model: Two leadership styles, one dimension.*

Job-Centered Leadership Style
Leadership Style ·· | ·················· **Employee-Centered Leadership Style**

ees while developing relationships. The leader is sensitive to subordinates and communicates to develop trust, support, and respect while looking out for their welfare. Review the even-numbered items in Self-Assessment Exercise 3-1 for examples of employee (people) oriented leadership behavior.

Based on Self-Assessment Exercise 3-1, is your leadership style more job (task) or employee (people) centered?

Applying the Concept 3-1

University of Michigan Leadership Styles

Identify each of these five behaviors by its leadership style. Write the appropriate letter in the blank before each item.

    a. job-centered   b. employee-centered

_____ 1. The manager is influencing the follower to do the job the way the leader wants it done.

_____ 2. The manager just calculated the monthly sales report and is sending it to all the sales representatives so they know if they met their quota.

_____ 3. The leader is saying a warm, friendly good morning to followers as they arrive at work.

_____ 4. The manager is in his or her office developing plans for the department.

_____ 5. The leader is seeking ideas from followers on a decision he or she has to make.

Ohio State University: Initiating Structure and Consideration Behavior

The Personnel Research Board of Ohio State University, under the principal direction of Ralph Stogdill, began a study to determine effective leadership styles. In the attempt to measure leadership styles, these researchers developed an instrument known as the Leader Behavior Description Questionnaire (LBDQ). The LBDQ had 150 examples of definitive leader behaviors, which were narrowed down from 1,800 leadership functions. Respondents to the questionnaire perceived their leader's behavior toward them on two distinct dimensions or leadership types, which they eventually called *initiating structure* and *consideration*.[9]

- *Initiating structure behavior.* The initiating structure leadership style is essentially the same as the job-centered leadership style; it focuses on getting the task done.

- *Consideration behavior.* The consideration leadership style is essentially the same as the employee-centered leadership style; it focuses on meeting people's needs and developing relationships.

Because a leader can be high or low on initiating structure and/or consideration, four leadership styles are developed. *The Ohio State University Leadership Model identifies four leadership styles: low structure and high consideration, high structure and high consideration, low structure and low consideration, and high structure and low consideration.* Figure 3-3 illustrates the four leadership styles and their two dimensions.

Leaders with high structure and low consideration behavior use one-way communications and decisions are made by the managers, whereas leaders with high consideration and low structure use two-way communications and tend to share decision making.[10] To determine your two-dimensional leadership style from Self-Assessment Exercise 3-1, put your two separate (Task and People) scores together and determine which of the

Ohio State University Leadership Model: identifies four leadership styles—(1) low structure and high consideration, (2) high structure and high consideration, (3) low structure and low consideration, and (4) high structure and low consideration.

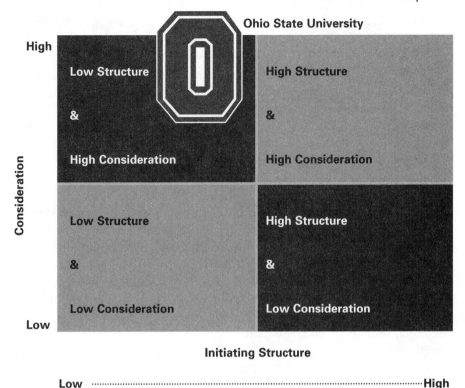

four styles in Figure 3-3 is the closest match. Police Commissioner William Bratton appears to use the high structure and high consideration leadership style, because of his participative leadership style.

Differences between Leadership Models—and Their Contributions

The Ohio State and University of Michigan leadership models are different in that the University of Michigan places the two leadership behaviors at opposite ends of the same continuum, making it one dimensional. The Ohio State University Model considers the two behaviors independent of one another, making it two dimensional; thus this model has four leadership styles.

The two leadership behaviors on which the models of both universities are based have strong research support. Leadership behaviors were developed, and repeatedly tested, using statistical factor analysis to narrow the dimensions down to structure/job-centered and consideration/employee-centered. The LBDQ and modified versions have been used in hundreds of studies by many different researchers.[11]

Research efforts to determine the one best leadership style have been weak and inconsistent for most criteria of leadership effectiveness. In other words, there is no one best leadership style in all situations; this is the first contribution, because it has helped lead researchers to the next paradigm— that of contingency leadership theory. Thus, the contribution of the behavioral leadership paradigm was to identify two generic dimensions of leadership behavior that continue to have importance in accounting for leader effectiveness today.[12]

Although there is no one best leadership style in all situations, there has been a consistent finding that employees are more satisfied with a leader who is high in consideration.[13] Prior to the two university leadership studies, many organizations had focused on getting the job done with little, if any, concern for meeting employee needs. So, along with other behavioral theory research, there was a shift to place more emphasis on the human side of the organization to increase productivity; this is a second contribution. The saying that a happy worker is a productive worker comes from this period of research.

Another important research finding was that most leadership functions can be carried out by someone besides the designated leader of a group.[14] Thus, due to behavioral leadership research, more organizations began training managers to use participative leadership styles. In fact, Rensis Likert at the University of Michigan later proposed that managers make extensive use of group supervision instead of supervising each subordinate separately. Likert proposed three types of leadership behavior, differentiated between effective and ineffective managers: job-centered behavior, employee-centered behavior, and participative leadership.[15] Thus, as a third contribution of these leadership models, Likert can be credited as being the first to identify the participative leadership style that is commonly used today.

THE LEADERSHIP GRID

In this section we discuss the Leadership Grid theory, including research and contributions of the high-concern-for-people and high-concern-for-production (team leader) leadership styles.

Leadership Grid Theory

Behavior leadership theory did not end in the mid-1950s with the University of Michigan and Ohio State University studies. Robert Blake and Jane Mouton developed the Managerial Grid® and published it in 1964, updated it in 1978 and 1985, and in 1991 it became the Leadership Grid® with Anne Adams McCanse replacing Mouton.[16] Behavioral leadership is still being researched today. The Leadership Grid was recently applied to project management by different researchers.[17]

The Leadership Grid builds on the Ohio State and Michigan studies; it is based on the same two leadership dimensions, which Blake and Mouton called *concern for production* and *concern for people*.[18] The concern for both people and production is measured through a questionnaire on a scale from 1 to 9. Therefore, the grid has 81 possible combinations of concern for production and people. However, *the* **Leadership Grid** *identifies five leadership styles: 1,1 impoverished; 9,1 authority compliance; 1,9 country club; 5,5 middle of the road; and 9,9 team leader.* See Figure 3-4 for an adaptation of the Leadership Grid.

Leadership Grid: identifies five leadership styles—1,1 impoverished; 9,1 authority compliance; 1,9 country club; 5,5 middle of the road; and 9,9 team leader.

Following are descriptions of leadership styles in the Leadership Grid:

- The *impoverished leader* (1,1) has low concern for both production and people. The leader does the minimum required to remain employed in the position.
- The *authority-compliance leader* (9,1) has a high concern for production and a low concern for people. The leader focuses on getting the job done as people are treated like machines.
- The *country-club leader* (1,9) has a high concern for people and a low concern for production. The leader strives to maintain a friendly atmosphere without regard for production.
- The *middle-of-the-road leader* (5,5) has balanced, medium concern for both production and people. The leader strives to maintain satisfactory performance and morale.
- The *team leader* (9,9) has a high concern for both production and people. This leader strives for maximum performance and employee satisfaction. According to Blake, Mouton, and McCanse, the team leadership style is generally the most appropriate for use in all situations.

To estimate your Leadership Grid leadership style, using Self-Assessment Exercise 3-1, use your Task score as your concern for production and your People score, and plot them on the Leadership Grid in Figure 3-4. Then select the closest of the five leadership styles. Commissioner Bratton, NYPD, tends to be a team leader.

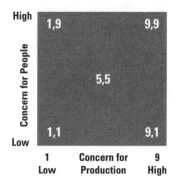

Figure 3-4 *Blake, Mouton, and McCanse Leadership Grid.*

Leadership Grid and High-High Leader Research and Contributions

The *high-high leader* has concern for both production and people; this is the team leadership style. However, authors of the Leadership Grid were not the only ones to conduct research to determine if the high-high style was the most effective leadership style in all situations. Blake and Mouton did conduct an extensive empirical research study that measured profitability before and after a 10-year period. In the study, one company subsidiary used an extensive Grid Organizational Development program designed to teach managers how to be 9,9 team leaders (experimental group), while

---

Applying the Concept 3-2

The Leadership Grid

Identify the five statements by their leader's style. Write the appropriate letter in the blank before each item.

a. 1,1 (impoverished)   c. 9,1 (authority compliance)   e. 9,9 (team)
b. 1,9 (country club)   d. 5,5 (middle of the road)

____ **1.** The group has very high morale; members enjoy their work. Productivity in the department is one of the lowest in the company. The manager is one of the best liked in the company.

____ **2.** The group has adequate morale; the employees are satisfied with their manager. They have an average productivity level compared to the other departments in the company.

____ **3.** The group has one of the lowest levels of morale in the company; most employees do not like the manager. It is one of the top performers compared to other departments.

____ **4.** The group is one of the lowest producers in the company; employees don't seem to care about doing a good job. It has a low level of morale, because the employees generally don't like the manager.

____ **5.** The group is one of the top performers; the manager challenges employees to continue to meet and exceed goals. Employees have high morale because they like the manager.

another subsidiary did not use the program (control group). The subsidiary using the team leadership style increased its profits four times more than the control subsidiary. Thus, the researchers claimed that team leadership usually results in improved performance, low absenteeism and turnover, and high employee satisfaction.[19] Blake and Mouton support the high-high leader style as a universal theory.

However, another researcher disagreed with these findings, calling high-high leadership a myth.[20] A more objective meta-analysis (a study combining the results of many prior studies) found that although task and relationship behavior tends to correlate positively with subordinate performance, the correlation is usually weak.[21] In conclusion, although there is some support for the universal theory, the high-high leadership style is not accepted as the one best style in all situations.

Critics suggested that different leadership styles are more effective in different situations.[22] Thus, a contribution of behavioral research is that it led to the shift in paradigm to contingency leadership theory. As you will learn in Chapter 5, contingency leadership theory is based on the behavioral theory of production and people leadership styles. Situational leadership models don't agree with using the same leadership style in all situations, but rather prescribe using the existing leadership style that best meets the situation.

A second contribution of behavioral leadership theory was the recognition that organizations need both production and people leadership. There is a generic set of production-oriented and people-oriented leadership functions that must be performed to ensure effective organizational performance. These two functions are an accepted universal theory; they apply across organizations, industries, and cultures. So in general, every organization on a global scale needs to perform production and people leadership functions to be successful. However, cultures vary on the value they assign to these leadership behaviors, and individuals from different cultures have different reactions to these leadership styles.[23] Consequently, a manager who is successful in America may not be successful in another country. In conclusion, production and people functions must be performed in all organizations; but how they are performed—or leadership styles—must vary with the situation. This is contingency leadership theory, which is the topic of Chapter 5.

A third related contribution of behavioral leadership theory supports co-leadership. The manager does not have to perform both production and people functions. Thus, strong production-oriented leaders can be successful if they have co-leaders to provide the people-oriented functions for them, and vice versa. Research suggests that group members who have the "best ideas" contributing to the decision are not necessarily the "best liked," and vice versa. When it is difficult for managers to be leaders of both production and people functions, co-leadership can be effective.[24] So if you tend to be more production- or people-oriented, seek co-leaders to complement your weaker area.

Humor is part of behavioral leadership, and it is considered important at successful organizations including Southwest Airlines and General Electric. Herb Kelleher, CEO of Southwest, tries to make work fun. Jack Welch, CEO of GE, said; "We have a lot of humor in our company. We spend a lot of time screwing around."[25]

Before we go on to motivation, let's tie personality traits from Chapter 2 together with what we've covered so far. Complete Self-Assessment Exercise 3-2 now.

Self-Assessment Exercise 3-2

Your Personality Traits and Leadership Styles

We stated in the first section that *traits affect leadership behavior.* How does this relate to you? For the University of Michigan Leadership Model, generally, if you had a high personality score for the Big Five surgency dimension in Self-Assessment Exercise 2-1 (dominance trait, high need for power), you most likely have a high score for the task (job-centered) leadership style. If you had a high score for agreeableness (sensitivity to others trait, high need for affiliation), you most likely have a high score for the people (employee-centered) leadership style. My U of M leadership style is primarily _____ _____.

For the Ohio State University Leadership Model, you need to score your personality for surgency and agreeableness as high or low. Then you combine them, and these personality scores should generally provide the same two-dimensional behaviors corresponding to one of the four leadership styles. My OSU leadership style is primarily _____ _____.

For the Leadership Grid, you need to score your personality for surgency and agreeableness on a scale of 1 to 9. Then you combine them on the grid, and these personality scores should generally provide about the same score as Self-Assessment Exercise 3-1. My leadership grid style is primarily _____ _____.

If you scored a Leader Motive Profile, your score for tasks should generally be higher than your score for people, because you have a greater need for power than affiliation. However, your leadership style on the Ohio State model could be high structure and high consideration, because this implies socialized power. You could also have a 9,9 team leader score on the Leadership Grid. My LMP is primarily _____ _____.

LEADERSHIP AND MAJOR MOTIVATION THEORIES

In this section we discuss motivation and leadership, the motivation process (which explains how motivation affects behavior), three classifications of motivation theories (content, process, and reinforcement) and three content motivation theories: hierarchy of needs, two-factor, and acquired needs theory. We also briefly describe the need to balance professional and personal needs.

Motivation and Leadership

motivation: anything that affects behavior in pursuing a certain outcome.

Motivation is anything that affects behavior in pursuing a certain outcome. From an organizational perspective, the outcomes managers want employees to pursue are organizational objectives. In our definition of leadership (Chapter 1), motivation is a key factor in the influencing process; the leader must motivate the followers to achieve organizational objectives. In the opening case, Commissioner Bratton had to motivate the 76 precinct commanders and 38,000 police workers to cut the crime rate by 10 percent the first year and another 15 percent the second year. In the rest of this chapter, you will learn the motivation theories Bratton used to motivate the NYPD.

There has been considerable interest in how motivation affects performance. Charles Shipley, a vice president of SL Industries, says that managers have to learn more about motivating workers and guiding them. Top managers must realize that motivation and leadership are the key to developing effective managers. Jack Welch, CEO of GE, said that his most important job is developing and motivating leaders. The ability to motivate yourself and your followers is critical to your success as a leader.[26]

The Motivation Process

motivation process: people go from need to motive to behavior to consequence to satisfaction or dissatisfaction.

*Through the **motivation process,** people go from need to motive to behavior to consequence to satisfaction or dissatisfaction.* For example, you are thirsty (need) and have a drive (motive) to get a drink. You get a drink (behavior) that quenches (consequence and satisfaction) your thirst. However, if you could not get a drink, or a drink of what you really wanted, you would be dissatisfied. Satisfaction is usually short-lived. Getting that drink satisfied you, but sooner or later you will need another drink. For this reason, the motivation process has a feedback loop. See Figure 3-5 for an illustration of the motivation process.

Some need or want motivates all behavior. However, needs and motives are complex: We don't always know what our needs are, or why we do the things we do. Have you ever done something and not known why you did it? Understanding needs will help you to better understand motivation and behavior. You will gain a better understanding of why people do the things they do.

Like traits, motives cannot be observed; but you can observe behavior and infer what the person's motive is. However, it is not easy to know why people behave the way they do, because people do the same things for different reasons. Also, people often attempt to satisfy several needs at once.

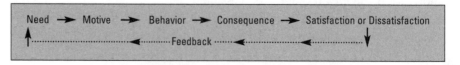

Figure 3-5 *The motivation process.*

An Overview of Three Major Classifications of Motivation Theories

There is no single universally accepted theory of how to motivate people, or how to classify the theories. We will discuss motivation theories and how you can use them to motivate yourself and others. In the following sections you will learn about content motivation theories, process motivation theories, and reinforcement theory. See Figure 3-6 for this classification with a listing of major motivation theories you will learn.

After studying all of the theories separately, we put them back together using the unifying motivation process to see the relationship between the theories. You can select one theory to use, or take from several to make your own theory, or apply the theory that best fits the specific situation.

CLASSIFICATION OF MOTIVATION THEORIES	SPECIFIC MOTIVATION THEORY
1. **Content motivation theories** focus on explaining and predicting behavior based on employee need motivation.	A. **Hierarchy of needs theory** proposes that employees are motivated through five levels of need—physiological, safety, social, esteem, and self-actualization.
	B. **Two-factor theory** proposes that employees are motivated by motivators (higher-level needs) rather than maintenance (lower-level needs) factors.
	C. **Acquired needs theory** proposes that employees are motivated by their need for achievement, power, and affiliation.
2. **Process motivation theories** focus on understanding how employees choose behaviors to fulfill their needs.	A. **Equity theory** proposes that employees will be motivated when their perceived inputs equal outputs.
	B. **Expectancy theory** proposes that employees are motivated when they believe they can accomplish the task, they will be rewarded, and the rewards for doing so are worth the effort.
	C. **Goal-setting theory** proposes that achievable but difficult goals motivate employees.
3. **Reinforcement theory** proposes that behavior can be explained, predicted, and controlled through the consequences for behavior.	<u>Types of Reinforcement</u> • Positive • Avoidance • Extinction • Punishment

Figure 3-6 *Major motivation theories.*

CONTENT MOTIVATION THEORIES

Before we present the content motivation theories, let's discuss content motivation theories in general. *Content motivation theories focus on explaining and predicting behavior based on people's needs.* However, the prediction of behavior does not include specific behavior that will be used to satisfy the need; predicting behavior refers to the person being motivated to behavior to satisfy the need. Motivation is also considered an inner desire to satisfy an unsatisfied need. Have you ever wondered why people do the things they do? The primary reason people do what they do is to meet their needs or wants to be satisfied. People want job satisfaction, and they will leave one organization for another to meet this need.

An employee who has job satisfaction usually has a higher level of motivation and is more productive than a dissatisfied employee. According to content motivation theorists, if you want to have satisfied employees you must meet their needs. When employees are asked to meet objectives, they have the question, although usually not asked, what's in it for me? The key to successful leaderships is to meet the needs of employees while achieving organizational objectives, as discussed in the topics of socialized power and ethics (Chapter 2).[27]

Hierarchy of Needs Theory

In the 1940s Abraham Maslow developed his hierarchy of needs theory,[28] which is based on four major assumptions: (1) Only unmet needs motivate. (2) People's needs are arranged in order of importance (hierarchy) going from basic to complex needs. (3) People will not be motivated to satisfy a higher-level need unless the lower-level need(s) has been at least minimally satisfied. (4) Maslow assumed that people have five classifications of needs, which are presented here in hierarchical order from low to high level of need.

Hierarchy of Needs. The **hierarchy of needs** *theory proposes that people are motivated through five levels of needs—physiological, safety, belongingness, esteem, and self-actualization.*

1. *Physiological needs:* These are people's primary or basic needs: air, food, shelter, sex, and relief or avoidance of pain.
2. *Safety needs:* Once the physiological needs are met, the individual is concerned with safety and security.
3. *Belongingness needs:* After establishing safety, people look for love, friendship, acceptance, and affection. Belongingness is also called social needs.
4. *Esteem needs:* After the social needs are met, the individual focuses on ego, status, self-respect, recognition for accomplishments, and a feeling of self-confidence and prestige.
5. *Self-Actualization needs:* The highest level of need is to develop one's full potential. To do so, one seeks growth, achievement, and advancement.

content motivation theories: focus on explaining and predicting behavior based on people's needs.

hierarchy of needs theory: proposes that people are motivated through five levels of needs: physiological, safety, belongingness, esteem, and self-actualization.

Maslow's work was criticized because it did not take into consideration that people can be at different levels of needs based on different aspects of their lives. Nor did he mention that people can revert back to lower-level needs. Today, Maslow and others realize that needs are not on a simple five-step hierarchy. Maslow's assumptions have recently been updated to reflect this insight, and many organizations today are using a variety of the management methods he proposed 30 years ago. Maslow has also been credited with influencing many management authors, including Douglas McGregor, Rensis Likert, and Peter Drucker.[29]

Motivating Employees with Hierarchy of Needs Theory. The major recommendation to leaders is to meet employees' lower-level needs so that they will not dominate the employees' motivational process. You should get to know and understand people's needs and meet them as a means of increasing performance. See Figure 3-7 for a list of ways in which managers attempt to meet these five needs.

Two-Factor Theory

In the 1960s, Frederick Herzberg published his two-factor theory.[30] Herzberg combined lower-level needs into one classification he called *hygiene* or *maintenance*; and higher-level needs into one classification he called *moti-*

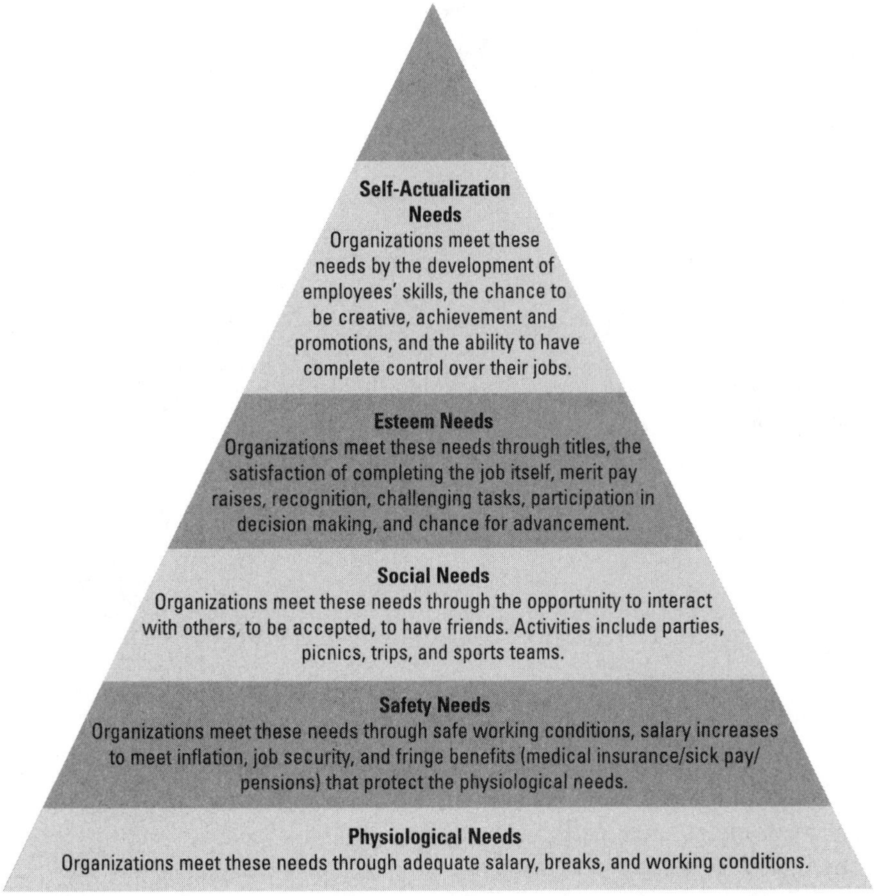

Self-Actualization Needs
Organizations meet these needs by the development of employees' skills, the chance to be creative, achievement and promotions, and the ability to have complete control over their jobs.

Esteem Needs
Organizations meet these needs through titles, the satisfaction of completing the job itself, merit pay raises, recognition, challenging tasks, participation in decision making, and chance for advancement.

Social Needs
Organizations meet these needs through the opportunity to interact with others, to be accepted, to have friends. Activities include parties, picnics, trips, and sports teams.

Safety Needs
Organizations meet these needs through safe working conditions, salary increases to meet inflation, job security, and fringe benefits (medical insurance/sick pay/pensions) that protect the physiological needs.

Physiological Needs
Organizations meet these needs through adequate salary, breaks, and working conditions.

Figure 3-7 *How organizations motivate with hierarchy of needs theory.*

two-factor theory: proposes that people are motivated by motivators rather than maintenance factors.

vators. ***Two-factor theory*** *proposes that people are motivated by motivators rather than maintenance factors.* Before you learn about two-factor theory, complete Self-Assessment Exercise 3-3.

Self-Assessment Exercise 3-3

Job Motivators and Maintenance Factors

Here are 12 job factors that contribute to job satisfaction. Rate each according to how important it is to you by placing a number from 1 to 5 on the line before each factor.

Very important		Somewhat important		Not important
5	4	3	2	1

_____ 1. An interesting job I enjoy doing

_____ 2. A good manager who treats people fairly

_____ 3. Getting praise and other recognition and appreciation for the work that I do

_____ 4. A satisfying personal life at the job

_____ 5. The opportunity for advancement

_____ 6. A prestigious or status job

_____ 7. Job responsibility that gives me freedom to do things my way

_____ 8. Good working conditions (safe environment, nice office, cafeteria, etc.)

_____ 9. The opportunity to learn new things

_____ 10. Sensible company rules, regulations, procedures, and policies

_____ 11. A job I can do well and succeed at

_____ 12. Job security and benefits

For each factor, write the number from 1 to 5 that represents your answer. Total each column (should be between 6 and 30 points).

Motivating factors	Maintenance factors
1. _____	2. _____
3. _____	4. _____
5. _____	6. _____
7. _____	8. _____
9. _____	10. _____
11. _____	12. _____
Totals _____	_____

Did you select motivators or maintenance factors as being more important to you? The closer to 30 (6) each score is, the more (less) important it is to you. Continue reading to understand the difference between motivators and maintenance factors.

Maintenance—Extrinsic Factors. Maintenance factors are also called *extrinsic motivators* because motivation comes from outside the person and the job itself. Extrinsic motivators include pay, job security, title; working conditions; fringe benefits; and relationships. These factors are related to meeting lower-level needs. Review Self-Assessment Exercise 3-3, the even-numbered questions, for a list of extrinsic job factors.

Motivators—Intrinsic Factors. Motivators are called *intrinsic motivators* because motivation comes from within the person through the work itself. Intrinsic motivators include achievement, recognition, challenge, and advancement. These factors are related to meeting higher-level needs. Doing something we want to do and doing it well can be its own reward. Organizations realize the importance of intrinsic motivation and are making jobs more interesting and challenging.[31] Review Self-Assessment Exercise 3-3, the odd-numbered questions, for a list of intrinsic job factors.

Herzberg's Two-Factor Motivation Model. Herzberg and associates, based on research, disagreed with the traditional view that satisfaction and dissatisfaction were at opposite ends of one continuum (a one-dimensional model). There are two continuums: not dissatisfied with the environment (maintenance) to dissatisfied, and satisfied with the job itself (motivators) to not satisfied (a two-dimensional model). See Figure 3-8 for Herzberg's motivation model. Employees are on a continuum from dissatisfied to not dissatisfied with their environment. Herzberg contends that providing maintenance factors will keep employees from being dissatisfied, but it will not make them satisfied or motivate them. In other words, maintenance factors will not satisfy or motivate employees; they will only keep them from being dissatisfied. For example, Herzberg believes that if employees are dissatisfied with their pay and they get a raise, they will no longer be dissatisfied. However, before long people get accustomed to the new standard of living and will become dissatisfied again. Employees will need another raise to not be dissatisfied again. The vicious cycle goes on. So Herzberg says you have to focus on motivators—the job itself.

Money as a Motivator. The current view of money as a motivator is that money matters more to some people than others, and that it may motivate some employees. However, money does not necessarily motivate employees to work harder.[32] Money also is limited in its ability to motivate. For example, many commissioned workers get to a comfortable point and don't push to make extra money; and some employees get to the point

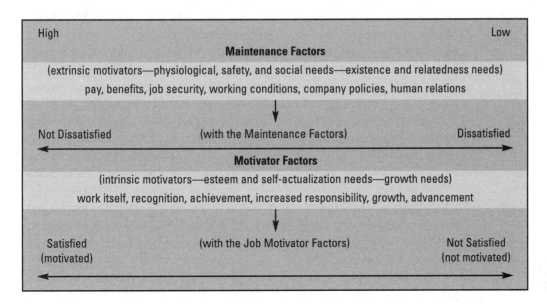

Figure 3-8 *Two-factor motivation theory.*

where they don't want overtime work, even though they are paid two or three times their normal wage.

But money is important. As GE's CEO Jack Welch says, you can't just reward employees with trophies; you need to reward them in the wallet too. Employees often leave one organization for another to make more money. High compensation (pay and benefits) based on performance is a practice of successful organizations. If you got a pay raise, would you be motivated and more productive?[33]

Motivating Employees with Two-Factor Theory. Under the old management paradigm, money (and other extrinsic motivators) was considered the best motivator. Under the new leadership paradigm, pay is important, but it is not the best motivator; intrinsic motivators are. Herzberg's theory has been criticized for having limited research support. However, it continues to be tested: Recently one study supported it, and another only partially supported it.[34] Herzberg fits the new paradigm: He says that managers must first ensure that the employees' level of pay and other maintenance factors are adequate. Once employees are not dissatisfied with their pay (and other maintenance factors), they can be motivated through their jobs. Herzberg also developed *job enrichment*, the process of building motivators into the job itself by making it more interesting and challenging. Job enrichment has been used successfully to motivate employees to higher levels of performance at many organizations, including AT&T, GM, IBM, Maytag, Monsanto, Motorola, Polaroid, and the Traveler's Life Insurance Company.

Acquired Needs Theory

acquired needs theory: proposes that people are motivated by their need for achievement, power, and affiliation.

Acquired needs theory *proposes that people are motivated by their need for achievement, power, and affiliation.* This is essentially the same definition given for achievement motivation theory in Chapter 2. It is now called acquired needs theory because David McClelland was not the first to study these needs, and because other management writers call McClelland's theory acquired needs theory. A general needs theory was developed by Henry Murray[35], then adapted by John Atkinson and David McClelland. However, McClelland's achievement motivation theory became more widely published than Atkinson's work. You have already learned about McClelland's work, so we will be brief here. It's important to realize how closely linked traits, behavior, and motivation are. Acquired need is also widely classified as both a trait and a motivation, since McClelland and others believe that needs are based on personality traits. McClelland's affiliation need is essentially the same as Maslow's belongingness need; and power and achievement are related to esteem, self-actualization, and growth. McClelland's motivation theory does not include lower-level needs for safety and physiological needs. This theory is still being researched; a recent study used it with nurse managers. The conclusion was that both need for achievement and power motives of nurse managers influence patient and staff outcomes in health care in the 1990s.[36]

Acquired needs theory says that all people have the need for achievement, power, and affiliation, but to varying degrees. Here are some ideas for motivating employees based on their dominant needs:

- *Motivating employees with a high n Ach.* Give them nonroutine, challenging tasks with clear, attainable objectives. Give them fast and frequent feedback on their performance. Continually give them increased responsibility for doing new things. Keep out of their way.

- *Motivating employees with a high n Pow.* Let them plan and control their jobs as much as possible. Try to include them in decision making, especially when they are affected by the decision. They tend to perform best alone rather than as team members. Try to assign them to a whole task rather than just part of a task.

- *Motivating employees with high n Aff.* Be sure to let them work as part of a team. They derive satisfaction from the people they work with rather than the task itself. Give them lots of praise and recognition. Delegate responsibility for orienting and training new employees to them. They make great buddies and mentors.

Police Commissioner Bratton is motivating his precinct commanders by focusing more on meeting higher-level needs—esteem and self-actualization (Maslow), motivators (Herzberg), and need for achievement (McClelland). Before we briefly discuss the need to balance professional and personal needs, see Figure 3-9 for a comparison of the three content theories of motivation.

The Need to Balance Professional and Personal Needs

The need to balance professional and personal needs is currently a hot topic, with the ascent of matrixed organizations working around the clock due to a global marketplace—and with the reengineered, downsizing, right-sizing world that focuses on how to get more done with fewer people. Successful leaders use socialized power and strive to meet the needs of people and the organization to create a win-win situation for all stakeholders. Two major things organizations are doing to help employees meet their personal needs are providing on-site day care centers—or giving employees information to help them find good day care—and offering flextime. Some leaders are also telling employees to go home and "get a life" before it is too

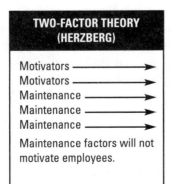

HIERARCHY OF NEEDS (MASLOW)	TWO-FACTOR THEORY (HERZBERG)	ACQUIRED NEEDS THEORY (MCCLELLAND)
Self-Actualization ⟶	Motivators ⟶	Achievement and Power
Esteem ⟶	Motivators ⟶	Achievement and Power
Belongingness ⟶	Maintenance ⟶	Affiliation
Safety ⟶	Maintenance ⟶	Not classified
Physiological ⟶	Maintenance ⟶	Not classified
Needs must be met in a hierarchical order.	Maintenance factors will not motivate employees.	Employees must be motivated differently based on their acquired needs.

Figure 3-9 *A comparison of content motivation theories.*

late.[37] To get more specific, up-to-date information on this topic, complete the Management General website exercises related to this topic.

PROCESS MOTIVATION THEORIES

Process motivation theories focus on understanding how people choose behavior to fulfill their needs. Process motivation theories are more complex than content motivation theories. Content motivation theories simply focus on identifying and understanding people's needs. Process motivation theories go a step further, attempting to understand why people have different needs, why their needs change, how and why people choose to try to satisfy needs in different ways, the mental process people go through as they understand situations, and how they evaluate their need satisfaction. In this section you will learn about three process motivation theories: equity theory, goal-setting theory, and expectancy theory.

process motivation theories: focus on understanding how people choose behavior to fulfill their needs.

Equity Theory

If employees perceive organizational decisions and managerial actions to be unfair or unjust, they are likely to experience feelings of anger, outrage, and resentment.[38] Equity theory is primarily J. Stacy Adams' motivation theory, in which people are said to be motivated to seek social equity in the rewards they receive (output) for their performance (input).[39] *Equity theory proposes that people are motivated when their perceived inputs equal outputs.*

equity theory: proposes that people are motivated when their perceived inputs equal outputs.

Rewarding People Equitably. Through the equity theory process, people compare their inputs (effort, experience, seniority, status, intelligence, and so forth) and outputs (praise, recognition, pay, benefits, promotions, increased status, supervisor's approval, etc.) to that of relevant others. A relevant other could be a co-worker or group of employees from the same or different organizations, or even from a hypothetical situation. Notice that our definition says *perceived* and not *actual* inputs to outputs.[40] Others may perceive that equity actually exists, and that the person complaining about inequity is wrong.

Equitable distribution of pay is crucial to organizations.[41] Unfortunately, many employees tend to inflate their own efforts or performance when comparing themselves to others. Employees also tend to overestimate what others earn. Employees may be very satisfied and motivated until they find out that a relevant other is earning more for the same job, or earning the same for doing less work. A comparison with relevant others leads to three conclusions: The employee is underrewarded, overrewarded, or equitably rewarded.[42] When inequity is perceived, employees attempt to reduce it by reducing input or increasing output.

Motivating with Equity Theory. Research supporting equity theory is mixed, because people who believe they are overrewarded usually don't change their behavior. Instead, they often rationalize that they deserve the outputs. One view of equity is that it is like Herzberg's maintenance factors.

When employees are not dissatisfied, they are not actively motivated; but maintenance factors do demotivate when employees are dissatisfied. According to equity theory, when employees believe they are equitably rewarded they are not actively motivated. However, when employees believe they are underrewarded, they are demotivated.

Using equity theory in practice can be difficult, because you don't always know who the employee's reference group is, nor their view of inputs and outcomes. However, this theory does offer some useful general recommendations:

1. Managers should be aware that equity is based on perception, which may not be correct. It is possible for the manager to create equity or inequity. Some managers have favorite subordinates who get special treatment; others don't.

2. Rewards should be equitable. When employees perceive that they are not treated fairly, morale and performance problems occur. Employees producing at the same level should be given equal rewards.

3. High performance should be rewarded, but employees must understand the inputs needed to attain certain outputs. When incentive pay is used, there should be clear standards specifying the exact requirements to achieve the incentive. A manager should be able to objectively tell others why one person got a higher merit raise than another did. Commissioner Bratton of the NYPD was concerned about equitably rewarding police based on their performance of decreasing the crime rate. Thus, those with lower crime rates got larger pay raises, and vice versa.

Expectancy Theory

Expectancy theory is based on Victor Vroom's formula: motivation = expectancy × instrumentality × valence.[43] *Expectancy theory proposes that people are motivated when they believe they can accomplish the task, they will get the reward, and the rewards for doing so are worth the effort.* The theory is based on the following assumptions: Both internal (needs) and external (environment) factors affect behavior; behavior is the individual's decision; people have different needs, desires, and goals; people make behavior decisions based on their perception of the outcome.

expectancy theory: proposes that people are motivated when they believe they can accomplish the task, they will get the reward, and the rewards for doing so are worth the effort.

Three Variables. All three variable conditions must be met in Vroom's formula for motivation to take place.

- *Expectancy* refers to the person's perception of his or her ability (probability) to accomplish an objective. Generally, the higher one's expectancy, the better the chance for motivation. When employees do not believe that they can accomplish objectives, they will not be motivated to try.

- *Instrumentality* refers to belief that the performance will result in getting the reward. Generally, the higher one's instrumentality, the greater the chance for motivation. If employees are certain to get the reward, they probably will be motivated. When not sure, employees may not be motivated. For example, Dan believes he would be a good manager and wants to get promoted. However, Dan has an external locus of control and believes that working hard will not result in a promotion anyway. Therefore, he will not be motivated to work for the promotion.

- *Valence* refers to the value a person places on the outcome or reward. Generally, the higher the value (importance) of the outcome or reward, the better the chance of motivation. For example, the supervisor, Jean, wants an employee, Sim, to work harder. Jean talks to Sim and tells him that working hard will result in a promotion. If Sim wants a promotion, he will probably be motivated. However, if a promotion is not of importance to Sim, it will not motivate him.

Motivating with Expectancy Theory. One study found that expectancy theory can accurately predict a person's work effort, satisfaction level, and performance—but only if the correct values are plugged into the formula. A more recent meta-analysis (a study using the data of 77 other prior studies) had inconsistent findings with some positive correlations. A more recent study found that expectancy theory can be used to determine if leaders can be trained to use ethical considerations in decision making.[44]

Therefore, this theory works in certain contexts but not in others. Expectancy theory also works best with employees who have an internal locus of control, because if they believe they control their destiny, their efforts will result in success. The following conditions should be implemented to make the theory result in motivation:

1. Clearly define objectives and the performance necessary to achieve them.

2. Tie performance to rewards. High performance should be rewarded. When one employee works harder to produce more than other employees and is not rewarded, he or she may slow down productivity.

3. Be sure rewards are of value to the employee. Managers should get to know employees as individuals. Develop good human relations.

4. Make sure your employees believe you will do what you say you will do. For example, employees must believe you will give them a merit raise if they do work hard. So that employees will believe you, follow through and show them you do what you say you'll do.

5. Use the Pygmalion effect (Chapter 2) to increase expectations. Your high expectation can result in follower self-fulfilling prophecy. As the level of expectation increases, so will performance.

Goal-Setting Theory

The research conducted by E. A. Locke and others has revealed that setting objectives has a positive effect on motivation and performance. High-achievement, motivated individuals consistently engage in goal setting.[45] ***Goal-setting theory*** *proposes that specific, difficult goals motivate people.* Our behavior has a purpose, which is usually to fulfill a need. Goals give us a sense of purpose as to why we are working to accomplish a given task.

goal-setting theory: proposes that specific, difficult goals motivate people.

Four parts of the model (Example from McDonald's*):							
(1) Infinitive	+	(2) action verb	+	(3) singular, specific, and measurable result to be achieved	+	(4) target date	
To		increase		the number of stores to 25,000		by December 2000.	
(1)	+	(2)	+	(3)		+	(4)

*"McDonald's," *Wall Street Journal*, 13 May 1998, p. 1.

Model 3-1 *Writing Effective Objectives Model*

Writing Objectives. To help you to write effective objectives that meet the criteria you will learn next, use the model. The parts of the **writing objectives model** are (1) Infinitive + (2) action verb + (3) singular, specific, and measurable result to be achieved + (4) target date. The model is shown in Model 3-1, which is adapted from Max E. Douglas's model.

Criteria for Objectives. For an objective to be effective, it should include the four criteria listed in steps 3 and 4 of the writing objectives model:

- *Singular result.* To avoid confusion, each objective should contain only one end result. When multiple objectives are listed together, one may be met but the other(s) may not.

- *Specific.* The objective should state the exact level of performance expected.

- *Measurable.* If people are to achieve objectives, they must be able to observe and measure their progress regularly to monitor progress and to determine if the objective has been met.

- *Target date.* A specific date should be set for accomplishing the objective. When people have a deadline, they usually try harder to get the task done on time. If people are simply told to do it when they can, they don't tend to get around to it until they have to. It is also more effective to set a specific date, such as October 29, rather than a set time, such as in two weeks, because you can forget when the time began and should end. Some objectives are ongoing and do not require a stated date. The target date is indefinite until it is changed.

In addition to the four criteria from the model, there are three other criteria that do not always fit within the model:

- *Difficult but achievable.* A number of studies show that individuals perform better when assigned difficult objectives rather than (1) easy objectives, (2) objectives that are too difficult, or (3) simply told "do your best."[46]

writing objectives model: (1) Infinitive + (2) action verb + (3) singular, specific, and measurable result to be achieved + (4) target date.

- *Participatively set.* Teams that participate in setting their objectives generally outperform groups with assigned objectives.
- *Commitment.* For objectives to be met, employees must accept them. If employees are not committed to striving for the objective, even if you meet the other criteria, they may not meet the objective. Using participation helps get employees to accept objectives.

Using Goal Setting to Motivate Employees. Goal theory is currently one of the most validated research approaches to work motivation. Setting objectives that meet the criteria for objectives results in higher levels of performance.[47] In the opening case, Commissioner Bratton's primary motivation method was goal theory. Recall that he asked for an immediate 10 percent drop in the crime rate, 15 for the next year, and the NYPD achieved a 27 percent cut in crime within two years. Clearly, these objectives meet the criteria for motivating the police.

REINFORCEMENT THEORY

B. F. Skinner, reinforcement motivation theorist, contends that to motivate employees it is not necessary to identify and understand needs (content motivation theories), nor to understand how employees choose behaviors to fulfill them (process motivation theories). All the manager needs to do is understand the relationship between behaviors and their consequences, and then arrange contingencies that reinforce desirable behaviors and discourage undesirable behaviors. **Reinforcement theory** *proposes that through the consequences for behavior, people will be motivated to behave in predetermined ways.* Reinforcement theory uses behavior modification (apply reinforcement theory to get employees to do what you want them to do) and operant conditioning (types and schedules of reinforcement). Skinner states that behavior is learned through experiences of positive and negative consequences. The three components of Skinner's framework are found in Figure 3-10, with an example.[48]

As illustrated in the example in Figure 3-10, behavior is a function of its consequences.[49] Employees learn what is, and is not, desired behavior as a result of the consequences for specific behavior. The two important concepts used to modify behavior are the types of reinforcement and the schedules of reinforcement.

reinforcement theory: proposes that through the consequences for behavior, people will be motivated to behave in predetermined ways.

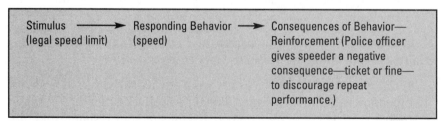

Figure 3-10 *Components of reinforcement theory.*

Types of Reinforcement

The four types of reinforcement are positive, avoidance, extinction, and punishment.

Positive Reinforcement. A method of encouraging continued behavior is to offer attractive consequences (rewards) for desirable performance. For example, an employee is on time for a meeting and is rewarded by the manager thanking him or her. The praise is used to reinforce punctuality. Other reinforcements are pay, promotions, time off, increased status, and so forth. Positive reinforcement is the best motivator for increasing productivity.

Avoidance Reinforcement. Avoidance is also called *negative reinforcement.* As with positive reinforcement, you are encouraging continued desirable behavior. The employee avoids the negative consequence. For example, an employee is punctual for a meeting to avoid the negative reinforcement, such as a reprimand. *Rules* are designed to get employees to avoid certain behavior. However, rules in and of themselves are not a punishment. Punishment is given only if the rule is broken.

Extinction. Rather than encourage desirable behavior, extinction (and punishment) attempts to reduce or eliminate undesirable behavior by withholding reinforcement when the behavior occurs. For example, an employee who is late for a meeting is not rewarded with praise. Or the manager may withhold a reward of value, such as a pay raise, until the employee performs to set standards.

From another perspective, managers who do not reward good performance can cause its extinction. In other words, if you ignore good employee performance, good performance may stop because employees think, "Why should I do a good job if I'm not rewarded in some way?"

Punishment. Punishment is used to provide an undesirable consequence for undesirable behavior. For example, an employee who is late for a meeting is reprimanded. Notice that with avoidance there is no actual punishment; it's the threat of the punishment that controls behavior. Other methods of punishment include harassing, taking away privileges, probation, fining, demoting, firing, and so forth. Using punishment may reduce the undesirable behavior; but it may cause other undesirable behavior, such as poor morale, lower productivity, and acts of theft or sabotage. Punishment is the most controversial method and the least effective in motivating employees. Figure 3-11 illustrates the four types of reinforcement.

Schedule of Reinforcement

The second reinforcement consideration in controlling behavior is determining when to reinforce performance. The two major classifications are continuous and intermittent.

Continuous Reinforcement. With a continuous method, each and every desired behavior is reinforced. Examples of this method would be a machine with an automatic counter that lets the employee know, at any

3. Select the appropriate reinforcement schedule.

4. Do not reward mediocre or poor performance.

5. Look for the positive and give praise, rather than focus on the negative and criticize. Make people feel good about themselves (Pygmalion effect).

6. Never go a day without giving sincere praise.

7. Do things for your employees, instead of to them, and you will see productivity increases.

As a manager, try the positive first. Positive reinforcement is a true motivator because it creates a win-win situation by meeting the needs of the employee as well as the manager and organization. From the employees' perspective, avoidance and punishment create a lose-win situation. The organization or manager wins by forcing them to do something they really don't want to do.

Giving Praise

Pay can increase performance. But it is not the only, nor necessarily the best, reinforcer for performance. Empirical research studies have found that feedback and social reinforcers (praise) may have as strong an impact on performance as pay. In the 1940s, Lawrence Lindahl conducted a survey revealing that what employees want most from a job is full appreciation for work done. Similar studies have been performed over the years with little change in results. Another survey showed that managers want personal recognition more than salary, by four to one. Another survey revealed that 27 percent of workers would quit to move to a company known for giving praise and recognition; 38 percent of workers said they rarely or never get praise from the boss.[56]

Although research has shown praise to be an effective motivator, and giving praise costs nothing and takes only a minute, few employees are getting a pat on the back these days. However, good leaders do commend more than they command.[57] When was the last time your manager thanked you or gave you some praise for a job well done? When was the last time your manager complained about your work? If you are a manager, when was the last time you praised or criticized your employees? What is the ratio of praise to criticism?

Giving praise develops a positive self-concept in employees and leads to better performance—the Pygmalion effect and self-fulfilling prophecy. Praise is a motivator (not maintenance) because it meets employees' needs for esteem and self-actualization, growth, and achievement. Giving praise creates a win-win situation. It is probably the most powerful, simplest, least costly, and yet most underused motivational technique there is.

Ken Blanchard and Spencer Johnson popularized giving praise through their best-selling book, *The One-Minute Manager*.[58] They developed a technique that involves giving one-minute feedback of praise. Model 3-2, Giving Praise, is an adaptation. *The steps in the **giving praise model** are (1) Tell the employee exactly what was done correctly. (2) Tell the employee why the*

giving praise model: includes four steps—(1) Tell the employee exactly what was done correctly. (2) Tell the employee why the behavior is important. (3) Stop for a moment of silence. (4) Encourage repeat performance.

behavior is important. (3) Stop for a moment of silence. (4) Encourage repeat performance. Blanchard calls it one-minute praise because it should not take more than one minute to give the praise. It is not necessary for the employee to say anything. The four steps are described below and illustrated in Model 3-2.

step 1. **Tell the employee exactly what was done correctly.** When giving praise, look the person in the eye. Eye contact shows sincerity and concern. It is important to be very specific and descriptive. General statements, like "you're a good worker," are not as effective. On the other hand, don't talk for too long, or the praise loses its effectiveness.

step 2. **Tell the employee why the behavior is important.** Briefly state how the organization and/or person benefits from the action. It is also helpful to tell the employee how you feel about the behavior. Be specific and descriptive.

step 3. **Stop for a moment of silence.** Being silent is tough for many managers.[59] The rationale for the silence is to give the employee the chance to "feel" the impact of the praise. It's like "the pause that refreshes." When you are thirsty and take the first sip or gulp of a refreshing drink, it's not until you stop, and maybe say, "Ah," that you feel your thirst quenched.

step 4. **Encourage repeat performance.** This is the reinforcement that motivates the employee to continue the desired behavior. Blanchard recommends touching the employee. Touching has a powerful impact. However, he recommends it only if both parties feel comfortable. Others say don't touch employees; it could lead to a sexual harassment charge.

As you can see, giving praise is easy, and it doesn't cost a penny. Managers trained to give praise say it works wonders. It's a much better motivator than giving a raise or other monetary reward. One manager stated that an employee was taking his time stacking cans on a display. He gave the employee praise for stacking the cans so straight. The employee was so pleased with the praise that the display went up with about a 100 percent increase in productivity. Note that the manager looked for the positive, and used positive reinforcement rather than punishment. The manager could have given a reprimand comment such as, "Quit goofing off and get the display up faster." That statement would not have motivated the employee to increase productivity. All it would have done was hurt human relations, and could have ended in an argument. The cans were straight. The employee was not praised for the slow work pace. However, if the praise had not worked, the manager should have used another reinforcement method.[60]

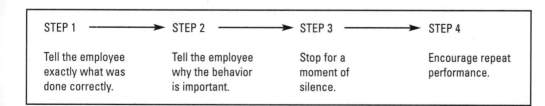

STEP 1 →	STEP 2 →	STEP 3 →	STEP 4
Tell the employee exactly what was done correctly.	Tell the employee why the behavior is important.	Stop for a moment of silence.	Encourage repeat performance.

Model 3-2 *Giving Praise*

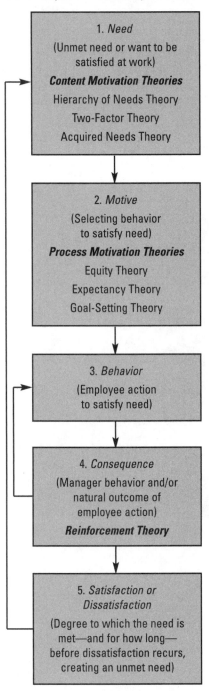

Figure 3-13 *The motivation process with the motivation theories.*

Putting the Motivation Theories Together within the Motivation Process

Motivation is important because it helps to explain why employees behave the way they do. At this point you may be wondering: How do these theories fit together? Is one the best? Should I try to pick the correct theory for a given situation? The groups of theories are complementary; each group of theories refers to a different stage in the motivation process. Each group of theories answers a different question. Content motivation theories answer the question: What needs do employees have that should be met on the job? Process motivation theories answer the question: How do employees choose behavior to fulfill their needs? Reinforcement theory answers the question: What can managers do to get employees to behave in ways that meet the organizational objectives?

In the first section of this chapter you learned that the motivation process went from need to motive to behavior to consequence to satisfaction or dissatisfaction. Now let's make the motivation process a little more complex by incorporating the motivation theories, or answers to the preceding questions, into the process. See Figure 3-13 for an illustration. Note that step 4 loops back to step 3 because, according to reinforcement theory, behavior is learned through consequences. Step 4 does not loop back to steps 1 or 2 because reinforcement theory is not concerned about needs, motives, or satisfaction; it focuses on getting employees to behave in predetermined ways, through consequences provided by managers. Also note that step 5 loops back to step 1 because meeting needs is ongoing; meeting our needs is a never-ending process. Finally, be aware that according to two-factor theory, step 5 satisfaction or dissatisfaction is not on one continuum but on two separate continuums (satisfied to not satisfied or dissatisfied to not dissatisfied), based on the level of need being met (motivator or maintenance).

Communication, Coaching, and Conflict Skills

M. Douglas Ivester took over as chairman of the board and CEO of Coca-Cola, replacing the late Cuban-born Roberto Goizueta, in 1997. Some questioned whether Ivester could fill the shoes of Goizueta, who was very successful at leading Coca-Cola to new record sales and profits. Ivester did not get much of a honeymoon when he started; Coke's earnings were being hammered by overseas economic woes. Its community credibility was also being hurt by a racial-discrimination lawsuit, by European Union officials' suspicions that Coke used its dominant market position to shut out competitors, and by the contamination scare in Belgium and France.

Coke CEO Ivester may have been hampered by his own management decisions. With no second-in-command (co-leader), he focused on product distribution instead of company image. Ivester's ambitious acquisition plans caused conflict between Coke and regulators in Europe and elsewhere, who have made things more difficult for Coke. GrassRoots Recycling Network ran paid advertisements in the *New York Times,* stating that Ivester was responsible for wasting billions of plastic Coke bottles every year.

CEO Ivester was also criticized for his communications during the Belgian and French crises in June 1999. Over 200 people in several Belgian and French towns reported illness—complaining of headaches, stomachaches, and nausea—after drinking Coca-Cola products. The French minister of consumer affairs, Marylise Lebranchu, complained that Coke took 48 hours to provide information on how to identify which soft-drink cans might pose further risks. She said that 48 hours is too long; the delay forced France to order that all canned Coke products be removed from store shelves to avoid risking further illnesses. Coke products were also removed from stores in Belgium; the Netherlands and Luxembourg restricted sales of certain Coke products, and Coke had to recall bottles of water in Poland. French and Belgian government officials scolded the company for not offering enough information on what caused the illness; Coke had to be asked to bring back more data to provide a satisfactory and conclusive explanation for the illnesses. Coke estimated the recall and lost sales would cost over $103 million, and its profits dropped 21 percent in the second quarter of 1999. The U.S. press questioned why it took Ivester a week to apologize, and asked if CEO Ivester could turn things around. After only two years as CEO of Coke, Ivester stepped down and recommended Douglas Daft to take his place, which the board approved. Ivester said he thought it was time for "a change" and "fresh leadership."

Despite these problems, the Coca-Cola Company is clearly the global soft-drink industry leader. Coke owns over 160 other soft-drink brands, manufactured and sold by the Coca-Cola Company and its subsidiaries in nearly 200 countries around the world. In fact, approximately 70 percent of sales and 80 percent of profits come from outside the United States. Coke views itself as being a worldwide business that is always local. Its bottling and distribution operations are, with some exceptions, locally owned and operated by independent businesspeople who are native to the nations in which they are located. Coke also owns the Minute Maid Company, which is the world's leading marketer of juices and juice drinks.

John Pemberton created Coca-Cola, and on May 8, 1886, he first sold it to local pharmacies as a soda-fountain drink priced at 5 cents a glass. In 1886, Coke's average sales were nine drinks per day; in 1998, average sales of all Coke products exceed 1 billion servings per day.[1]

■ *Go to the Internet:* For more updated information about M. Douglas Ivester, his successor Douglas Daft, and Coca-Cola, go to the Web. Do a name search on the Internet, and visit the Coke website at **http://www.cocacola.com**.

Ivester was the hand-picked successor of Goizueta. What led to his early retirement? In this chapter we examine M. Douglas Ivester's leadership as it relates to the topics of this chapter. The focus of the chapter is on three related topics. We begin with sending and receiving communications, because it is the foundation for coaching and managing conflict. Next we discuss feedback as it relates to both communication and coaching. Based on this foundation, you will learn how to coach followers, and then how to manage conflicts.

COMMUNICATION

communication: the process of conveying information and meaning.

Communication is the process of conveying information and meaning. True communication takes place only when all parties understand the message (information) from the same perspective (meaning). At all organizational levels, it has been estimated that at least 75 percent of each workday is consumed in communication. Thus, every successful person is in the communication business. Your ability to speak, read, and write will have a direct impact on your career success: Organizations recruit people with good communication skills, and organizations offer communication training programs.[2] In this section we discuss the importance of communication in leadership and examine the communication process of sending and receiving messages.

Communication and Leadership

Communication is a major competency for leaders, because effective communication is part of leadership style. Empirical research supports the statement that effective leaders are also effective communicators; there is a positive relationship between communication competency and leadership performance.[3]

Good interpersonal and communication skills drive effective leadership.[4] For example, from Chapter 1, our definition of leadership is based on communication: Leaders play informational roles, and the shift in paradigm from management to leadership includes differences in communication skills. From Chapter 2, personality affects the type of communication used: Ethical leaders with integrity will use open and honest communications; the Pygmalion effect requires communication of attitudes. From Chapter 3, communication varies with leadership style: The autocratic leader uses one-way communication to tell employees what to do, while the democratic leader uses two-way communication as the team decides what to do and how to do it. Leaders use communication to motivate followers.

Organizations with effective communication systems are more likely to be successful. One important part of organizational communications is to convey the mission, vision, and values so that all employees understand the big picture of what is trying to be accomplished. However, research based on 10,000 firms indicates that leaders are not doing an effective job in this area. You will learn more about strategic leadership in Part Three, Chapters

10 and 11. Lee Iacocca, former top executive credited with saving Chrysler from bankruptcy, said, "The most important thing I learned in school was how to communicate." Two important parts of leadership communication are sending and receiving messages; for example, a study by Pitney-Bowes found that each day its workers send and receive an average of 201 messages of all types.[5]

Sending Messages and Giving Instructions

Managers use the communication process of sending a variety of messages in person, on the phone, and in writing. An important part of a manager's job is to give instructions, which is sending a message. Have you ever heard a manager say, "This isn't what I asked for"? When this happens, it is usually the manager's fault. Managers often make incorrect assumptions and do not take 100 percent of the responsibility for ensuring their message is transmitted with mutual understanding. As a manager, how well you give instructions directly affects your ability to motivate your employees, as well as their satisfaction with your supervisory leadership.[6] Before sending a message, you should carefully plan the message. Then, give the message orally using the message-sending process, or send the message in writing.

Planning the Message. Before sending a message, you should plan it, answering these questions:

- *What is the goal of the message?* Is it to influence, to inform, to express feeling, or all of these things? What do you want as the end result of the communication? Set an objective. After considering the other planning dimensions, determine exactly what you want to say to meet your objective. In today's diverse global economy, you also need to be culturally sensitive in deciding what to say in a message.[7]

- *Who should receive the message?* Have you included everyone who needs to receive your message?

- *How will you send the message?* With the receivers in mind, plan how you will convey the message so that it will be understood. Select the appropriate method (see Applying the Concept 4-1 for a list) for the audience and situation. As a general guide, use rich oral channels for sending difficult and unusual messages, less rich written channels for transmitting simple and routine messages to several people, and combined channels for important messages that employees need to attend to and understand. You should also avoid giving too much detail.[8]

- *When will the message be transmitted?* Timing is important. For example, if it is going to take 15 minutes to transmit a message, don't approach an employee five minutes before quitting time. Wait until the next day. Make an appointment when appropriate.

- *Where will the message be transmitted?* Decide on the best setting— your office, the receiver's workplace, and so forth. Remember to keep distractions to a minimum.

oral message-sending process:
(1) develop rapport; (2) state your communication objective; (3) transmit your message; (4) check the receiver's understanding; (5) get a commitment and follow up.

The Oral Message-Sending Process. Be careful not to talk too fast when sending oral messages over the phone or in person.[9] It is helpful to follow the steps in the **oral message-sending process:** *(1) develop rapport; (2) state your communication objective; (3) transmit your message; (4) check the receiver's understanding; and (5) get a commitment and follow up.* Model 4-1 lists these steps.

step 1. **Develop rapport.** Put the receiver at ease. It is usually appropriate to begin communications with small talk correlated to the message. It helps prepare the person to receive the message.

step 2. **State your communication objective.** The common business communication objectives are to influence, inform, and express feelings. With the goal of influencing, it is helpful for the receiver to know the end result of the communication before covering all the details.

step 3. **Transmit your message.** If the communication objective is to influence, tell the people what you want them to do, give instructions, and so forth. Be sure to set deadlines for completing tasks. If the objective is to inform, tell the people the information. If the objective is to express feeling, do so.

step 4. **Check the receiver's understanding.** About the only time you may not want to check understanding during one-to-one or small-group communication is when the objective is to express feelings. When influencing and giving information, you should ask direct questions, and/or use paraphrasing. To simply ask, "Do you have any questions?" does not check understanding. In the next section of this chapter, you will learn how to check understanding by using feedback.

step 5. **Get a commitment and follow up.** When the goal of communication is to inform or express feelings, a commitment is not needed. However, when the goal of communication is to influence, it is important to get a commitment to the action. The leader needs to make sure that followers can do the task and have it done by a certain time or date. For situations in which the follower does not intend to get the task done, it is better to know this when sending the message, rather than to wait until the deadline before finding out. When followers are reluctant to commit to the necessary action, leaders can use persuasive power within their authority. When communicating to influence, follow up to ensure that the necessary action has been taken.

Written Communication and Writing Tips. With information technology and the Internet, you can communicate with anyone in the world—in real time. Because the use of e-mail will continue to increase, your written communication skills are more important than ever.[10] So we have included some simple but important writing tips that can help you to improve your writing.

- Lack of organization is the number one writing problem.[11] Before you begin writing, set an objective for your communication. Keep the audience in mind. What do you want them to do? Make an outline,

Applying the Concept 4-1

Methods of Sending Messages

For each of these ten communication situations, select the most appropriate channel for transmitting the message. Write the appropriate letter in the blank before each item.

Oral communication
a. face-to-face
b. meeting
c. presentation
d. telephone

Written communication (includes e-mail and traditional methods)
e. memo
f. letter
g. report
h. bulletin board
i. poster
j. newsletter

_____ **1.** You are waiting for an important letter to arrive by FedEx, and you want to know if it is in the mail room yet.

_____ **2.** Employees have been leaving the lights on in the stock room when no one is in it. You want them to shut the lights off.

_____ **3.** José, Jamal, and Sam will be working on a new project as a team. You need to explain the project to them.

_____ **4.** John has come in late for work again, and you want this practice to stop.

_____ **5.** You have exceeded your departmental goals. You want your manager to know about it, because it should have a positive influence on your upcoming performance appraisal.

_____ **6.** Your spouse sells Avon products and wants you to help her advertise where you work. However, you don't want to ask anyone directly to buy Avon.

_____ **7.** People in another department sent a message asking for some numbers relating to your work.

_____ **8.** You have been asked to be the speaker for a local nonprofit organization.

_____ **9.** You enjoy writing, and you want to become better known by more people throughout your firm.

_____ **10.** You have been given a written complaint from a customer and asked to take care of it.

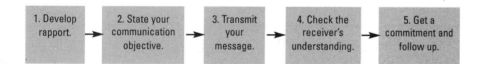

Model 4-1 *The oral message-sending process.*

using letters and/or numbers, of the major points you want to get across. Now put the outline into written form. The first paragraph states the purpose of the communication. The middle paragraphs support the purpose of the communication: facts, figures, and so forth. The last paragraph summarizes the major points and clearly states the action, if any, to be taken by you and other people.

• Write to communicate, not to impress. Keep the message short and simple. Limit each paragraph to a single topic and an average of five sentences. Sentences should average 15 words. Vary paragraph and sentence length, but a paragraph should not exceed one-half a page. Write in the active voice (I recommend...) rather than the passive voice (it is recommended...).

• Edit your work and rewrite where necessary. To improve sentences and paragraphs, add to them to convey full meaning, cut out unnecessary words and phrases, and/or rearrange the words. Check your work with the computer spelling and grammar checkers. Have others edit your work as well.

Receiving Messages

The second communication process that leaders are involved in is receiving messages. With oral communications, the key to successfully understanding the message is listening. Thus, leaders need to be patient and listen to others.[12] Complete Self-Assessment Exercise 4-1 to determine how good a listener you are, then read the tips for improving listening skills in the message-receiving process.

Self-Assessment Exercise 4-1

Listening Skills

Select the response that best describes the frequency of your actual behavior. Write the letter A, U, F, O, or S on the line before each of the 15 statements.

A—almost always   U—usually   F—frequently
O—occasionally   S—seldom

____ 1. I like to listen to people talk. I encourage others to talk by showing interest, smiling, nodding, and so forth.

____ 2. I pay closer attention to people who are more similar to me than I do to people who are different from me.

____ 3. I evaluate people's words and nonverbal communication ability as they talk.

____ 4. I avoid distractions; if it's noisy, I suggest moving to a quiet spot.

____ 5. When people come to me and interrupt me when I'm doing something, I put what I was doing out of my mind and give them my complete attention.

____ 6. When people are talking, I allow them time to finish. I do not interrupt, anticipate what they are going to say, or jump to conclusions.

____ 7. I tune people out who do not agree with my views.

____ 8. While the other person is talking, or professors are lecturing, my mind wanders to personal topics.

____ 9. While the other person is talking, I pay close attention to the nonverbal communications to help me fully understand what they are trying to communicate.

____ 10. I tune out and pretend I understand when the topic is difficult for me to understand.

____ 11. When the other person is talking, I think about and prepare what I am going to say in reply.

____ 12. When I think there is something missing or contradictory, I ask direct questions to get the person to explain the idea more fully.

____ 13. When I don't understand something, I let

the other person know I don't understand.

_____ 14. When listening to other people, I try to put myself in their position and see things from their perspective.

_____ 15. During conversations I repeat back to the other person what has been said in my own words to be sure I correctly understand what has been said.

If people you talk to regularly were to answer these questions about you, would they have the same responses that you selected? To find out, have friends fill out the questions with you in mind rather than themselves. Then compare answers.

To determine your score, give yourself 5 points for each A, 4 for each U, 3 for each F, 2 for each O, and 1 for each S for statements 1, 4, 5, 6, 9, 12, 13, 14, and 15. Place the numbers on the line next to your response letter. For items 2, 3, 7, 8, 10, and 11 the score reverses: 5 points for each S, 4 for each O, 3 for each F, 2 for each U, and 1 for each A. Place these score numbers on the lines next to the response letters. Now add your total number of points. Your score should be between 15 and 75. Place your score on the continuum to the right. Generally, the higher your score, the better your listening skills.

15–20–25–30–35–40–45–50–55–60–65–70–75

Poor listener   *Good listener*

An oral message cannot be received accurately unless the receiver listens. When asked, "Are you a good listener?" most people say yes. In reality, 75 percent of what people hear, they hear imprecisely—and 75 percent of what they hear accurately, they forget within three weeks. In other words, most people are really not good listeners. One of the skills we need to develop most is listening. The key to effective leadership is sensitive listening. Listening's greatest value is that it gives the speaker a sense of worth. People have a passionate desire to be heard.[13]

The Message-Receiving Process. *The **message-receiving process** includes listening, analyzing, and checking understanding.* To improve your listening skills, spend one week focusing your attention on listening, by concentrating on what other people say and the nonverbal communications they send when they speak. Notice if their verbal and nonverbal communication are consistent. Do the nonverbal messages reinforce the speaker's words or detract from them? Talk only when necessary, so that you can listen and "see" what others are saying. If you apply the following tips, you will improve your listening skills. The tips are presented in the message-receiving process (Figure 4-1): We should listen, analyze, and then check understanding.

message-receiving process: listening, analyzing, and checking understanding.

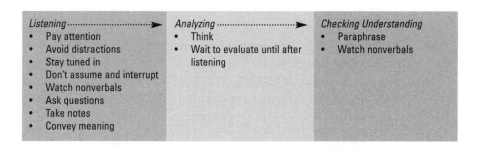

Figure 4-1 *The message-receiving process.*

Listening. *Listening* is the process of giving the speaker your undivided attention. As the speaker sends the message, you should listen by:

- *Paying attention.* When people interrupt you to talk, stop what you are doing and give them your complete attention immediately. Quickly relax and clear your mind, so that you are receptive to the speaker. This will get you started correctly. If you miss the first few words, you may miss the message.

- *Avoiding distractions.* Keep your eye on the speaker. Do not fiddle with pens, papers, or other distractions. For important messages, put your phone on "take a message." If you are in a noisy or distracting place, suggest moving to a quiet spot.

- *Staying tuned in.* While the other person is talking or the professor is lecturing, do not let your mind wander to personal topics. If it does wander, gently bring it back. Do not tune out the speaker because you do not like something about the person, or because you disagree with what is being said. If the topic is difficult, do not tune out; ask questions. Do not think about what you are going to say in reply, just listen.

- *Not assuming and interrupting.* Do not assume you know what the speaker is going to say, or listen to the beginning and jump to conclusions. Most listening mistakes are made when people hear the first few words of a sentence, finish it in their own minds, and miss the second half. Listen to the entire message without interrupting the speaker.

- *Watching nonverbal cues.* Understand both the feelings and the content of the message. People sometimes say one thing and mean something else. So watch as you listen to be sure that the speaker's eyes, body, and face are sending the same message as the verbal message. If something seems out of sync, get it cleared up by asking questions.

- *Asking questions.* When you feel there is something missing, contradictory, or you just do not understand, ask direct questions to get the person to explain the idea more fully.

- *Taking notes.* Part of listening is writing important things down so you can remember them later, and document them when necessary. This is especially true when you're listening to instructions. You should always have something to take notes with, such as a pen and a notebook or some index cards.

- *Conveying meaning.* The way to let the speaker know you are listening to the message is to use verbal clues, such as, "you feel ...," "uh huh," "I see," and "I understand." You should also use nonverbal communication such as eye contact, appropriate facial expressions, nodding of the head, or leaning slightly forward in your chair to indicate you are interested and listening.

Analyzing. *Analyzing* is the process of thinking about, decoding, and evaluating the message. Poor listening occurs in part because people speak at an average rate of 120 words per minute, while they are capable of listening at a rate of over 500 words per minute. The ability to comprehend words more than four times faster than the speaker can talk often results in minds wandering. As the speaker sends the message, you should analyze by:

- *Thinking.* To help overcome the discrepancy in the speed between your ability to listen and people's rate of speaking, use the speed of your brain positively. Listen actively by organizing, summarizing, reviewing, interpreting, and critiquing often. These activities will help you to do an effective job of decoding the message.

- *Waiting to evaluate until after listening.* When people try to listen and evaluate what is said at the same time, they tend to miss part or all of the message. You should just listen to the entire message, then come to your conclusions. When you evaluate the decision, base your conclusion on the facts present rather than on stereotypes and generalities.

Checking Understanding. *Checking understanding* is the process of giving feedback. After you have listened to the message—or during the message if it's a long one—check your understanding of the message by:

- *Paraphrasing.* Begin speaking by giving feedback, using paraphrasing to repeat the message to the sender. When you can paraphrase the message correctly, you convey that you have listened and understood the other person. Now you are ready to offer your ideas, advice, solution, decision, or whatever the sender of the message is talking to you about.

- *Watching nonverbal cues.* As you speak, watch the other person's nonverbal cues. If the person does not seem to understand what you are talking about, clarify the message before finishing the conversation.

Do you talk more than you listen? To be sure your perception is correct, ask your manager, coworkers, and friends who will give you an honest answer. If you spend more time talking than listening, you are probably failing in your communications, and boring people too. Regardless of how much you listen, if you follow these guidelines, you will improve your conversation and become a person that people want to talk to, instead of a person they feel they have to listen to. To become an active listener, take the responsibility for ensuring mutual understanding.

Work to change your behavior to become a better listener. Review the 15 statements in Self-Assessment Exercise 4-1. To improve your listening skills practice doing items 1, 4, 5, 6, 9, 12, 13, 14, and 15; and avoid doing items 2, 3, 7, 8, 10, and 11. Effective listening requires responding to the message to ensure mutual understanding takes place.

In the opening case, Coca-Cola Company was slow to send the message with the information the Belgian and French governments wanted. Even when Coke sent the information, the governments criticized the company for not giving them complete information. Did Coke listen to the governments' request? If Coke were not so slow, and if it had provided full information, could the company have prevented the mass recall of Coke products, and would Coke have been able to resume selling its products sooner?

The most common cause of messages not resulting in communication is the lack of getting feedback that ensures mutual understanding. The proper use of questioning and paraphrasing can help you ensure that your messages are communicated.

How to Get Feedback on Messages

Here are four guidelines you should use when getting feedback on messages. They are appropriate for managers and nonmanagers.

- *Be open to feedback.* There are no dumb questions. When someone asks a question, you need to be responsive, and patiently answer questions and explain things clearly. If people sense that you get upset if they ask questions, they will not ask questions.

- *Be aware of nonverbal communication.* Make sure that your nonverbal communications encourage feedback. For example, if you say, "I encourage questions," but when people ask questions you look at them as though they are stupid, or you are impatient, people will learn not to ask questions. You must also be aware of, and read, peoples' nonverbal communications. For example, if you are explaining a task to Larry and he has a puzzled look on his face, he is probably confused but may not be willing to say so. In such a case, you should stop and clarify things before going on.

- *Ask questions.* When you send messages, it is better to know whether the messages are understood before action is taken, so that the action will not have to be changed or repeated. Communicating is the responsibility of both the message sender and receiver. So you should ask questions to check understanding, rather than simply asking, "Do you have any questions?" Direct questions dealing with the specific information you have given will indicate if the receiver has been listening, and whether he or she understands enough to give a direct reply. If the response is not accurate, try repeating, giving more examples, or elaborating further on the message. You can also ask indirect questions to attain feedback. You can ask "how do you feel?" questions about the message. You can also ask "if you were me" questions, such as, "If you were me, how would you explain how to do it?" Or you can ask third-party questions, such as, "How will employees feel about this?" The response to indirect questions will often tell you other people's attitudes.

- *Use paraphrasing.* The most accurate indicator of understanding is paraphrasing. How you ask the receiver to paraphrase will affect his or her attitude. For example, if you say "Joan, tell me what I just said so that I can be sure you will not make a mistake as usual," would probably result in defensive behavior on Joan's part. Joan would probably make a mistake. Here are two examples of proper requests for paraphrasing:

  > "Now tell me what you are going to do, so we will be sure that we are in agreement."

"Would you tell me what you are going to do, so that I can be sure that I explained myself clearly?"

Notice that the second statement takes the pressure off the employee. The sender is asking for a check on his or her ability, not that of the employee. These types of requests for paraphrasing should result in a positive attitude toward the message and the sender. They show concern for the employee and for communicating effectively.

360-Degree Multirater Feedback

So far, we have discussed the informal methods of getting feedback. We now turn to a formal evaluation process using 360-degree multirater feedback. The use of feedback from multiple sources has become popular as a means of improving performance. Almost all of the Fortune 500 companies are using some type of multirater feedback instrument to evaluate their managers and key individual contributors. General Electric's CEO Jack Welch has stated that these tools have been critical to GE's success.[20]

As the name implies, ***360-degree feedback** is based on receiving performance evaluations from many people*. Most 360-degree evaluation forms are completed by the person being evaluated, his or her manager, peers, and subordinates when applicable. Customers, suppliers, and other outside people are also used when applicable. See Figure 4-2 for an illustration of the 360-degree feedback process.

When the employee's final evaluation is based on multiple sources, it may be more objective than one completed only by the manager. However, the manager may be the one who gives the final evaluation, or their evaluation may be given the most weight. If you are serious about getting ahead, it is critical for you to focus on the feedback from your manager and do what it takes to receive a good evaluation. Employees usually receive the results of their 360-degree evaluation from someone in the human resources department or from an external consultant, who often helps the person develop an action plan for improving performance. The manager also has input into the plan for improvement and works with the employee during the next evaluation period.

Coca-Cola's M. Douglas Ivester found out about Coke's creating health problems in Europe through feedback. Through feedback, decisions had to be made about how to solve the problem of Coke making people ill.

360-degree feedback: a formal evaluation process based on receiving performance evaluations from many people.

Figure 4-2 *360-degree feedback sources.*

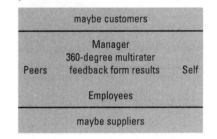

COACHING

Coaching has been called the latest leadership fad.[21] Coaching is based on feedback and communications: It involves giving feedback, which requires communication. In this section we discuss coaching and leadership, and we explain how to give coaching feedback. We then present a coaching model you can use on the job, and end by briefly discussing mentoring, which may be considered a form of coaching.

Coaching and Leadership

coaching: the process of giving motivational feedback to maintain and improve performance.

Coaching is the process of giving motivational feedback to maintain and improve performance. Coaching is designed to maximize employee strengths and minimize weaknesses. Coaching helps leaders concentrate on goals, develop resiliency, and build interpersonal savvy. One of its goals is to make life better for employees and the organization. Managers from the management paradigm didn't see coaching in their job description. However, leaders from the leadership paradigm view developing effective followers as a key part of a leader's job. As a means of improving performance, organizations are training their managers to be coaches, and this trend is expected to continue. Coaching boosts performance. Nine of ten workers who have received job coaching think it is an effective developmental tool.[22]

Developing your coaching skills is an important part of your leadership development. Whether you are a manager or not, you can be a leader and coach others, including your manager. Coaching is especially important when an employee is new to the job and organization.

How to Give Coaching Feedback

When people hear the word *coaching*, they often think of athletes, but managers should also be looking for steady performance and continual improvement. Athlete-coaching skills are being used successfully in the business world.[23] If you have ever had a good coach, think about the behavior he or she used that helped to maintain and improve your performance and that of other team members. The next time you watch a sporting event, keep an eye on the coaches and learn some ways to coach employees.

We next discuss some guidelines that will help you to be an effective coach; the guidelines are also shown in Figure 4-3. The guidelines are designed primarily for use with employees who are doing a good job. As in the definition of coaching, the focus is on maintaining and continually improving performance. In the next section we present more specific guidelines and a coaching model for leading employees who are not performing as expected.

Develop a Supportive Working Relationship. Research has shown that the most important contributor to employee success and retention is their relationship with their manager. The relationship will be based on personality styles, and the manager and employee do not have to be friends and socialize together. People who are very different and don't really like each other personally can still have a good working relationship. Your relationship with followers needs to convey your concern for them as an individual and your commitment to coach them to success. A supportive working relationship can build enthusiasm and commitment to continual performance improvement.[24]

You should periodically ask employees if there is anything you could do to help them do a better job. Take the time to listen to them. There will seldom be big problems. Problems are often caused by petty annoyances that an employee believes are too trivial to bother the manager with. Your job as a manager is to run interference, to remove the stumbling blocks for the

1. Develop a supportive working relationship.
2. Give praise and recognition.
3. Avoid blame and embarrassment.
4. Focus on the behavior, not the person.
5. Have employees assess their own performance.
6. Give specific and descriptive feedback.
7. Give coaching feedback.
8. Provide modeling and training
9. Make feedback timely, but flexible.
10. Don't criticize.

Figure 4-3 *Coaching guidelines.*

employees to improve their performance and that of the business unit.[25]

Give Praise and Recognition. Why should you give recognition to employees for doing their job? The reason is simple: It motivates employees to maintain and increase performance. In Chapter 3 you learned the importance of giving praise, and how to use the giving praise model. We cannot overemphasize the importance of giving praise and recognition, and you cannot give too much of it. Recognition includes praise, awards, and recognition ceremonies. Awards include certificates of achievement, a letter of commendation, a pin, a plaque, a trophy, a medal, a ribbon, clothing, cash, trips, meals, employee of the month, and so on. Awards are symbolic acts of thanks for contributions to the success of the organization. Recognition ceremonies ensure that individual, team, and work-unit achievements are acknowledged by others in the organization. Most highly successful organizations celebrate their success in some way. Mary Kay owes much of the success of her cosmetics business to her elaborate recognition systems, with the ultimate award of the pink Cadillac. True leaders are always quick to give recognition to their followers.[26]

Avoid Blame and Embarrassment. The objective of coaching is to develop employees' knowledge, abilities, and skills. Thus, any leadership behavior that focuses on making the person feel bad does not help to develop the employee. Some things are best not said. For example, if an employee makes a mistake and realizes it, verbalizing it is not needed; doing so only makes them feel bad. Besides, effective leaders treat mistakes as learning experiences. Statements like, "I'm surprised that you did XYZ," or "I'm disappointed in you" should also be avoided.

Focus on the Behavior, not the Person. The purpose of coaching is to achieve desirable behavior, not to belittle the person. Let's use examples to illustrate the difference between coaching by focusing on changing behavior rather than by focusing on the person. Notice that the statements focusing on the person would be placing blame and embarrassment—or belittling the person.

- *Situation 1.* The employee is dominating the discussion at a meeting.
  Focus on person—You talk too much; give others a chance.
  Focus on behavior—I'd like to hear what some of the other group members have to say.

- *Situation 2.* The employee is late for a meeting again.
  Focus on person—You are always late for meetings; why can't you be on time like the rest of us?
  Focus on behavior—This is the second time in a row that you arrived late for our meeting. The group needs your input right from the start of the meeting.

Have Employees Assess Their Own Performance. Here are some examples of criticism and self-evaluation coaching feedback to help explain the difference.

- *Situation 3.* The employee has been making more errors lately.
  Criticism—You haven't been working up to par lately; get on the ball.

Self-evaluation—How would you assess the amount of errors you have been making this week?

- *Situation 4.* The employee is working on a few reports, and one is due in two days. The manager believes the employee may not meet the deadline.
  Criticism—Are you going to meet the deadline for the report?
  Self-evaluation—How are you progressing on the cost-cutting report that's due this Thursday? Is there something I can do to help?

Can the criticism statements result in defensive behavior, not listening, feeling bad about oneself, and disliking the task and the manager? Do the self-evaluation statements create different feelings and behavior?

Give Specific and Descriptive Feedback. *Specific feedback* is needed to avoid confusion over which particular behavior needs to be improved. Compare the preceding criticism statements, which are not specific, to the self-evaluation statements, which are specific. Can you understand how the person being criticized may not understand specifically what the manager is talking about, so may be unable to change even if they are willing to do so?

Descriptive feedback can be based on *facts* or *inferences*. Facts can be observed and proven; inferences cannot. In situation 3, the manager can observe and prove that the employee made more errors this week than in prior weeks. However, the manager cannot observe or prove why. The manager may infer many reasons for the changed behavior, such as laziness, illness, a personal problem, and so on. In situation 4, the manager cannot prove that the report will be late; the manager is inferring that it will be and attempting to coach the employee to make sure it is completed on time. Give factual rather than inferential feedback, because factual tends to be positive, while inferential tends to be more negative criticism.

Give Coaching Feedback. Self-assessment can work well, especially when performance needs to be maintained rather than improved. However, it is not always appropriate; if overused, it can have limited success. There are often times when you will want to offer coaching feedback without self-assessment. It is important to respond positively to negative behavior and outcomes, and the way to do this is not by pointing out mistakes but by selling the benefits of positive behavior.[27] Here are some examples of how to coach versus criticize.

- *Situation 5.* The manager just saw an employee, who knows how it should be done, incorrectly pick up a fairly heavy box.
  Criticism—You just picked up the box wrong. Don't let me catch you again.
  Coaching feedback—If you don't want to injure your back, use your legs—not your back.

- *Situation 6.* A student sees a fellow student going to the MG website by typing in the entire address, **http://www.mgeneral.com.**
  Criticism—You just wasted time typing in the entire MG website address. Don't use the entire address, or make it a favorite address.

Coaching feedback—Would you like me to show you a faster way to get to the MG home page?

- *Situation 7.* A worker is completing a task by following an inefficient, step-by-step procedure.
  Criticism—You're not doing that the best way. Do X, Y, then Z from now on.
  Coaching feedback—Have you given any thought to changing the sequence of steps for completing that task to X, Y, then Z?

Provide Modeling and Training. A good manager leads by example. If employees see the manager doing things in an effective manner, they will tend to copy the manager. As illustrated in situations 4 and 5, coaching often requires some training. Failing to train and coach new employees is failing to lead. Training tasks should be done in a step-by-step process.[28] The job instructional training (JIT) method is widely used (see Model 4-2). *The* ***job instructional training*** *steps include (1) trainee receives preparation; (2) trainer presents the task; (3) trainee performs the task; and (4) trainer follows up.* Remember that tasks we know well seem very simple, but they are usually difficult for the new trainee. You can also use co-leadership and have others do the training, especially if they are better at training than you are.

job instructional training: (1) trainee receives preparation; (2) trainer presents task; (3) trainee performs task; and (4) trainer follows up.

step **1.** **Trainee receives preparation.** Put the trainee at ease as you create interest in the job and encourage questions. Explain the quantity and quality requirements and why they are important.

step **2.** **Trainer presents the task.** Perform the task yourself at a slow pace, explaining each step several times. Once the trainee seems to have the steps memorized, have the trainee explain each step as you slowly perform the task again. For complex tasks with multiple steps, it is helpful to write them out and to give a copy to the trainee.

step **3.** **Trainee performs task.** Have the trainee perform the task at a slow pace, while explaining each step to the trainer. Correct any errors and be patiently willing to help the trainee perform any difficult steps. Continue until the trainee is proficient at performing the task.

step **4.** **Trainer follows up.** Tell the trainee who to ask for help with any questions or problems. Gradually leave the trainee alone. Begin by checking quality and quantity frequently, and decrease checks based on the trainee's skill level. Observe the trainee performing the task, and be sure to correct any errors or faulty work procedures before they become a habit. As you follow up, be sure to be patient and encouraging. Praise a good effort at first, and good performance as skills develop.

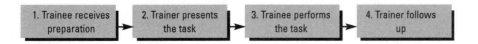

| 1. Trainee receives preparation | → | 2. Trainer presents the task | → | 3. Trainee performs the task | → | 4. Trainer follows up |

Model 4-2 *Job instructional training steps.*

Make Feedback Timely, but Flexible. Feedback should be given *as soon as possible* after the behavior has been observed. For example, in situation 5 you would want to give the coaching feedback as soon as you saw the employee lift the box incorrectly. To tell the employee about it a few days later would have less impact on changing the behavior, and the employee could be injured by then. The *flexibility* part comes into play (1) when you don't have the time to do the full coaching job, and (2) when emotions are high. For example, if you were late for an important meeting and wanted to sit down with the employee to fully discuss the problem of lifting incorrectly, a later date could be set. If you were really angry and yelled at the employee and the employee yelled back, it is usually a good idea to make an appointment to discuss it later when emotions have calmed, to rationally discuss the matter using coaching feedback. Besides, yelling does not work; [29] it is a form of criticism. Even if you yelled in anger while following every other coaching guideline, it would be criticism.

Remember that everyone can be a coach. Coaches can be effective by following simple guidelines,[30] presented here. So don't criticize, start coaching—today. These general guidelines apply to any leadership situation, such as being a parent or guardian. Next we focus on how to coach the employee who is performing below expected standards.

Don't Criticize. Jack Falvey, management consultant and author, takes the positive versus negative feedback to the point of recommending only positive feedback:

> Criticism is to be avoided at all costs (there is no such thing as constructive criticism; all criticism is destructive). If you must correct someone, never do it after the fact. Bite your tongue and hold off until the person is about to do the same thing again and then challenge the person to make a more positive contribution.[31]

What Is Criticism and Why Doesn't It Work?

Falvey's statement may seem a bit extreme, but it is true. Placing blame and embarrassment and focusing on the person are types of criticism. Criticism is rarely effective. Criticism involves a judgment, which is that either the person is right or wrong. Criticism is also the process of pointing out mistakes, which places blame and is embarrassing. Once you tell a person they are wrong or made a mistake, directly or indirectly, four things usually happen: (1) They become defensive and justify their behavior, or they blame it on someone or something. (2) They don't really listen to so-called constructive feedback. (3) They are embarrassed and feel bad about themselves, or they view themselves as losers. (4) They begin to dislike the task or job, as well as the critic. The more criticism employees receive, the more defensive they become. They listen less, they are in conflict as their self-concept is threatened or diminishes, they eventually hate the task or job and usually the critic, and they often quit the job, get a transfer, or are fired. Giving praise has an opposite, positive effect on employees, their behavior, and their performance.

The Sandwich Approach to Criticism, and Why It Doesn't Work. The sandwich approach offers both praise and criticism at the same time, to help offset the negative. But, if your manager tells you five good things about how you are doing and one bad thing, which do you remember? Similarly, suppose that today ten good things and one bad thing happened to the average person. If you ask that person how their day is going, will they say "I'm having a great day," and talk about some of the ten good things that happened? Or will they say, "I'm having a bad day," and talk only about the one bad thing? How would you respond?

Demotivating. Employees with overly critical managers tend to develop the attitude of, "My manager doesn't care about me or appreciate my work, so why should I work hard to do a good job?" They play it safe by doing the minimum, taking no risk, focusing on not making errors, and covering up any errors so they aren't criticized. They avoid contact with the manager and they feel stress just seeing the manager approach them. They think, "What did I do this time?"

The Difference between Criticism and Coaching Feedback. By now you probably agree that criticism usually does not work; in fact, it often makes the behavior worse. But you may be thinking that you can't always catch an employee in the act and challenge them to perform better. What do you do? The major difference between criticism and coaching feedback is that *coaching feedback is based on a good, supportive relationship; it is specific and descriptive; and it is not judgmental criticism.* And coaching is often based on the employee doing a self-assessment of performance. Criticism makes employees feel like losers; praise and coaching feedback makes them feel like winners. And nothing breeds success like good coaches. Before getting into how to give coaching feedback, with examples of criticism and coaching praise, we discuss its components.

coaching feedback: feedback that is (1) based on a good, supportive relationship; (2) specific and descriptive; and (3) not judgmental criticism.

The Coaching Model for Employees Who Are Performing Below Standard

When managers are giving feedback to employees who are performing below standard, all ten of the coaching guidelines are important. However, most managers are more apt to use embarrassment, to focus on the person, and to criticize the person who is performing below standard than

---

Applying the Concept 4-2

Criticism or Coaching Feedback

Identify each of these five statements as criticism or coaching feedback. For each criticism only, write a coaching feedback statement to replace it.

a. criticism   b. coaching feedback

_____ **1.** You just dropped it on the floor.

_____

_____ **2.** This is still dirty. You are going to have to clean it again.

_____

_____ **3.** I couldn't help overhearing your conflict with Jack. Would you like me to tell you how you can minimize this problem in the future?

_____

_____ **4.** You are a poor speller. Make sure you don't forget to use the spell check before you pass in your work.

_____

_____ **5.** *In a loud, angry voice:* Let me help you with that.

_____

the person who is doing a good job. Avoid this temptation, because it doesn't really work. Don't exclude the poor performer and develop negative relationships with them. They need your one-on-one coaching, at its best. Be patient but persistent; don't give up on them.[32] Before getting into the coaching model, let's discuss attribution theory and the performance formula because they affect the coaching model.

attribution theory: used to explain the process managers go through in determining the reasons for effective or ineffective performance and deciding what to do about it.

Attribution Theory. *Attribution theory is used to explain the process managers go through in determining the reasons for effective or ineffective performance and deciding what to do about it.* The reaction of a manager to poor performance has two stages. First, the manager tries to determine the cause of the poor performance, and then he or she selects an appropriate corrective action.[33] To help you determine the cause of poor performance, we provide you with the performance formula; and to take corrective action, the coaching model.

Managers tend to attribute the cause of poor performance by certain employees to internal reasons (ability and/or motivation) within their control, and poor performance by other employees to external reasons (resources) beyond their control. Managers are less critical of those employees whose poor performance is attributed to external reasons beyond their control. Effective leaders try to avoid this problem. (Chapter 6 examines these "in-group" and "out-group" relationships to depth.)

performance formula: explains performance as a function of ability, motivation, and resources.

Determining the Cause of Poor Performance and Corrective Coaching Action. The **performance formula** *explains performance as a function of ability, motivation, and resources.* Model 4-3 is a simple model that can help you determine the cause of poor performance and the corrective action to take based on the cause. When ability, motivation, or resources are low, performance will be lower.

When the employee's *ability* is the reason for keeping performance from being optimal, the corrective coaching action is training (JIT). When *motivation* is lacking, motivational techniques (discussed in Chapter 3) such as giving praise might help. Talk (coach) to the employee, and work together to develop a plan to improve performance. When *resources* (tools, material, equipment, information, others did not do their part, bad luck or timing, and so on) are the problem, you need to get the resources. When obstacles are getting in the way of performance, you need to overcome them.

Performance (f)*
Ability, Motivation, and Resources

*(f) = is a function of

Model 4-3 *The performance formula.*

Improving Performance with the Coaching Model. The steps in the coaching model are (1) describe current performance; (2) describe desired performance; (3) get a commitment to the change; and (4) follow up. Again, use all ten guidelines to coaching within the framework of the coaching model.

step 1 ▪ **Describe current performance.** In detail, using specific examples, describe the current behavior that needs to be changed.

For example, for an ability or motivation problem, say something like, "There is a way to lift boxes that will decrease your chances of getting injured."

step 2. **Describe desired performance.** Tell the employee exactly what the desired performance is, in detail. If *ability* is the reason for poor performance, modeling and training the employee with JIT are very appropriate. If the employee knows the proper way, the reason for poor performance is *motivational*. Demonstration is not needed; just describe desired performance as you ask the employee to state why the performance is important.

For example, *Ability*—"If you squat down and pick up the box using your legs instead of your back, it is easier and there is less chance of injuring yourself. Let me demonstrate for you." *Motivation*—"Why should you squat and use your legs rather than your back to pick up boxes?"

step 3. **Get a Commitment to the Change.** When dealing with an *ability* performance issue, it is not necessary to get employees to verbally commit to the change if they seem willing to make it. However, if employees defend their way, and you're sure it's not as effective, explain why your proposed way is better. If you cannot get the employee to understand and agree based on rational persuasion, get a verbal commitment through coercive power, such as a threat of discipline. Also, for *motivation* performance issues, this is important because, if the employee is not willing to commit to the change, he or she will most likely not make the change.

For example, *Ability*—the employee will most likely be willing to do it correctly, so skip the step. *Motivation*—"Will you squat rather than use your back from now on?"

step 4. **Follow up.** Remember, some employees do what managers inspect, not what they expect. You should follow up to ensure that the employee is behaving as desired.

When you are dealing with an *ability* performance issue, and the person was receptive and you skipped step 3, say nothing. But watch to be sure the task is done correctly in the future. Coach again, if necessary. For a *motivation* problem, make a statement that you will follow up, and describe possible consequences for repeat performance.

For example, *Ability*—say nothing, but observe. *Motivation*—"Picking up boxes with your back is dangerous; if I catch you doing it again, I will take disciplinary action." See Model 4-4 for a review of the steps in the coaching model.

Mentoring

Mentoring is a form of coaching in which a more experienced manager helps a less experienced protégé. Thus, the ten tips for coaching apply to mentoring. However, mentoring includes more than coaching, and it is more involved and personal than coaching. The formal mentor is usually at a higher level of management and is not the protégé's immediate manager. Family, friends, and peers can also be mentors. The primary responsibility is to coach the

mentoring: a form of coaching in which a more experienced manager helps a less experienced protégé.

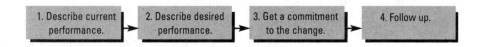

1. Describe current performance. → 2. Describe desired performance. → 3. Get a commitment to the change. → 4. Follow up.

Model 4-4 *Coaching model.*

protégé by providing good, sound career advice and to help develop leadership skills necessary for a successful management career. However, the protégé should not try to become just like the mentor; we all need to learn from others yet we need to be ourselves to be effective.

Research studies have found that mentoring results in more career advancement and job satisfaction for the protégé.[35] Based on success of mentoring, many organizations—including the IRS, Hewlett-Packard, and IBM—have formal mentoring programs, while others have informal mentoring. Former Coca Cola CEO Roberto Goizueta hand-picked M. Douglas Ivester to be his successor; Goizueta served as his coach and mentor.

We all need mentors, so don't wait for someone to ask you.[36] Seek out a mentor. If your organization has a formal mentoring program, try to sign up for it. If it is informal, ask around about getting a mentor, and remember that a mentor can be from another organization. Whenever you have job- or career-related questions and would like advice, contact your mentor.

MANAGING CONFLICT

conflict: exists whenever people are in disagreement and opposition.

A *conflict exists whenever people are in disagreement and opposition*. In the workplace, conflict is inevitable because people don't see things exactly the same way, nor should they. Organizational success is based on how well it deals with business conflicts.[37] In this section we discuss conflict and leadership and present five conflict management styles you can use to resolve conflicts.

Conflict and Leadership

Many leaders are constantly exposed to conflict. Research suggest that managers devote approximately one-fifth of their time to handling conflict. Thus, handling conflict constructively is an important leadership skill. Your ability to resolve conflicts will have a direct effect on your leadership success. With the trend toward teamwork, conflict skills are increasingly important to team decision making. In the global economy, you need to be sensitive to cultural differences so that you don't create additional conflicts.[38]

Conflict Can Be Dysfunctional or Functional. Conflict is an inherent part of organizational activity. People often think of conflict as fighting and view it as disruptive. When conflict is not resolved effectively, negative consequences occur. When conflict prevents the achievement of organizational objectives, it is negative or *dysfunctional conflict*. However, it can be positive. *Functional conflict* exists when disagreement and opposition supports the achievement of organizational objectives. Functional conflict increases the quality of group decisions, and leads to innovative changes.[39] The question today is not whether conflict is negative or positive, but how to manage conflict to benefit the organization.

Conflict Can Be Problem- or Relationship-Oriented. The appropriate action to resolve a conflict depends on the type of conflict. Problem-oriented conflict resolution focuses on finding a mutually satisfactory solution to the conflict problem. Relationship-oriented conflict resolution focuses on reducing hostility and distrust.[40] However, as discussed with coaching, you need to focus on the behavior, not the person; and you need good communication skills and feedback to resolve conflicts effectively.

Conflict Management Styles

Conflict management skills can be developed with appropriate training.[41] In this discussion, we focus more on resolving conflicts in your own personal and professional lives, and less on mediating conflicts between others.

When you are in conflict, you have five conflict management styles to choose from. The five styles are based on two dimensions of concerns: concern for others' needs and concerns for your own needs. These concerns result in three types of behavior:

- A low concern for your own needs and a high concern for others' needs results in passive behavior.
- A high concern for your own needs and a low concern for others' needs results in aggressive behavior.
- A moderate or high concern for your own needs and others' needs results in assertive behavior.

Each conflict style behavior results in a different combination of win-lose situations. The five styles, along with concern for needs and win-lose combinations, are presented in Figure 4-4 and discussed here in order of passive, aggressive, and assertive behavior. The conflict style that you tend to use the most is based on your personality and leadership style.[42] There is no one best conflict management style for all situations; in this section you will learn the advantages and disadvantages and the appropriate use of each conflict management style.

Avoiding Conflict Style. The *avoiding conflict style* user attempts to passively ignore the conflict rather than resolve it. When you avoid a conflict, you are being unassertive and uncooperative. People avoid conflict by refusing to take a stance, or escape conflict by mentally withdrawing and

Figure 4-4 *Conflict management styles.*

physically leaving. A lose-lose situation is created because the conflict is not resolved.

Advantages and Disadvantages of the Avoiding Conflict Style. The advantage of the avoiding style is that it may maintain relationships that would be hurt through conflict resolution. The disadvantage of this style is that conflicts do not get resolved. An overuse of this style leads to conflict within the individual. People tend to walk all over the avoider. Some managers allow employees to break rules without confronting them. Avoiding problems usually does not make them go away; the problems usually get worse. And the longer you wait to confront others, the more difficult the confrontation usually is.

Appropriate Use of the Avoiding Conflict Style. The avoiding style is appropriate to use when: (1) the conflict is trivial; (2) your stake in the issue is not high; (3) confrontation will damage an important relationship; (4) you don't have time to resolve the conflict; or (5) emotions are high. When you don't have time to resolve the conflict or people are emotional, you should confront the person(s) later. However, it is inappropriate to repeatedly avoid confrontation until you get so upset that you end up yelling at the other person(s). This passive-aggressive behavior tends to make the situation worse by hurting human relations. Often people do not realize they are doing something that bothers you (that you are in conflict), and when approached properly, they are willing to change.

Accommodating Conflict Style. The *accommodating conflict style* user attempts to resolve the conflict by passively giving in to the other party. When you use the accommodating style, you are being unassertive but cooperative. You attempt to satisfy the other party, neglecting your own needs by letting others get their own way. A win-lose situation is created.

Differences between the Avoiding and Accommodating Styles. A common difference between the avoiding and accommodating styles is based on behavior. With the avoiding style, you don't have to do anything you really did not want to do; with the accommodating style, you do. For example, if you are talking to someone who makes a statement that you disagree with, to avoid a conflict you can say nothing, change the subject, or stop the conversation. However, suppose you have to put up a display with someone who says, "Let's put up the display this way." If you don't want to do it the other person's way, but say nothing and put it up the other person's way, you have done something you really did not want to do.

Advantages and Disadvantages of the Accommodating Conflict Style. The advantage of the accommodating style is that relationships are maintained by doing things the other person's way. The disadvantage is that giving in may be counterproductive. The accommodating person may have a better solution, such as a better way to put up a display. An overuse of this style tends to lead to people taking advantage of the accommodator, and the type of relationship the accommodator tries to maintain is usually lost.

Appropriate Use of the Accommodating Conflict Style. The accommodating style is appropriate when (1) the person enjoys being a follower; (2) maintaining the relationship outweighs all other considerations; (3)

the changes agreed to are not important to the accommodator, but are to the other party; (4) the time to resolve the conflict is limited. This is often the only style that can be used with an autocratic manager who uses the forcing style.

Forcing Conflict Style. The *forcing conflict style* user attempts to resolve the conflict by using aggressive behavior to get their own way. When you use the forcing style, you are uncooperative and aggressive, doing whatever it takes to satisfy your own needs—at the expense of others, if necessary. Forcers use authority, threaten, intimidate, and call for majority rule when they know they will win. Forcers commonly enjoy dealing with avoiders and accommodators. If you try to get others to change without being willing to change yourself, regardless of the means, then you use the forcing style.[43] A win-lose situation is created.

Advantages and Disadvantages of the Forcing Style. The advantage of the forcing style is that better organizational decisions will be made, when the forcer is correct, rather than less effective compromised decisions. The disadvantage is that overuse of this style leads to hostility and resentment toward its user. Forcers tend to have poor human relations.

Appropriate Use of the Forcing Style. Some managers commonly use their position power to force others to do what they want them to do. The forcing style is appropriate to use when (1) unpopular action must be taken on important issues; (2) commitment by others to proposed action is not crucial to its implementation—in other words, people will not resist doing what you want them to do; (3) maintaining relationships is not critical; or (4) the conflict resolution is urgent.

Negotiating Conflict Style. The *negotiating conflict style* user attempts to resolve the conflict through assertive, give-and-take concessions. This is also called the compromising style. When you use the compromising approach, you are moderate in assertiveness and cooperation. An I win some, you win some situation is created through compromise.

Advantages and Disadvantages of the Negotiating Conflict Style. The advantage of the compromise style is that the conflict is resolved relatively quickly, and working relationships are maintained. The disadvantage is that the compromise often leads to counterproductive results, such as suboptimum decisions. An overuse of this style leads to people playing games such as asking for twice as much as they need in order to get what they want. It is commonly used during management and labor collective bargaining.

Appropriate Use of the Negotiating Conflict Style. The compromise style is appropriate to use when (1) the issues are complex and critical, and there is no simple and clear solution; (2) parties have about equal power and are interested in different solutions; (3) a solution will be only temporary; and (4) time is short.

Collaborating Conflict Style. The *collaborating conflict style* user assertively attempts to jointly resolve the conflict with the best solution agreeable to all parties. It is also called the problem-solving style. When you use the collaborating approach, you are being assertive and cooperative. Although avoiders and accommodators are concerned about others' needs, and forcers are concerned about their own needs, the collaborator is concerned about finding the best solution to the problem that is satisfactory to all parties. Unlike the forcer, the collaborator is willing to change if a better solution is presented. While negotiating is often based on secret information, collaboration is based on open and honest communication. This is the only style that creates a true win-win situation.

Differences between the Negotiating and Collaborating Styles. A common difference between negotiating and collaborating is the solution. Let's continue with the example of putting up a display. With negotiation, the two people may trade off by putting up one display one person's way and the next display the other person's way. This way they each win and lose. With collaboration, the two people work together to develop one display method that they both like. It may be a combination of both, or simply one person's if after an explanation, the other person really agrees that the method is better. The key to collaboration is agreeing that the solution is the best possible one.

Advantages and Disadvantages of the Collaborating Style. The advantage of the collaborating style is that it tends to lead to the best solution to the conflict, using assertive behavior. The disadvantage is that the skill, effort, and time it takes to resolve the conflict are usually greater and longer than the other styles. There are situations, mentioned under "Negotiating Conflict Style," when collaboration is difficult, and when a forcer prevents its use. The collaborating style offers the most benefit to the individual, group, and organization.

Appropriate Use of the Collaborating Conflict Style. The collaborating style is appropriate when (1) you are dealing with an important issue that requires an optimal solution, and compromise would result in suboptimiz-

---

Applying the Concept 4-3

Selecting Conflict Management Styles

For each of these five conflict situations, identify the most appropriate conflict management style. Write the appropriate letter in the blank before each item.

a. avoiding   b. accommodating   c. forcing   d. negotiating   e. collaborating

_____ 1. You have joined a committee in order to meet people. Your interest in what the committee does is low. While serving on the committee, you make a recommendation that is opposed by another member. You realize that you have the better idea. The other party is using a forcing style.

_____ 2. You are on a task force that has to select a new computer. The four alternatives will all do the job. It's the brand, price, and service that people disagree on.

_____ 3. You are a sales manager. Beth, one of your competent salespeople, is trying to close a big sale. The two of you are discussing the next sales call she will make. You disagree on the strategy to use to close the sale.

_____ 4. You're late and on your way to an important meeting. As you leave your office, at the other end of the work area you see Chris, one of your employees, goofing off instead of working.

_____ 5. You're over budget for labor this month. It's slow, so you ask Kent, a part-time employee, to leave work early. Kent tells you he doesn't want to go because he needs the money.

ing; (2) people are willing to place the group goal before self-interest, and members will truly collaborate; (3) maintaining relationships is important; (4) time is available; and (5) it is a peer conflict.

In the opening case, Coca-Cola was in conflict with the governments of Belgium and France over the health risk of its products. Coke did not want to have to wait for a period of time before restocking the store shelves with its drinks. Thus, Coke managers were in continual communication with these two governments to negotiate a solution that allowed its products to be sold again.

Of the five styles, the most difficult to implement successfully, due to the complexity and level of skill needed, is the collaborative style. It is most likely to be underutilized when it would have been appropriate. Organizations around the globe, including Coca-Cola, are training employees to resolve conflicts using collaboration.[44] Therefore, in order to develop your conflict skills, the collaborative style is the only one that we cover in detail, in the next section. You will learn how to negotiate in Chapter 9.

COLLABORATING CONFLICT MANAGEMENT STYLE MODELS

Effective leaders encourage conflict resolution and build collaboration throughout the organization. They challenge all of us to learn to get along with each other. Although you can help prevent conflict, you will not eliminate it completely—nor should you try to, because it can be functional. You will develop your skill to assertively confront (or be confronted by) people you are in conflict with, in a manner that resolves the conflict without damaging interpersonal relationships. The model of conflict management can be used to develop conflict skills. We provide a model with the steps you can follow when initiating, responding to, and mediating a conflict resolution. The same steps for resolving conflict effectively are applicable to coworkers, people we live with, and international political situations.[45]

Initiating Conflict Resolution

An initiator is the person who confronts the other person(s) to resolve the conflict. Confronting others you are in conflict with is usually the better solution to conflict, rather than avoiding or accommodating.[46] When initiating a conflict resolution using the collaborating style, use the following model: *The **initiating conflict resolution model** steps are (1) plan a BCF statement that maintains ownership of the problem; (2) present your BCF statement and agree on the conflict; (3) ask for, and/or give, alternative conflict resolutions; and (4) make an agreement for change.* This model is part of behavior modeling, which is an effective training method to develop your conflict resolution leadership skills.

initiating conflict resolution model:
(1) plan a BCF statement that maintains ownership of the problem; (2) present your BCF statement and agree on the conflict; (3) ask for, and/or give, alternative conflict resolutions; and (4) make an agreement for change.

----

step 1 ▪ **Plan a BCF statement that maintains ownership of the problem.** Planning is the starting management function, and the starting point of initiating a conflict resolution. Let's begin by stating what *maintains ownership of the problem* means. Assume you don't smoke, and someone visits you while smoking. Is it you or the smoker who has a problem? The smoke bothers you, not the smoker. It's your problem. Open the confrontation with a request for the respondent to help you solve your problem. This approach reduces defensiveness and establishes an atmosphere of problem solving that will maintain the relationship.

BCF model: describes a conflict in terms of behavior, consequences, and feelings.

The **BCF model** *describes a conflict in terms of behavior, consequences, and feelings.* When you do B (behavior), C (consequences) happens, and I feel F (feelings). For example, when you smoke in my room (behavior), I have trouble breathing and become nauseous (consequence), and I feel uncomfortable and irritated (feeling). You can vary the sequence by starting with a feeling or consequence to fit the situation and to provide variety. For example, I fear (feeling) that the advertisement is not going to work (behavior), and that we will lose money (consequences).

When developing your opening BCF statement, as shown in the examples just given, be descriptive, not evaluative. Keep the opening statement short. The longer the statement, the longer it will take to resolve the conflict. People get defensive when kept waiting for their turn to talk. Avoid trying to determine who is to blame for something, or who is right and wrong. Both parties are usually partly to blame or correct. Fixing blame or correctness only gets people defensive, which is counterproductive to conflict resolution. Timing is also important. If others are busy, see them later to discuss the conflict. In addition, don't confront a person on several unrelated issues at once.

After planning your BCF statement, you should practice saying it before confronting the other party.[47] In addition, think of some possible alternatives you can offer to resolve the conflict. However, be sure your ideas show high concern for others rather than just for yourself; create a win-win situation. Try to put yourself in the other person's position. If you were the other person, would you like the ideas presented by the confronter?

step 2 ■ **Present your BCF statement and agree on the conflict.** After making your short, planned BCF statement, let the other party respond. If the other party does not understand or avoids acknowledgment of the problem, persist. You cannot resolve a conflict if the other party will not even acknowledge its existence. Repeat your planned statement several times by explaining it in different terms until you get an acknowledgment or realize it's hopeless. But don't give up too easily. If you cannot agree on a conflict, you may have to change your approach and use one of the other four conflict management styles.

step 3 ■ **Ask for, and/or give, alternative conflict resolutions.** Begin by asking the other party what can be done to resolve the conflict. If you agree, great; if not, offer your resolution. However, remember that you are collaborating, not simply trying to change others. When the other party acknowledges the problem, but is not responsive to resolving it, appeal to common goals. Make the other party realize the benefits to him or her and the organization as well.

step 4 ■ **Make an agreement for change.** Try to come to an agreement on specific action you will both take to resolve the conflict. Clearly state, or better yet for complex change, write down the specific behavior changes necessary by all parties to resolve the conflict. Again, remember that you are collaborating, not forcing. The steps are also listed in Model 4-5.

Initiating Conflict Resolution	Responding to Conflict Resolution	Mediating Conflict Resolution
Step 1. Plan a BCF statement that maintains ownership of the problem.	Step 1. Listen to and paraphrase the conflict using the BCF model.	Step 1. Have each party state his or her complaint using the BCF model.
Step 2. Present your BCF statement and agree on the conflict.	Step 2. Agree with some aspect of the complaint.	Step 2. Agree on the conflict problem(s).
Step 3. Ask for, and/or give, alternative conflict resolutions.	Step 3. Ask for, and/or give, alternative conflict resolutions.	Step 3. Develop alternative conflict resolutions.
Step 4. Make an agreement for change.	Step 4. Make an agreement for change.	Step 4. Make an agreement for change.
		Step 5. Follow up to make sure the conflict is resolved.

Model 4-5 *The collaborating conflict style.*

Responding to Conflict Resolution

As the responder, an initiator has confronted you. Here's how to handle the role of the responder to a conflict. Most initiators do not follow the model. Therefore, the responder must take responsibility for successful conflict resolution by following the conflict resolution model steps:

1. Listen to and paraphrase the conflict using the BCF model.
2. Agree with some aspect of the complaint.
3. Ask for, and/or give, alternative conflict resolutions.
4. Make an agreement for change.

The steps are also listed in Model 4-5.

Mediating Conflict Resolution

Frequently, conflicting parties cannot resolve their dispute alone. In these cases, a mediator should be used. A *mediator* is a neutral third party who helps resolve a conflict. In nonunionized organizations, managers are commonly the mediators. But some organizations have trained and designated employees as mediators. In unionized organizations, the mediator is usually a professional from outside the organization. However, a conflict resolution should be sought internally first.[48]

Before bringing the conflicting parties together, the mediator should decide whether to start with a joint meeting or conduct individual meetings. If one employee comes to complain, but has not confronted the other party, or if there is a serious discrepancy in employee perceptions, meet one-on-one with each party before bringing them together. On the other hand, when both parties have a similar awareness of the problem and motivation to solve it, you can begin with a joint meeting when all parties are calm. The manager should be a mediator, not a judge. Get the employees to resolve the conflict, if possible. Remain impartial, unless one party is violating company policies. Do a good job of coaching. Avoid blame and embarrassment. Don't make comments such as, "I'm disappointed in you two," or "you're acting like babies."

When bringing conflicting parties together, follow the mediating conflict model steps. These steps are listed in Model 4-5.

mediator: a neutral third party who helps resolve a conflict.

If either party blames the other, make a statement such as, "We are here to resolve the conflict; placing blame is not productive." Focus on how the conflict is affecting their work. Discuss the issues by addressing specific behavior, not personalities. If a person says, "We cannot work together because of a personality conflict," ask the parties to state the specific behavior that is bothering them. The discussion should make the parties aware of their behavior and the consequences of their behavior. The mediator may ask questions or make statements to clarify what is being said. The mediator should develop one problem statement that is agreeable to all parties, if possible.

If the conflict has not been resolved, an arbitrator may be used. *An arbitrator is a neutral third party who makes a binding decision to resolve a conflict.* The arbitrator is like a judge, and their decision must be followed. However, the use of arbitration should be kept to a minimum because it is not a collaborative conflict style. Arbitrators commonly use a negotiating style in which each party wins some and loses some. Mediation and then arbitration tends to be used in management labor negotiations, when collective bargaining breaks down and the contract deadline is near.

As we end this chapter, you should understand how important communications, feedback, coaching, and conflict resolutions are to leadership effectiveness at Coca-Cola and all organizations. Self-Assessment Exercise 4-2 will help you to understand how your personality traits affect your communications, feedback, coaching, and conflict management style.

arbitrator: a neutral third party who makes a binding decision to resolve a conflict.

Self-Assessment Exercise 4-2

Your Personality Traits and Communication, Feedback, Coaching, and Conflict Management Style

Let's tie personality traits from Chapter 2 together with what we've covered in this chapter. We are going to present some general statements about how your personality may affect your communication, feedback, coaching, and conflict. For each area, determine how the information relates to you. This will help you better understand your behavior strengths and weaknesses, and identify areas you may want to improve.

Communication. If you have a high *surgency* personality, you most likely are an extravert and have no difficulty initiating and communicating with others. However, you may be dominating during communication and may not listen well and be open to others' ideas. Be careful not to use communications simply as a means of getting what you want; be concerned about others and what they want. If you are low in surgency, you may be quiet and reserved in your communications. You may want to be more vocal.

If you are high in *agreeableness* personality trait, you are most likely a good listener and communicator. Your *adjustment* level affects the emotional tone of your communications. If you tend to get emotional during communications, you may want to work to keep your emotions under control. We cannot control our feelings, but we can control our behavior. If you are high in *conscientiousness*, you tend to have reliable communications. If you are not conscientious, you may want to work at returning messages quickly. People who are open to *new experience* often initiate communication, because communicating is often part of the new experience.

Feedback and Coaching. If you have a high *surgency* personality, you have a need to be in control. Watch the tendency to give feedback, but not listen to it. You may need to work at *not* criticizing. If you have low surgency, you may want to give more feedback and do more coaching. If you have a high *agreeableness* personality, you are a people person and probably enjoy coaching others. However, as a manager, you must also discipline when needed, which may be difficult for you. If you are high on the *adjustment* personality trait, you may tend to give positive coaching; people with low *adjustment* need to watch the negative criticism. If you have a high *conscientiousness* with a high need for achievement, you may tend to be more concerned about your own success. This is also true of people with a high *surgency* personality. Remember that an important part of leadership is coaching others. If you have a low *conscientiousness*, you may need to put forth effort to be a good coach. Your *openness to experience* personality affects whether you are willing to listen to others' feedback and make changes.

Conflict Styles. Generally, the best conflict style is collaboration. If you have a high *surgency* personality, you most likely have no problem confronting others when in conflict. However, be careful not to use the forcing style with others; remember to use social, not personal power. If you have a high *agreeableness* personality, you tend to get along well with others. However, be careful not to use the avoiding and accommodating styles to get out of confronting others; you need to satisfy your needs too. *Adjustment* will affect how to handle a conflict situation. Try not to be low in adjustment and get too emotional. If you are *conscientious*, you may be good at conflict resolution; but again, be careful to meet others' needs too. *Openness to experience* affects conflicts, because their resolution often requires change; be open to new things.

Action Plan. Based on your personality, what specific things will you do to improve your communication, feedback, coaching, and conflict management style?

_____

_____

_____

II

Team Leadership

5 Contingency Leadership Theories

Carleton Fiorina left Lucent Technology to become president and CEO of Hewlett-Packard (HP) to lead HP's adaptation to the Internet era. HP is not afraid to look at fresh approaches and will do whatever is required to stay on top. Fiorina, called Carly, is the first outsider to run HP and the first woman to head one of the nation's largest public firms. HP is among the top 20 on the Fortune 500 list, as well as among its top five most admired companies and top ten best companies to work for in America. Fiorina's decision-making record at Lucent was a key factor in her getting the CEO position at HP. One challenge any outsider faces in taking on a top-level management job is making peace with the followers, especially with those who wanted the newcomer's job. Fiorina works relentlessly, but also has quick wit and a warm way of asserting herself. She says that she feels like she's working all the time—"it's relentless; the pace is blistering."

HP was founded in 1939 by Bill Hewlett and Dave Packard, who started the company in a garage. Today HP is one of the world's largest computer companies and the foremost producer of test and measurement instruments. It sells more than 29,000 products used by people for personal use and in industry, business, engineering, science, medicine, and education in more than 120 countries.

The company's management style is called "The HP Way." HP believes the achievements of an organization are the result of the combined efforts of each person in the organization, working toward common objectives. These objectives should be realistic, should be clearly understood by everyone in the organization, and should reflect the organization's basic character and personality. Seven corporate objectives provide a framework for group and individual goal-setting in which all employees participate. HP's management objective is to foster initiative and creativity by allowing the individual great freedom of action in attaining well-defined objectives.[1]

■ *Go to the Internet:* For more information about Carleton Fiorina and HP, and for updated information provided in this case, do a name search on the Internet and visit the HP website at **http://www.hp.com.**

As you read this chapter, you will learn more about Fiorina's leadership style as it relates to five contingency leadership theories. We begin with an overview of contingency leadership theories. Next we present five contingency leadership models: contingency leadership, leadership continuum, path-goal, normative leadership, and the situational leadership model. Then we put the behavioral (Chapter 3) and contingency leadership theories together. We end by discussing leadership theory substitutes.

CONTINGENCY LEADERSHIP THEORIES AND MODELS

Both the trait and behavioral leadership theories were attempts to find the one best leadership style in all situations. In the late 1960s, it became apparent that there is no one best leadership style in all situations. Managers need to adapt different leadership styles to different situations.[2] Thus, contingency leadership theory became the third major leadership paradigm (Chapter 1), and the leadership styles used in its models are based on the behavioral leadership theories.

In this chapter you will learn about the contingency, continuum, path-goal, normative, and situational leadership models. This is the historical sequence by the date each model was published. We also put the behavioral and contingency leadership theories together and present leadership substitute theory. In this section, we discuss the contingency theory factors and the need for global contingency leadership.

Leadership Theories versus Leadership Models

As defined in Chapter 1, a *leadership theory* is an explanation of some aspect of leadership; theories have practical value because they are used to better understand, predict, and control successful leadership. A *leadership model is an example for emulation or use in a given situation.* In earlier chapters we talked about leading by example, which is emulation or the hope that followers will imitate the leader's behavior. In this chapter we discuss using models in a given situation to improve performance of leaders, followers, or both.

leadership model: an example for emulation or use in a given situation.

All of the contingency leadership theories in this chapter have leadership models. The leadership theory is the longer text that explains the variables and leadership styles to be used in a given contingency situation. The leadership model is the short (one page or less) summary of the theory to be used when selecting the appropriate leadership style for a given situation.

Contingency Theory and Model Variables

Contingency means "it depends." One thing depends on other things, and for a leader to be effective there must be an appropriate fit between the leader's behavior and style and the followers and the situation. Recall from Chapter 1 that *contingency leadership theories* attempt to explain the appropriate leadership style based on the leader, followers, and situation. Thus, if managers can properly diagnose a situation and followers, and use the appropriate leadership style, successful outcomes are highly likely.

See Figure 5-1 for a list of general contingency leadership variables that can be used as a framework in which to place all the contingency leadership model variables for analyzing leadership.[3] Throughout this chapter, each contingency leadership model's variables are described in terms of this framework. For each model, the *leader* variable also includes the leadership styles of each model.

FOLLOWERS	LEADER	SITUATION
Capability	Personality traits	Task
Motivation	Behavior	Structure
	Experience	Environment

Figure 5-1 *Framework for contingency leadership variables.*

Managers are responsible for providing the most effective leadership to each person and for linking individual personal objectives with the department and organization's objectives. This is true at HP, where the relationships and objectives vary from worker to worker for the same manager. Different groups also prefer different leadership styles. Leaders display a range of behavior in different situations, because leadership is largely shaped by contextual factors that not only set the boundaries within which leaders and followers interact but also determine the demands and constraints confronting the leader.[4]

Global Contingency Leadership

Before we get into all the theories, let's take a minute to quickly help you realize how important contingency leadership is in the global economy of today. Global companies like McDonald's, with restaurants all over the world, realize that successful leadership styles can vary greatly from place to place. In Europe and other parts of the world, managers have more cultural than technical aspects as they deal with diverse value systems and religious backgrounds. Management is organized more as a language than a set of techniques. More companies are now looking for graduates with an international openness and flexibility who can master the complexity of the global economy.[5]

Back in the 1970s, Japan was increasing its rate of productivity at a faster pace than that of the United States. William Ouchi found that Japanese firms were managed and led differently than U.S. organizations. He identified seven major differences between the two countries. The Japanese had: (1) longer periods of employment, (2) more collective decision making, (3) more collective responsibility, (4) slower process of evaluating and promoting employees, (5) more implicit mechanisms of control, (6) more unspecialized career paths, and (7) more holistic concern for employees.[6] Ouchi combined practices of U.S. and Japanese companies in what he called Theory Z. Over the years, many American companies have adopted more collective decision making and shared leadership responsibilities. On the other side of the ocean, the Japanese have also been influenced by American management practices, because many Japanese citizens come to the United States to earn business degrees.

CONTINGENCY LEADERSHIP THEORY AND MODEL

In 1951, Fred E. Fiedler began to develop the first situational leadership theory. It was the first theory to specify how situational variables interact with leader personality and behavior. He called the theory "Contingency Theory of Leader Effectiveness."[7] Fiedler believed that leadership style is a reflection of personality (trait theory oriented) and behavior (behavioral theory oriented), and that leadership styles are basically constant. Leaders do not change styles, they change the situation. *The **contingency leadership model** is used to determine if a person's leadership style is task- or relationship-oriented, and if the situation (leader-member relationship, task structure, and position power) matches the leader's style to maximize performance.* In this section we discuss Fiedler's leadership styles, situational favorableness, determining the appropriate leadership style for the situation, and research by Fiedler and others. See Figure 5-2 to see how Fiedler's model fits into the framework of contingency leadership variables.

contingency leadership model: determines if a person's leadership style is task- or relationship-oriented, and if the situation (leader-member relationship, task structure, and position power) matches the leader's style to maximize performance.

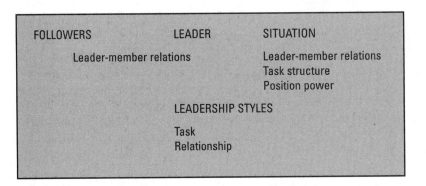

Figure 5-2 *Contingency leadership model variables within the contingency leadership framework.*

Leadership Style and the LPC

Although you may be able to change your behavior with different followers, you also have a dominant leadership style. The first major factor in using Fiedler's model is to determine your dominant leadership style as being task-motivated or relationship-motivated. People primarily gain satisfaction from task accomplishment or from forming and maintaining relationships with followers. To determine leadership style, using Fiedler's model, you must complete the least preferred coworker (LPC) scales. The LPC essentially answers the question, are you more task-oriented or relationship-oriented? The two leadership styles are (1) *task* and (2) *relationship*. Approximately 200 tests revealed that people who completed the LPC scales did in fact use the preferred leadership style in simulated situations and actual job situations.[8]

Note that Fiedler developed two leadership styles, which is a one-dimensional model. The leadership styles part of Fiedler's model is similar to the University of Michigan Leadership Model, in that it is based on only two leadership styles: one focusing on the task (job-centered leadership) and the other focusing on relationship (employee-centered). To determine your Fiedler leadership style, complete Self-Assessment Exercise 5-1.

Self-Assessment Exercise 5-1

Your Fiedler LPC Leadership Style

Return to Chapter 3, Self-Assessment Exercise 3-1, and place your score for tasks on the following Task line and your score for people on the Relationship line.

10 — 9 — 8 — 7 — 6 — 5 — 4 — 3 — 2 — 1

*High **Task** Leadership Style*

10 — 9 — 8 — 7 — 6 — 5 — 4 — 3 — 2 — 1

*High **Relationship** Leadership Style*

According to Fiedler, you are primarily either a task- or relationship-oriented leader. Your highest score is your primary leadership style. Neither leadership style is the one best style. The one appropriate leadership style to use is based on the situation, our next topic.

Situational Favorableness

After determining your leadership style, you determine the situational favorableness. *Situation favorableness* refers to the degree a situation enables the leader to exert influence over the followers. The more control the leader has over the followers, the more favorable the situation is for the leader. The three variables, in order of importance, are

1. *Leader-member relations.* This is the most powerful determinant of overall situational favorableness. Is the relationship good (cooperative and friendly) or poor (antagonistic and difficult)? Do the followers trust, respect, accept, and have confidence in the leader (good)? Is there much tension (poor)? Leaders with good relations have more influence. The better the relations, the more favorable the situation.

2. *Task structure.* Second in potency; is the task structured or unstructured? Do employees perform repetitive routine, unambiguous, standard tasks that are easily understood? Leaders in a structured situation have more influence. The more structured the jobs are, the more favorable the situation.

3. *Position power.* The weakest factor; is position power strong or weak? Does the leader have the power to assign work, reward and punish, hire and fire, give raises and promotions? The leader with position power has more influence. The more power, the more favorable the situation.

The relative weights of these three factors together create a continuum of situational favorableness of the leader. Fiedler developed eight levels of favorableness, going from 1 (highly favorable) to 8 (very unfavorable). See Figure 5-3 for an adapted model.[9]

Determining the Appropriate Leadership Style

To determine whether task or relationship leadership is appropriate, the user answers the three questions pertaining to situational favorableness, using the Fiedler contingency theory model (Figure 5-3). The user starts with question 1 and follows the decision tree to Good or Poor depending on the relations. The user then answers question 2 and follows the decision tree to Repetitive or Nonrepetitive. When answering question 3, the user ends up in one of eight possible situations. If the LPC leadership style matches, the user does nothing, since they may be successful in that situation.

Changing the Situation. However, if the leadership style does not match the situation, the leader may be ineffective. One option is to change to a job that matches the leadership style. Fiedler recommends (and trains people to) change the situation, rather than their leadership styles. Here are a few general examples of how to change the situation variables to make it a more favorable match for the leader's style.

- The leader generally would not want to change the *relationship* from good to poor, but rather the task structure or position power. If relations are poor, the leader can work to improve them by showing interest in followers, listening to them, and spending more time getting to know them personally.
- The *task* can be more or less structured by stating more or less spe-

Figure 5-3 *Fiedler contingency leadership model.*

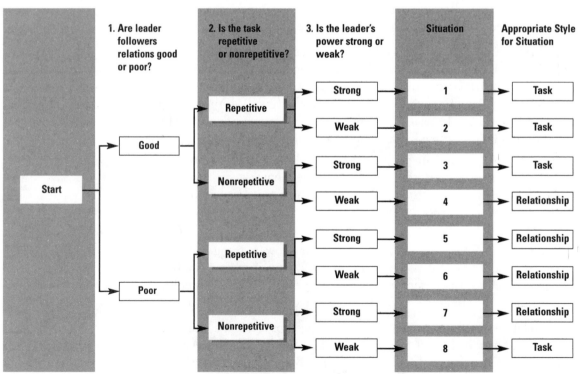

If the manager's LPC leadership style matches the situation, the manager does nothing. If the LPC leadership style does not match the situation, the manager changes the situation to match his or her LPC leadership style.

cific standards and procedures for completing the task, and giving or not giving clear deadlines.

- A leader with strong *position power* does not have to use it; downplay it. Leaders with weak power can try to get more power from their manager and play up the power by being more autocratic.

Fiorina's Leadership Style. Based on prior management jobs, Carly Fiorina will have *good* relations with followers at HP, the task of CEO is *unstructured* or *nonrepetitive*, and Carly's position power as CEO is *strong*. This is Situation 3, in which the appropriate leadership style is *task*. If Fiorina's LPC style is task, Fiedler would say that she need do nothing. However, if her LPC style is relationship, Fiedler would suggest that she change the situation to meet her relationship style.

Research

Despite its groundbreaking start to contingency theory, Fiedler's work was criticized in the 1970s for conceptual reasons, and because of inconsistent empirical finding and inability to account for substantial variance in group performance.[10] Fiedler disagreed with some of the criticism and published rejoinders to both studies.[11] Over the past 20 years, numerous studies have tested the model. Two meta-analyses concluded that the research tends to support the model, although not for every situation and not as strongly for field studies as for laboratory studies.[12] Thus, the debate continues over the validity of the model.

One criticism is of Fiedler's view that the leader should change his or

---

Applying the Concept 5-1

Contingency Leadership Theory

Using Figure 5-3, determine the situation number with its corresponding appropriate leadership style. Select two answers, writing the appropriate letters in the blanks before each item.

a. 1 b. 2 c. 3 d. 4 e. 5 f. 6 g. 7 h. 8

A. task-oriented   B. relationship-oriented

___ ___ **1.** Saul, the manager, oversees the assembly of mass-produced containers. He has the power to reward and punish. Saul is viewed as a hard-nosed manager.

___ ___ **2.** Karen, the manager, is from the corporate planning staff. She helps the other departments plan. Karen is viewed as being a dreamer; she doesn't understand the various departments. Employees tend to be rude in their dealings with Karen.

___ ___ **3.** Juan, the manager, oversees the processing of canceled checks for the bank. He is well liked by the employees. Juan's manager enjoys hiring and evaluating his employees' performance.

___ ___ **4.** Sonia, the principal of a school, assigns teachers to classes and has various other duties. She hires and decides on tenure appointments. The school atmosphere is tense.

___ ___ **5.** Louis, the chairperson of the committee, is highly regarded by its volunteer members from a variety of departments. The committee members are charged with recommending ways to increase organizational performance.

her style rather than the situation. The other situational writers in this chapter suggest changing leadership styles, not the situation. Fiedler has helped contribute to the other contingency theories. Based on the contingency leadership model, Fiedler teamed up with J. E. Garcia to develop cognitive resources theory (CRT).[13]

CRT is a person-by-situation interaction theory in which the person variables are leader intelligence and experience, and the situational variable is stress experienced by leaders and followers. CRT has important implications for leader selection and for situational management. Fiedler recommends a two-step process for effective utilization of leaders: (1) recruiting and selecting individuals with required intellectual abilities, experience, and job-relevant knowledge, and (2) enabling leaders to work under conditions that allow them to make effective use of the cognitive resources for which they were hired.[14] Fiedler has empirical support for his new CRT, but again, it is not without critics.[15]

Despite the critics, Fiedler's contingency leadership model and cognitive resources theory are considered the most validated of all leadership theories by some scholars.[16] However, if there were only one accepted valid motivation theory (Chapter 3) and only one leadership theory, this book would not be presenting several of them.

LEADERSHIP CONTINUUM THEORY AND MODEL

Robert Tannenbaum and Warren Schmidt also developed a contingency theory in the 1950s.[17] They stated that leadership behavior is on a continuum from boss-centered to subordinate-centered leadership. Their model focuses on who makes the decisions. They noted that a leader's choice of a leadership pattern should be based on forces in the boss, forces in the subordinates, and forces in the situation. Look at Figure 5-4 to see how Tannenbaum and Schmidt's variables fit within the framework of contingency leadership variables.

Tannenbaum and Schmidt identify seven major styles the leader can choose from. Figure 5-5 is an adaptation of their model, which lists the seven styles.[18] *The **leadership continuum model** is used to determine which one of seven styles to select, based on the use of boss-centered versus subordinate-centered leadership, to meet the situation (boss, subordinates, situation/time) in order to maximize performance.*

Before selecting one of the seven leadership styles, the leader must consider the following three forces or variables:

- *Boss.* The leader's personality and behavioral preferred style—based on experience, expectation, values, background, knowledge, feeling of security, and confidence in the subordinates—is considered in selecting a leadership style. Based on personality and behavior, some leaders tend to be more autocratic and others more participative.

- *Subordinates.* The followers' preferred style for the leader is based

leadership continuum model: determines which of seven styles to select, based on the use of boss-centered versus subordinate-centered leadership, to meet the situation (boss, subordinates, situation/time) in order to maximize performance.

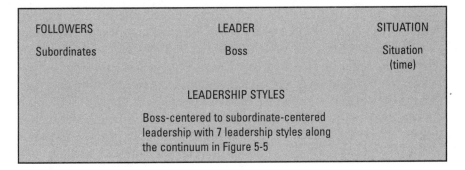

on personality and behavior, as with the leader. Generally, the more willing and able the followers are to participate, the more freedom of participation should be used, and vice versa.

• *Situation (time).* The environmental considerations, such as the organization's size, structure, climate, goals, and technology, are considered in selecting a leadership style. Upper-level managers also influence leadership styles. For example, if a middle manager uses an autocratic leadership style, the leader may tend to use it too.

The *time* available is another consideration. It takes more time to make participative decisions. Thus, when there is no time to include followers in decision making, the leader uses an autocratic leadership style.

In a 1986 follow-up by Tannenbaum and Schmidt to their original 1958 and 1973 articles, they recommended that (1) the leader become a group member when allowing the group to make decisions; (2) the leader clearly state the style (follower's authority) being used; (3) the leader not try to trick the followers into thinking they made a decision that was actually made by the leader; and (4) it's not the number of decisions the followers make, but their significance that counts.[19]

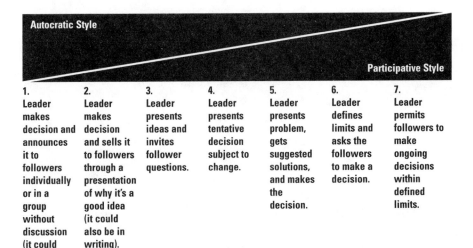

Figure 5-5 *Tannenbaum and Schmidt's leadership continuum model.*

Note that Tannenbaum and Schmidt developed two major leadership styles, with seven continuum styles, which is a one-dimensional model. The leadership styles part of their model is similar to the University of Michigan Leadership Model, in that it is based on two major leadership styles: one focusing on boss-centered behavior (job-centered leadership) and the other focusing on subordinate-centered behavior (employee-centered).

Although the leadership continuum model was very popular, it did not undergo research testing like the contingency leadership model. One major criticism of this model is that the three factors to consider when selecting a leadership style are very subjective. In other words, determining which style to use, and when, is not clear in the model. The situational leadership and the normative leadership models thus took over in popularity, most likely because they clearly identified which leadership style to use in a given, clearly defined situation.

Although Carly Fiorina of HP changes leadership styles to meet the needs of the situation, she tends to make greater use of the participative styles. You will determine your major leadership continuum style later, in Self-Assessment Exercise 5-3, which puts together three of the contingency leadership styles (continuum, path-goal, and normative).

PATH-GOAL LEADERSHIP THEORY AND MODEL

The path-goal leadership theory was developed by Robert House, based on an early version of the theory by M.G. Evans, and published in 1971.[20] House formulated a more elaborate version of Evans's theory, one that included situational variables. House intended to reconcile prior conflicting findings concerning task- and relationship-oriented leader behavior. His theory specified a number of situational moderators of relationships between task- and person-oriented leadership and their effects.[21] House attempted to explain how the behavior of a leader influences the perform-

---

Applying the Concept 5-2

Leadership Continuum

Using Figure 5-5, identify these five statements by their style. Write the appropriate letter in the blank before each item.

      a. 1   b. 2   c. 3   d. 4   e. 5   f. 6   g. 7

____ **1.** "Chuck, I selected you to be transferred to the new department, but you don't have to go if you don't want to."

____ **2.** "Sam, go clean off the tables right away."

____ **3.** "From now on, this is the way it will be done. Does anyone have any questions about the procedure?"

____ **4.** "These are the two weeks we can go on vacation. You select one."

____ **5.** "I'd like your ideas on how to stop the bottleneck on the production line. But I have the final say on the solution we implement."

FOLLOWERS	LEADER	SITUATION
Subordinates (authoritarianism, locus of control, ability)	None	Environment (task structure, formal authority, and work group)

LEADERSHIP STYLES

Directive
Supportive
Participative
Achievement-oriented

Figure 5-6 *Path-goal leadership model variables within the contingency leadership framework.*

ance and satisfaction of the followers (subordinates). Look at Figure 5-6 to see how House's model fits into the framework of contingency leadership variables. Note that unlike the earlier contingency leadership models, House's model does not have a leader trait and behavior variable. The leader is supposed to use the appropriate leadership style (one of four), regardless of preferred traits and behavior.

*The **path-goal leadership model** is used to select the leadership style (directive, supportive, participative, or achievement-oriented) appropriate to the situation (subordinate and environment) to maximize both performance and job satisfaction.* Note that path-goal leadership theory is based on motivation theories of goal-setting and expectancy theory.[22] The leader is responsible for increasing followers' motivation to attain personal and organizational goals. Motivation is increased by (1) clarifying the follower's path to the rewards that are available, or (2) increasing the rewards that the follower values and desires. *Path clarification* means that the leader works with followers to help them identify and learn the behaviors that will lead to successful task accomplishment and organizational rewards.

The path-goal model is used to determine employee objectives and to clarify how to achieve them using one of four leadership styles. It focuses on how leaders influence employees' perceptions of their goals and the paths they follow toward goal attainment. As shown in Figure 5-7 (an adaptation of the model), the situational factors are used to determine the leadership style that affects goal achievement through performance and satisfaction.

path-goal leadership model: determines the leadership style (directive, supportive, participative, or achievement-oriented) appropriate to the situation (subordinate and environment) to maximize both performance and job satisfaction.

Figure 5-7 *House path-goal leadership model.*

Situational Factors

Subordinate.   Subordinate situational characteristics include:

1. *Authoritarianism* is the degree to which employees defer to and want to be told what to do and how to do the job.

2. *Locus of control* (Chapter 2) is the extent to which employees believe they control goal achievement (internal), or if goal achievement is controlled by others (external).

3. *Ability* is the extent of the employees' ability to perform tasks to achieve goals.

Environment.   Environment situational factors include:

1. *Task structure* is the extent of repetitiveness of the job.

2. *Formal authority* is the extent of the leader's position power. Note that task structure and formal authority are essentially the same as Fiedler's.

3. *Work group* is the extent to which coworkers contribute to job satisfaction, or the relationship between followers. Note that House identifies work group as a situational variable. However, under the contingency framework, it would be considered a follower variable.

Leadership Styles

Based on the situational factors in the path-goal model, the leader can select the most appropriate leadership style by using the following general guidelines for each style. The original model included only the directive (based on initiating structure, job-centered style) and supportive (based on consideration and employee style) leadership styles (from the Ohio State and University of Michigan behavioral leadership studies). The participative and achievement-oriented leadership styles were added in a 1974 publication by House and Mitchell.[23]

Directive.   The leader provides high structure. Directive leadership is appropriate when the followers want authority leadership, have external locus of control, and the follower ability is low. Directive leadership is also appropriate when the environmental task is complex or ambiguous, formal authority is strong, and the work group provides job satisfaction.

Supportive.   The leader provides high consideration. Supportive leadership is appropriate when the followers do not want autocratic leadership, have internal locus of control, and follower ability is high. Supportive leadership is also appropriate when the environmental tasks are simple, formal authority is weak, and the work group does not provide job satisfaction.

Participative.   The leader includes employee input into decision making. Participative leadership is appropriate when followers want to be involved, have internal locus of control, and follower ability is high; when the environmental task is complex, authority is either strong or weak, and job satisfaction from coworkers is either high or low.

Achievement-Oriented.   The leader sets difficult but achievable goals, expects followers to perform at their highest level, and rewards them for doing so. In essence, the leader provides both high directive (structure) and high supportive (consideration) behavior. Achievement-oriented leadership is appropriate when followers are open to autocratic leadership, have external locus of control, and follower ability is high; and when the environmental task is simple, authority is strong, and job satisfaction from coworkers is either high or low.

Research

A meta-analysis based on 120 studies examined directive and supportive behavior, and showed that support for path-goal theory was significantly greater than chance, but results were quite mixed. An extensive review of the research on moderator variables in leaders also had inconclusive findings.[24] Recent reviews of the history of path-goal theory have concluded that it has not been adequately tested, possibly because it is such a complex model. It continues to be tested; a recent study used a survey of 1,000 respondents from governmental and public auditing sample.[25]

Although path-goal theory is more complex and specific than leadership continuum, it is also criticized by managers because it is difficult to know which style to use when. As you can see, there are many situations in which not all six situational factors are exactly as presented in the guidelines for when to use the style. Judgment calls are required to select the appropriate style as necessary.

Despite its limitations, the path-goal model has already made an important contribution to the study of leadership by providing a conceptual framework to guide researchers in identifying potentially relevant situa-

---

Applying the Concept 5-3

Path-Goal Leadership

Using Figure 5-7, and text descriptions, identify the appropriate leadership style for the five situations. Write the appropriate letter in the blank before each item.

a. directive   b. supportive   c. participative   d. achievement

_____ 1. The manager has a new, complex task for her department, and she is not sure how it should be done. Her employees are experienced and like to be involved in decision making.

_____ 2. The manager is putting together a new task force that will have an ambiguous task to complete. The members all know each other and get along well.

_____ 3. The manager has decided to delegate a new task to an employee who has been doing a good job. The employee, however, tends to be insecure and may feel threatened by taking on a new task, even though it is fairly easy and the

manager is confident that the employee can do the job easily.

_____ 4. The department members just finished the production quarter and easily met the quota. The manager has strong position power and has decided to increase the quota to make the job more challenging.

_____ 5. The manager has an employee who has been coming in late for work, with no apparent good reason. The manager has decided to take some corrective action to get the employee to come in on time.

tional variables. It also provides a useful way for leaders to think about motivating followers.[26]

Charismatic Leadership and Value-Based Leadership Theory. Path-goal leadership theory led to the development of the theory of charismatic leadership in 1976. You will learn about charismatic leadership in Chapter 10. Path-goal theory was considerably broadened in scope, and in 1996 House referred to it as value-based leadership theory.[27] Because value-based Leadership theory is new and relatively untested, we do not present it here. However, see note 27 for House's further-developed theory.

Fiorina's Leadership Style. As a successful CEO, Carly Fiorina most likely uses the four different leadership styles that are appropriate for her followers and situations. You will determine your major path-goal leadership style in Self-Assessment Exercise 5-3, which puts together the contingency leadership styles.

NORMATIVE LEADERSHIP THEORY AND MODELS

An important leadership question today is, "When should the manager take charge and when should the manager let the group make the decision?" In 1973, Victor Vroom and Philip Yetton published a decision-making model to answer this question while improving decision-making effectiveness. Vroom and Arthur Jago refined the model and expanded it to four models in 1988.[28] The four models are based on two variable factors: individual or group decisions and time-driven or development-driven decisions.

normative leadership model: has four decision trees, used in determining the leadership style (autocratic, AI–AII; consultative, CI–CII; and group, GII) appropriate to the situation (ten variables) to maximize decisions.

The *normative leadership model* uses four decision trees that enable users to determine the leadership style (autocratic, AI–AII; consultative, CI–CII; and group, GII) appropriate to the situation (ten variables) to maximize decisions. Look at Figure 5-8 to see how the normative leadership models fit into the framework of contingency leadership variables.

Leadership Styles

Vroom and Yetton identified five leadership styles. Two are autocratic (AI and AII), two are consultative (CI and CII), and one is group oriented (GII).

- *AI.* The leader makes the decision alone, using information available to him or her without input from anyone else.

- *AII.* The leader gets information from followers but makes the decision alone. Followers may or may not be told what the problem is. They are asked only for information, not for their input into the decision; followers do not generate or evaluate alternative decisions.

- *CI.* The leader meets individually with relevant followers, explains the situation, and gets information and ideas on the decision to be made. The leader makes the final decision alone. The leader may or may not use the followers' input.

FOLLOWERS	LEADER	SITUATION
Developmental-Driven	LI Leader Information	Time-Driven
Design Model		Decision Model
CR Commitment	LEADERSHIP STYLES	QR Quality Requirement
Requirement	Individual and Group Decision Models	ST Problem Structure
CP Commitment Probability	Autocratic	
GC Goal Congruence	AI, AII	
CO Subordinate Conflict	Consultative	
SI Subordinate Information	CI,CII	
	Group	
	GII	

Figure 5-8 *Normative leadership model variables within the contingency leadership framework.*

- *CII.* The leader meets with followers as a group, explains the situation, and gets information and ideas on the decision to be made. The leader makes the decision alone after the meeting. Leaders may or may not use the followers' input.

- *GII.* The leader meets with the followers as a group, explains the situation, and the decision is made by group consensus. The leader does not try to influence the group to adopt his or her decisions and is willing to implement any decision that has the support of the entire group. If there is no consensus, then the leader makes the final decision based on the group input.

Determining the Model and Appropriate Leadership Style

The first step is actually to select one of the four normative leadership models based on the decision. Thus, the first variable is based on the type of decision to be made: Is it individual or group? The second variable is based on the decision being driven: Is it driven by time, or by development of followers?

To determine the appropriate style for a specific situation, you answer eight questions, some of which may be skipped based on the model used and prior questions. The questions are sequential, presented in a decision-tree format similar to the Fiedler model, leading you to the appropriate style to use. In some situations more than one leadership style is appropriate, and you can select any one.

Decision Quality and Acceptance. Although there are eight variable questions to answer, based on prior research, the quality requirements of a decision and likelihood of follower acceptance before choosing a decision style are considered the most important.[29] The eight diagnostic questions to answer as you follow the decision tree are as follows:

- *QR—Quality Requirement.* Is there a quality requirement such that one solution is likely to be more rational than another?

- *CR—Commitment Requirement.* How important is follower commitment? Is followers' acceptance of the decision critical to effective implementation?

- *LI—Leader Information.* Do I have sufficient information to make a high-quality decision without getting input from others?

- *ST—Problem Structure.* Is the problem structured? (similar to Fiedler)

- *CP—Commitment Probability.* If I were to make the decision by myself, is it reasonably certain that my followers would accept it, and would they be committed to the decision?

- *GC—Goal Congruence.* Do followers share the organizational goals to be attained in solving the problem?

- *CO—Subordinate Conflict.* Is conflict among followers likely in the preferred solution? (not relevant to individual problems)

- *SI—Subordinate Information.* Do followers have sufficient information to make a high-quality decision?

With four models, five leadership styles, and eight decision diagnostic questions to answer, normative leadership is the most complex contingency theory. The questions were originally answered as yes or no. However, questions now have five multiple choices. The latest computer software version of this model, which replaces decision rules with mathematical functions, is recommended to apply the model in its complete form.[30] Therefore, we do not provide a copy of the model(s). However, in Chapter 7 we present an adapted version of it—the situational management decision-making model, which is part of behavior modeling, in Skill Building Exercise 7-1. It is in Chapter 7 because it fits better with the decision-making discussion in that chapter.

Research

Numerous studies have tested the normative leadership model. In general, the results of empirical research have supported the model. Vroom and Jago conducted research concluding that managers using the style recommended in the model have a 62 percent probability of a successful decision, whereas those not using the recommended style have only a 37 percent probability of a successful decision.[31] However, the model is not without its critics. For example, the studies compared only people who used the model. There is no evidence to show that leaders who use the model are more effective overall than leaders who do not use the model.[32] Although the same has been said by different researchers regarding the contingency leadership model, a different author states that the normative leadership model is probably the best supported of the contingency leadership theories of effective leadership behavior.[33] Again, there is no one leadership model accepted as the best by researchers.

Vroom and Yetton's model tends to be popular in the academic community, because it is based on research. However, it is not as popular with managers, who find it cumbersome to select from four models, pull out the model, and follow an eight-question decision tree every time they have to make a decision. Our next, and last, contingency leadership theory—before we put them together and discuss leadership substitute theory—is situational leadership theory.

Fiorina's Leadership Style. As a successful CEO, Carly Fiorina uses different leadership styles that are appropriate for her followers and situations. However, we don't know if she actually uses the normative leadership model. You will determine your major normative leadership style later in Self-Assessment Exercise 5-3, which puts together the contingency leadership styles.

SITUATIONAL LEADERSHIP THEORY AND MODEL

Before you learn about the situational leadership model, complete Self-Assessment Exercise 5-2 to determine your preferred situational leadership style.

Self-Assessment Exercise 5-2

Determining Your Preferred Situational Leadership Style

Following are 12 situations. Select the one alternative that most closely describes what you would do in each situation. Don't be concerned with trying to pick the right answer; select the alternative you would really use. Circle a, b, c, or d. Ignore the M/C _____ and S _____ parts, which will be explained later in this chapter and used in class in Skill-Building Exercise 5-2.

M/C _____ 1. Your rookie crew seems to be developing well. Their need for direction and close supervision is diminishing. What do you do?
   a. Stop directing and overseeing performance unless there is a problem. S _____
   b. Spend time getting to know them personally, but make sure they maintain performance levels. S _____
   c. Make sure things keep going well; continue to direct and oversee closely. S _____
   d. Begin to discuss new tasks of interest to them. S _____

M/C _____ 2. You assigned Jill a task, specifying exactly how you wanted it done. Jill deliberately ignored your directions and did it her way. The job will not meet the customer's standards. This is not the first problem you've had with Jill. What do you decide to do?
   a. Listen to Jill's side, but be sure the job gets done right. S _____
   b. Tell Jill to do it again the right way, and closely supervise the job. S _____
   c. Tell her the customer will not accept the job, and let Jill handle it her way. S _____
   d. Discuss the problem and possible solutions to it. S _____

M/C _____ 3. Your employees work well together; the department is a real team. It's the top performer in the organization. Because of traffic problems, the president okayed staggered hours for departments. As a result, you can change your department's hours. Several of your workers have suggested changing. You take what action?

a. Allow the group to decide its hours. S _____

b. Decide on new hours, explain why you chose them, and invite questions. S _____

c. Conduct a meeting to get the group members' ideas. Select new hours together, with your approval. S _____

d. Send around a memo stating the hours you want. S _____

M/C _____ 4. You hired Bill, a new employee. He is not performing at the level expected after one month's training. Bill is trying, but he seems to be a slow learner. What do you decide to do?

a. Clearly explain what needs to be done and oversee his work. Discuss why the procedures are important; support and encourage him. S _____

b. Tell Bill that his training is over and it's time to pull his own weight. S _____

c. Review task procedures and supervise Bill's work closely. S _____

d. Inform Bill that his training is over, and tell him to feel free to come to you if he has any problems. S _____

M/C _____ 5. Helen has had an excellent performance record for the last five years. Recently you have noticed a drop in the quality and quantity of her work. She has a family problem. What do you do?

a. Tell Helen to get back on track and closely supervise her. S _____

b. Discuss the problem with Helen. Help her realize that her personal problem is affecting her work. Discuss ways to improve the situation. Be supportive and encourage her. S _____

c. Tell Helen you're aware of her productivity slip, and that you're sure she'll work it out soon. S _____

d. Discuss the problem and solution with Helen, and supervise her closely. S _____

M/C _____ 6. Your organization does not allow smoking in certain areas. You just walked by a restricted area and saw Joan smoking. She has been with the organization for 10 years and is a very productive worker. Joan has never been caught smoking before. What action do you take?

a. Ask her to put it out, and then leave. S _____

b. Discuss why she is smoking, and ask what she intends to do about it. S _____

c. Give her a lecture about not smoking, and check up on her in the future. S _____

d. Tell her to put it out, watch her do it, and tell her you will check on her in the future. S _____

M/C _____ 7. Your department usually works well together with little direction. Recently a conflict between Sue and Tom has caused problems. As a result, you take what action?

a. Call Sue and Tom together and make them realize how this conflict is affecting the department. Discuss how to resolve it and how you will check to make sure the problem is solved. S _____

b. Let the group resolve the conflict. S _____

c. Have Sue and Tom sit down and discuss their conflict and how to resolve it. Support their efforts to implement a solution. S _____

d. Tell Sue and Tom how to resolve their conflict and closely supervise them. S _____

M/C _____ 8. Jim usually does his share of the work with some encouragement and direction. However, he has migraine headaches occasionally and doesn't pull his weight when this happens. The others resent doing Jim's work. What do you decide to do?

a. Discuss his problem and help him come up with ideas for maintaining his work; be supportive. S _____

b. Tell Jim to do his share of the work and closely watch his output. S _____

c. Inform Jim that he is creating a hardship for the others and should resolve the problem by himself. S _____

d. Be supportive, but set minimum performance levels and ensure compliance. S _____

M/C _____ 9. Barbara, your most experienced and productive worker, came to you with a detailed idea that could increase your department's productivity at a very low cost. She can do her present job and this new assignment. You think it's an excellent idea; what do you do?

a. Set some goals together. Encourage and support her efforts. S _____

b. Set up goals for Barbara. Be sure she agrees with them and sees you as being supportive of her efforts. S _____

c. Tell Barbara to keep you informed and to come to you if she needs any help. S _____

d. Have Barbara check in with you frequently, so that you can direct and supervise her activities. S _____

M/C _____ 10. Your boss asked you for a special report. Frank, a very capable worker who usually needs no direction or support, has all the necessary skills to do the job. However, Frank is reluctant because he has never done a report. What do you do?

a. Tell Frank he has to do it. Give him direction and supervise him closely. S _____

b. Describe the project to Frank and let him do it his own way. S _____

c. Describe the benefits to Frank. Get his ideas on how to do it and check his progress. S _____

d. Discuss possible ways of doing the job. Be supportive; encourage Frank. S _____

M/C _____ 11. Jean is the top producer in your department. However, her monthly reports are constantly late and contain errors. You are puzzled because she does everything else with no direction or support. What do you decide to do?

a. Go over past reports with Jean, explaining exactly what is expected of her. Schedule a meeting so that you can review the next report with her. S _____

b. Discuss the problem with Jean, and ask her what can be done about it; be supportive. S _____

c. Explain the importance of the report. Ask her what the problem is. Tell her that you expect the next report to be on time and error free. S _____

d. Remind Jean to get the next report in on time without errors. S _____

M/C _____ 12. Your workers are very effective and like to participate in decision making. A consultant was hired to develop a new method for your department using the latest technology in the field. What do you do?

a. Explain the consultant's method and let the group decide how to implement it. S _____

b. Teach them the new method and closely supervise them. S _____

c. Explain the new method and the reasons that it is important. Teach them the method and

make sure the procedure is followed. Answer questions. S _____

d. Explain the new method and get the group's input on ways to improve and implement it. S _____

To determine your preferred management style, follow these steps:

1. In this chart, circle the letter you selected for each situation.

The column headings (S1 through S4) represent the management style you selected.

S1 = Telling, S2 = Selling,
S3 = Participating, S4 = Delegating

	S1T	S2S	S3P	S4D
1	c	b	d	a
2	b	a	d	c
3	d	b	c	a
4	c	a	d	b
5	a	d	b	c
6	d	c	b	a
7	d	a	c	b
8	b	d	a	c
9	d	b	a	c
10	a	c	d	b
11	a	c	b	d
12	b	c	d	a

Totals   _____   _____   _____   _____

2. Add up the number of circled items per column. The column with the highest total is your preferred situational leadership style. Is this the style you tend to use most often?

Your management style flexibility is reflected in the distribution of your answers. The more evenly distributed the numbers are between telling, selling, participating, and delegating, the more flexible your style is. A score of 1 or 0 in any column may indicate a reluctance to use the style.

Note: There is no "right" leadership style. This part of the exercise is designed to enable you to better understand the style you tend to use or prefer to use. In Skill-Building Exercise 5-2, you will use the situational leadership model to try to determine the most appropriate leadership style for these 12 situations.

Paul Hersey and Ken Blanchard published the Life Cycle Theory of Leadership in 1969. They revised it, and in 1977 published the Situational Leadership® Model. Unlike the other contingency theories, situational leadership is not called a theory by its authors, because it does not attempt to explain why things happen.[34] However, other authors do call it a theory. The primary contingency variable of situational leadership is the maturity level of the followers. Like the path-goal model, situational leadership does not have a leader variable, and the situational variable—task—is actually included within the follower variable because it is closely related to follower maturity. Thus, task is not included within the model as a separate variable. Look at Figure 5-9 to see how the situational leadership variables fit into the framework of contingency leadership variables.

*The **situational leadership model** is used to determine which of four leadership styles (telling, selling, participating, and delegating) matches the situation (followers' maturity level to complete a specific task) to maximize performance.* For the most part, situational leadership is an adaptation of the Ohio State University Leadership Model. Thus, unlike the one-dimensional contingency model with two styles (more similar to University of Michigan model), situational leadership is two-dimensional—with four leadership styles. See Figure 5-10 to find out how Hersey and Blanchard adapted the Ohio State model.

So to use the situational leadership model, you first determine the maturity level of the follower(s) and then follow by choosing the leadership style that matches the maturity level. We now discuss the theory components of the model.

situational leadership model: determines which leadership style (telling, selling, participating, and delegating) matches the situation (followers' maturity level to complete a specific task) to maximize performance.

Determining Follower Maturity

Follower maturity is measured on a continuum from low to high, which you, as a manager, determine. You select the one capability level that best describes the followers' ability and willingness or confidence to complete the specific task. These levels follow:

- *Low (M1)—unable and unwilling or insecure.* The followers can't or won't do the specific task without detailed directions and close supervision, or they are insecure and need supervision.

- *Low to Moderate (M2)—unable but willing or confident.* The followers have moderate ability to complete the task but need specific

Figure 5-9 *Situational leadership model variables within the contingency leadership framework.*

FOLLOWERS	LEADER	SITUATION
Follower Maturity	None	Task
	LEADERSHIP STYLES	
	Telling	
	Selling	
	Participating	
	Delegating	

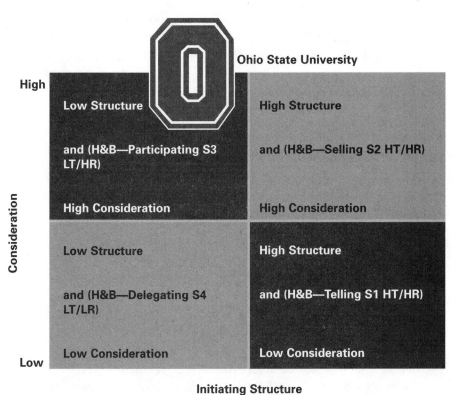

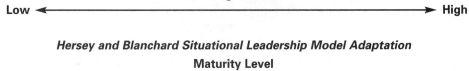

Leadership Styles—Rather than call the leadership style by its two dimensions, which Hersey and Blanchard (H&B) call high or low (H/L) task—T and relationship—R, they gave each leadersh style a name, as shown in the Ohio model.

Maturity Level—H&B also placed a bell-shaped curve within the four leadership style quadrants, and added the maturity continuum to the bottom of the leadership style model to indicate which leadership style should be used to match the followers' maturity level.

Matching the Maturity Level to	the Leadership Style
M1—Unable and unwilling or insecure	S1 Telling—HT/LR
M2—Unable but willing or confident	S2 Selling—HT/HR
M3—Able but unwilling or insecure	S3 Participating—LT/HR
M4—Able and willing or confident	S4 Delegating—LT/LR

direction/task and support/relationship to get the task done properly. The employees may be highly motivated and willing, but still need task direction due to lack of ability.

- *Moderate to High (M3)—able but unwilling or insecure.* The followers have high ability but may lack the confidence due to insecurity to do the job. What they need most is support and encouragement to motivate them to get the task done.

- *High (M4)—able and willing or confident.* The followers are capable of doing the task without task direction or supportive relationship. They can be left on their own to do the job.

Leadership Styles and Selection

The four leadership styles are based on task and relationship behavior. In other words, when you interact with your followers, you can be focusing on getting the task done, developing supportive relationships, both behaviors, or neither.

Telling (S1)—high-task/low-relationship behavior (HT/LR). This style is appropriate when leading low-maturity followers (M1). When interacting with employees, give very detailed instructions, describing exactly what the task is and when, where, and how to perform it. Closely oversee performance and give some support, but the majority of time with the employees is spent giving directions. Make decisions without input from the employees.

Selling (S2)—high-task/high-relationship behavior (HT/HR). This style is appropriate when leading low- to moderate-maturity followers (M2). You give specific instructions as well as oversee performance at all major stages through completion. At the same time, support the followers by explaining why the task should be performed as requested and answering their questions. Work on relationships as you sell the benefits of completing the task your way. Give fairly equal amount of time to directing and supporting employees. When making decisions, you may consult employees, but still have the final say. Once you make the decision, which can incorporate employees' ideas, direct and oversee their performance.

Participating style (S3)—low-task/high-relationship behavior (LT/HR). This style is appropriate when leading followers with high-moderate maturity (M3). When interacting with followers, spend a small amount of time giving general directions with the majority of time spent giving encouragement. Spend limited time overseeing performance, letting employees do the task their way while focusing on the end result. Support the employees by encouraging them and building up their self-confidence. If a task needs to be done, don't tell them how to do it; ask them how they will accomplish it. Make decisions together, or allow employees to make the decision subject to your limitations and approval.

Delegating style (S4) involves low-task/low-relationship behavior (LT/LR). This style is appropriate when leading followers with high maturity (M4). When interacting with these followers, merely let them know what needs to be done. Answer their questions, but provide little, if any, direction. It is not necessary to oversee performance. These employees are highly motivated and need little, if any, support. Allow these employees to make their own decisions subject to your limitations, although approval will not be necessary. Another term for delegating would be laissez-faire—hands off, leave them alone to do their own thing.

Changing Leadership Styles. Using the model, you change your leadership style with different followers, and with the same follower. Most people perform a variety of tasks on the job. It is important to realize that followers' maturity may vary depending on the specific task. For example, a bank teller may be at an M4 maturity level for routine transactions but may be an M1 for opening new or special accounts.

Developing Followers. Employees tend to start working with an M1 capability, needing close direction and supervision. As their ability to do the job increases, you can begin to be more supportive, develop a working relationship, and probably stop supervising closely. As a manager, you should gradually develop your employees from M1 levels to M3 or M4 over time. The idea of developing followers was better indicated under the original name—the life cycle.

Research

Hersey and Blanchard have not provided any evidence that people who use their model are more effective leaders with higher levels of performance. Prior tests of the model have shown mixed results, indicating that the model may hold for only certain types of employees. It has been criticized for having inconsistency in its instruments and model.[35] A more recent test also criticized the model.[36] Although not as a direct answer to the criticism of the model, Hersey uses this baseball metaphor: I can't give you the way

---

Applying the Concept 5-4

Situational Leadership

For each of these five statements, using Figure 5-10, identify the maturity level of the employees and the appropriate leadership style to get the job done. Write the appropriate letter in the blank before each item.

a. low maturity (M1) *telling* style (S1-HT/LR)
b. low to moderate maturity (M2) *selling* style (S2-HT/HR)
c. moderate to high maturity (M3) *participating* style (S3-LT/HR)
d. high maturity (M4) *delegating* style (S4-LT/LR)

_____ **1.** Mary Ann has never done a report before, but you know she can do it with a minimum of help from you.

_____ **2.** You told Angelo to fill the customer order to your specifications. However, Angelo deliberately ignored your directions. The customer returned the order to you with a complaint.

_____ **3.** Tina is an enthusiastic employee. You have decided to expand her job responsibilities to include a difficult task, which she has never done before.

_____ **4.** Part of Pete's job, which he has done properly many times, is to take out the trash in your office when it's full. It's full now.

_____ **5.** Carlos usually does an excellent job and gets along well with coworkers. For the past two days you have seen a drop in the quality of his work and noticed him arguing with coworkers. You want Carlos to return to his usual level of performance.

to hit a home run every time at bat, but I can help you increase your batting average. That's what we are doing for people with the Situational Leadership model.

Commonly Used in Training Programs. Even though situational leadership has the least research support, it has been used in more management training workshops than any other contingency leadership model. Hersey and Blanchard and their associates go all over the world and train managers to be situational leaders. The Situational Leadership material has been translated into 19 or more languages. Hersey himself has trained more than 4 million managers from over 1,000 organizations in more than 125 countries. Many more trainers use the Situational Leadership material, rather than having Hersey or Blanchard and associates do the training. Situational Leadership is probably so popular because it is a relatively easy model to understand and use, based on a commonsense approach to leadership. Hersey and Blanchard's Situational Selling Model and Situational Parenting Model are also popular.[37]

Contributions. An important contribution of the model is the emphasis on flexibility in adapting the leadership style. Hersey and Blanchard remind us that it is essential to lead followers differently, to lead the same follower differently for different tasks, and to coach followers to develop their maturity level.[38] Carly Fiorina, CEO of HP, changes leadership styles with her followers and tends to use the relationship leadership styles more often than the task leadership styles. She may have attended a leadership training program and learned to use the situational leadership model.

Adaptations. Situational management, in Skill-Building Exercise 5-2, is an adaptation of Hersey and Blanchard's Situational Leadership. Skill-Building Exercises 7-1 (Situational Decision Making), 4-1 (Situational Communications), and 8-1 (Situational Group Leadership) are adapted from Hersey and Blanchard, and Vroom and Yetton. Others have also modified situational leadership.[39]

PUTTING THE BEHAVIORAL AND CONTINGENCY LEADERSHIP THEORIES TOGETHER

Figure 5-11 is a review of different words that are used to describe the same two leadership behavior concepts; it also includes the number of leadership styles based on the two behavior concepts. Figure 5-12 includes the different names given to the leadership styles. You should realize that all the leadership styles are based on the same two behavior concepts. We developed Figures 5-11 and 5-12 to put all these contingency leadership theories together with behavioral leadership styles. These figures should help you to better understand the similarities and differences between these theories.

As we put the leadership theories together, we acknowledge the brilliant synthesizer Russell Ackoff, founder of systems theory, and present his advice on leadership. Ackoff warns against the continued reliance by man-

	LEADERSHIP	BEHAVIOR/STYLE	NUMBER OF LEADERSHIP STYLES BASED ON BEHAVIOR CONCEPTS
Behavioral Theories			
Iowa State University	Autocratic	Democratic	2
University of Michigan	Job-centered	Employee-centered	2
Ohio State University	Structure	Consideration	4
Leadership Grid	Concern for production	Concern for people	5
Contingency Theories			
Contingency model	Task	Relationship	2
Leadership continuum	Boss-centered	Subordinate-centered	7
Path-goal model	Directive	Supportive	4
Normative model	Autocratic	Group	5
Situational leadership	Task	Relationship	4
*Situational management	Directive	Supportive	4

*Presented in Skill-Building Exercise 5-2.

Figure 5-11 *Names given to the same two leadership behavior concepts.*

agement on fads, and he advocates systems leadership. Systems leadership requires an ability to bring the will of followers into agreement with that of the leader so they follow him or her voluntarily, with enthusiasm and dedication.[40]

Prescriptive and Descriptive Models

One last difference between models, not shown in any figures, is the difference between prescriptive and descriptive models. The contingency leadership model, the normative leadership model, and the situational leadership model are all prescriptive models. *Prescriptive leadership models tell the user exactly which style to use in a given situation.* However, the continuum and path-goal leadership models are descriptive models. *Descriptive leadership models identify contingency variables and leadership styles without specifying which style to use in a given situation.* In other words, users of the descriptive model select the appropriate style based more on their own judgment. Look at all the leadership models and you will see what we mean.

Many managers prefer prescriptive models; this is a reason why the normative and situational leadership models are more commonly used in organizational leadership training programs than the descriptive leadership models. Many managers also prefer simple prescriptive models, and this is a reason why situational leadership is more commonly used than normative. On the other hand, many academic researchers scoff at prescriptive models, especially simple ones, and prefer the more complex descriptive models based on sold theoretical foundations.

prescriptive leadership models: tell the user exactly which style to use in a given situation.

descriptive leadership models: identify contingency variables and leadership styles without specifying which style to use in a given situation.

Figure 5-12 *Putting the Behavioral and Contingency Leadership Theories Together*

	LEADERSHIP STYLES				CONTINGENCY VARIABLES	CONTINGENCY CHANGE	DESIRED OUTCOME
BEHAVIORAL THEORIES							
U of Michigan	Job Centered		Employee Centered				
Ohio State U	High Structure/ Low Consideration	High Structure/ High Consideration	Low Structure/ High Consideration	Low Structure/ Low Consideration			
CONTINGENCY THEORIES							
Contingency Leadership Model	Task		Relationship		Leader/Follower Relations Task Structure Position Power	The Situation	Performance
Leadership Continuum Model	1	2 & 3	4 & 5	6 & 7	Manager Subordinates Situation/time	Leadership Style	Performance
Path-Goal Model	Directive	Achievement	Supportive	Participative	Subordinate (authoritarianism, locus of control, ability) Environment (task structure, formal authority, work group)	Leadership Style	Performance Job Satisfaction
Normative Leadership Model	Autocratic AI & AII	Consultative CI & CII		Group GII	Development or Time Driven and Individual or Group Model LI, CR, CP, GC, CO, SI, QR, ST	Leadership Style	Decisions
Situational Leadership Model	Telling	Selling	Participating	Delegating	Follower Maturity for the Task	Leadership Style	Performance
*Situational Management Model	Autocratic	Consultative	Participative	Empowerment	Follower Capability for the Task	Leadership Style	Performance

*Presented in Skill-Building Exercise 5-2.

Self-Assessment Exercise 5-3

Your Continuum, Path-Goal, and Normative Preferred Leadership Styles

You have already determined your LPC contingency leadership style (Self-Assessment Exercise 5-1) and your preferred situational leadership style (Self-Assessment Exercise 5-2). Using Self-Assessment Exercise 5-3, you can determine your other preferred styles by following these steps: (1) Circle your situational leadership style in the first column. (2) In the same row, the columns to the right show your other preferred leadership styles.

SITUATIONAL LEADERSHIP STYLE	LEADERSHIP CONTINUUM STYLE	PATH-GOAL LEADERSHIP STYLE	NORMATIVE LEADERSHIP STYLE
Telling	1 Boss-centered	Directive	Autocratic—AI, AII
Selling	2 or 3	Achievement	Consultative—CI, CII
Participating	4 or 5	Supportive	Consultative—CI, CII
Delegating	6 or 7 Subordinate-centered	Participative	Group—GII

Self-Assessment Exercise 5-4

Personality Traits and Leadership Style

The personality traits and behavior and leadership style are the same as those in Chapters 2 and 3, so for a full discussion return to those chapters. In this chapter, the main thing we want to make you aware of is the need to be flexible and to change your leadership style to match the contingency situation with different followers, and with the same follower for different tasks.

Two ways to check your willingness to change leadership styles are (1) Does your personality profile, Chapter 2, include high openness to experience? (2) More directly, review your situational leadership style profile for the 12 situations in Self-Assessment Exercise 5-2. Are you open to changing leadership

styles? Place your score for each of the 4 styles here _____ _____ _____ _____. The more evenly distributed your answers are, the more willing you are to change leadership styles.

In the self-assessment exercises in this chapter, you have learned your preferred contingency leadership styles. However, according to four contingency theories, you should not always use the same leadership style. Therefore, you need to be aware of your preferred style, to know whether you are reluctant to change leadership styles, and to focus on diagnosing the contingency situation so that you use the appropriate leadership style for the model you are following. In other words, if you use a contingency leadership model, you should improve your ability to change leadership styles while improving your leadership and follower performance.

The easiest model to use on the job without an actual copy, because you can simply remember it and go through the process in your mind, is situational leadership and its adapted situational management model. You can develop your skill at using this model in Skill-Building Exercise 5-2.

LEADERSHIP SUBSTITUTES THEORY

The five leadership theories presented assume that some leadership style will be effective in each situation. However, in keeping with contingency theory, there are factors outside the leader's control that have a larger impact on outcomes than do leadership actions. Contingency factors provide guidance and incentives to perform, making the leader's role unnecessary in some situations.[41] Steven Kerr and John Jermier argued that certain situational variables prevent leaders from affecting subordinates' (followers') attitudes and behaviors.[42] *Substitutes for leadership include characteristics of the subordinate, task, and organization that replace the need for a leader or neutralize the leader's behavior.*

substitutes for leadership: include characteristics of the subordinate, task, and organization that replace the need for a leader or neutralize the leader's behavior.

Substitutes and Neutralizers

Thus, *substitutes* for leadership make a leadership style unnecessary or redundant. For example, highly skilled workers do not need a leader's task behavior to tell them how to do their job. *Neutralizers* reduce or limit the effectiveness of a leader's behavior. For example, managers who are not near an employee cannot readily give task-directive behavior. Carly Fiorina, CEO of HP, has highly competent presidents of various divisions from around the world reporting to her, thus substituting for and neutralizing her leadership style. See Figure 5-13 to see how the substitutes for leadership fit into the framework of contingency leadership variables. Then, read a description of each substitute.

The following variables may substitute or neutralize leadership by providing task-oriented direction and/or people-oriented support rather than a leader:

1. *Characteristics of followers.* Ability, knowledge, experience, training. Need for independence. Professional orientation. Indifference toward organizational rewards.

2. *Characteristics of the task.* Clarity and routine. Invariant methodology. Provision of own feedback concerning accomplishment. Intrinsic satisfaction. This characteristic is similar to Fiedler and others' task behavior.

Figure 5-13 *Substitute for leadership variables within the contingency leadership framework.*

3. *Characteristics of the organization.* Formalization (explicit plans, goals, and areas of responsibility). Inflexibility (rigid, unbending rules and procedures). Highly specified and active advisory and staff functions. Closely knit, cohesive work groups. Organizational

FOLLOWERS	LEADER	SITUATION
Subordinates	None	Task organization

rewards not within the leader's control. Spatial distance between leader and followers.

Leadership Style

Leaders can analyze their situation and better understand how these three characteristics substitute or neutralize their leadership style and thus can provide the leadership and followership most appropriate for the situation. The leader role is to provide the direction and support not already being provided by the task, group, or organization. The leader fills the gaps in leadership. As with situational leadership, high-maturity followers don't need leadership. Thus with the delegating leadership style, you delegate leadership to the follower.

Changing the Situation

Like Fiedler suggested, leaders can change the situation rather than their leadership style. Thus, substitutes for leadership can be designed in organizations in ways to complement existing leadership, to act in leadership absence, and to otherwise provide more comprehensive leadership alternatives. After all, organizations have cut middle-management numbers, and something has to provide the leadership in their absence. One approach is to make the situation more favorable for the leader by removing neutralizers. Another way is to make leadership less important by increasing substitutes such as job enrichment, self-managing teams, and automation.[43]

Research

A study of nursing work indicated that the staff nurses' education, the cohesion of the nurses, and work technology substituted for the head nurse's leadership behavior in determining the staff nurses' performance. Another study found that situational variables directly affect subordinate satisfaction or motivation; however, it also found little support for moderating effects of situational variables on the relationship between leader behavior and subordinate motivation. Another study found that need for supervision moderates the relationship between task-oriented leadership and work stress, but not between task-oriented leadership and job satisfaction; however, a robust relationship between human-oriented leadership and job satisfaction was found.[44]

A meta-analysis was conducted to estimate more accurately the bivariate relationships between leadership behaviors, substitutes for leadership, followers' attitudes, and role perceptions and performance; and to examine the relative strengths of the relationships between these variables. It was based on 435 relationships obtained from 22 studies containing 36 independent samples. Overall, the theory was supported. In summary, as with the other theories, results are mixed. Research has found support for some aspects of the theory, but other aspects have not been tested or supported. Therefore, it is premature to assess the validity and utility of leadership substitute theory.[45]

6

Dyadic Relationships, Followership, and Delegation

Kim Wung made wood furniture, beautifully handcrafted with Asian artistic designs. Most of her items were tables and chairs, which she sold to a local furniture store. Ms. Wung's main employment was with the Los Angeles Department of Motor Vehicles (DMV). As demand for her unique furniture increased, Ms. Wung found it increasingly difficult to balance her part-time hobby with her full-time job. With so many orders coming in, Ms. Wung could no longer fill all of them by working only nights and weekends. The endless cycle of work was beginning to take its toll on her physically.

With 20 years of service to the state, she retired at age 42 with a small pension and devoted herself full time to Wung Furniture. But even working full-time, Ms. Wung could not keep up with the demand for her furniture. Over a few years, as her business grew, she moved out of her basement into a shop and hired more employees. Kim Wung now has three separate areas or departments making furniture. Each department has seven or eight employees and a crew leader. All three departments make one standard-size set, and each department makes a few other products as well. The crew leaders are Yeng-Lee, Chang, and Sung-Mee.

Feeling that the business has grown to the size she is comfortable with, Ms. Wung has resolved to maintain a no-growth strategy for the foreseeable future. However, she is not satisfied with the rate of productivity. Ms. Wung has very few meetings with her three crew leaders, and they are not informed of each other's productivity rates. Crew leaders work alongside the employees. The only real management responsibilities they have are staffing and leadership. Ms. Wung does the planning, organizing, and controlling for all three crews. She sets up independent jobs and evaluates and rewards employees on an individual basis.

Yeng-Lee's crew has the highest rate of productivity. Members help each other and get along well; they usually go on breaks and eat lunch together. Yeng-Lee and all her crew members seem to do about the same amount of work. She encourages her crew to develop and maintain a team spirit.

Chang's crew has the middle rate of productivity. His team members seem to be split. Chang and three employees get along well and produce at about the same high rate. The other four members seem to be individual-oriented. One is very fast, one produces at about the same rate as the group of three, and the other two are slow. They just seem to take it slow and easy, and Chang and the others do not say anything to them about their productivity level.

Sung-Mee's crew has the lowest productivity rate. All but one of the members seems to work at a slow, easy pace. Sung-Mee and the one fast worker get along well; but the two of them do not get along well with the rest of the crew members, who seem to want the other members to slow down the production rate to their level.

Ms. Wung has called a meeting with Yeng-Lee, Chang, and Sung-Mee to discuss her observations and to discuss ways of increasing productivity throughout the company.

In this chapter you will learn more about the dyadic relationship between Wung and her crew leaders and between the crew leaders and their followers. We will discuss the evolution of dyadic theory, including the vertical dyadic linkage (VDL) theory, followed by in-depth coverage of leader-member exchange (LMX) theory. Then we will turn our attention to follower-based approaches to leadership. The last section of the chapter covers delegation, including a model that can help you develop your delegation skills.

EVOLUTION OF THE DYADIC APPROACH

Most of the early theory and research on leadership has focused on leaders and not paid much attention to followers. Dyadic theorists emphasize the concept of exchange between a leader and a follower. A *dyad* is a group of two. For our purposes, **dyadic** *refers to the relationship between a leader and each follower in a work unit*. **Dyadic theory** *is an approach to leadership that attempts to explain why leaders vary their behavior with different followers*. The dyadic viewpoint argues that a single leader will form different relationships with different followers. For instance, if we were to sample the opinions of different followers about one leader, they would reveal different dyadic relationships. One group of followers may characterize their relationship with the leader in positive terms, while another group characterizes their relationship with the same leader in negative terms. This would appear to be

dyadic: refers to the relationship between a leader and each follower in a work unit.

dyadic theory: attempts to explain why leaders vary their behavior with different followers.

Figure 6-1 *Dyadic approach: Stages of development.*

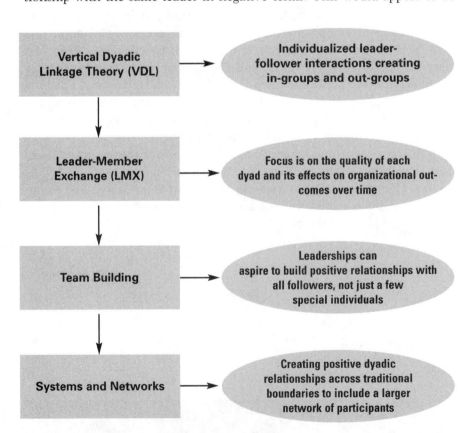

true for Chang's crew in the opening case. To understand leadership in this context, we begin by taking a closer look at the nature of the relationship in each leader-follower dyad (see Figure 6-1). Particular attention is paid to the leader-member exchange theory (LMX). The significance of this theory lies in its excellent attempt to explain why one subgroup in a unit is part of a cohesive team with the leader, and another subgroup is excluded. The leader-member exchange model proposes that leaders develop unique working relationships with members and by so doing, they create in-groups and out-groups. These relationships affect the types of power and influence tactics leaders use. You will learn more about influencing and power in Chapter 9.

As shown in Figure 6-1, the four stages of development in the dyadic approach are VDL, LMX, team building, and systems and networks. Relationship-based approaches to leadership theory have been in development over the past 25 years, and they continue to evolve.[1] The first developmental stage was the awareness of a relationship between a leader and a follower, rather than between a leader and a group of followers. The second stage described specific attributes of the exchange between a leader and a follower. The third stage explored the question of why leaders could not intentionally develop partnerships with each follower, rather than a select few, and the fourth stage expanded the view of dyads to include larger systems and networks.[2]

Dyadic theory reveals three trends worth mentioning: (1) that the size of the dyad expands from a "one-on-one" to a network between the leader and followers, with each stage of development; (2) that the quality of each dyadic relationship affects performance; and (3) that the combined effects of expanded relationships, and the quality of such relationships within a larger structure, greatly enhance organizational performance. The four stages of dyadic theory are presented separately.

Vertical Dyadic Linkage (VDL) Theory

Before we begin, determine the dyadic relationship with your manager by completing Self-Assessment Exercise 6-1.

Self-Assessment Exercise 6-1

Dyadic Relationship with Your Manager

Select a present or past manager and answer each question describing your relationship using the following scale:

1 — 2 — 3 — 4 — 5

*Is descriptive of
our relationship*

*Is not descriptive
of our relationship*

_____ 1. I have quick, easy access to talk with my manager anytime I want to.

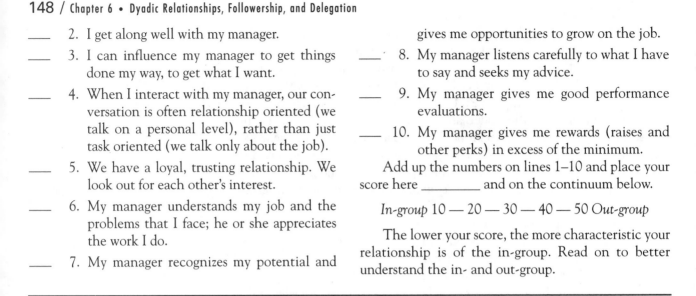

____ 2. I get along well with my manager.

____ 3. I can influence my manager to get things done my way, to get what I want.

____ 4. When I interact with my manager, our conversation is often relationship oriented (we talk on a personal level), rather than just task oriented (we talk only about the job).

____ 5. We have a loyal, trusting relationship. We look out for each other's interest.

____ 6. My manager understands my job and the problems that I face; he or she appreciates the work I do.

____ 7. My manager recognizes my potential and gives me opportunities to grow on the job.

____ 8. My manager listens carefully to what I have to say and seeks my advice.

____ 9. My manager gives me good performance evaluations.

____ 10. My manager gives me rewards (raises and other perks) in excess of the minimum.

Add up the numbers on lines 1–10 and place your score here _____ and on the continuum below.

In-group 10 — 20 — 30 — 40 — 50 *Out-group*

The lower your score, the more characteristic your relationship is of the in-group. Read on to better understand the in- and out-group.

vertical dyadic linkage (VDL) theory: attempts to understand how a leader creates in-groups and out-groups.

in-group: includes followers with strong social ties to their leader in a people-oriented relationship characterized by high mutual trust, exchange, loyalty, and influence.

out-group: includes followers with little or no social ties to their leader in a strictly task-oriented relationship characterized by low exchange, lack of trust, and influence.

Vertical dyadic linkage (VDL) theory attempts to understand how a leader creates in-groups and out-groups. Central to VDL theory are two kinds of relationships (in- and out-group) that occur among leaders and followers, and how these relationships affect the types of power and influence tactics leaders use.[3] *The **in-group** includes followers with strong social ties to their leader in a people-oriented relationship characterized by high mutual trust, exchange, loyalty, and influence.* Leaders primarily use expert, referent, and reward power to influence members of the in-group. *The **out-group** includes followers with little or no social ties to their leader in a strictly task-oriented relationship characterized by low exchange, lack of trust and loyalty, and top-down influence.* Leaders mostly use reward, as well as legitimate and coercive power, to influence out-group members (these types of power are discussed in more detail in Chapter 9). To satisfy the terms of the exchange relationship, out-group followers need only comply with formal role requirements (such as duties, rules, standard procedures, and legitimate direction from the leader). As long as such compliance is forthcoming, the out-group follower receives the standard benefits for the job (such as a salary) and no more. In the opening case, Sung-Mee's crew exhibits all the symptoms of a work unit divided into in-groups and out-groups. Sung-Mee gets along with one crew member that he describes as a fast worker, and the two of them don't get along with the rest of the crew. Leaders have considerably more influence with in-group followers. However, this greater degree of influence also has a price. If leaders use legitimate or coercive power with in-group members, they risk losing the high levels of loyalty and commitment in-group members feel toward them.

Members of the in-group are invited to participate in important decision making, are given added responsibility, and have greater access to the leader. Members of the out-group are managed according to the requirements of the employment contract. They receive little inspiration, encouragement or recognition. In terms of influence and support, in-group members experience greater mutual influence and collaborative effort with the leader, while out-group members tend not to experience positive relationships and influence. The in-group versus out-group status also reveals an element of reciprocity or exchange. The leader grants special favors to in-group members in exchange for their loyalty, commitment, and above-average production.

These differences are based on the dyad between the leader and each follower. Thus, by focusing on the relationship between a leader and each follower, VDL research has found great variance of leader style and impact within a group of followers.

Leader-Member Exchange (LMX) Theory: An Overview

A shift of the theoretical emphasis to LMX is seen as the second stage in the evolution of the dyadic approach, focusing on the quality of the dyadic relationship and its effects on organizational outcomes over time.[4] **Leader-member exchange (LMX) theory** *attempts to understand the quality of each dyadic relationship and its effects on organizational outcomes over time.* As you can see by our definitions of VDL and LMX, LMX is an extension of, or based on, VDL. We present an overview of LMX here and go into greater detail in the next section.

leader-member exchange (LMX) theory: attempts to understand the quality of each dyadic relationship and its effects on organizational outcomes over time.

Some researchers argue that leaders do not treat each member in an exchange relationship equally; instead, each member is treated somewhat differently. The type of relationship between a leader and a member is assumed to differ on the basis of quality. In theory, the difference lies on a continuum of low quality to high quality. With group members on the top half of the continuum, the leader has a good relationship; with those on the lower half of the continuum, the leader has a poor relationship. Each of these pairs of relationships, or dyads, must be judged based on whether a group member is "in" or "out" with the leader.[5] Studies evaluating characteristics of LMX relationships explored such factors as communication frequency, turnover, job satisfaction, performance, job climate, commitment, and characteristics of followers. Being a member of the in-group is related to several predictable outcomes. For example, in-group followers receive higher performance ratings than do out-group followers.[6] In addition, out-group followers have higher levels of turnover than do in-group followers, and in-group fol-

---

Applying the Concept 6-1

In-Groups vs. Out-Groups

For each of the following statements made by a follower, identify which group he or she belongs to. Write the appropriate letter in the blank before each item.

a. in-group   b. out-group

_____ **1.** My manager and I are similar in a lot of ways.

_____ **2.** When I am not sure what is going on, I can count on my manager to tell me the truth even if it will hurt my feelings.

_____ **3.** When I have a major problem at work or in my personal life, my manager does only what's required of him or her as my manager without going out of his way.

_____ **4.** As far as my feelings toward my manager go, we relate to each other strictly along professional lines and work.

_____ **5.** I seldom have any direct contact with my manager unless something is wrong with how I have done my job.

lowers have more positive ratings of organizational climate than do out-group followers. Finally, it appears that higher levels of job performance by followers are more closely related to strong leader-member relations than they are to strong organizational relations.[7] Overall, these studies found that the quality of the LMX relationship was substantially higher for in-group members than out-group members. The benefits to the leader from an in-group relationship are evident. When the leader has tasks that require considerable initiative and effort on the part of some group members to be carried out successfully, the assistance and commitment of followers in the in-group becomes an invaluable asset to the leader. In the opening case, Yeng-Lee's crew works together as a team. She has a high-quality relationship with all her crew, and they help each other and get along well. As a result, Yeng-Lee's crew has the highest productivity of the three crews.

However, the special relationship with in-group followers creates certain obligations and constraints for the leader. To maintain the relationship, the leader must continuously pay attention to in-group members, remain responsive to their needs and feelings, and rely more on time-consuming influence methods such as persuasion and consultation. The leader cannot resort to coercion or heavy-handed use of authority without endangering the quality of the relationship.[8]

The basis for establishing a deeper exchange relationship with in-group members is the leader's control over outcomes that are desirable to the followers. These outcomes include such benefits as helping with a follower's career (for example, recommending advancement), giving special favors (bigger office, better work schedule), allowing participation in decision making, delegating greater responsibility and authority, more sharing of information, assigning in-group members to interesting and desirable tasks, and giving tangible rewards such as a pay increase. In return for sharing in these benefits, in-group members have certain obligations and expectations beyond those required of out-group members. In-group members are expected to be loyal to the leader, to be more committed to task objectives, to work harder, and to share some of the leader's administrative duties. Unless this cycle of reciprocal reinforcement of leader and member behavior is interrupted, the relationship is likely to develop to a point where there is a high degree of mutual dependence, support, and loyalty.[9]

In a revision of LMX theory, the development of relationships in a leader-member dyad was described as a "life cycle model" with three possible stages.[10] In the first stage, the leader and follower conduct themselves as strangers, testing each other to identify what kinds of behavior are acceptable. Each relationship is negotiated informally between each follower and the leader. The definition of each group member's role determines what the leader expects the member to do. Here, impressions management by the follower would play a critical role in influencing how the leader perceives him or her. *Impressions management is a follower's effort to project a favorable image in order to gain an immediate benefit or improve long-term relationships with the leader.* Impressions management is most critical during the early stages (stage 1 and 2) of the life-cycle model. Research has shown that impressions management tactics such as ingratiation can influence the

impressions management: a follower's effort to project a favorable image in order to gain an immediate benefit or improve long-term relationships with the leader.

leader in some important ways.[11] ***Ingratiation*** *is the effort to appear support-ive, appreciative, and respectful.* Most studies find a positive correlation between ingratiation by a follower and affection (or liking) of the leader for the follower. Affection in turn is positively related to the quality of the exchange relationship and the leader's assessment of the follower's compe-tence, loyalty, commitment, and work ethic.

Now that you understand LMX, complete Self-Assessment Exercise 6-2.

ingratiation: the effort to appear supportive, appreciative, and respectful.

Self-Assessment Exercise 6-2

In-Group and Out-Group

Based on Self-Assessment Exercise 6-1, and your reading of VDL and LMX theory, place the people who work or have worked for your present or past manager in the in-group or out-group. Be sure to include yourself.

In-Group Members

_____
_____
_____
_____

Out-Group Members

_____
_____
_____
_____

In the second stage, as the leader and follower become acquainted, they engage in further refining the roles they will play together. Mutual trust, loyalty, and respect are developed. Relationships that remain at the first stage may deteriorate and remain at the level of an out-group member. Some exchange relationships advance to a third stage as the roles reach maturity. Here, exchange based on self-interest is transformed into mutual commitment to the mission and objectives of the work unit. This is charac-teristic of relationships at the in-group level. Thus, it would appear that the end result of the life-cycle model is the creation of a clear distinction between in-group and out-group members. Critics point out that a sharply differentiated in-group is likely to create feelings of resentment and under-mine team identification among followers in the out-group.[12] Hostility between the two groups is likely to undermine necessary cooperation and teamwork for the work unit as a whole.

Team Building

The third stage in the development of dyadic theory advances the notion that effective leaders should aspire to establish relationships with all group members, not just with a few special individuals.[13] The emphasis is on how a leader might forge a partnership with each follower without alienating anyone. Effective leaders know that while it is not possible to treat all followers in exactly the same way, it is important that each person perceive that he or she is an important and respected member of the team rather than a "second-class citizen." Therefore, the manager must provide all employees access to high-quality leader-member exchanges that are based on mutual trust, supportiveness, respect, and loyalty. For instance, not every employee may desire greater responsibility, but each should feel that there is equal opportunity based on competence rather than on being part of some in-group in the organization. Of the three crew leaders in the opening case, Yeng-Lee's crew best represents a team in the way they work and relate to each other.

Studies have shown that when leaders are trained to develop and nurture high-quality relationships with all of their followers, the results on follower performance have been dramatic. Followers who feel they have developed a positive relationship one-on-one with the leader tend to exhibit higher productivity and performance gains. As these relationships mature, the entire work group becomes more cohesive, and the payoffs are evident to all participants. In some sense, partnership building enables a leader to meet both the personal and work-related needs of each group member, one at a time.[14] Through the leader's support, encouragement and training, the followers feel a sense of self-worth, appreciation, and value for their work, and they respond with high performance. The concept of leading teams is covered in detail in Chapters 7 and 8.

Systems and Networks

The most recent version of dyadic theory prescribes that leader dyads can be expanded to larger systems. A systems-oriented perspective examines how a dyadic relationship can be created across traditional boundaries to include a larger system. This version of the theory focuses on the larger network that may cut across functional, divisional, and even organizational boundaries rather than on leaders and followers.[15] Proponents of this view contend that leader relationships are not limited to followers, but include peers, customers, suppliers, and other relevant stakeholders in the broader community.

Support for the systems and network view of dyadic theory stems from events of the past that have brought us to the current state of work relationships. After so many years of being bossed around, of working within confining roles, of unending reorganization, downsizing, reengineering, mergers, and acquisitions, most people are cynical, exhausted, focused on self-protection, and unwilling to continue playing the passive follower role. In the new global world of rapid change, it is time for leaders at every level to become committed about what's best in all workers, not just those in the in-group; and to create organizations that value creativity, contribution, and compassion in a collective sense. Leaders must create processes and structures that bring all workers together to talk to one another, listen to one another's stories, and reflect together. Developing relationships of trust, where people do what they say, speak truthfully, and refuse to act from petty self-interest would no doubt avoid the polarization that dominates organizations characterized by in-groups and out-groups. There is increasing evidence that many courageous companies, and their leaders, are adopting the systems and network view of dyadic theory. As Margaret Wheatley, scholar, researcher, author, former professor of management and now a consultant at Kellner-Rogers and Wheatley, Inc., notes, we must embrace community and create a global culture of diverse yet interwoven communities. As she puts it, "it is time to . . . reach out and invite those we have excluded, . . . recognize that no one person or leader has the answer, that we need everybody's creativity to find our way through this strange world."[16]

Applying the Concept 6-2

Stages of Development of the Dyadic Approach

Which stage is described by the following statements? Write the appropriate letter in the blank before each item.

a. vertical dyadic linkage theory   c. team building
b. leader-member exchange theory   d. systems and networks

_____ **1.** A dyadic approach that focuses on creating positive dyadic relationships across traditional boundaries to include more participants.

_____ **2.** A hierarchical relationship in which leader-follower dyads develop, and the emphasis is on the quality of each relationship and its effects on organizational outcomes over time.

_____ **3.** A dyadic approach that encourages leaders to aspire to having positive relationships with all followers, not just a few special individuals.

_____ **4.** A relationship in which leader-follower interactions lead to the creation of in-groups and out-groups.

THE LEADER-MEMBER EXCHANGE MODEL

There is a general acceptance of the notion that effective leadership consists in part of good relationships between leaders and followers. But several questions about such relationships remain, and their answers are not intuitively obvious:[17]

- What are the attributes (or rational characteristics) of high-quality relationships?

- Which influential factors and leader behaviors enhance high-quality leader-member exchange relationships?

- What are the effects of variance in the quality of relationships as revealed through research?

- To what extent does bias affect the quality of relationships between leaders and followers, and how does it influences their affective, behavioral, and organization-related performance?

Attributes of High-Quality LMX Relationships

The first question concerns the characteristics of the LMX relationship itself. According to LMX literature, high-quality relationships are characterized by greater levels of loyalty, commitment, respect, affection, mutual trust, and possibly mutual liking between leaders and followers.[18] It is not clear, however, that these are universal attributes of high-quality relationships. The way in which LMX has been defined and measured has varied somewhat from study to study. Most studies have measured LMX with a questionnaire scale filled out by the follower. The LMX-7 scale is the most commonly used instrument for defining and measuring the quality of relationships. Examples of questions featured on the LMX-7 scale included structured questions, such as:

- How well does your leader understand your job problems and needs? (Not a bit, A little, A fair amount, Quite a bit, and A great deal)
- How well does your leader recognize your potential? (Not at all, A little, Moderately, Mostly, and Fully)
- How would you characterize your working relationship with your leader? (Extremely ineffective, Worse than average, Average, Better than average, and Extremely effective)

In studies using this scale, the quality of relationships is usually assumed to involve attributes such as mutual trust, respect, affection, and loyalty. Complete Self-Assessment Exercise 6-3 to determine your LMX relationship with your manager.

Self-Assessment Exercise 6-3

Your LMX Relationship with Your Manager

Self-Assessment Exercise 6-1 is a form of measuring your LMX relationship with your manager. Note that some of the questions are similar to the LMX-7 questions. The score, ranging from 10 to 50, gives you more than a simple in-group or out-group assessment. Place your score here _____ and on the following continuum.

```
10  —  20  —  30  —  40  —  50
High-quality              Low-quality
LMX relationship          LMX relationship
```

The lower your score, generally, the better is your relationship with your manager. We say generally, because you could have a manager who does not have a good relationship with any employee. Thus, a good LMX can be a relative measure.

Other researchers have recently used more diverse questionnaires in an attempt to identify separate dimensions of LMX relationships and unique attributes.[19] The new measures appear to combine quality of the relationship with determinants of the relationship such as perceived competence or behavior of the other person. These findings are examined in the next section, "Antecedents to High-Quality LMX Relationships." It is not clear yet whether the newest scales offer any advantages over a single scale in identifying and measuring attributes that can be described as more broad-based or universal. Only a few studies have measured LMX from the perception of both the leader and the follower.[20] Contrary to expectations of high correlations on LMX attribute agreement, the correlation between leader-rated LMX and follower-rated LMX is low enough to raise questions about scale validity for one or both sources. It is unclear whether the low correlation reflects instrument reliability or actual differences in the perception of LMX attributes. Characteristics of LMX deemed positive to the exchange relationship may vary among leaders and followers, depending on key influencing factors. More research is obviously needed to determine if there are any universal attributes of high-quality LMX relationships.

Antecedents to High-Quality LMX Relationships

High-quality relationship antecedents include (1) follower attributes, (2) situational factors, and (3) leader's perceptions and behaviors. LMX theory does not specify these, but implies that the behavior of followers influences leaders to show support, delegate to followers a substantial amount of work, allow followers more discretion in conducting their work, engage in open communication, and encourage mutual influence between themselves and their followers. Most of the current research on LMX theory since the initial studies of the 1970s has focused on examining how the quality of LMX relationships is related to this interaction between the leader and follower.[21]

One set of studies narrowed its focus on the factors that predict the quality of the exchange relationship for a dyad based on the leader's first impressions of the follower. Overall, these studies found that a favorable relationship is more likely when the follower is perceived to be competent and dependable, and the follower's values and attitudes are similar to those of the leader.[22] The leader's first impression of a group member's competency plays an important role in defining the quality of the LMX relationship. Another key linking factor is whether the leader and team members have a positive or negative relationship. We can assume that group members who make effective use of impressions management tactics such as ingratiation and self-promotion increase their chances of positively influencing the LMX relationship. *Self-promotion* is the effort to appear competent and dependable.

self-promotion: the effort to appear competent and dependable.

A field study seems to confirm that first impressions make a difference. Researchers gathered ratings of six aspects of the manager–group-member dyad: the group members' perceived similarity with the leader, the follower's feelings about the leader, the member's view of the leader-member exchange relationship, the leader's expectation of the member, the leader's liking of the follower, and the leader's view of the leader-member exchange relationship. Results showed that the initial leader expectations of members and member expectations of the leader were good predictors of the leader-member exchanges at two weeks and at six weeks. Member expectations of the leader also accurately predicted member assessments of the quality of the leader-member exchange at six months. An important interpretation of these results is that the leader-member exchange is formed in the first several days of the relationships. As the saying goes, "You have only one chance to make a first impression." Situational factors such as demographics and organizational variables may also affect the quality of LMX relationships, but there has been little research on this front to reach a firm conclusion.[23]

Another set of studies examined how the quality of an LMX relationship affects leader and follower behavior. A favorable exchange relationship is said to correlate with more supportive behavior by the leader toward the follower, less close monitoring, more mentoring, and more involvement and delegation. Regarding follower behavior, a more favorable exchange relationship is correlated with more support for the leader, fewer pressure tactics (for example, threats and demands) to influence the leader, and more open communication with the leader.[24]

Earlier in this chapter, in describing the role of vertical dyadic theory (VDL) in the dyadic approach, the point was made that follower behavior and performance were the key determinants of in-group and out-group status. One more determinant is follower reaction to "tryouts," described as "role episodes."[25] For example, a manager asks a new employee to do something beyond what the formal employment agreement calls for. The new employee's reaction ("sure, glad to help," versus a "grumble," or "that's not my job" attitude) indicates potential loyalty, support, and trustworthiness, and leads to more—or fewer—opportunities for responsibility, personal growth, and other positive experiences.

In describing what leaders should do (rather than what they do), research began to shift emphasis toward how LMX can influence outcomes such as follower performance, commitment, satisfaction, and citizenship behavior. Also, there is the implication that any leader behavior that has a positive effect on LMX quality will be effective. However, precisely what these behaviors are is not explicitly clear, because the appropriate leader behavior is dependent on anticipated follower response. Specifying the attributes of high-quality LMX—trust, respect, commitment, latitude of discretion, and openness—is as close as the theory comes to describing or prescribing specific leader behaviors. In the next section we examine the findings of some research studies focusing on these behavioral attributes and performance.

Research on the Quality of LMX Relationships

A number of studies have reported a positive correlation between measures of relationship quality reported by followers and citizenship behavior, commitment, performance, and satisfaction.[26] However, a closer examination reveals that empirical findings relating LMX quality to dependent variables such as those listed earlier are mixed, and they do not support the argument put forth by proponents of a strong correlation. For example, four studies cited for their consistent results in finding a positive correlation between LMX quality and citizenship were later found to have varying results. One of the studies addresses the relationship between LMX and decision influence, not LMX and citizenship behavior.[27] Another citation is a review of empirical literature on citizenship and not an empirical study.[28] The remaining two studies did indeed find a positive relationship between quality of leader-follower relationships and citizenship behavior.[29] Studies that have assessed the association between LMX and employee turnover are also mixed.[30]

The association between LMX and performance has also inspired quite a few studies. Correlations ranging from .02 to .33 have been reported in these studies.[31] It is easy to see from these coefficients that the association between LMX and performance is not very strong. Another problem with these studies is that many of them used leaders' ratings to measure performance. As one researcher points out, this measurement process may introduce correlated response errors. In other words, such measures are likely to be correlated with measures of leader-member exchange quality, because the leaders are themselves parties to the LMX relationship. When objective measures are used, associations between LMX and performance are less reliable: A key issue to consider is the potential problem of social reciprocity serving as an influence on ratings obtained from leader-follower dyads.[32]

Several conclusions can be drawn from the preceding discussion. First, both LMX quality and performance ratings may jointly reflect the influence of multiple biases. For example, if quality of LMX is high, as perceived by followers, and if the leader-follower perceptions are mutual, there is a strong likelihood that leaders will both like followers, and rate their performance as high due to this liking—rather than due to the followers' actual performance. Research on the influence of this bias has found positive relationships between leaders' ratings of followers and familiarity of leaders with followers, and leaders' liking of these same followers.[33] Based on this conclusion, a second conclusion can then be made that LMX relationships are as much a function of the characteristics and behavior of followers as the behavior of leaders. A third conclusion is that LMX is a better explanation of the development of leader-follower relationships than of the effects of leaders on followers in a holistic sense.[34] As such, some scholars have argued that LMX theory may be more accurately viewed as a theory of dyadic relationships and their subjective consequences, rather than a theory that focuses primarily on leadership.[35] In the next section we focus on the subjectivity of LMX theory as it relates to bias in the quality of the relationship.

The Pygmalion Effect and Bias in LMX Relationships

There is the question of the extent to which bias affects the quality of relationships between leaders and followers, and its influence on their affective, behavioral, and career goals. Bias is imbedded in the LMX process itself. For whatever reasons—ability level, familiarity, liking, loyalty, reputation of followers, or prior performance—selected pairs of leaders and followers develop high-quality LMX relationships. Leaders express positive attitudes such as trust and respect toward these followers. Leaders also express a desire for reciprocal influence with followers and imply that they expect a high level of mutual support and loyalty in return.

From a leader's perspective, these explicit and implicit exchanges convey expectations of follower loyalty, commitment, mutual obligation, and liking. This information induces a Pygmalion effect, or what others have described as self-fulfilling prophecy and social reciprocation.[36] Recall that we discussed the Pygmalion effect in Chapter 2. Here we apply it to LMX, and consider how it applies to performance evaluation. The *Pygmalion effect* occurs when selected group members demonstrate loyalty, commitment, dedication, and trust and as a result, win the liking of leaders who subsequently give them higher performance ratings. These ratings, which may or may not be tied to actual performance, then influence the member's reputation, and often become a matter of record. The ratings may ultimately be used—formally or informally—in future selection, development, and promotion decisions. Consequently, followers with a history of high performance ratings are those who get promoted to higher-level positions. Thus, a positive Pygmalion effect could well result not only in high follower commitment, satisfaction, and performance ratings by leaders, but also in enhanced career development.

On its face, this would be judged to be a good or effective process of follower growth and promotion—were it not for the possible adverse implications it might have for the development and career advancement of group members who are not similar, familiar, and well liked by their leaders. The resulting quality of LMX will be high within the in-groups and low in the out-groups. This will likely result in disproportional allocation of organizational rewards to "in-group" members to the exclusion of "out-group" members.

The preceding scenario describes what seems to be a naturally occurring process. It does not imply intentional favoritism, discrimination, or bias toward selected individuals or minorities. However, it does explain one important process by which unintended bias can occur in organizations. The conclusion to be drawn from this discussion is that leaders, managers, and Human Resource Management specialists need to be made aware of the potential biasing processes associated with high-quality LMX relationships. Procedural checks and balances need to be applied to minimize such biases, if this is indeed possible. Otherwise, the development of high-quality LMX relations could result in organizationally dysfunctional consequences and discrimination against out-group followers. One possible approach to minimizing selective bias that produces favored treatment toward some members consists of training leaders to offer high-quality LMX relationships to all followers, a practice described earlier as partnership building.

FOLLOWERSHIP

Because leaders are more visible than followers, most leadership literature has focused on leaders and ignored the role of followers in explaining organizational successes or failures.[37] Also, to a large extent, misconceptions about followers have contributed to our limited understanding of followership. Webster defines a *follower* as "one that follows the opinions or teachings of another."[38] This definition implies that followers are inactive partners of the leader-follower dyad until they receive explicit instructions from a leader and then proceed to follow those instructions in an unquestionable manner.

Recall from Chapter 1 that we defined *leadership* as "the influencing process of leaders and followers to achieve organizational objectives through change." A *follower* is a person who is being influenced by a leader. Although a manager has authority to influence employees, followers are also influenced by other employees. And as we have stated in earlier chapters, followers also influence the manager. Good followers who give input that influences managers are vital to the success of any organization. In this section we discuss follower influencing characteristics, effective leader feedback, effective followership, guidelines for effective followership, and the dual roles of being a leader and follower.

follower: a person who is being influenced by a leader.

Follower Influencing Characteristics

From the perspective of the individual, this section briefly examines how followers' power position, locus of control, and education and experience can affect the relationships among followers and between leaders and followers (see Figure 6-2).

Follower Power Position. In today's workplace, followers can and do command greater degrees of influence, both with other followers and with their leaders. Leaders need to realize that they are no longer the sole possessors of power and influence in their work units. Followers with valuable skills and experience may be able to use their expert power to influence other followers and the leader. Popular followers may be able to use their charm or charisma to influence others. In looking at the leader's in-group and out-group, it is easy to see how followers in a leader's in-group with power (referent or charismatic) may wield even greater influence on the leader than followers in the out-group. Even the employee at the bottom rung of the corporate ladder has personal and position-based sources of power that can be used to boost upward influence, thereby affecting the organization and acquiring an active role in the leadership of the organization. Personal sources of power include knowledge, expertise, effort, and persuasion. This is further elaborated on when discussing the follower's education and experience as key influencing characteristics. Position sources of power include information, location, and access.[39]

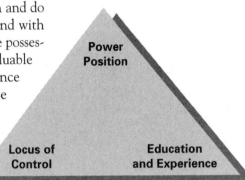

Figure 6-2 *Follower key influencing characteristics.*

A position that is key to the transmission of information can establish that position, and the follower in it, as critical—thus, influential—to those who seek the information. A central location provides influence to a follower, because the follower is known to many and contributes to the work of many. Finally, access to people and information in an organization gives the follower in that position a way to establish relationships with others. With a network of relationships resulting from a follower's formal position, there is no doubt that he or she has greater opportunities to influence others at different levels of the organization. In certain situations, followers may even exercise coercive powers over leaders. How these different bases of follower power and influence affect leader-follower and inter-follower relationships is of importance to leaders and researchers. Leaders cannot afford to ignore followers with significant power and influence, because these followers ultimately can facilitate or hinder the leader's performance.

locus of control: is on a continuum between an external and internal belief over who has control of a person's destiny.

Follower Locus of Control. As discussed in Chapter 2, **locus of control** *is on a continuum between an external and internal belief over who has control of a person's destiny.* People who believe they are "masters of their own destiny" are said to have an *internal locus of control*; they believe that they can influence people and events in their workplace. Some research suggests that a leader's effectiveness may indeed depend on the match between the leader's personality and the followers' personality. Though many personality traits exist, only locus of control has been used consistently in this research area. People who believe they are "pawns of fate" are said to have an *external locus of control;*[40] they believe they have no influence or control at work. The findings of one study revealed that followers' locus of control influenced their choice of preferred leadership style. Followers with an internal locus of control preferred a participative style, while followers with an external locus of control preferred a directive style. On the leader's locus of control, managers with an internal locus of control were more people-oriented.[41]

More research needs to be conducted on how other personality traits such as followers' values, self-confidence, dominance, tolerance to stress, commitment, and reliability can affect how they relate to leaders and other followers. Given the link between a follower's locus of control and preferred leadership style for effectiveness, these characteristics must be taken into account as leaders seek to develop meaningful relationships with their followers. Followers with an internal locus of control would seek to balance the quality of work and their quality of life, and demand more from work than just a fair compensation. This includes a work environment that facilitates communication with leaders, participation in decision-making, and opportunities to be creative.[42]

Follower Education and Experience. To be more effective, leaders will need to understand and appreciate their followers' education, experiences, training, and backgrounds—and how these characteristics influence their behavior. This requirement is dictated by the fact that leaders and followers today work in an environment of constant change. Today's workers—most of them followers—are far more educated and younger than the workforce of 20 years ago; yet, the need for continuing education and training on the job will only increase. One reason for this is the increasing pace of technological change at work. To keep up, workers need to regularly update their knowledge and skills to stay ready for new task requirements. Along with technological change is the ongoing flattening of organizational structures. As many organizations reduce middle-management positions, much of the responsibility and authority previously reserved for that level are being delegated to followers.[43] As a result, organizations are increasingly assuming a flat rather than tall structure.

Not all followers have the same level of education or experience. These differences can have a major impact on the relationships among followers, and between leaders and followers. Followers in new job positions with little or no experience tend to need more guidance, coaching, and feedback; whereas followers in long-term employment positions with experience often need only minimal guidance and periodic feedback in order to achieve high levels of performance. To improve their performance, inexperienced employees often seek the assistance of experienced employees.

These facts point to one direction; that to succeed in the work environment of the future, it will take a different kind of leadership and a different kind of followership. One implication for leadership is that followers have more options and greater expectations of having input in the design and description of their jobs. One out of every four workers between the ages of 25 and 64 is college educated—twice as many as 20 years ago—and 85 percent have at least a high-school education. Coupled with constant updates in their skills and education, workers' job mobility and assertiveness tends to be higher than that of workers 20 years ago. Another implication for leadership involves a shift away from the sort of top-down directive style of managing workers that was common when tasks were highly structured and power tended to be centralized in managers' hands toward a more decentralized, participative style of managing.[44] Leaders who ignore this imperative would face higher employee dissatisfaction and turnover. The era of the passive follower, it would appear, is a thing of the past.

> ## Applying the Concept 6-3
>
> **Follower Influencing Characteristics**
>
> Identify the specific follower influencing characteristic in each of these statements. Write the appropriate letter in the blank before each item.
>
> a. power position   b. locus of control   c. education and experience
>
> _____ **1.** When it comes to selling my points to peers, I easily get them to see things my way rather than the manager's way due to my seniority and popularity in this division.
> _____ **2.** Many of my peers depend on me for direction, because I am the only one in the department who has been trained to work with this new machine successfully.
> _____ **3.** It's not what you know, it's who you know that counts around here.

A key part of every leader's job is to appraise followers' performance and offer constructive feedback on how the follower can improve. However, few leaders are ever trained on how to perform this task effectively. In the next section we offer some guidelines for effective feedback by leaders.

Effective Leader Feedback

In this section, we continue from Chapter 4, our discussion of feedback. Effective followership involves performing the job effectively and efficiently. However, when this does not happen, it is the leader's responsibility to provide appropriate feedback to the followers on their performance. As most leaders will attest, this is an important but difficult managerial responsibility. People in general tend to be defensive about criticism, because it questions their abilities and threatens their self-esteem. Many leaders avoid confronting followers about below-average performance because of the potential for such actions to degenerate into personal conflict that fails to deal with the underlying problem, or does so only at the cost of shattered respect and trust between the leader and follower. Correcting a follower's performance deficiencies may be required to help the follower improve, but the way it is done can preserve or strain the leader-follower relationship. Recognizing that followers are not a homogeneous group, but rather individuals with distinct characteristics, should help leaders choose appropriate feedback approaches for their followers.

Much work has been done in the areas of conflict and counseling on the most effective way to provide corrective feedback. As discussed, given the changing nature of work and the increasing power and influence of followers at work, effective leaders are learning to take a supportive, problem-solving approach when dealing with inappropriate behavior or deficient performance by followers. Leaders must learn to stay calm and professional when followers overreact to corrective feedback. Leaders must avoid a rush to judgment when followers don't perform. The leader must be specific in stating the deficiency, calmly explaining the negative impact of ineffective behavior, helping the follower identify reasons for poor performance, and suggesting remedies for change. At the conclusion of an evaluation session, the follower must come away believing that the leader showed a genuine desire to be of help, and that both parties arrived at a mutual agreement on specific action steps for improvement. The follower's self-confidence should remain intact or be enhanced through feedback, rather than shattered. Figure 6-3 presents 11 guidelines for effective leader feedback. Note that these 11 guidelines are not in sequential order; however, some of them are more effective if introduced early in the feedback process rather than later. Thus, Figure 6-3 splits the guidelines into two groups: the early and later stages of feedback.

In the next section we examine follower attributes about leaders, and discuss how followers can contribute to effective leadership.

Effective Followership

Organizational successes and failures are often attributed to effective or ineffective leadership, although followers may have been the true reason behind the outcome. Unfortunately, due to the limited research focusing on the role of followers, there does not appear to be much evidence supporting a perfect and direct relationship between effective followership and successful leadership. However, when examining the question of what distinguishes high-performance teams and organizations from average ones, most scholars and practitioners agree that high-performing organizations have good leaders and good followers.[45] Competent, confident, and motivated followers are key to the successful performance of any leader's work group or team. Increasingly, many people are replacing old negative conceptions of followers with positive conceptions. Rather than the conforming and passive role in which followers have been cast, effective followers are described as courageous, responsible, and proactive.

Research on followership described five followership styles, categorized according to two dimensions.[46] The first dimension is the quality of independent, critical thinking versus dependent, uncritical thinking. Independent-minded thinkers go beyond manuals and procedures; when

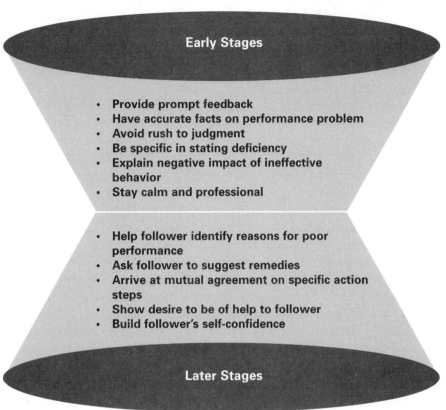

Figure 6-3 *Guidelines for effective leader feedback.*

rationality calls for independent actions or decisions, they are willing to follow their convictions. They are creative, innovative, and willing to offer constructive criticism when it's appropriate. Conversely, a dependent, uncritical thinker sticks to the procedure or preset instructions with very little deviation—even when circumstances warrant it. He or she accepts the leader's ideas without independent evaluation. The second dimension of followership style is active versus passive behavior. The active individual takes initiative in problem solving and decision making, is highly visible throughout the work unit, and interacts with coworkers at many different levels. The passive individual is barely noticeable within the work unit. Their level of involvement or interaction is limited to doing what they are told to do. They avoid responsibility beyond what their job description calls for, and need constant supervision.

The extent to which a follower is active or passive—and is a critical, independent thinker or a dependent, uncritical thinker—determines whether he or she is an alienated follower, a passive follower, a conformist, a pragmatic survivor, or an effective follower. *The **alienated follower** is a passive yet independent, critical thinker.* The alienated follower is someone who feels cheated or unappreciated by his or her organization for exemplary work. Often cynical in their behavior, alienated followers are capable but unwilling to participate in developing solutions to problems. They are just happy to dwell on the negatives and ignore the positives as far as organizational life goes. *The **conformist follower** is an active yet dependent, uncritical*

alienated follower: a passive yet independent, critical thinker.

conformist follower: an active yet dependent, uncritical thinker.

passive follower: exhibits neither critical, independent thinking nor active participation.

effective follower: is both a critical, independent thinker and active in the group.

pragmatic follower: exhibits a little of all four styles, depending on which style fits with the prevailing situation.

thinker. In other words, conformists are the "yes people" of the organization. They carry out all orders without considering the consequences of such orders. A conformist would do anything to avoid conflict. Authoritarian leaders prefer conformist followers. *The passive follower exhibits neither critical, independent thinking nor active participation.* The passive follower looks to the leader to do all the thinking and does not carry out his or her tasks with enthusiasm. Lacking in initiative and a sense of responsibility, the passive follower requires constant supervision and never goes beyond the job description. They are often described by their leaders as lazy, unmotivated, and incompetent. *The effective follower is both a critical, independent thinker and active in the group.* The effective follower presents a consistent image of commitment, innovation, creativity, and hard work for achieving organizational goals. Effective followers are not risk averse nor shy of conflict. They have the courage to initiate change and put themselves at risk or in conflict with others, even their leaders, to serve the best interest of the organization. They are effective in self-managed teams. *The pragmatic follower exhibits a little of all four styles—depending on which style fits with the prevailing situation.* Pragmatic followers are "stuck in the middle" most of the time. Because it is difficult to discern just where they stand on issues, they present an ambiguous image with positive and negative sides. On the positive side, when an organization is going through desperate times, the pragmatic follower knows how to "work the system to get things done." On the negative side, this same behavior can be interpreted as "playing political games," or adjusting to maximize self-interest.

Before reading more about how to be an effective follower, and examining some guidelines, complete Self-Assessment Exercise 6-4.

Self-Assessment Exercise 6-4

Effective Followership

Select a present or past manager and answer each question about your behavior using the following scale.

5 — 4 — 3 — 2 — 1
I do this regularly

5 — 4 — 3 — 2 — 1
I do not do this

_____ 1. I offer my support and encouragement to my manager when things are not going well.

_____ 2. I take initiative to do more than my normal job without having to be asked to do things.

_____ 3. I counsel and coach my manager when it is

appropriate, such as with a new, inexperienced manager, and in unique situations in which the manager needs help.

_____ 4. When the manager does not have a good idea, I raise concerns and try to improve the plans, rather than simply implement a poor decision.

_____ 5. I seek and encourage the manager to give me honest feedback, rather than avoiding it and acting defensively when it is offered.

_____ 6. I try to clarify my role in tasks by making sure I understand my manager's expectations of me and my performance standards.

_____ 7. I show my appreciation to my manager, such as saying thanks when he or she does something in my interest.

_____ 8. I keep the manager informed; I don't withhold bad news.

_____ 9. I would resist inappropriate influence by the boss; if asked, I would not do anything illegal or unethical.

Add up the numbers on lines 1–9 and place your score here _____ and on the continuum below.

9 — 15 — 25 — 35 — 45
Ineffective follower   _Effective follower_

The higher your score, generally the more effective you are as a follower. However, your manager also has an effect on your followership. A poor manager can affect your followership behavior; however, make sure you do try to be a good follower. Read on to better understand how to be an effective follower.

To be effective as a follower, it is important to acquire the skills necessary to combine two opposing follower roles; namely, to execute decisions made by a leader and to raise issues about those decisions when they are deemed as misguided or unethical. Though it is not always practical, followers must be willing to risk the leader's displeasure with such feedback. Developing a high level of mutual trust and respect can mitigate this risk. In such a relationship, a leader is likely to view criticism and dissenting views as an honest effort to facilitate achievement of shared objectives and values, rather than as an intentional expression of personal disagreement or disloyalty.

How followers perceive a leader plays a critical role in their ability to help the leader grow and succeed. Just as leaders make attributions about follower competence, followers make attributions about leader competence and intentions. Followers assess whether the leader's primary motivation is more for his or her personal benefit or career advancement than their welfare and the organization's mission. Credibility is increased and follower commitment is enhanced when the leader makes self-sacrifices to gain support for his or her ideas rather than imposing on followers. Leaders who appear insincere or motivated only by personal gain create an atmosphere in which integrating the two opposing follower roles is impossible. Here, followers would play the passive role of conforming to the leader's expectations without offering any constructive criticism, even when it is called for in a leader's decisions and actions.

Recommendations for Effective Followership

Research on followership has identified certain guidelines on how to become a more effective follower. The guidelines, it is assumed, will help distinguish followers on top-performing teams from their counterparts on more average teams. Issues such as how to improve the relationship, how to resist improper influence, and how to challenge flawed plans and actions are dealt with through these guidelines. Also underlying these guidelines are themes such as maintaining credibility and trust, adhering to your own values and convictions, and taking personal responsibility for team performance and for your own life.[47] Figure 6-4 presents nine guidelines for effective followership; note that the nine questions in Self-Assessment Exercise 6-4 are based on these guidelines.

a. **Offer support to leader.**
b. **Take initiative.**
c. **Play counseling and coaching roles to leader, when appropriate.**
d. **Raise issues and/or concerns when necessary.**
e. **Seek and encourage honest feedback from the leader.**
f. **Clarify your role and expectations.**
g. **Show appreciation.**
h. **Keep the leader informed.**
i. **Resist inappropriate influence of leader.**

Figure 6-4 *Recommendations for effective followership.*

Offer Support. A good follower looks for ways to express support and encouragement to a leader who is encountering resistance in trying to introduce needed change in his or her organization. Successful organizations are characterized by followers whose work ethic and philosophy are in congruence with those of the leader.

Take Initiative. Effective followers take the initiative to do what is necessary without being told, including working beyond their normally assigned duties. They look for opportunities to make a positive impact on the organization's objectives. When serious problems arise that impede the organization's ability to accomplish its objectives, effective followers take the risk to initiate corrective action by pointing out the problem to the leader, suggesting alternative solutions, or if necessary, resolving the problem outright. While taking the initiative often involves risks, if done carefully and properly, it can make the follower a valuable part of the team and a member of the leader's in-group.

Play Counseling and Coaching Roles to Leader, When Appropriate. Contrary to the falsehood that leaders have all the answers, most people now recognize that followers also have opportunities to coach and counsel the leader, especially when a leader is new and inexperienced. The existence of a mutually trusting relationship with the leader facilitates upward coaching and counseling. An effective follower must be alert for opportunities to provide helpful advice, and ask questions, or simply be a good listener when the leader needs someone to confide in. Because some leaders may be reluctant to ask for help, it is the followers' responsibility to recognize such situations and step in when appropriate. For example, a leader whose interpersonal relationship with another follower may be having a different effect than the leader intended could be counseled to see the ineffectiveness of his approach or style ("I am sure you intended for Bob to see the value of being on time when you said . . . , but that is not how he took it") by another follower.

Raise Issues/Concerns When Necessary. When there are potential problems or drawbacks with a leader's plans and proposals, a follower's ability to bring these issues or concerns to light is critical. How the follower raises these issues is critical, because leaders often get defensive in responding to negative feedback. Followers can minimize such defensiveness by acknowledging the leader's superior status and communicating a sincere desire to be of help in accomplishing the organization's goals, rather than personal objectives. When challenging a leader's flawed plans and proposals, it is important for the follower to pinpoint specifics rather than vague generalities, and to avoid personalizing the critique.

In some cases a leader's refusal to listen to a follower's concerns about a decision or policy that is unethical, illegal, or likely to have significant adverse consequences on the organization may require the follower to use influence tactics, such as threatening to resign or warning of public exposure. However, such drastic steps are appropriate only after other less drastic alternatives (such as rational persuasion or the use of group pressure) have failed to influence the leader. The threat to resign as an influence tactic should not be issued lightly; it should be expressed with the conviction to follow through, or it should not be used at all. Also, the follower must not express such a threat with personal hostility.

Seek and Encourage Honest Feedback from the Leader. Followers can play a constructive role in how their leaders evaluate them. Some leaders are uncomfortable with expressing negative concerns about a follower's performance, so, they tend to focus only on the follower's strengths. One way to build mutual trust and respect with the leader is to encourage honest feedback about his or her evaluation of your performance. Encourage the leader to point out the strongest and weakest aspects of your work. To ensure that you have a comprehensive evaluation, consult the leader for his or her input on other things you can do to be more effective, and find out if he or she has concerns about any other aspects of your work performance.

Clarify Your Role and Expectations. Where there is some question of role ambiguity or uncertainty about job expectations, this must be clarified with the leader. As revealed in Chapter 7 on leading effective teams, it is the leader's responsibility to clearly communicate role expectations for followers. Nevertheless, many leaders fail to communicate clear job expectations, followers' scope of authority and responsibility, performance targets that must be attained, and appropriate deadlines. Followers must insist on clarification in these areas with their leaders. In some cases the problem is that of role conflict. The leader directs a follower to perform mutually exclusive tasks and expects results on all of them at the same time. Followers should be assertive but diplomatic about resolving role ambiguity and conflict.

Show Appreciation. Everyone, including leaders, loves to be appreciated when they perform a good deed that benefits others. When a leader makes a special effort to help a follower such as helping to protect the follower's interest, or nurturing and promoting the follower's career, it is appropriate for the follower to show appreciation. Even if the leader's actions don't directly benefit a particular follower but represent a significant accomplishment for the organization (for example, negotiating a difficult joint venture, completing a successful restructuring task, securing a greater share of resources for the group), it is still an appropriate gesture for followers to express their appreciation and admiration for the leader. Recognition and support of this kind only reinforces desirable leadership behavior. Although some may argue that praising a leader is a form of ingratiation easily used to influence the leader, when sincere, it can help to build a productive leader-follower exchange relationship.

Keep the Leader Informed. Leaders rely on their followers to relay important information about their actions and decisions. Accurate and timely information enables a leader to make good decisions and to have a complete picture of where things stand in the organization. Leaders who appear not to know what is going on in their organizations do feel and look incompetent in front of their peers and superiors. It is embarrassing for a leader to hear about events or changes taking place within his or her unit from others. This responsibility of relaying information to the leader includes both positive and negative information. Some followers tend to withhold bad news from their leaders; this is just as detrimental as providing no information at all.

Resist Inappropriate Influence of Leader. A leader may be tempted to use his or her power to influence the follower in ways that are not appropriate (legally or ethically). Despite the power gap between the leader and follower, the follower is not required to comply with inappropriate influence attempts, or to be exploited by an abusive leader. Effective followers would challenge the leader in a firm, tactful, and diplomatic way. Reminding the leader of his or her ethical responsibilities, insisting on your rights, and pointing out the negative consequences of complying are various ways in which a follower can resist inappropriate influence attempts by a leader. It is important to challenge such behavior early, before it becomes habitual, and to do it without personal hostility. We conclude this section on followership with a brief discussion of the dual role of being a leader and a follower and the challenges it presents.

Dual Role of Being a Leader and a Follower

As mentioned earlier, leadership is not a one-way street. And as the guidelines for effective followership just revealed, good leadership is found in highly effective followers. It is important to recognize that even when someone is identified as a leader, the same person often holds a complementary follower role. It is not at all uncommon to switch between being a leader and being a follower several times over the course of a day's work. For example, within an organization, middle managers answer to vice presidents, who answer to CEOs, who answer to the board of directors; within the school system, teachers answer to the principal, who answers to the school superintendent, who

---

Applying the Concept 6-4

Guidelines for Effective Followership

Referring to Figure 6-4 on page 226, identify each guideline by a letter from a through i in the blank before each situation.

____ **1.** We started a new project today, and I did not understand what I was supposed to do. So I went to talk to my manager on what we may do about it.

____ **2.** We have a new manager, and I've been filling her in on how we do things in our department.

____ **3.** My manager and I have short daily meetings.

____ **4.** Employees have not been following safety rules as they should, and the manager hasn't done anything about it. So I went to talk to him about it.

____ **5.** We have performance reviews only once a year. But I wanted to know what my manager thinks of my work, so we had a meeting to discuss my performance.

____ **6.** My manager gave me a new assignment that I wanted, so I thanked him.

____ **7.** I showed up early for the meeting and the conference room was messy, so I cleaned up.

____ **8.** My manager hinted about having a sexual relationship, so I reminded her that I was happily married, clearly told her I was not interested, and asked her not to talk about it again.

answers to school board members. How to integrate these diverse roles is an interesting question with valuable lessons for leadership effectiveness. As one researcher on high-performance teams revealed, the most successful teams were those that had a great deal of role switching among the "followers" concerning who is serving a leadership role at any given time.[48]

To execute both roles effectively, it is necessary to find a way to integrate them. This is not an easy task, given the high potential for role conflicts and ambiguities. Leaders are held responsible for everything that happens in their work unit, and are also required to delegate much responsibility and authority to their followers to empower them in resolving problems on their own. Leaders are also expected to train and develop followers, which may involve training someone who eventually wants the leader's job—even if he or she is not ready to give it up. How to balance these competing and often conflicting demands and perform the dual roles of leader and follower effectively is a subject that deserves much more research focus than it has received.

DELEGATION

So far in this chapter, we have discussed dyadic relationships and followership. We now focus on developing followers by delegating tasks to them. *Delegation is the process of assigning responsibility and authority for accomplishing objectives.* Telling employees to perform the tasks that are part of their job design is issuing orders, not delegating. *Delegating* refers to giving employees new tasks. The new task may become a part of a redesign job, or it may simply be a one-time task. In this section we discuss delegating, delegation decisions, and delegating with a model.

delegation: the process of assigning responsibility and authority for accomplishing objectives.

Delegating

Let's begin by discussing the benefits of delegation, the obstacles to delegation, and signs of delegating too little.

Benefits of Delegation. When managers delegate, they have more time to perform high-priority tasks. Delegation gets tasks accomplished and increases productivity. Delegation trains employees and improves their self-esteem as well as eases the stress and burden on managers.[49] It is a means of developing followers by enriching their jobs. Delegating can result in increased performance and work outcomes.

Obstacles to Delegation. Managers become used to doing things themselves. Managers fear that the employee will fail to accomplish the task. You can delegate responsibility and authority, but not your accountability. Managers believe they can perform the task more efficiently than others.[50] Some managers don't realize that delegation is an important part of their job, others don't know what to delegate, and some don't know how to delegate. If you let these or other reasons keep you from delegating, you could end up like Dr. Rudenstine, president of Harvard University, who became ill due to job stress by trying to do too much by himself.

Signs of Delegating Too Little. There are certain behaviors associated with leaders who are reluctant to delegate to their subordinates. These behaviors are signs that a leader is delegating too little. Some of these behaviors include taking work home, performing employee tasks, being behind in work, a continual feeling of pressure and stress, rushing to meet deadlines, requiring that employees seek approval before acting, and not completing tasks on time. Unfortunately, in many of today's cost-cutting environments, you don't always have someone you can delegate some of your tasks to.

Delegation Decisions

An important part of delegation is knowing which tasks to delegate. Successful delegation is often based on selecting what task to delegate, and who to delegate it to.[51]

What to Delegate. As a general guide, use your prioritized to-do list and delegate anything that you don't have to be personally involved with because of your unique knowledge or skill. Some possibilities include the following:

- *Paperwork.* Reports, memos, letters, and so on.
- *Routine tasks.* Checking inventory, scheduling, ordering, and so on.
- *Technical matters.* Have top employees deal with technical questions and problems.
- *Tasks with developmental potential.* Give employees the opportunity to learn new things. Prepare them for advancement by enriching their job.
- *Employees' problems.* Train employees to solve their own problems; don't solve problems for them, unless their capability is low.

What Not to Delegate. As a general guide, do not delegate anything that you need to be personally involved with because of your unique knowledge or skill. Here are some typical examples:

- *Personnel matters.* Performance appraisals, counseling, disciplining, firing, resolving conflicts, and so on.
- *Confidential activities.* Unless you have permission to do so.
- *Crises.* There is no time to delegate.
- *Activities delegated to you personally.* For example, if you are assigned to a committee, do not assign someone else without permission.

Determining Whom to Delegate To. Once you have decided what to delegate, you must select an employee to do the task. When selecting an employee to delegate to, be sure that he or she has the capability to get the job done right by the deadline. Consider your employees' talents and interests when making a selection. You may consult with several employees to determine their interest before making the final choice.

Before you learn how to delegate with the use of a model, complete

Self-Assessment Exercise 6-5 to learn how your personality may affect your followership and delegation.

Self-Assessment Exercise 6-5

Followership and Personality

Personality Differences

Generally, if you have an agreeableness Big Five personality type, which is a high need for affiliation, you will have a good relationship with your manager, because having a good relationship with everyone helps you to meet your needs. If you have a lower need for power, you prefer to be a follower, rather than a leader. Generally, you will be willing to delegate authority.

If you have a surgency/high need for power, you may have some problems getting along with your manager. You prefer to be in control, or to be a leader rather than a follower. However, if you don't get along well with your manager, you will have difficulty climbing the corporate ladder. You may have some reluctance to delegate authority because you like to be in control—and when you delegate, you lose some control.

If you have a conscientiousness/high need for achievement, you may not be concerned about your relationship with your manager, other than getting what you want to get the job done. However, if you don't get along well with your manager, you will have difficulty getting what you want. You may also be reluctant to delegate tasks that you like to do, because you get satisfaction from doing the job itself, rather than having someone else to do it.

Being well adjusted also helps you to have a good relationship with your manager. Being open to experience, which includes an internal locus of control (Chapter 2), helps you to get along with others since you are willing to try new things.

Gender Differences

Although there are exceptions, generally, women tend to seek relationships that are on a more personal level than men. For example, two women who work together are more apt to talk about their family life than two men. Men do socialize, but it is more frequently about other interests such as sports. It is not unusual for women who have worked together for months to know more about each other's personal and family life than men who have worked together for years. Men who do enjoy talking about their personal life tend to talk more about their families in dyads with women than in those with men. One of the reasons men enjoy working with women is because they often bring a personal-level relationship to the job.

How does your personality affect your dyadic relationships, followership and delegation?

_____

_____

_____

_____

_____

_____

_____

Delegating with the Use of a Model

After determining what to delegate and to whom, you must plan for and delegate the tasks. *The **delegation model** steps are (1) explain the need for delegating and the reasons for selecting the employee; (2) set objectives that define responsibility, level of authority, and deadline; (3) develop a plan; (4) establish control checkpoints and hold employees accountable.* Following these four steps

delegation model: (1) explain the need for delegating and the reasons for selecting the employee; (2) set objectives that define responsibility, level of authority, and deadline; (3) develop a plan; (4) establish control checkpoints and hold employees accountable.

can increase your chances of successfully delegating. As you read, you will see how the delegation model is used with the job characteristics model, core job dimensions, and critical psychological states to influence perform-ance and work outcomes.

step 1. **Explain the need for delegating and the reasons for selecting the employee.** It is helpful for the employee to understand why the assignment must be completed. In other words, how will the department or organization benefit? Informing employees helps them realize the importance of the task (experienced meaningfulness of work). Telling the employee why he or she was selected should make him or her feel valued. Don't use the "it's a lousy job, but someone has to do it" approach. Be positive; make employees aware of how they will benefit from the assignment.[52] If step 1 is completed successfully, the employee should be motivated, or at least willing, to do the assignment.

step 2. **Set objectives that define responsibility, level of authority, and dead-line.** The objectives should clearly state the end result the employee is responsi-ble for achieving by a specific deadline. You should also define the level of authority the employee has, as the following choices illustrate:

- Make a list of all supplies on hand, and present it to me each Friday at 2:00 (inform authority).
- Fill out a supply purchase order, and present it to me each Friday at 2:00 (recommend authority).
- Fill out and sign a purchase order for supplies; send it to the purchas-ing department with a copy put in my in-basket each Friday by 2:00 (report authority).
- Fill out and sign a purchase order for supplies, and send it to the purchasing department each Friday by 2:00, keeping a copy (full authority).

step 3. **Develop a plan.** Once the objective is set, a plan is needed to achieve it. It is helpful to write the objective, with the level of authority, and the plan. When developing a plan, be sure to identify the resources needed to achieve the objec-tives, and give the employee the authority necessary to obtain the resources. Inform all parties with whom the employee must work about his or her authority. For example, if an employee is doing a personnel report, you should contact the per-sonnel department and tell them the employee must have access to the necessary information.

step 4. **Establish control checkpoints and hold employees accountable.** For simple, short tasks a deadline without control checkpoints is appropriate. However, it is often advisable to check progress at predetermined times (control checkpoints) for tasks that have multiple steps and/or will take some time to complete. This builds information flow into the delegation system right from the start. You and the employee should agree on the form (phone call, visit, memo, or detailed report) and time frame (daily, weekly, or after specific steps are completed but before going on to the next step) for information regarding the assignment. When establishing con-trol, you consider the employee's capability level. The lower the capability, the more frequent the checks; the higher the capability, the less frequent the checks.

It is helpful to list the control checkpoints in writing on an operational planning sheet, making copies of the finished plan, so that the parties involved and you as the delegating manager have a record to refer to. In addition, all parties involved should record the control checkpoints on their calendars. If the employee to whom the task was delegated does not report as scheduled, follow up to find out why the person did not report, and get the information. You should evaluate performance at each control checkpoint to date and upon completion, to provide feedback that develops knowledge of the results of work. Providing praise for progress and completion of the task motivates employees to do a good job.[53] You will learn how to give praise in Chapter 11.

The four steps of the delegation process are summarized in Model 6-1. In Skill-Building Exercise 6-2, you will have the opportunity to use the model to delegate a task, and to develop your delegation skills.

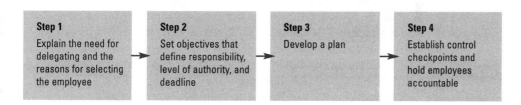

Step 1
Explain the need for delegating and the reasons for selecting the employee

Step 2
Set objectives that define responsibility, level of authority, and deadline

Step 3
Develop a plan

Step 4
Establish control checkpoints and hold employees accountable

Model 6-1 *Steps in the delegation model.*

Leading Effective Teams

Milacron Plastic Technologies Group Vice President Harold J. Faig, a 31-year veteran of the plastic processing industry, was recently honored as a "hero of U.S. manufacturing" by *Fortune* magazine. The article, which appeared in the May 24, 1999, edition of *Fortune,* is the latest recognition for Faig, whose tenacity helped pull the Plastics Technologies Group through a difficult period in the 1980s and put it on the road to number one in injection-molding machinery in the United States in the 1990s.

In the 1980s, the United States led the world in making machine tools. Cincinnati Milacron was the leading player in the United States, especially in plastics-molding machinery. During the 1970s and 1980s, Milacron was growing rapidly. It expanded and diversified its lines of machines to process many types and sizes of plastic products—primarily through injection molding, blow molding, and extrusion technologies. These systems helped Milacron's customers produce products as varied as car parts, toys, pipes, electronic components, medical utensils, and packaging. But Japanese competition in the mid-1980s and Milacron's slow response to it—giving up some of the low end of the product line—soon threatened Milacron's market share and reputation.

As U.S. companies were being driven out of the market in the mid-1980s, Milacron fought back with a new machine called Vista and a new way of developing its products—teamwork. Faig and a group of like-minded managers got together and figured out what characteristics a new machine would need to have to compete with Japanese products. They decided that a new machine would have to be 40 percent less expensive than its predecessors, 40 percent faster and more effective, and developed in a year, one-half the normal development period. Faig and his managers realized that this goal could be achieved only through teamwork in the organization.

Faig put together a team of ten, with people from purchasing, marketing, inventory, manufacturing, and engineering. They moved their offices close together and reported directly to the vice president. They kept logs of their work, so future teams could learn from their successes and failures. They agreed not to talk about their project with outsiders and to ease members' worries about being ridiculed for suggesting ideas outside their expertise. They met as a group only once a week and, whenever problems arose, avoided making decisions too quickly.

The group began by interviewing prospective customers and looking at competing machines. Group members made commonsense decisions that might have been rejected if they had been working through normal departmental channels. For instance, they decided to work with the metric rather than the English system of measurement. They strove to use readily available U.S.-made parts and to cut down the number of parts as much as possible. Instead of searching for inexpensive parts, they looked for sensible, inexpensive ways to put those parts together.

The result? In its first year of production, Vista outsold its predecessor by 2.5 times. It uses 50 percent fewer parts and costs 40 percent less. And those team log books left Milacron with a legacy that the company is not likely to ignore.[1] The Plastics Technologies Group has since been recognized in favorable articles in *Fortune, Business Week, Industry Week,* and other leading business/trade magazines. With the company's estimated 1999 sales nearing $1.8 billion, Milacron remains a world leader in technology systems and tooling for processing plastic and metal. It has major manufacturing facilities in North America and Europe and 12,000 employees worldwide.

■ *Go to the Internet:* For more information on Harold Faig and Milacron, Inc., and to update the information provided in this case, do a name search on the Internet and visit Milacron's website at **http://www.milacron.com.**

Faig's decision to introduce cross-functional teams in response to competitive pressures from its Japanese rivals obviously paid off. Team members demonstrated a shared sense of purpose and collective responsibility that is characteristic of effective teams. The focus of this chapter is on how organizations can develop and lead effective teams to achieve organizational goals. We explore the importance of incorporating teams into the organization's structure, and discuss the different types of team formats commonly found in organizations. We describe team development, looking at the team leader's and organization's roles in building effective teams. The process of team learning is described using two approaches—post-activity review and dialogue sessions. Emphasis is also given to organizational and management practices that support and encourage team creativity. Finally, we examine decision making in teams and leadership skills for conducting effective team meetings.

THE IMPORTANCE OF TEAMWORK IN ORGANIZATIONS

The concept of teamwork is not new to organizations, yet as many scholars have recently pointed out, teamwork is becoming a fundamental unit of organizational structure.[2] Everyone talks about teams, but it takes more than an ad hoc group of people to make up a winning team. In the Milacron case, the team was a conscious response to changing competitive market conditions. Faig and his team of managers decided to put together a cross-functional team that could effectively and efficiently address Milacron's competitive disadvantage compared to its Japanese counterparts. In this section we will first define teams, examine the types of teams that exist in organizations, and then discuss the advantages and disadvantages of using teams.

What Is a Team?

team: a unit of two or more people with complementary skills who are committed to a common purpose, set of performance goals, and expectations, for which they hold themselves accountable.

A **team** *is a unit of two or more people with complementary skills who are committed to a common purpose, set of performance goals, and expectations, for which they hold themselves accountable.*[3] This definition contains three key points to remember. First, teams are made up of two or more people. Teams can be large; but most tend to be small, with fewer than 15 people. Second, people in teams work together on a continuing basis for the duration of the team. Third, people in a team share a goal, whether it be to build a home, design a network system, or launch a space shuttle. Increasingly, employees are frequently assigned to complete assignments as teams. The Milacron team had these features.

Groups versus Teams: What Is the Difference?

All teams are groups, but not all groups are teams. A manager can put together a group of people and never build a team. Extensive research in the workplace has confirmed that there are indeed some differences between teams and groups.[4] The team concept implies a sense of shared mission and collective responsibility, but the commitment within a group might not be as strong. Team members have common goals or tasks; group members sometimes work slightly more independently. Members of a group have a strong leader; a team has shared leadership roles. In a team there is individual and mutual accountability; in contrast, a group emphasizes individual accountability.[5] Teams are characterized by equality; in the best teams, there are no individual "stars" and everyone suppresses individual ego for the good of the whole. It is important to bear in mind that these distinctions probably reflect only matters of degree. Teams might also be considered to be highly specialized groups.

Types of Teams

Many types of teams can and do exist within organizations. We will examine three important types of teams: functional teams, cross-functional teams, and self-managed teams.

Functional Teams. A *functional team consists of a line manager and his or her subordinates.* It is generally associated with the traditional vertical hierarchy. In organizations structured along functional lines (such as production, accounting, marketing, research and development, and human resource management), a functional team typically makes up a single department. For example, the quality control department at Ben & Jerry's, Inc., in Burlington, Vermont, is a functional team that tests all incoming ingredients and outgoing finished products to make sure only the best products go into the company's ice cream. There is no consensus on the specific leadership style employed by functional team leaders. Using Vroom and Yetton's taxonomy of leadership styles, a functional team leader can employ either the autocratic, consultative, or group-oriented leadership styles. However, in many situations, the size of the team, task description, and

functional team: consists of a line manager and his or her subordinates.

Applying the Concept 7-1

Group or Team

Based on each statement, identify it as characteristic of a group or a team. Write the appropriate letter in the blank before each item.

a. group   b. team

_____ **1.** My manager conducts my performance appraisals, and I get good ratings.

_____ **2.** We don't have any departmental goal; we just do the best we can to accomplish the mission.

_____ **3.** My compensation is based primarily on my department's performance.

_____ **4.** I get the assembled product from Jean; I paint it and send it to Tony for packaging.

_____ **5.** There are about 30 people in my department.

membership mix may play a role in determining what leadership style is employed. For instance, functional team leaders in small-to-medium size groups generally tend to have a more centralized and hierarchical leadership style in place. Functional teams with routine, standardized tasks generally have leaders who employ a centralized leadership style. Functional teams grew in popularity in response to broader strategic moves by expanding businesses, but they are on the decline as companies look for ways to better serve customers and increase speed, flexibility, and quality.[6] An unintended negative consequence of the functional team is the tendency for team members to focus on local versus overall company mission. This has led to a shift toward cross-functional teams.

cross-functional team: made up of members from different departments/units within the organization.

Cross-Functional Teams. A *cross-functional team* is made up of members from different departments/units within the organization. Team membership may also include representatives from outside organizations such as suppliers, clients, and joint-venture partners.[7] The team is given responsibility for planning and conducting a project that requires considerable coordination, cooperation, and input from all parties involved; for example, creating a new product in a manufacturing organization or developing an interdisciplinary course for a college or university. The Milacron team in the opening case exemplifies a cross-functional team.

Separate cross-functional teams may be formed in an organization for different activities, projects, or customer groups. They may be either temporary or permanent additions to the formal structure of the organization. Most members of a cross-functional team are also members of a functional or product/service department in the organization, which often creates role conflicts and competing social identities.[8] Cross-functional teams typically have a specific team leader selected by higher management. Team leaders play a crucial role in cross-functional teams. They can affect a team's effort, cohesion, goal selection, and goal attainment. The cross-functional team manager should begin by ensuring that everyone has the same understanding of the team's objective; define roles and deliverables up-front with each team member; negotiate with team members' managers to establish the time and other resources that members will give to the team; be prepared to deal with personal conflicts, role conflicts, goal conflicts, and performance conflicts; act more like a facilitator than a manager; share leadership responsibilities; be willing to seek outside help; and finally, monitor and assess the continuing process and progress of the team.[9]

Cross-functional teams offer many potential benefits to an organization.[10] Bringing together the right people gives the team more expertise than that in individual functional departments to make important design and operating decisions. Coordination is improved and many problems are avoided when people from different functions come together to work on a project at the same time, rather than working on it sequentially. The diversity of member backgrounds fosters creativity in the generation of ideas and problem solutions. Working on a cross-functional team helps members learn to view a problem or challenge from different perspectives, rather than from only a narrow functional viewpoint. Members can learn new skills that will be carried back to their functional jobs and to subsequent teams. Finally, the positive synergy that occurs in effective teams can help them achieve a level of performance that exceeds the sum of the individual performances of members.[11] Cross-functional teams are often an organization's first step toward greater employee participation and empowerment.[12] These teams may gradually evolve into self-managed teams, which represent a fundamental change in how work is organized. The group-centered approach to leadership would seem to fit the requirements of the cross-functional team. Under this leadership approach, the leader's role in a cross-functional team is to serve as a consultant, advisor or facilitator, rather than as a manager in an order-giving role. This style of leadership falls under Vroom and Yetton's consultative (CI and CII) and group-oriented (GII) categories.

Self-Managed Teams. A *self-managed team (SMT)* consists of members from different departments/units within the organization who are given the authority and responsibility for managerial decisions in achieving the team's goals.[13] Top management usually determines the mission, scope of operations, and the budget for self-managed teams. Operating decisions such as setting performance goals, determining work assignments and schedules, evaluating team member performance, and handling conflict are delegated to the team. The amount of delegated authority varies from one organization to another. For example, in some organizations, SMTs may be given the primary responsibility for personnel decisions such as selecting the team leader, hiring and firing team members, and determining compensation rates (within specified limits). In other organizations, such decisions are reserved for higher management. Self-managed teams have been used most often for manufacturing work, but they are finding increasing application in the service sector. Companies are finding out that SMTs create a work environment that stimulates people to become self-motivated. Besides speeding up decision making and innovation, SMTs inspire employees to connect with the company's vision in a very special way: They see the company as the means by which they can affect key issues and develop their leadership skills.[14] The group-centered leadership style prevails in self-managed team situations. According to this style of leadership, the group as a whole must share the responsibility for leadership functions.

> **self-managed team (SMT):** consists of members from different departments/units within the organization who are given the authority and responsibility for managerial decisions in achieving the team's goals.

To create the right environment for the introduction of self-directed teams and to support the team concept, adjustments are required to an organization's leadership practices, incentive systems, communications support, and career development policies. In addition, managers need to understand the costs and challenges involved in making teams work. Self-directed work teams can boost productivity and quality. At their best, teams succeed because most people are goal-directed social beings who gain a feeling of satisfaction from achieving goals with others. However, to attain this ideal, the members of a team must have a common objective, precise roles and goals, the resources required to work productively, and enough loyalty to see a project through to completion.[15]

Figure 7-1 summarizes our discussion of team types and their evolution.

In summary, the functional team represents grouping individuals by common skills and activities within the traditional hierarchical structure.

Figure 7-1 *Evolution of teams and team leadership.*

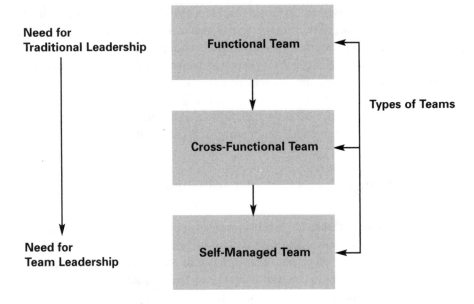

Leadership is based on the vertical hierarchy. In cross-functional teams, members have more freedom from the hierarchy, but the team typically is still leader-centered and leader-directed. The leader is most often assigned by the organization and is usually a supervisor or manager from one of the departments represented on the team. Leaders do, however, have to give up some of their control and power at this stage in order for the team to function effectively. In the highest stage of evolution, team members work together without the direction of managers, supervisors, or assigned team leaders. Self-directed teams are member- rather than leader-centered and directed.[16]

The Importance of Teamwork

Teamwork is an understanding of and commitment to group goals on the part of all team members. The increased acceptance and use of teams suggests that their usage offers many advantages. In this section we specify several of these advantages as well as examine the potential problems of working in teams.

Advantages of Teamwork. First, in a team situation it is possible to achieve synergy, whereby the team's total output exceeds the sum of the various individuals' contribution. Synergy involves creative cooperation, described by one scholar as similar to two hands working together in order to perform several times the work of one hand.[17] Second, team members often evaluate one another's thinking, so the team is likely to avoid major errors. This habit of mutual support and peer evaluation helps teams make better decisions and can give an organization immunity against disruptive surprises. Third, teams can and do contribute well to continuous improvement and innovation. For example, a number of companies worldwide have found that self-managed teams create a work environment that stimulates people to become self-motivated. Besides speeding up decision making and

teamwork: an understanding of and commitment to group goals on the part of all team members.

innovation, team members report greater satisfaction with their jobs.[18] Finally, being a member of a team makes it possible to satisfy more needs than when one person works alone; among these are the need for affiliation, security, self-esteem, and self-fulfillment.

Disadvantages of Teamwork. Teamwork has some potential disadvantages for both organizations and individuals. A common problem is that members face pressure to conform to group standards of performance and conduct. A team member may be ostracized for being much more productive than his or her coworkers. Shirking of individual responsibility, also known as "social loafing," is another problem frequently noted in groups. *Social loafing is a phenomenon of reduced effort by people when they are not individually accountable for their work.* Many students who have worked on team projects (like group term papers) have encountered a social loafer.

Another well-known disadvantage associated with highly cohesive groups or teams is groupthink. *Groupthink is when members of a cohesive group tend to agree on a decision not on the basis of its merit, but because they are less willing to risk rejection for questioning a majority viewpoint or presenting a dissenting opinion.*[19] The group culture values getting along more than getting things done. The group often becomes more concerned with striving for unanimity than in objectively appraising different courses of action. Dissenting views are suppressed in favor of consensus.

Though cohesiveness is a desirable quality of teams, at their worst, teams that are extremely cohesive can also become a source of conflict with other teams. They may become too cohesive, to the point that they resemble cliques with minimal outside interaction or influence, thus creating the potential for significant inter-group conflicts. A production team might devote significant energy to creating problems for the marketing team because the latter requires constant changes in product designs to fit customer needs. Complete Self-Assessment Exercise 7-1 to evaluate teamwork from your own work experience.

social loafing: a phenomenon of reduced effort by people when they are not individually accountable for their work.

groupthink: when members of a cohesive group tend to agree on a decision not because of its merit, but because they are less willing to risk rejection for questioning a majority viewpoint or presenting a dissenting opinion.

Applying the Concept 7-2

Type of Team

Based on each statement, identify it as characteristic of the following team types. Write the appropriate letter in the blank before each item.

a. functional   b. cross-functional   c. self-managed

_____ **1.** We are developing a team to speed up processing our orders, and we are including two of our major customers.

_____ **2.** Our team has been charged with developing a new product within three months, and we get to come up with it any way we want to.

_____ **3.** The manager is conducting a department meeting.

_____ **4.** We don't really have a manager in our team.

_____ **5.** The manager is setting up a team with three of her employees to come up with ideas to increase productivity.

Self-Assessment Exercise 7-1

Assessing Teamwork in Your Group

Based on experiences you are having or have had with teams, indicate whether your team has (or had) the following characteristics by placing a check mark in the appropriate column.

In my team:

	Mostly True	Mostly False
1. There is a common understanding and commitment to group goals on the part of all team members.	____	____
2. Members support and provide constructive feedback to one another's ideas.	____	____
3. Members do not feel the pressure to conform to group standards of performance and conduct.	____	____

In my team:

	Mostly True	Mostly False
4. Dissenting views are accepted and discussed rather than suppressed in favor of consensus.	____	____
5. There is a high level of interpersonal interaction among members.	____	____
6. Much of the responsibility and authority for making important decisions is turned over to the team.	____	____
7. There is an open communication channel for all members to voice their opinions.	____	____

In my team:

	Mostly True	Mostly False
8. Members are provided with the opportunity for continuous learning and training in appropriate skills.	____	____
9. Every team member is treated equally.	____	____
10. Members are more likely to provide backup and support for one another without the team leader's instruction.	____	____
11. Rewards and recognition are linked to individual as well as team results.	____	____

In my team:

	Mostly True	Mostly False
12. There are clearly established roles and responsibilities for performing various tasks.	____	____

Add up the number of mostly true answers and place the total on the continuum below.

$$12 - 11 - 10 - 9 - 8 - 7 - 6 - 5 - 4 - 3 - 2 - 1$$
Effective teamwork   *Ineffective teamwork*

The higher the score, the more effective is the teamwork. Self-assessment exercises like this can be used by groups during team building to improve teamwork. You will learn more about the team leader's role in building effective teams in the next section, and about self-managed teams in the next chapter.

DEVELOPING TEAM LEADERSHIP SKILLS

team effectiveness: the achievement of four performance outcomes— innovation/adaptation, efficiency, quality, and employee satisfaction.

Team effectiveness is defined as the achievement of four performance outcomes—innovation/adaptation, efficiency, quality, and employee satisfaction.[20] Innovative or adaptive teams are those with the capability to rapidly respond to environmental needs and changes. Efficient teams enable the organization to attain goals with fewer resources. Quality pertains to the team's ability to achieve superior results with fewer resources and exceed customer expectations. Satisfaction measures the team's ability to maintain employee commitment and enthusiasm by meeting the personal needs of its members. Teams vary in their effectiveness. Some are successful and some are not. The obvious question therefore becomes, what makes one team successful and another unsuccessful? We will discuss the team leader's personal role and the organization's role in creating and sustaining effective teams in this next section.

The Team Leader's Role in Building Effective Teams

Although an important goal of a team-based organization is for group members to participate in leadership (as in the case of self-managed teams), leaders still play an important role. Instead of the leader's job disappearing, leaders learn to lead in new ways. To be an effective team leader requires a shift in mind-set and behavior for those who are accustomed to working in traditional organizations where managers make all the decisions. Team-based organizations need leaders who are knowledgeable in the team process and who can help with the interpersonal demands of teams. If they are to establish satisfied, productive, and loyal team members, managers must recognize the broad needs of their people. These needs include challenging work that gives employees the opportunity to use all of their talents, opportunity for advancement, a sense of security and being part of a team, a healthy work environment, and effective leadership. Without effective leadership, teams can get off course, go too far or not far enough, lose sight of their mission, and become blocked by interpersonal conflict.[21] Therefore, team leaders have an important personal role to play in building effective teams. The key roles of a leader in building an effective team are summarized in Figure 7-2.

- Emphasize group recognition and rewards.
- Identify and build on the team's strengths.
- Develop trust and a norm of teamwork.
- Develop the team's capabilities to anticipate and deal with change effectively.
- Empower teams to accomplish their work with minimal interference.
- Inspire and motivate teams toward higher levels of performance.
- Recognize individual and team needs and attend to them in a timely fashion.
- Encourage and support team decisions.
- Provide teams with challenging and motivating work.

Figure 7-2 *The team leader's role in creating effective teams.*

The Organization's Role in Building Effective Teams

In assessing a team's effectiveness, top management needs to critically evaluate the performance of the team on an ongoing basis. Where the team concept is not achieving expected results in the organization, top management must ask itself some key questions:

- Does the team fully understand why it was set up—that is, its mission?
- Is the team getting the support and information that it needs from top management?
- Have appropriate leadership, communication, and task structures been set up for team operations?

- Top management's unconditional support
- Adequate information and other resources
- Flexible task structure
- Appropriate size and membership mix
- Clearly defined mission statement and goals
- Appropriate power-sharing structure—shared leadership
- Competent team leadership
- Evaluation and solicitation of feedback on team effectiveness
- Adequate socialization of team members

Figure 7-3 *The organization's role in creating effective teams.*

• Does the organizational culture/environment support teamwork and have reward programs that motivate and reinforce team behavior?[22]

These questions address the role of the organization in providing an infrastructure and culture that supports effective teamwork. Figure 7-3 summarizes the key roles an organization can play in creating an effective team. These roles are further discussed in Chapter 8 on building self-managed teams.

FACILITATING TEAM LEARNING

It can be argued that an important determinant of long-term team effectiveness is the extent to which the team can learn to work effectively and adapt its performance strategies to its environment. This is probably more true today than before, given the dynamic nature of the environment in which most teams operate. Team leaders and members can encourage and facilitate the process of team learning.

Team Learning Approaches

Learning can occur in many ways. Conceptually, team members can learn through the training and education received from their managers before the actual task, or in group sessions where problems are discussed and solutions reached. The benefits of classroom learning or group discussions depend on the methodology used by team leaders. One-way directional instructions have been found to be inadequate in helping employees learn key tasks. At best they provide employees with some information; at worst, they confuse theory and practice. Group discussions can degenerate into shouting matches in which nothing is accomplished. The other method of learning is from feedback after a team has completed a team project. The process of learning during and after a team project is critical, because there is a reference point of behavior. Meetings between team members and the team leader become key learning grounds. The leader's skill in conducting these types of meetings determines the level of learning that members can get out of such meetings. Against this background, two leader-led activities that have been identified as useful for facilitating team learning are post-activity reviews and dialogue sessions.[23] We will discuss both in this section.

Post-Activity Review. The **post-activity review** *is a procedure for collectively analyzing the processes and resulting outcomes of a team activity.* The expression "experience is the best teacher" is definitely a truism implied in post-activity reviews. When a systematic analysis is made after an important team activity is finished to discover the reasons for success or failure, it is described as learning from experience. The post-activity review goes by other names, such as an "after-activity" or "postmortem." The objective for team members is to review what was done well in the activity, and discuss what

post-activity review: a procedure for collectively analyzing the processes and resulting outcomes of a team activity.

can be improved the next time a similar task is undertaken. They review their initial goals and objectives for the activity, the methods/procedures used to carry out the activity, the difficulties or obstacles encountered in doing the activity, key decisions that were made, and the outcomes.[24]

A post-activity review may be conducted by the team leader or an outside facilitator. The role of the leader/facilitator is to guide and focus the group's energies on constructive problem solving. The potential exists for reviews to turn into criticisms of individuals for what they did or did not do. The job of the leader is to encourage objective analysis of what happened and find ways to improve performance in the future.

Groups with authoritarian leaders have some obvious difficulties that tend to limit feedback about effective and ineffective leader behavior. In a team headed by a powerful leader who does not welcome honest feedback on his or her actions from subordinates, the post-activity review will be one-sided and ineffective because subordinates will be afraid to point out the leader's mistakes. Feedback about leadership and interpersonal relationships is most likely when the leader and team members are emotionally mature, trust and respect each other, and are flexible and nondefensive. In self-managed teams with no formal leaders, there may be less inhibition; but even in this situation, reluctance about criticizing teammates tends to reduce accurate feedback.

Though post-activity reviews are generally accepted as a key step in facilitating team learning, there has been little research to evaluate their benefits, the facilitating conditions, or the best procedures. In reviewing the literature on feedback, some scholars have identified and recommended several leadership behaviors by individual leaders that can improve the effectiveness of post-activity reviews:[25]

- Near the beginning, make a self-critique that acknowledges shortcomings.

- Encourage feedback from others and model nondefensive acceptance of it.

- Ask members to identify effective and ineffective aspects of team performance.

- Encourage members to examine how group processes affected team performance.

- Keep the discussion focused on behaviors rather than on individuals.

- If necessary, provide your own assessment of team performance.

- Recognize improvements in team performance.

- Ask members for suggestions on how to improve team performance.

- Propose improvements not already included in the team's suggestions.

Dialogue Sessions. *Dialogue sessions are open discussions between team members without one or a few persons dominating the meeting, thus giving members the opportunity to understand each other's perceptions and implicit assumptions about task issues.*[26] Problem solving is more difficult when team

dialogue sessions: open discussions between team members without one or a few persons dominating the meeting, thus giving members the opportunity to understand each other's perceptions and implicit assumptions about task issues.

members have different assumptions about the cause of the problem, and these assumptions are not openly examined and evaluated. When this happens, any discussion or dialogue is likely to become a debate about competing proposals, with little consideration of implicit assumptions.

Implicit assumptions are unlikely to be examined closely when there is excessive advocacy by team members.[27] ***Excessive advocacy*** *is when team members act as if the group discussions are a debate to be won or involve personal agendas to be protected.* Members may make exaggerated claims, present inferences as facts, make assertions or forecasts unsupported by any evidence, and try to dismiss or refute dissent with little or no consideration. Little effort is made to understand the feelings and assumptions of people who take a different position on an issue. This type of inflexibility makes it hard for team members to have any kind of meaningful dialogue. Without meaningful dialogue, team learning is hampered. To facilitate mutual understanding, improve problem solving, and increase team learning, researchers caution that advocacy should be balanced with inquiry. Inquiry occurs when assumptions are openly discussed, evidence is carefully examined, and risks are identified along with benefits.[28]

To analyze the effectiveness of a dialogue session, different approaches have been suggested. One such approach recommends that after a meeting, each member should rate on a scale of 1 to 10 (with 10 the highest) the performance of the leader and the team in several key areas, including the following:

- Was participation in the discussion equally balanced among all members?
- Were your opinions and thoughts solicited by the team?
- Do you feel you influenced the final outcome?
- Do you feel others influenced the final product?
- Do you feel the final outcomes were creative?[29]

ENCOURAGING TEAM CREATIVITY

In a fast-changing global economy such as we have today, any company not actively developing new ideas is seriously jeopardizing its survival. The companies that survive and thrive will not be those that have the greatest financial resources, but those that can make use of the creativity of their workforce.[30] More organizations are discovering the power of teams to accomplish tasks and contribute innovative solutions to organizational problems/challenges. For teams to play the role of facilitating continuous change, the organization must provide the right type of environment that supports creativity, and the team leader must have a matching mind-set for such an environment. In this section we examine organizational practices that help create a climate that encourages creativity and leadership practices that help nourish team creativity within such environments. But first, we present a definition and some background on the concept of organizational creativity.

excessive advocacy: when team members act as if the group discussions are a debate to be won or involve personal agendas to be protected.

Organizational creativity is the creation of a valuable, useful new product, service, idea, procedure, or process by individuals working together in a complex social system.[31] To implement creativity in organizations, managers must combine the following components: creativity skills, environment, and application. Creativity skills are the techniques used by individuals and teams to identify problems, generate problem-solving ideas, and evaluate and implement ideas to create change. Environment focuses on the systems, structures, and atmosphere of the organization in which people are employed. Application means that, once the skills are developed for creativity and the organization supports these skills, there must be a focus. When these three ingredients work together effectively, the result is creative output.[32] Much of the discussion in this chapter on building effective teams and facilitating team learning bears directly on team creativity. Thus, the key issue here is establishing both the organization's and the team leader's role in facilitating and encouraging creativity.

Establishing a climate for team creativity is imperative if innovation is to take place. In today's knowledge economy, many organizations unknowingly kill off employee creativity. In the pursuit of productivity, efficiency, and control, creativity is undermined. But researchers in this area believe that business imperatives can readily coexist with creativity if organizations and the leaders they employ adjust their thinking.[33] Perhaps the most important point top management should remember is that their primary role is not so much to be creative themselves as to build an environment where others can be creative. Specifically, top management needs to understand that for team members, creativity comprises having expertise, being able to think in a flexible and imaginative manner, and feeling motivated.

organizational creativity: the creation of a valuable, useful new product, service, idea, procedure, or process by individuals working together in a complex social system.

Organizational Practices That Support Team Creativity

Creating an organizational structure and climate that supports and encourages creativity provides the framework against which managerial practices can take hold. Without the appropriate organizational support, individual managerial attempts at encouraging and fostering creativity will be ineffective and unsuccessful. The suggestions that follow are ways an organization can make its position on creativity known throughout the organization.[24]

- *Provide adequate and quality resources.* Creative workers have a high degree of self-motivation, and therefore want to achieve high-quality output. This is characteristic of self-managed teams, discussed earlier. To achieve high quality, teams need not just adequate but also quality resources and state-of-the-art equipment. In allocating scarce resources, top management has to make this a top priority if it intends to stay innovative.

- *Provide appropriate recognition and rewards.* Organizations should be aware of the effect various sorts of incentives or rewards can have on creativity; certain types of motivation are more conducive to creativity than others. Research has shown that people tend to generate more creative solutions when they are motivated by intrinsic (that is, a sense of accomplishment) rather than extrinsic (pay) rewards.[35] To foster creativity, an organization and its leaders must find the right balance of intrinsic-to-extrinsic rewards for team members. Despite the high intrinsic motivation of creative teams, they also need extrinsic motivation.

- *Provide flexibility and a minimum amount of structure.* Many creative workers (whether in teams or as individuals) regard the tall hierarchical structure as the death knell of creativity. "Structure" for creative teams means rules and regulations, many layers of approval, strict dress codes, fixed office hours, and rigid assignments. The organization must strive to provide greater flexibility and a more decentralized, organic structure for creativity to take place.

- *Provide free time.* Employees need to be able to experiment and dream outside of their regular functional area. The organization can establish a culture whereby team leaders can give members free time for activities that are not officially sanctioned. One study of creativity found that in almost every case, the essence of the creative act came during the "unofficial" time period. One of the best-known results of this practice is 3M's Post-it Notes, one of the five most popular 3M products and one that resulted from an engineer's free-time experiments with another worker's "failure"—a not-very-sticky glue. 3M lets employees spend 15 percent of their time (also known as the 15 percent rule) on any projects of their own choosing, without management approval.[36]

Managerial Practices That Support Creativity

According to one researcher, the managerial practices that can encourage employee creativity include matching people with the right assignments, giving people autonomy, deciding the correct amount of time and money to give to a team or project, paying careful attention to the design of teams, and emphasizing teamwork.[37] While this list is not exhaustive, it highlights many of the operational decisions and actions team managers have to make or take into account when trying to achieve team goals. Just because top management's practices establish broad policies and standards does not mean that they will automatically be implemented at the team level. That's why it is still important to emphasize, in this section, specific managerial practices that implement the organization's broad policies.

- *Matching members with the right assignments.* Team members from different functional groups come with different expertise and capabilities. It is the team leader's responsibility to make sure that team members are matched with tasks that fit their competence. People are more creative in areas where they feel the most comfortable either due to prior training, experience, or education. An example would be a manager conducting tasks analysis, needs assessment, and a skills inventory of prospective team members before forming a team, and then using that information as the basis for designing the team and specifying the task for which it will be responsible.

- *Give members autonomy.* Team members need the freedom to think and engage in creative processes. A team leader who restricts this type of activity or attempts to micromanage the process will stifle creativity. Creativity can be achieved in different ways; but because it is a mental process that often requires using all the senses in a not-so-structured manner, not having the autonomy to follow one's instincts as conditions demand will greatly hamper the process. An example of giving autonomy would be allowing teams to experiment with their ideas (within specific boundaries) before revealing any details to other groups or the leadership.

- *Adequate time and money.* Although it is top management's responsibility to allocate the budget for the team, the team leader/manager has the responsibility of administering the budget after it has been allocated. Organizing a team to accomplish its work requires that enough time and money be made available to the team. Creativity is not a free activity. Team leaders must be willing to implement the organization's policies on rewards and recognition at the team level. Creativity is possible but difficult in a structured environment; as mentioned earlier, team leaders must be willing to provide adequate time for teams to engage in creative endeavors. The team leader must be willing to use money to create comfortable physical surroundings and support for creative activities by team members. Examples may include comfortable office spaces, computers and network systems, and free recreational amenities that are made available to team members during creativity sessions.

- *Protect against "creativity blockers."* In designing and managing a team, a leader must be aware of what has been described by some scholars as "creativity blockers." Examples of creativity blockers include designing teams with members who practice "functional fixedness." ***Functional fixedness*** *refers to the belief that there is only one way to do something.* The prevalence of this type of attitude in a team will discourage creativity.[38] This is a liability of functional teams, and it explains the preference for cross-functional teams. The team leader's leadership style could be a creativity blocker. An authoritarian leader who is inflexible and close-minded will not enhance creativity in his or her team. Another creativity blocker is the managerial practice of structuring team discussions in ways that do not allow for maximum idea generation from the whole group. An example would be allowing team members to criticize and judge ideas as soon as they are offered. This practice has two dysfunctional outcomes. People in the group may censor themselves (not share all their ideas with the group), because even mild rejection or criticism has a significant dampening effect, or they may prematurely reject others' ideas by focusing on an idea's flaws rather than its possibilities.[39] Given these findings, leaders may want to follow the practice of postponing evaluation of new ideas until they are all on the table, and encouraging other team members to do the same. Removing self-

functional fixedness: the belief that there is only one way to do something.

censors is necessary in developing a climate of creativity. Self-Assessment Exercise 7-2 should help you assess the climate for creativity in your organization or institution.

Self-Assessment Exercise 7-2

Assessing the Climate for Creativity

Place a check mark in the appropriate column for each question.

	Mostly Agree	Mostly Disagree
1. Organizational practices generally encourage creativity.		
2. The reward system has been carefully designed to encourage creativity.		
3. People are not restricted by rules and regulations or many layers of approval when they want to try new ideas.		
4. "Doing things the way they have always been done" is not a slogan that applies in this organization.		
5. People are able to experiment and dream outside their regular functional area on company time.		
6. The organization's culture values and appreciates input from members.		
7. People feel they have been properly matched with tasks that fit their skills, interests, and experiences.		

	Mostly Agree	Mostly Disagree
8. Employees have greater autonomy to think and act freely than they would in another organization.		
9. In looking around, it is certain that the work environment has been carefully designed to encourage creativity.		
10. Managerial practices in this organization would lead to the conclusion that creativity and innovation are highly valued at all levels.		

Add up the number of "mostly agree" checkmarks on the following statements and place the sum on the continuum below.

The higher the score, the more supportive the organizational climate is of creativity and innovation. Self-assessment exercises like this can be used to encourage students to relate their work environments to the concepts in ways that allow others to benefit from the experience.

10 — 9 — 8 — 7 — 6 — 5 — 4 — 3 — 2 — 1
Supportive climate   *Unsupportive climate*

DECISION MAKING IN TEAMS

The uncertainty, ambiguity, and ever-changing circumstances of today's environment require that leaders have the courage to make difficult decisions. We will examine decision making in the context of the team, including the advantages and disadvantages of team decision making over decisions made by an individual manager, the determinants of effective team decisions, and leadership roles in team decisions.

Applying the Concept 7-3

Managing Creative Teams

Identify which strategy for creative teams each statement relates to. Write the appropriate letter in the blank before each item.

a. quality resources   c. flexibility
b. recognition and rewards   d. free time

_____ **1.** They gave me this pin for five years of service to the company.

_____ **2.** How does management expect us to make a quality product when they get these cheap parts from our supplier?

_____ **3.** There sure are a lot of rules and regulations to know to work here.

_____ **4.** I wish I could take my break, and on time, regularly.

_____ **5.** I don't know why the manager keeps checking to make sure I'm doing my job according to the proper company procedures.

Team vs. Individual Decision Making

When it comes to solving problems and making decisions, organizations have relied on both individuals and teams. Teams are preferred over individuals when relevant information and expertise are scattered among different people, when participation is needed to obtain necessary commitment, when concentrating power in a single individual hurts the group, or when controversial decisions need to be made. Using a group to make a decision offers several potential advantages over decisions made by an individual manager.

Advantages.   Team decisions have the following advantages:

- Can improve decision quality by facilitating the pooling of relevant knowledge and stimulating creative ideas

- Can improve decision quality when they involve the interdependent activities of different functions, subunits, or parties

- Allow responsibility to be diffused among several people, thereby facilitating some types of unpopular decisions such as budget cutbacks and disciplinary actions

- Help members understand the nature of the problem and the reasons for the final choice of a solution; this understanding helps members implement the decision effectively

- Are likely to result in higher commitment by team members to implement decisions as compared to decisions made by a manager alone

Disadvantages.   Team decisions have these disadvantages:

- Usually take longer than decisions made by a manager alone, and the cost in participant time is greater

- Are not necessarily better than those made by a single manager, who has all of the relevant information and knowledge needed to make the decision; and in some cases, team decisions may even be inferior

- May be self-serving and contrary to the best interests of the organization, if team members have objectives and/or priorities that are different from those of the manager

- May end up being a poor compromise rather than an optimal solution, when team members cannot agree among themselves about the team's objectives and priorities

- May symbolize a team's tendency to support each other in defensive avoidance of evidence that existing policies are no longer valid or adequate

Determinants of Effective Team Decisions

Several factors have been associated with effective team decisions. Researchers and practitioners have referred to several of these factors. The contribution of information and ideas by team members—in other words, the degree of team-member participation in decision making—has been cited as a key determinant of effective team decisions. The size and composition of the team, as mentioned earlier, also makes a difference in the quality of decisions. The clarity of communication coupled with member knowledge and open-mindedness will determine how effectively members share information with each other and the extent to which group discussion stays focused on the problem. The degree of team cohesiveness, the manner in which disagreement is resolved, and status differentials among members have also been referenced as important factors influencing effective decision making within the team. Finally and most important, the leader's skills, experience, and style in dealing with all these factors cannot be ignored.[40] We will explore five of these factors in greater detail.

Team Size and Composition.   Team size affects the decision process in several ways. The larger the team, the greater the depth of knowledge and variety of perspectives on a problem. However, the downside of a large group or team is that communication becomes more difficult as members increase and less time is available for each person to speak. The potential for a few members to dominate group discussions increases. The rest of the team members are less able to contribute to the discussion and tend to feel threatened and dissatisfied. As group size increases, cliques and coalitions are likely to develop, creating greater potential for conflict. Meetings require more time, and a consensus agreement becomes more difficult to achieve. Given this trade-off between costs and benefits as group size increases, it is imperative for group leaders to determine what size is optimal in a given situation.[41]

Members' Status.   In groups where there are obvious status differences among members, honest debate and discussion of ideas may be inhibited. Low-status members may be reluctant to criticize or disagree with high-status members. Research results reveal that the ideas and opinions of high-status members have more influence and tend to be evaluated more favorably, even when the basis of their status is irrelevant to the decision being made. Suggested remedies for group leaders or management to minimize the influence of status differences on group decisions include (i) keep meetings free of obvious status symbols, and (ii) develop a norm of mutual respect and appreciation for each member's ideas and contributions, regardless of member status.

Team Cohesiveness.   *Team cohesiveness* is defined as the extent to which members stay together and remain united in the pursuit of a common goal.[42] Where members share similar values, attitudes, and cultural backgrounds, group cohesiveness is likely to be much stronger. However, a high degree of group cohesiveness can be a mixed blessing. For example, a cohesive group is more likely to agree on a decision, but members may tend to agree too quickly without a critical evaluation of the alternatives. This can lead to the phenomenon known as groupthink: when members of a cohesive group tend to agree on a decision not because of its merit, but because they are less willing to risk rejection for questioning a majority viewpoint or presenting a dissenting opinion. This tendency undermines creativity and effective decision making during problem solving. Basically, groupthink is an extreme form of consensus. The group thinks as a unit, believes it is impervious to outside criticism, and begins to have illusions about its own invincibility.

The positive consequences of team cohesiveness are higher team member morale and performance. As a general rule, employee morale is much higher in cohesive teams because of increased communication, a friendly atmosphere, team loyalty, and member participation in decisions and activities. Regarding team performance, it seems that cohesiveness and performance are generally positively related, although research results are mixed. One study found a positive correlation between cohesiveness and performance when team interdependence was high, requiring frequent interaction, coordination, and communication.[43]

Traits and Values of Team Members.   Research results have revealed that teams with compatible members (similar traits, values, personality) are more productive, especially when joint action is necessary under conditions of time pressure.[44] Members with similar traits and values will more likely have a common frame of reference when making decisions. Personality traits affect team performance. Complete Self-Assessment Exercise 7-3 to better understand how your personality affects your teamwork.

Quality of Leadership.   Quality of leadership is considered one of the most important determinants of effective group decision making. An effective leader ensures that the group uses an objective, systematic decision process, but does not dominate the discussion. A considerable amount of skill is needed to achieve a delicate balance between passive and domineering behavior as a leader. Effective leaders know how to create that balance.

Self-Assessment Exercise 7-3

Personality Traits and Teams

Answer the following two questions, and then read how your personality profile can affect your teamwork.

I enjoy being part of a team and working with others more than I enjoy working alone:

7 — 6 — 5 — 4 — 3 — 2 — 1
Strongly agree   *Strongly disagree*

I enjoy achieving team goals more than individual accomplishments:

7 — 6 — 5 — 4 — 3 — 2 — 1
Strongly agree   *Strongly disagree*

The stronger you agree with the two statements, the higher the probability that you will be a good team player. However, lower scores do not mean that you are not a good team player. Here is some information on how the Big Five personality dimensions and their related motive needs can affect your teamwork.

- *Urgency—high need for power.* If you have a high need for power, whether you are the team leader or not, you have to be careful not to dominate the group. Seek others' input, and work on knowing when to lead and follow. Even when you have great ideas, be sensitive to others so they don't feel that you are bullying them, and stay calm (adjustment) as you influence them. Also be aware of your motives, to make sure you use socialized rather than personalized power. You have the potential to make a positive contribution to the team with your influencing leadership skills. If you have a low need for power, try to be assertive so that others don't take advantage of you, and speak up when you have good ideas.

- *Agreeableness—high need for affiliation.* If you have a high need for affiliation, you tend to be a good team player. However, don't let the fear of hurting relationships get in your way of influencing the team when you have good ideas. Don't be too quick to give in to others; it doesn't help the team's performance when you have a better idea that is not implemented. You have the potential to be a valuable asset to the team as you contribute your skills of working well with others and making them feel important. If you have a low need for affiliation, be careful to be sensitive to others.

- *Conscientiousness—high need for achievement.* If you have a high need for achievement, you must watch your natural tendency to be more individual- than team-oriented. It's good to have your own goals, but if the team and organization fail, so do you. Remember that there is usually more than one good way to do anything; your way is not always the best. In a related issue, don't be a perfectionist, because you can create problems with team members. Being conscientious, you have the potential to help the team do a good job and reach its full potential. If you have a low need for achievement, push yourself to be a valuable contributor to the group, and pull your own weight.

Leadership Roles in Group Decisions

The way a manager runs a meeting greatly affects whether the ideas of the team members are expressed. If a manager takes a power position and uses directive questions, the responses will tend to be guarded and cautious. If a manager uses facilitative skills, however, such as asking open-ended questions, encouraging cross-discussion, actively listening, "playing back" what he or she hears another person saying, openly accepting the ideas of others, and recognizing how others feel about a proposal, the meeting will be more productive. Facilitation skills lead to better problem solving and better decisions, which can result in higher productivity and increased quality. Over the years, these two opposing perspectives have received considerable attention from behavioral scientists. One scholar refers to these two contrasting leader behavior models as the "traditional approach" and the "group-centered" approach.[45]

Traditional Approach. According to this approach, the leader should exercise his or her power to initiate, direct, drive, instruct, and control team members. This view of the leader's role points to the following prescriptions:

- The leader should focus on the task and ignore personal feelings and relationships whenever possible.
- The leader should seek opinions and try to get agreement but never relinquish the right to make final choices.
- The leader should stay in control of the group discussion at all times and should politely but firmly stop disruptive acts and irrelevant discussion.
- The leader should discourage members from expressing their feelings and should strive to maintain a rational, logical discussion without any emotional outbursts.
- The leader should guard against threats to his or her authority in the group and should fight if necessary to maintain it.

While this kind of leadership role produces some favorable results, some behavioral scientists argue that it comes at a price. Meetings are conducted in an orderly fashion and decisions are made, but members become apathetic and resentful, which leads to a decrease in participation and a reduction in quality of decisions. Acceptance of decisions by group members may also be jeopardized if members feel pressured and unable to influence the decisions significantly.

Group-Centered Approach. Based on experience and research by behavioral scientists, the group-centered approach of leadership has emerged as the better of the two. According to the group-centered view of leadership, the group as a whole must share the leadership responsibility. Sharing the responsibility for leadership functions will make members more satisfied with the group.[46] The following prescriptions for leaders are indicated by group-centered leadership:

- The leader should listen attentively and observe nonverbal cues to be aware of member needs, feelings, interactions, and conflict. In doing so, the leader should view the group as a collective entity or social system rather than as merely a collection of individuals.
- The role of the leader should be to serve as a consultant, advisor, teacher, and facilitator, rather than as a director or manager of the group.

- The leader should model appropriate leadership behaviors and encourage members to learn to perform these behaviors themselves.
- The leader should establish a climate of approval for expression of feelings as well as ideas.
- The leader should encourage the group to deal with any maintenance needs and process problems within the context of the regular group meetings. However, the leader should not try to move too quickly in encouraging group self-evaluation.
- The leader should relinquish control to the group and allow the group to make the final choice in all appropriate kinds of decisions.

There are difficulties with implementing group-centered leadership. Leaders who are accustomed to the traditional approach may be afraid to risk sharing control with group members, fearing that if they do, they will appear weak or incompetent. Resistance may also come from some group members who prefer to avoid assuming more responsibility for leadership functions in the group. Despite these difficulties, group-centered leadership sounds very appealing. It has been found to be effective in some groups, but further research is needed to determine the limits of its usefulness. This research is likely to indicate the need for a contingency theory of meeting leadership, as discussed in the next section. Such a theory would prescribe more sharing of leadership functions in some situations than others.

Normative Leadership Model

Recall that in Chapter 5, "Contingency Leadership Theories," we discussed the normative leadership model. That model is also very applicable to group decision making, because it is used to determine when groups should be included in decision making (GII leadership style). Skill-Building Exercise 7-1 presents a contingency leadership decision-making model that is adapted from the normative leadership model and the situational leadership model. Although it is a simpler model, it uses the same leadership styles as situational leadership or management.

MEETING LEADERSHIP SKILLS

With a group structure, managers spend a great deal of time in management meetings. There are generally few meetings involving employees. However, most teams include employees, and it is common for teams to have daily meetings. With the trend toward teams, meetings are taking up an increasing amount of time. Therefore, the need for meeting management skills is stronger than ever. The success of meetings depends on the leader's skill at managing group process. The most common complaints about meetings are that there are too many of them, they are too long, and they are unproductive. Meeting leadership skills can lead to more productive meetings. Ford Motor Company spent $500,000 to send 280 employees to a three-day meeting with three one-day meetings to follow. After the training, fewer employees complained of meetings being too long or unproductive.

Managers had gained the necessary meeting leadership skills and were putting this knowledge to practice. Ford's investment had obviously paid off. In this section, we learn how to plan and conduct a meeting and how to handle problem group members.[47]

Planning Meetings

The leaders' and members' preparation for the meeting has a direct effect on the meeting. Unprepared leaders tend to conduct unproductive meetings. There are at least five areas where planning is needed: objectives, selecting participants and making assignments, the agenda, the time and place for the meeting, and leadership. A written copy of the plan should be sent to members before the meeting (see Figure 7-4).

Objectives. Probably the single greatest mistake made by those who call meetings is that they often have no clear idea and purpose for the meeting. Before calling a meeting, clearly define its purpose and set objectives to be accomplished during the meeting. The only exception may be for regularly scheduled information-disseminating or brainstorming meetings.

Participants and Assignments. Before calling the meeting, decide who should attend the meeting. The more members who attend a meeting, the smaller the chance that any work will get done. Does the full group or

---

- **Time.** List date, place (if it changes), and time (both beginning and ending).

- **Objective.** State the objectives and/or purpose of the meeting. The objectives can be listed with agenda items, as shown below, rather than as a separate section. But be sure objectives are specific.

- **Participation and Assignments.** If all members have the same assignment, if any, list it. If different members have different assignments, list their name and assignment. Assignments may be listed as agenda items, as shown for Ted and Karen.

- **Agenda.** List each item to be covered, in order of priority, with its approximate time limit. Accepting the minutes of the preceding meeting may be an agenda item. Here is an example agenda:

GOLD TEAM MEETING

November 22, 2000, Gold room, 9:00 to 10:00 A.M.

Participation and Assignments

All members will attend and should have read the enclosed six computer brochures before the meeting. Be ready to discuss your preferences.

Agenda

1. Discussion and selection of two PCs to be presented to the team at a later date by PC representatives—45 minutes (note that this is the major objective: the actual selection takes place later).

2. Ted will give the Venus project report—5 minutes.

3. Karen will present an idea for changing the product process slightly, without discussion—5 minutes. Discussion will take place at the next meeting, after members have given the idea some thought.

Figure 7-4 *Meeting plans.*

team need to attend? Should some nongroup specialist be invited to provide input? On controversial issues, the leader may find it wiser to meet with key members before the meeting to discuss the issue. Participants should know in advance what is expected of them at the meeting. If any preparation is expected (read material, do some research, make a report, and so forth), they should have adequate notice.

Agenda. Before calling the meeting, identify the activities that will take place during the meeting in order to achieve the objective of the meeting. The agenda tells the members what is expected and how the meeting will progress. Having a set time limit for each agenda item helps keep the group on target; needless discussion and getting off the subject are common at meetings. However, you need to be flexible and allow more time when really needed. Agenda items may also be submitted from members. If you include agenda items that require action, they should have objectives.

Place agenda items in order of priority. Then if the group does not have time to cover every item, the least important items carry forward. In meetings where the agenda items are not prioritized, the tendency is for the leader to put all the so-called quick items first. When this happens, the group gets bogged down and either rushes through the important items or puts them off until later.

Date, Time, and Place. To determine which day(s) and time(s) of the week are best for meetings, get members' input. Members tend to be more alert early in the day. When members are close, it is better to have more frequent, shorter meetings focusing on one or just a few items. However, when members have to travel, fewer but longer meetings are needed. Be sure to select an appropriate place for the meeting, and plan for the physical comfort of the group. Check that seating provides eye contact for small discussion groups, and plan enough time so that the members do not have to rush. If reservations are needed for the meeting place, make them far enough in advance to get a proper meeting room.

With advances in technology, telephone conferences and meetings are becoming quite common. Videoconferences are also gaining popularity. These techniques have saved travel costs and time, and they have resulted in better and quicker decisions. Companies using videoconferencing include Aetna, Arco, Boeing, Ford, IBM, TRW, and Xerox. The personal computer has been said to be the most useful tool for running meetings since Robert's Rules of Order. The personal computer can be turned into a large-screen "intelligent chalkboard" that can dramatically change meeting results. Minutes (notes on what took place during the last meeting) can be taken on the personal computer, and a hard copy can be distributed at the end of the meeting.

Leadership. The leader should determine the appropriate leadership style for the meeting. Each agenda item may need to be handled differently. For example, some items may simply call for disseminating information; others may require a discussion, vote, or a consensus; still other items may require a simple, quick report from a member; and so forth. An effective way to develop group members' ability is to rotate the role of the group moderator or leader for each meeting.

Conducting Meetings

At the first meeting, the group is in the orientation stage. The leader should use the high-task role. However, the members should be given the opportunity to spend some time getting to know one another. Introductions set the stage for subsequent interactions. A simple technique is to start with introductions, then move on to the group's purpose, objectives, and members' job roles. Some time during or following this procedure, have a break that enables members to interact informally. If members find that their social needs will not be met, dissatisfaction may occur quickly.

The Three Parts of Meetings.   Each meeting should include the following parts:

1. *Identifying objectives.*   Begin the meetings on time; waiting for late members penalizes the members who are on time and develops a norm for coming late. Begin by reviewing progress to date, the group's objectives, and the purpose or objective for the specific meeting. If minutes are recorded, they are usually approved at the beginning of the next meeting. For most meetings it is recommended that a secretary be appointed to take minutes.

2. *Covering agenda items.*   Be sure to cover agenda items in priority order. Try to keep to the approximate times, but be flexible. If the discussion is constructive and members need more time, give it to them; however, if the discussion is more of a destructive argument, move ahead.

3. *Summarizing and reviewing assignments.*   End the meeting on time. The leader should summarize what took place during the meeting. Were the meeting's objectives achieved? Review all of the assignments given during the meeting. Get a commitment to the task that each member should perform for the next or a specific future meeting. The secretary and/or leader should record all assignments. If there is no accountability and follow-up on assignments, members may not complete them.

Leadership.   The team leader needs to focus on group structure, process, and development. As stated, the leadership style needed changes with the group's level of development. The leader must be sure to provide the appropriate task and/or maintenance behavior when it is needed.

Handling Problem Members

As members work together, personality types tend to emerge. Certain personality types can cause the group to be less efficient. Some of the problem members you may have in your group are the silent, talker, wanderer, bored, and arguer.

Silent.   To be fully effective, all group members should participate. If members are silent, the group does not get the benefits of their input. It is the leader's responsibility to encourage the silent member to participate without being obvious or overdoing it. One technique the leader can use is the rotation method, in which all members take turns giving their input. This method is generally less threatening than directly calling on them. However, the rotation method is not appropriate all the time. To build up the silent member's confidence, call on them with questions they can easily answer. When you believe they have convictions, ask them to express them. Watch their nonverbal communication as indicators of when to call on them. If you are a silent type, try to participate more often. Know when to stand up for your views and be assertive. Silent types generally do not make good leaders.

Talker. Talkers have something to say about everything. They like to dominate the discussion. However, if they do dominate, the other members do not get to participate. The talker can cause intragroup problems such as low cohesiveness and conflicts. It is the leader's responsibility to slow talkers down, not to shut them up. Do not let them dominate the group. The rotation technique is also effective with talkers. They have to wait their turn. When not using a rotation method, gently interrupt the talker and present your own ideas or call on other members to present their ideas. Prefacing questions with statements like "let's give those who have not answered yet a chance" can also slow the talker down. If you tend to be a talker, try to slow down. Give others a chance to talk and do things for themselves. Good leaders develop others' ability in these areas.

Wanderer. Wanderers distract the group from the agenda items. They tend to change the subject, and often like to complain. The leader is responsible for keeping the group on track. If the wanderer wants to socialize, cut it off. Be kind, thank the member for the contribution, and then throw a question out to the group to get it back on track. However, if the wanderer has a complaint that is legitimate and solvable, allow the group to discuss it. Group structure issues should be addressed and resolved. But, if an issue is not resolvable, get the group back on track. Griping without resolving anything tends to reduce morale and commitment to task accomplishment. If the wanderer complains about unresolvable issues, make statements like, "We may be underpaid, but we have no control over our pay. Complaining will not get us a raise; let's get back to the issue at hand." If you tend to be a wanderer, try to be aware of your behavior and stay on the subject at hand.

Bored. Your group may have one or more members who are not interested in the job. The bored person may be preoccupied with other issues and not pay attention or participate in the group meeting. The bored member may also feel superior and wonder why the group is spending so much time on the obvious.

The leader is responsible for keeping members motivated. Assign the bored member a task such as writing ideas on the board, or recording the minutes. Call on bored members; bring them into the group. If you allow them to sit back, things may get worse and others may decide not to participate either. If you tend to be bored, try to find ways to help motivate yourself. Work at becoming more patient and in control of behavior that can have negative effects on other members.[48]

Arguer. Like the talker, the arguer likes to be the center of attention. This behavior can occur when you use the devil's advocate approach, which is helpful in developing and selecting alternative courses of action. However, arguers enjoy arguing for the sake of arguing, rather than helping the group. They turn things into a win-lose situation, and they cannot stand losing.

The leader should resolve conflict, but not in an argumentative way. Do not get into an argument with arguers; that is exactly what they want to happen. If an argument starts, bring others into the discussion. If it is personal, cut it off. Personal attacks only hurt the group. Keep the discussion moving on target. If you tend to be an arguer, strive to convey your views in an assertive debate format, not as an aggressive argument. Listen to others' views and be willing to change if they have better ideas.

Whenever you work in a group, do not embarrass, intimidate, or argue with any members, no matter how they provoke you. If you do, the result will make a martyr of them and a bully of you to the group. If you have serious problem members who do not respond to the techniques just described, confront them individually outside of the group. Get them to agree to work in a cooperative way.

Applying the Concept 7-4

Group Problem People

Identify the problem type in each of these situations. Write the appropriate letter in the blank before each item.

a. silent   b. talker   c. wanderer   d. bored   e. arguer

_____ **1.** Charlie is always first or second to give his ideas. He is always elaborating on ideas. Because Charlie is so quick to respond, others sometimes make comments to him about it.

_____ **2.** One of the usually active group members is sitting back quietly today for the first time. The other members are doing all the discussing and volunteering for assignments.

_____ **3.** As the group is discussing a problem, Billy asks the group if they heard about the company owner and the mailroom clerk.

_____ **4.** Eunice is usually reluctant to give her ideas. When asked to explain her position, Eunice often changes her answers to agree with others in the group.

_____ **5.** Dwayne enjoys challenging members' ideas. He likes getting his own way. When a group member does not agree with Dwayne, he makes wise comments about that member's past mistakes.

8

Leading Self-Managed Teams

Norman E. Garrity, president of Corning Technologies, and member of the board of directors of the parent company, Corning Inc., had the vision and wisdom of turning the company around through the use of self-managed teams (SMTs). The ability to adapt and evolve with the times is a trait almost unique to any successful business. In this age, when ever-improving technology is rapidly changing the way business is conducted, it is a testament to American ingenuity when a company can leverage what originally made it successful and keep right on going, even as those around them stumble or fall away. Consider the 148-year-old Corning, Inc. Most Americans know it for its hugely popular Corning Ware products and later from its ill-fated venture into silicone breast implants with Dow Chemical. That's all in the past now.

Through a strategically smart move, people will soon know Corning for its role in the red-hot telecommunications arena. Corning changed direction in the mid-1980s when markets matured for its television tubes and light bulbs, and competition increased from foreign competitors that could operate at lower costs. Led by Garrity, top management decided to respond by emphasizing quality, adding automation, and improving inventory controls. But an analysis led by Garrity found that half the potential benefits of such moves would be lost unless the company eliminated layers of management and empowered production employees to make decisions. Garrity urged the creation of self-managed teams and used them to reopen a plant in Blacksburg, Virginia, to produce high-quality automobile filters.

With union approval, Corning reduced job classifications from 47 to 4, enabling production employees to rotate jobs upon learning new skills. The company hired 150 people with good problem-solving abilities and organized them into 14-person teams to make managerial decisions, to discipline fellow employees, and to learn new skills. One result of their skill and job flexibility is that these highly trained employees can retool a line to produce a different type of filter six times faster than employees in a traditional filter plant. The effects on employee morale have been very positive. The employees say they like the additional responsibilities and believe they can improve their job security by turning out quality products.

The plant turned a $2 million profit in its first eight months, instead of losing $2.3 million during startup as projected. Corning had similar success with flexible, highly trained, self-managing teams at a new ceramic filter plant, which production employees helped to design. Teams of production employees (called "ceramics associates") worked with teams
of engineers and relationship specialists to
continually improve the production process, dramatically reducing error rates and improving delivery times. Corning is one of the world's leading producers of fiber-optic cable. It operates within a wide variety of markets: communications, aerospace, automotive, television and video, computers, consumer products, and medical laboratory markets, to name a few.

The challenge facing Corning is how to convert its other plants to self-managing teams. Garrity and his managers worry that the success at Blacksburg and Corning will be difficult to duplicate at plants that are already built and staffed. Garrity must also decide what to do with the supervisors that self-managed teams will supplant. They could be moved into advisory and coaching roles, but in the meantime these first-line managers worry whether they will have jobs after the transition to teams.

■ *Go to the Internet:* For more information on Norman Garrity and Corning, Inc., and to update the information provided in this case, do a name search on the Internet and visit Corning's website at **www.corning.com.**

SELF-MANAGED TEAMS

As the opening case illustrates, some American corporations have turned to self-directed or self-managed teams (SMTs) as a part of their response to today's intense competitive pressure to continuously improve performance in meeting and exceeding customers' expectations.[1] These companies have found that self-management creates a work environment that stimulates employees to become self-motivated. Some of the potential motivational effects of self-management on a company's employees are evident in Garrity's group at Corning, Inc. In this section we discuss the unique nature of self-managed teams, their effectiveness, and SMT research findings.

The Nature of Self-Managed Teams

Besides speeding up decision making and innovation, self-managed teams inspire employees to connect with the company's vision and mission in a very special way.[2] A sense of belonging and ownership in one's work helps to create a linkage between individual goals and aspirations and the company's long-term visions and mission. *Self-managed teams (SMTs) are relatively autonomous work groups in which the responsibilities and obligations traditionally maintained by management have been transferred to a group of people who perform a complex task with highly interdependent activities.*[3] Workers are trained to carry out all the jobs in their unit. The workers typically have no direct supervisor and often make many of the management decisions previously made by first-line supervisors. It is this shifting of control, authority, and responsibility further down the organization that differentiates self-managed teams from various other group-oriented participative management applications.

Self-managed teams cannot be formed by decree. The evolution from work group to team must be made consciously, using an explicit transition process. Team members must accept the responsibility of making decisions and practicing leadership from the beginning. For an SMT program to succeed, careful consideration must be given to the formation and development of the team. There must be a commitment and involvement of top management, and preparation of all program participants.[4] The Corning case illustrates the importance of these factors and how the Blacksburg plant, under Garrity's leadership, dealt with them.

Self-managed teams were once restricted to manufacturing activities. But they are finding increasing application in the service sector as well. The successful use of teams in any organization depends on good planning, sufficient support, and the choice of the right kind of team for the situation.[5] While the concept of teams is not new, the primary function of a regular team is to solve a specific organizational problem or complete a limited task, whereas self-managed teams (an extension of the regular team concept) are more likely to be given total responsibility for a particular corporate function.[6] They take on greater responsibility and authority than the regular team. Self-managed teams are common at several different companies. However, in many of these companies—as in the case of Corning—self-managed teams are not yet a company-wide policy. Only certain units are

self-managed teams (SMTs): relatively autonomous work groups in which the responsibilities and obligations traditionally maintained by management have been transferred to a group of people who perform a complex task with highly interdependent activities.

experimenting with self-managed teams within the company. A few noted examples include GM's Saturn Corp., Motorola's Space Division, the U.K.'s Nationwide Building society, PB Norge of British Petroleum, Honeywell's Defense Avionics Systems unit, London Life Insurance Co.'s Information Services group, and eastern North Carolina Perdue Farms' Human Resources department.

Decision-Making Latitude

Self-managed teams are usually empowered to make operating decisions such as setting performance goals and quality standards, assigning work, planning work schedules, creating task procedures, acquiring supplies and materials, interacting with customers, performing team member evaluations, and dealing with conflicts. Depending on the type of decisions, the amount of authority vested in a team varies greatly from one organization to another. For instance, in some organizations, the teams are given the primary responsibility for personnel decisions such as selecting the team leader, hiring and firing team members, and determining compensation (within specified limits). In other organizations, such decisions are left up to top management. Teams are usually allowed to make small expenditures for supplies and equipment without prior approval, but in most organizations management must approve any recommendations for large purchases. According to a survey of employer-sponsored training in the United States, of the 76 percent of companies that have teams, 38 percent classify some of these teams as self-managed, self-directed, or "semiautonomous." The same survey found that while creating work schedules continues to be the most common management function performed by self-managed teams, conducting training and performance appraisals jumped 10 percent. The only function that showed a decline in comparison to the previous year's survey was purchasing of equipment and services.[7]

Effectiveness of Self-Managed Teams

Self-managed teams are far more effective than traditional work groups, because the very nature of self-managed team operation leads to greater improvements in quality and speed than are possible in a traditional command-and-control structure.[8] With motivation and commitment, self-managed team members can release the energy and the drive needed to help their organizations reach new levels of quality and accomplishment. A well-thought-out implementation process can ease the transition to self-managed teams, because overcoming old attitudes and behaviors can be among the most difficult aspects of such a transition. However, not every self-managed team is effective. Virtually identical self-managed teams can be radically different in their success or failure. What makes one team effective and another ineffective is a question of interest to many researchers in this field. Studies addressing this question have identified, at the team level, certain key characteristics differentiating successful from unsuccessful teams.[9] An effective self-managed team:

- Has a clear mission and high performance standards. Team members know what the team is trying to accomplish and their role in making it happen.

- Spends considerable time taking stock of its equipment, training facilities, and other resources that the team will need in order to do its job effectively.

- Devotes significant amounts of time to planning and organizing in order to make optimal use of available resources and to assess members' technical skills before assigning tasks.

- Exhibits high levels of communication. This helps to minimize interpersonal conflict in the team, which often distracts the team from its stated mission.[10]

These characteristics, identified through research, have given leadership practitioners many ideas about how they may be able to increase the effectiveness of their work units or teams. Effective self-managed teams offer an organization significant benefits that cannot be realized through other work forms.

Potential Benefits of Using Self-Managed Teams

Self-managed teams may offer a number of potential benefits, including stronger commitment of team members to the work, improved quality and efficiency, more satisfied employees, lower turnover and absenteeism, and faster product development. Cross-trained team members offer flexibility in dealing with personnel shortages resulting from illness or turnover. Also, their extensive knowledge of work processes helps team members solve problems and suggest improvements.[11] These benefits are possible because of the unique nature of self-managed teams, explained earlier. Although it

---

Applying the Concept 8-1

Types of Teams

Identify each statement with one of these key terms. Write the appropriate letter in the blank before each item.

a. group   b. functional team   c. cross-functional   d. self-managed team

_____ **1.** In my department, a couple of us sometimes get together to discuss ways of improving our work processes.

_____ **2.** In my organization, I work in a team where leadership roles are rotated and shared, with each of us taking initiative at appropriate times for the good of the group.

_____ **3.** At the Appalachian Ice Cream factory, the quality control department headed by a unit supervisor is in charge of testing all incoming ingredients to make sure only the best products go into the company's ice cream.

_____ **4.** At Norton Telecom International, a team with members from information technology, finance, customer service, and quality control oversaw an ambitious system—an integration project that spanned operations in the United States and Canada.

_____ **5.** The thing I really like about my work unit is that most decisions are made by the group. For example, we decide who gets hired, and we do peer performance evaluations.

is still not clear if these results have been supported by the findings of more objective scientific studies, there is a large body of anecdotal evidence to support these benefits. In the next section we discuss research findings on self-managed teams.

Self-Managed Team Effectiveness Research

Evidence of the effectiveness of self-managed teams is supported by anecdotal reports published in business periodicals and case studies, but such reports are probably biased toward positive results (because organizations are less likely to report failure than success). Few experimental or quasi-experimental field studies have been conducted to evaluate self-managed teams. A longitudinal study in a mineral-processing firm in Australia compared self-managed teams with traditionally managed groups at a newly established facility and at an older facility. The researchers found that employees in self-managed teams were more satisfied and had higher organizational commitment, but there was no significant difference in absenteeism or turnover.[12] In another study comparing self-managed teams in a telecommunications company with traditionally managed teams performing the same type of work, researchers found that self-managed teams had higher job satisfaction and were rated more effective by top management. However, no significant differences were found with regard to organizational commitment, absenteeism, or objective measures of performance between the two groups.[13] In a railroad-car repair facility in Australia, a study compared traditional work groups with self-managed teams of workers that had been formed several months earlier. The researcher found that the self-managed teams had lower absenteeism and fewer accidents. In the most recent case, a longitudinal study conducted in a manufacturing company that had converted its assembly lines from traditional to self-managed teams found mixed results. Productivity and quality improved significantly for only one of the four assembly lines included in the study.[14]

It is evident from these experimental field studies that there are some favorable outcomes to self-managed teams, but the results vary from study to study. This calls for more empirical SMT research. In the opening case, Corning employees in self-managed teams at the Blacksburg, Virginia, plant increased their productivity, produced higher-quality goods, and showed greater commitment to the company's mission. Self-managed teams were successful at Corning because top management gave the teams wide decision-making latitude.

TEAM FORMATION

A successful self-managed team is described as one in which team members have a strong identification with the team, the degree of mutual cooperation and trust is high, and there is strong cohesiveness between members. For this standard to be achieved, the team formation process must ensure a good start. This is critical because some teams' failure or inability to function effectively can be traced to having been set up inappropriately from the start.

Figure 8-1 *Team formation variables.*

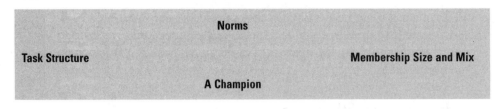

Researchers have identified four variables that need to be in place from the start if a self-managed team is going to be able to work effectively and efficiently.[15] *The **team formation variables** are norms, task structure, membership size and mix, and a champion.* See Figure 8-1 for a list of the four variables discussed in this section.

team formation variables: norms, task structure, membership size and mix, and a champion.

Norms

An effective self-managed team must possess an appropriate set of norms that govern all members' behavior. *A **norm** is a standard of conduct that is shared by team members and guides their behavior.*[16] A newly formed self-managed team can acquire its norms in one of two ways: (1) the norms of the organization of which the team is a subgroup can be assumed as the team's norms; or (2) norms can be created by the team itself as conditions demand. If a self-managed team is to have an effective working relationship over time, it must ensure from the start that conflicting norms do not confuse team members. Even after formation, the team needs to perform regular audits of existing norms to ensure that they still support overall team objectives.

norm: a standard of conduct that is shared by team members and guides their behavior.

Task Structure

Task structure was discussed in Chapter 5, "Contingency Leadership Theories." ***Task structure** refers to how clearly defined and repetitive the job is.* Structure is on a continuum from structured, repetitive, and routine to unstructured, nonrepetitive, and nonroutine. Asking the right questions about the team's tasks at the time of team formation will clarify and resolve any future misunderstandings. This is of particular importance to a self-managed team, given the absence of a formal leader whose responsibility is to establish and communicate the task structure as he or she would in a conventional group or team. At the formation of a self-managed team, it is important for members to know what the team's task is, and whether such a task is clearly defined and consistent with the mission of the team. Does the team have sufficient autonomy to perform its task and access to information about its desired results? Have conditions been created in which authority can shift between members to appropriately match the demands of the situation?

task structure: how clearly defined and repetitive the job is.

Membership Size and Mix

There are critical issues about membership size and mix that need to be addressed from the start. ***Membership size and mix** refers to the number and diversity of team members.* Is the collective membership of the team appro-

membership size and mix: the number and diversity of team members.

priate for the task to be performed? In other words, are there too few or too many members? According to some scholars, the optimal size for self-managed teams is usually the smallest number needed to do the task.[17]

Regarding membership mix or composition, do the team members collectively have sufficient knowledge, experience, and skills to perform the task? Along with task skills, it must be determined that team members possess sufficient maturity and interpersonal skills to work together cooperatively and to resolve conflict constructively when it happens. Is there diversity on the team? An appropriate amount of diversity contributes to innovative problem solving and performance of different subtasks requiring a variety of skills. Finally, on this variable, SMT formation must address the issue of membership stability. Effective self-managed teams usually have a fairly stable membership, as compared with the traditional project teams, which have a shorter life span and changing membership over the duration of the project. Stability of membership facilitates the development of team identification and the process of learning to self-manage.

A Champion

Successful self-managed teams are those that were formed with someone within the organization championing their cause. A *champion is an advocate of the SMT program whose responsibility is to help the program obtain necessary resources and gain political support from top management and other subunits of the organization.* This advocacy role is especially critical when the SMT concept is being applied on a broader scale throughout the company, and when there is hostility and distrust by other managers who are afraid the self-managed groups will cause major shifts of power and authority in the organization. The champion is therefore constantly engaged in "buying

champion: an advocate of the SMT program whose responsibility is to help the program obtain necessary resources and gain political support from top management and other subunits of the organization.

Applying the Concept 8-2

Team Formation Variables

Identify the team formation variables referred to in these statements. Write the appropriate letter in the blank before each item.

a. norms   b. task structure   c. membership size and mix   d. champion

_____ **1.** At the time of team formation, it is important to determine if team members possess appropriate task skills, sufficient members, and good interpersonal skills to work together cooperatively and to resolve conflicts constructively.

_____ **2.** When there is hostility and distrust by other managers who are afraid that self-managed teams will cause major shifts of power and authority in the organization, it is important to have an advocate who is responsible for helping the program win the support of top management and other subunits of the organization.

_____ **3.** At the formation of a self-managed team, it is important to determine whether the team has sufficient autonomy to perform its work; and whether conditions have been created so that authority can shift between members to appropriately match the demands of the situation.

_____ **4.** Self-managed teams need behaviors that are shared by all team members.

_____ **5.** If you start a self-managed team, you need to carefully consider who will be a team member.

in" and gaining commitment at all levels, while effectively communicating the benefits of SMTs. Here are some strategic actions a champion undertakes to create a successful SMT program:[18]

- Articulating a vision of what self-managed teams can accomplish for the organization
- Communicating clear expectations about the new responsibility of team members for regulating their own behavior
- Making sure that what SMT members do meets the needs and goals of the entire organization
- Coordinating the efforts of different self-managed teams so that their efforts support each other
- Finding ways to help self-managed teams reach decisions that every employee can support
- Facilitating continuous learning by team members
- Building and maintaining trust between team members and the rest of the organization

At Corning, the self-managed teams developed their positive norms and task structure, two factors that contributed to the teams' increased productivity. Each self-managed team had 14 members, bringing diverse skills, background, and experience to the team. Garrity is Corning's champion.

FACILITATING SUCCESS FACTORS FOR SELF-MANAGED TEAMS

The health and longevity of an SMT program depends on putting sound structures in place at the outset. Without a sound infrastructure, organizations can intentionally or unintentionally undermine the work of self-managed teams. Sometimes problems begin right at the top of the organization. For instance, management may cause problems when it charges the team with too many duties at once, superimposes a new SMT program on an existing system and procedures without proper assessment, is unsure of what it wants the team to do, takes back delegated responsibilities, or does not model the type of behavior it wants to create in self-managed teams.[19] To avoid these and other problems, researchers of self-managed teams suggest several facilitating factors, which may be used to ensure that the potential advantages of self-managed teams are realized.[20] See Figure 8-2 for a list of the seven factors affecting success that are discussed in this section.

1. **Top management support and commitment**
2. **Unambiguous goals and objectives**
3. **Appropriate compensation structure**
4. **Appropriate task design and measurement system**
5. **Appropriate scope of authority**
6. **Adequate information system**
7. **Strong and experienced facilitator**

Figure 8-2 *Self-managed group success factors.*

Top Management Support and Commitment

Moving to self-managed teams requires managers to make significant adjustments. They have the most to lose in the transformation from a hierarchical system to an empowered workplace. Functional departments such as marketing, production, and human resources will lose power as self-managed teams gain more influence over decisions formerly controlled by these departments. Strong support by top management is essential to ensure that managers and other members of the organization support the effort to implement self-managed teams rather than undermine it. Top management must be committed to allocating adequate resources for the teams to perform their tasks effectively, creating an organizational culture compatible with the self-management concept, helping managers go from autocrats to coaches and facilitators, and empowering teams. Only with this kind of support and commitment will initial success turn to long-term success of an SMT program.[21]

Unambiguous Goals and Objectives

Without clearly stated objectives, self-managed teams are likely to place their own objectives above the needs of the organization and work at cross-purposes. Self-managed teams are not totally independent entities; they perform tasks that contribute to the overall mission of the organization they are a part of. Thus to say that self-managed teams need direction from the organization on their mission and objectives is not a contradiction of the concept. Self-managed teams perform tasks that are interdependent with work carried out by other parts of the organization. Therefore, shared objectives and priorities that are clearly understood and accepted serve to guide task decisions, facilitate coordinated effort across teams, and provide a common ground for evaluating progress and adjusting performance strategies.

Appropriate Compensation Structure

A compensation structure that makes rewards and recognition contingent upon team performance will add to the motivational effects of self-managed teams. Rather than emphasize individual rewards, the compensation package should reward individuals for their contributions to the overall performance of the team. Although not every organization is willing to allow self-managed teams to determine their pay and benefits, the team should have considerable influence in determining how rewards such as bonuses are distributed among their members. It is also important to ensure that team members perceive the compensation structure as equitable and balanced. Team members appreciate intangible rewards (such as recognition), but members also need to benefit from tangible rewards (profits) for the team's contribution to the financial success of the organization. A prevailing view of exploitation by top management can adversely affect team performance.

Appropriate Task Design and Measurement System

Meaningful tasks, with important implications for the organization, that allow self-managed teams to experience personal responsibility for the work are likely to make teams more effective. An appropriate task design must also provide objective measurement systems that allow for accurate and timely feedback about work progress and outcomes. The team concept is strengthened by a task that requires cooperation and can be accomplished only if members work together and coordinate their efforts. The task must be a comprehensive and challenging one that requires a variety of skills, abilities, experience, and knowledge. Task design must allow SMT members to rotate through many different but interdependent tasks to learn new skills.

Appropriate Scope of Authority

A self-managed team should have adequate authority to carry out its responsibilities without interference by top management or other managers. When a self-managed team does not have the authority to make operational decisions about work assignments, work procedures, and work-related conflicts, its effectiveness can be seriously undermined. Though the scope of authority in various decision areas will vary from one organization to another, sufficient authority to make key operational decisions—including membership issues—will more likely add to the effectiveness of self-managed teams. This action can be suggested by the sense of empowerment that members feel in the team.

Adequate Information System

Information is the lifeblood of any organization, and so it is with self-managed teams. The introduction of self-managed teams into an organization is likely to require some modification of the existing information systems. Once-sensitive information about revenues, costs, and profits is now needed for the self-managed team to make informed decisions about products or services and work methods. In traditional organizations, such information is still restricted to managers and is rarely shared with operating employees, regardless of team status.

Strong and Experienced Facilitator

As more companies empower their employees to manage themselves, some scholars have assumed that team members will carry out most of the leadership functions, thus making a team leader position redundant. Others argue that the team leader is important for the success of self-managed teams, not only when they are initially formed, but later as well.[22] Supporters of this position maintain that as more companies empower their employees to manage themselves, former group or command leaders need to be trained to function more as facilitators than as leaders in the conventional sense.[23]

Self-managed teams link employees by process rather than by function, thus requiring the team leader to play the role of neutral facilitator or external leader. A *neutral facilitator* is an external leader of a self-managed team whose job is to create a supportive environment in which team members take on responsibilities to work productively and solve complex problems on their own. Considerable coaching and encouragement are usually necessary from the facilitator to get a new team off to a successful start.

neutral facilitator: an external leader of a self-managed team whose job is to create a supportive environment in which team members take on responsibilities to work productively and solve complex problems on their own.

Allowing teams to manage themselves frees facilitators from doing so and gives them time to focus on team development.[24] A facilitator would engage in team-building activities such as:

- Creating intervention sessions for mutual understanding
- Opening forums for resolving interpersonal difficulties
- Creating opportunities for social interaction
- Increasing mutual acceptance and respect among diverse team members
- Maintaining an open communication policy
- Highlighting mutual interest, not differences, of team members
- Increasing team identification through the use of ceremonies, rituals, and symbols
- Using team-oriented incentives

These activities can ensure that there is strong identification with the team, especially as pride in the team's accomplishments grows. Also, they will strengthen cohesiveness and the level of mutual cooperation between team members.

Self-managed teams are a success at Corning because they have top-management support and commitment. Self-managed teams set clear goals and objectives. They also gave input to the compensation structure, which created a win-win situation for employees and the company. The self-managed teams develop their own task design and measurement systems, and have a wide scope of authority, adequate information, and strong and experienced facilitators.

Applying the Concept 8-3

Team Facilitating Factors

Identify which factor is missing in the following statements. Write the appropriate letter in the blank before each item.

a. top-management support and commitment
b. unambiguous goals and objectives
c. appropriate compensation structure
d. appropriate task design and measurement system

e. appropriate scope of authority
f. adequate information system
g. strong and experienced facilitator

_____ 1. I get frustrated with this team because no one seems to know what we are doing.

_____ 2. Management expects us to give input into which products we should make. However, they don't give us the numbers we need to make effective decisions.

_____ 3. What bothers me is that we don't have a clear agreement on the quality of the product.

_____ 4. We really need a better manager if we are going to improve our team performance.

_____ 5. The team members are not taking our new self-directed status seriously, because they believe self-managed teams are just the latest fad, that management will drop it for the next hot topic.

DISTRIBUTED LEADERSHIP

Few people will argue against the appropriateness of participative management today. If you ask managers if they use participative management, most will say yes. But are the majority of American businesses truly using participative management at the lowest levels in the organization? The answer is no.[25]

According to Edward Lawler, world expert on high-involvement management (a form of distributive leadership), to be successful in the global economy organizations need to increase employee participation in management. *High-involvement management moves power, information, knowledge, and rewards farther down the organization.* To be truly effective, all four must move down the organization to the lowest level. Many top-performing companies are using high-involvement management as a competitive advantage to continually redesign the organization and stay ahead of competitors.[26] This change in leadership style was the major reason for Corning's recent success.

Although self-managed teams are becoming more common in the workplace, their success is still dependent on how well individuals in leadership roles can create an environment where employees take on responsibilities to work productively in self-managed, self-starting teams that identify and solve complex problems on their own. Scholars agree that a distributed leadership model is uniquely suited to the SMT concept.[27] *Distributed leadership is a collection of roles and behaviors that can be divided, shared, rotated, and used sequentially or concomitantly in an SMT environment.* Supporting this position, a study of 11 manager-less teams in manufacturing and 4 teams in education found that the most successful teams were those that demonstrated and distributed leadership. Different individuals with different strengths and abilities took on the leadership role over the course of the projects studied, a rotation that seemed to have contributed to the teams' success.[28]

The most extreme form of distributed leadership in self-managed teams occurs when there is no authority hierarchy of any sort; the organization's top management allows the team to make all important decisions collectively, and all leadership responsibilities are shared among members. Though still a rare concept in many organizations, teams with this much autonomy are most likely to be found in small employee-owned businesses. Distributed leadership is more complicated in larger organizations that cannot operate effectively as a single self-defining team.[29] Large corporations are experimenting with self-managed teams on a case-by-case basis, but few if any are at the stage where they are ready to grant complete autonomy to these teams. In other words, self-managed teams in large corporations do not determine their own mission, compensation structure, scope of activities, or membership mix, nor do they decide when to form or disband.

Achieving coordination and reaching agreement on strategic issues may be difficult in a large corporation with many self-managed teams. When teams with interdependent activities also have considerable autonomy to pursue different objectives and strategies, more conflicts are likely to

high-involvement management: moves power, information, knowledge, and rewards farther down the organization.

distributed leadership: a collection of roles and behaviors that can be divided, shared, rotated, and used sequentially or concomitantly in an SMT environment.

occur among the teams. In the opening case, the challenge facing Corning is how to convert its other existing plants to self-managed teams. Garrity and his managers are aware of these potential problems as they weigh the possibilities. It has to be understood that turning the whole corporation into autonomous teams will decrease the power of the center (top management). This makes cooperation increasingly dependent on a strong culture with shared values and beliefs, strong organizational commitment, and a willingness on the part of top executives to defer to the will of the majority on strategic decisions.

While small businesses and newly created organizational subunits have been successful in implementing distributed leadership, managers need to implement the SMT concept in traditional existing organizations. Although implementing high-involvement management in traditional organizations takes more time and effort than creating new organizations, it can be worth it if the implementation is carefully planned, and if commitment of key stakeholders is gained by allowing them to be involved in planning. Companies, including Honeywell, have redesigned traditional organizations to be run by high-involvement management and distributive leadership.[30]

TEAM DEVELOPMENT AND LEADERSHIP

In keeping with the preceding section illustrating the changing role of leadership to a more distributive approach, and with contingency theories of leadership (Chapter 5), in this section we discuss the development stages teams go through. At the same time, we examine which situational leadership style is appropriate for use during each development stage.

After a team has been created, it goes through distinct stages of development. The evolution from a simple work group to a team is not always guaranteed; events can happen along the way to prevent full attainment of the performing stage. The challenge for the organization, and its leadership, is to recognize the stages of team development and to help teams move through them successfully, while also realizing that different stages of development require different styles of leadership.

Research suggests that all groups go through the same stages as they grow from a collection of individuals to a well-functioning team.[31] One model describing these stages is presented in this section and summarized in Model 8-1. The **stages of group development** are *forming, storming, norming, performing, and adjourning.* These five stages generally occur in sequence, although there can be overlap, and groups may never get past the storming stage. Situational leadership can be applied to the stages of development.[32] In other words, because each stage confronts team members and leaders with unique problems and challenges, the appropriate leadership style changes with the level of team development. See Model 8-1 on the next page for an overview of the stages of group development and the appropriate leadership style for each stage.

stages of group development:
forming, storming, norming, performing, and adjourning.

Model 8-1 *Stages of team development and the appropriate leadership style for each stage.*

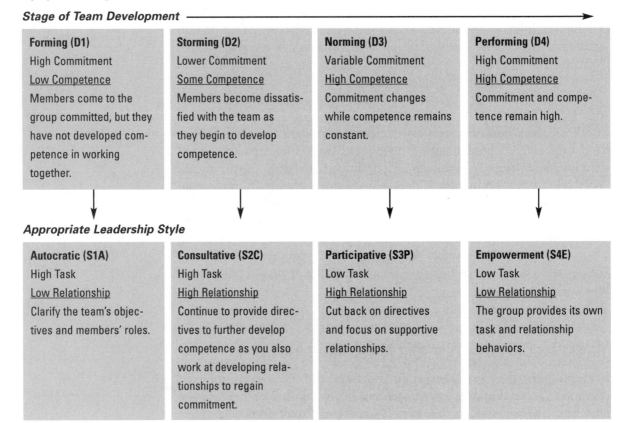

Stage of Team Development ⟶

Forming (D1)	Storming (D2)	Norming (D3)	Performing (D4)
High Commitment	Lower Commitment	Variable Commitment	High Commitment
<u>Low Competence</u>	<u>Some Competence</u>	<u>High Competence</u>	<u>High Competence</u>
Members come to the group committed, but they have not developed competence in working together.	Members become dissatisfied with the team as they begin to develop competence.	Commitment changes while competence remains constant.	Commitment and competence remain high.

Appropriate Leadership Style

Autocratic (S1A)	Consultative (S2C)	Participative (S3P)	Empowerment (S4E)
High Task	High Task	Low Task	Low Task
<u>Low Relationship</u>	<u>High Relationship</u>	<u>High Relationship</u>	<u>Low Relationship</u>
Clarify the team's objectives and members' roles.	Continue to provide directives to further develop competence as you also work at developing relationships to regain commitment.	Cut back on directives and focus on supportive relationships.	The group provides its own task and relationship behaviors.

Stage 1: Forming—Autocratic Leadership Style

team forming stage: characterized by low development (D1—high commitment and low competence); the appropriate leadership style is autocratic (high task/low relationship behavior).

The **team forming stage** *is characterized by low development (D1—high commitment and low competence), and the appropriate leadership style is autocratic (high task/low relationship behavior).*

Forming Stage. This is a period of getting to know each other (thus, it is also called the orientation stage). The immediate need is to determine what behavior is acceptable to others, explore bonding possibilities, and obtain task orientation. Uncertainty is high because no one knows how members will fit in (status), what will be required of them (roles and norms), who has the power to do what (power or authority), what the group will be like (cohesiveness), how decisions will be made, and how members will get along (conflict). These group processes and uncertainties must be resolved in order to progress to the next stage of development.

Autocratic Leadership Style. During the forming stage, the appropriate leadership style is directive (high task/low relationship). When a group first comes together, the leader's primary challenge is to spend time helping the group clarify its objectives and providing clear expectations of members. The leader's secondary challenge is to facilitate communication and interaction among members, helping them get to know one another and establishing guidelines for how the team will work together.

Stage 2: Storming—Consultative Leadership Style

*The **team storming stage** is characterized by moderate development (D2—lower commitment with some competence), and the appropriate leadership style is consultative (high task/high relationship behavior).*

Storming Stage. This is also called the dissatisfaction stage. Conflict and disagreement mark this stage as individual personalities emerge more clearly, and members become more assertive in clarifying their roles. There may be disagreements over the team's mission or goals. Team unity and cohesiveness may be in question as team members experience frustrations and feelings of incompetence. It is critical that the group work on resolving these structural and interpersonal issues, or it may not make it to the next stage of development.

Consultative Leadership Style. During the storming stage, the appropriate leadership style is consultative (high task/high relationship). The leader's role is to help the members meet their needs, debate ideas, resolve conflicts, and work through the uncertainties and conflicting perceptions about team tasks and goals. At the same time, the leader needs to continue to emphasize task behavior necessary to help the group develop its level of competence.

team storming stage: characterized by moderate development (D2—lower commitment with some competence); the appropriate leadership style is consultative (high task/high relationship behavior).

Stage 3: Norming—Participative Leadership Style

*The **team norming stage** is characterized by high development (D3—variable commitment with high competence), and the appropriate leadership style is participative (low task/high relationship behavior).* Norming is the development of norms, which is one of the four team formation variables.

Norming Stage. This stage is also called the resolution stage. It is characterized by less conflict, increased team unity, and greater harmony. With time, members have come to understand and accept one another. Consensus develops on acceptable leadership structure and group norms. Roles are clearly defined, and cohesiveness and team decision making are high. As members develop competence and confidence in their abilities, they often become more satisfied with the group. This allows for relationships to develop that satisfy members' affiliation needs.

As group interaction increases, so does the potential for conflict and other dysfunctions. If the group does not deal effectively with group process difficulties, the group may regress to stage two or plateau. If the group is successful at developing a positive group norm and process, it will develop to the next stage.

Participative Leadership Style. During the norming stage, the appropriate leadership style is participative (low task/high relationship). Once group members achieve unity, cohesiveness, role and task clarification, and competence, there is little need to use task behavior leadership. The team leader should encourage openness within the group and continue to facilitate communication and clarify team roles, values, and expectations. The leader needs to focus on strengthening relationships with and among team members in order to reduce the potential for conflicts. If the leader contin-

team norming stage: characterized by high development (D3—variable commitment with high competence); the appropriate leadership style is participative (low task/high relationship behavior).

ues to provide directives that are not needed, the group can become dissatisfied and regress or plateau at this level.

Stage 4: Performing—Empowerment Leadership Style

team performing stage: characterized by outstanding development (D4—high commitment and high competence); the appropriate leadership style is empowerment (low task/low relationship behavior).

*The **team performing stage** is characterized by outstanding development (D4—high commitment and high competence), and the appropriate leadership style is empowerment (low task/low relationship behavior).*

Performing Stage. High levels of commitment and competence characterize the performing stage, also called the production stage. The emphasis is on achieving the team's goals. The group has developed effective structures and processes that allow for optimum interactions, better coordination of actions, and a better approach to resolving disagreements. Team members confront and resolve problems in the interest of task accomplishment. The members are very productive, which leads to positive feelings and high levels of satisfaction. This positive and productive atmosphere may change with time, but the maturity of the group helps it to quickly overcome any problems because members are open with each other.

Empowerment Leadership Style. At this stage the appropriate leadership style is empowerment (low task/low relationship). Groups that develop to this stage have members who are competent and able to perform the appropriate task and relationship roles. The leader does not need to play either role, unless there is a major breakdown in the team structure, because the group has effectively become a self-managed team with shared leadership. The leader's role changes to one of a facilitator helping the team self-manage to reach its goals.

Stage 5: Adjourning

team adjourning stage: occurs when the team terminates, and leadership is no longer needed.

*The **team adjourning stage** of development happens when the team terminates, and leadership is no longer needed.*

The adjourning, also called terminating, stage is not reached in command groups unless there is some drastic reorganization. However, task or project groups do terminate. In groups that have progressed through all four stages of group development, the members may feel a sense of loss because the group is ending. However, in groups that experienced significant dysfunction and failed to progress through the stages of development, members often experience a feeling of relief at this stage.

Comparisons of Changes in Development Stages

The first development variable identified throughout each stage—level of commitment (which includes cohesiveness and team identity)—does not progress in successive fashion throughout the four stages of development. Commitment starts high in stage 1, drops in stage 2, and then rises through stages 3 and 4. Cohesiveness and team identity start low in stages 1 and 2 and increase through stages 3 and 4. The second development variable—level of member competence—increases through each of the first four stages.

Using the Appropriate Leadership Style

The ability to take a self-managed team through the four stages of development was clearly illustrated at Corning through Garrity's leadership. As a leader of a team, it is important for you to be aware of the group's development stage and the influencing variables at each stage. Using the appropriate leadership style will help you to effect positive results at each stage. In Skill-Building Exercise 8-1, Team Development Situational Management, you will develop your ability to identify group development stages and select the appropriate leadership style for the group or team by using Model 8-1. You may find it helpful to review Model 8-1 again now.

Self-Managed Teams at the Performing Level

In addition to Corning, self-managed teams have been successfully used at Motorola, Saturn, Honeywell, Whirlpool, and other companies, which demonstrates what happens when the vast untapped reservoir of creativity locked up in a traditional organization is released by empowering people to manage their own activities.[33] We will highlight examples of self-managed teams in action at four different companies.

Saturn Corporation. Since it was established, the Saturn Corporation has organized its key operations by self-managed teams with no supervisors, inspectors, time clocks, or union stewards. Saturn's self-managed teams are responsible for their activities, including quality, cost, production, and people. Without management commitment and a supportive environment at Saturn, the effectiveness of its self-managed teams would be in question. At Saturn, management and union leaders see themselves as guardians of the

---

Applying the Concept 8-4

Team Development Stage and Leadership Style

Using Model 8-1, identify the development stage and leadership style for each team. Write the appropriate letter in the blank before each item.

a. forming—autocratic style
b. storming—consultative style
c. norming—participative style

d. performing—empowerment style
e. terminating—no leadership needed

_____ **1.** The team is doing a good job of meeting objectives without being told to do so. However, some of the members show more interest and do more work than others.

_____ **2.** The task force interviewed all candidates and has just completed its meeting with the president to give its input on which controller to hire.

_____ **3.** The company has decided to form a committee to review the budget. Members are at the first budget meeting with the vice president of finance.

_____ **4.** Some of the SMT members are complaining about how the team operates and the way members interact as they work. However, they are beginning to work better together as a team.

_____ **5.** The team just beat its objective for the quarter. It is a top producer in the company. The members get along really well.

belief that making mistakes is permissible, a view that encourages employees to take risk without fear of punishment if they fail. Saturn's compensation system also motivates self-managed, integrated teams to take risks by rewarding them for meeting quality and productivity goals. Saturn human resource manager Joy Rodes confirms that the compensation system works because it is fully integrated with training, the sharing of decision making within teams, and the way Saturn treats its employees. Saturn has consistently been ranked one of the top-performing divisions at General Motors, and its employee and customer satisfaction surveys have been among the best in the industry.[34]

Honeywell's Defense Avionics Systems. The SMT concept is not new to Honeywell Inc.'s Defense Avionics Systems (DAS) unit—a maker and designer of avionics control systems for military aircraft. The eight-year-old effort of DAS to overhaul its logistics function has led to impressive results. The three teams that perform inventory control and distribution (IC&D) functions at DAS are practically self-managed, according to Tom Biederwolf, team leader of the production and engineering stockroom. DAS' self-managed teams perform work that was once done by 12 separate departments.[35]

London Life Insurance Co.'s Information Services (IS) Group. This is the case of a unit that made the transition from traditional work groups to highly effective teams. The goal for London Life Insurance Company was to create a team environment in which professional staff are empowered to actively manage their own skills and career growth. Toward this end, the IS unit formed a small team called the Self-Managed Team, which later evolved into the Performance Improvement Team, or PIT Crew. The team's activities included developing a 30-page booklet presenting the IS group's version of self-managed teams, conducting a 2-hour workshop on the concept for all IS staff, and establishing a measure to track ongoing performance of the teams based on 15 critical factors. While IS teams have achieved significant improvements in their processes, they have also learned some key lessons for effective SMT concept implementation. Their efforts have shown that communication and active, sustained top-management support are essential to the success of self-managed teams. IS self-managed teams also learned that goals and performance measures must be established from the outset. [36]

Perdue Farms. This is yet another example of using self-managed teams in a service rather than manufacturing setting. The human resources (HR) manager for the eastern North Carolina division of Perdue Farms explains how his department successfully changed into a self-managed work team. Serving as a pilot for the division's first team effort, the HR department set out to become a fully functioning self-managed work team within one year. During the early phase of implementation, the team was resistant to participating in discussions and in the decision-making process. Through training and coaching, team members were encouraged to lead discussions and make decisions on their own. Eventually, team members became more comfortable and productive and began thinking of themselves as a team. Team members have since learned to perform beyond job descriptions and think more about achieving the departmental mission developed by the team. Although the department did not achieve any major accomplishments in its first year of implementation, the HR manager noted that it did realize a higher level of performance in just one year.[37] The organization learned some key lessons during this process. For instance, it became apparent to the team that training, coaching, and offering team members steady feedback do greatly facilitate the transition from traditional work groups to self-managed teams. Providing positive reinforcement and realizing that behavior does not change overnight also facilitates continuous learning and builds trust with employees.

OUTDOOR TRAINING AND TEAM DEVELOPMENT

Another technique gaining popularity among corporations is outdoor training. Outdoor training environments vary from the mundane (community playgrounds) to the extreme (rough wilderness terrain). This experiential approach to building teamwork is especially critical to the SMT concept, given the absence of a formal or appointed leader in such teams. Self-managed teams often perform complex tasks with highly interdependent activities. This requires a cross-functional composition of the membership, and therein lies the challenge of creating a cohesive, self-managed team. Through the process of learning by doing, participants at outdoor training seminars acquire leadership and teamwork skills, which it is assumed helps them become better self-managed team members.

Goals of Outdoor Training

To understand the nature of outdoor training programs, it is important to seek answers to a few key questions: What specific objectives do these programs seek to achieve for their clients, what activities are undertaken to achieve these objectives, and what is their effectiveness?

In stating its goals, an outdoor training program will indicate its intentions to help participants discover how they work together as a team, to identify their strengths and weaknesses, to test their limits, to discover their inner self and what they are made of, to have the opportunity to break down self-imposed barriers, and above all to have fun. The emphasis is on building not only teamwork but also self-confidence for leadership.

Activities intended to accomplish the goals of outdoor training include desert backpacking, mountain backpacking, skiing and winter camping, canoe expeditions, sailing, rope climbing, kayaking, horseback riding, and survival games. Here, the outdoors is the classroom, and the instructors draw analogies between activities and the workplace. All activities are designed to stretch members to the limit, forcing them to rely on skills they never knew they had, and on one another, to complete the program.

Teamwork is enhanced as participants focus their attention on the process of getting things done by working with other people. Participants also practice their communication skills by giving clear, succinct instructions to one another on how to perform different activities. At the same time, participants have to learn to trust one another, because for most of these activities, completion and even survival appear to depend on trust.

Benefits of Outdoor Training

Proponents of outdoor training believe that a work team that experiences outdoor training will work more cooperatively back at the office. Among the most important benefits, according to proponents, are the opportunities to build greater self-confidence, discover hidden strengths, and learn to work better with people. To facilitate the transfer of these benefits from the outdoors to the office, good program trainers hold debriefing and follow-up sessions. Debriefing is a post-activity session in which participants review what they learned and discuss how they will apply their lessons to the job. The program's effectiveness is further enhanced by follow-up sessions, held periodically to assess progress in applying the knowledge and skills learned during outdoor training.

There are many who question the safety and effectiveness of outdoor training. Although outdoor training companies claim a near-zero risk of accidents, opponents believe that a threat to health and life does exist. Opponents also question the claim that teamwork learned in outdoor training does transfer to the work environment. As one researcher on the topic explains, the workplace is a different environment from the wilderness. Teams tend to gain and lose their members as teammates are transferred, promoted, or quit. This mobility, it is argued, often negates all the team-building efforts that take place during the outdoor experience. Another problem is simply that when teams return to work, they often revert to the old ways of doing things.

III

Organizational Leadership

9

Influencing: Power, Politics, and Negotiation

H. Ross Perot is a highly successful business founder, billionaire, social activist, founder of the political Reform party, and two-time candidate for U.S. president. Perot supporters say that he has a genuine desire to create a good life for others and to serve others. He has given away more than $100 million to various causes. However, others regard Perot as a leader obsessed with power and self-importance. But most people do agree that he is a very powerful man. Legend has it that Ross Perot started his business career as a boy delivering newspapers in a Texarkana, Texas, ghetto and became a successful young salesperson for IBM by meeting his annual sales quota in the first month.

Perot started Electronic Data Systems, Inc. (EDS) and became a powerful self-made billionaire. EDS assists client organizations in the development of computer information systems designed to address and solve business problems. Perot later sold EDS to General Motors (GM), becoming a member of GM's board of directors and a GM stockholder. He was very outspoken against GM management practices and car quality and pressed for drastic changes. Perot was so powerfully intimidating and successful at building a political network that GM management decided to buy his GM stock at a pre-mium price to get rid of him. Perot went on to recruit EDS employees away from GM when he created a competing company, Perot Systems, in 1988. Although Ross Perot is basically an autocratic leader, he has always been against bureaucracy and hierarchy and for informal communication.

According to Doron Levin, author of *Irreconcilable Differences: Ross Perot versus General Motors,* Perot's motives are money, attention, and power. His need for attention and power influenced his decision to spend millions of dollars running for the U.S. presidency and to develop the Reform party, a third political party, to compete with the Republican and Democratic parties. Out of the Reform party, members split from Ross Perot to start the American Reform party.[1]

■ *Go to the Internet:* For more information about H. Ross Perot, visit his personal website **http://www.perot.org** and read his biography to learn of his contributions to America. To learn more about his prior company, EDS, visit **http://www.eds.com**. To learn more about Perot Systems, visit **http://www.perotsystems.com**. The Reform party website is **http://www.reformparty.org**, and the American Reform party website is **http://www.americanreform.org**. You can also do a name search for Perot and these organizations to find out what others have to say about them.

Ross Perot is an example of a powerful man who has interactions with various groups of people. Each group's perception of his use of power may be different depending on their goals. The focus of this chapter is on helping you accomplish your goals, without taking advantage of others, by developing your skills in the following four areas. We will explore nine influencing tactics and the appropriate situations in which to use them. The seven types and two sources of power are identified, and you will learn ways to increase each type of power. Emphasis is also placed on guidelines for developing useful political skills. Finally, you will examine and learn to use a negotiation model.

INFLUENCING

Besides excellent work, what does it take to get ahead in an organization? To climb the corporate ladder, you will have to influence people—to gain power, play organizational politics, and negotiate to get what you want. These related concepts are the topics of this chapter. Recall from our definition of leadership (Chapter 1) that leadership is the "influencing" process of leaders and followers to achieve organizational objectives through change. Leaders and followers influence each other, because we are all potential leaders.[2] Influencing is so important that it is called the essence of leadership. **Influencing** *is the process of affecting others' attitudes and behavior in order to achieve an objective.* Research has revealed that management influence has a direct effect on organizational performance.[3] Power, politics, and negotiation are all ways of influencing others. In this section we discuss the influencing processes and outcomes, as well as influencing tactics.

influencing: the process of affecting others' attitudes and behavior in order to achieve an objective.

Influencing Processes and Outcomes

The Influencing Processes. There is a distinction between three different types of influencing processes.[4] The *influencing processes* are instrumental compliance, internalization, and identification.

Instrumental Compliance. The follower carries out a requested behavior for the purposes of obtaining a reward or avoiding a punishment controlled by the leader. The follower motivation is instrumental—the reward, or avoiding a punishment. If rewards and punishment are no longer important to the follower, or the leader loses power to give them to the follower, influence on behavior will stop.

Internalization. Followers become committed to the leader's influence because of the appeal to their values, beliefs, and self-image. Commitment occurs regardless of whether any tangible benefit is expected, and the followers' loyalty is to the ideas themselves, not to the leader who communicates them. The leader's influence is derived from insight about the followers' values and beliefs and the ability to communicate a request or proposal in a way that is consistent with them. In other words, the followers agree with the leader and are influenced. Influence would be lost if the followers no longer agreed with the leader's ideas.

Identification. The follower is committed to imitate the leader's behavior, or adopts the same attitudes to please the leader and to be like the leader. The motivation to develop and maintain a relationship with the leader may come from the need for affiliation and acceptance. Influence is based on affiliation and thus is lost if the follower no longer cares about the relationship with the leader.

Outcomes of Influence Attempts. It is useful to differentiate among three qualitatively distinct outcomes of influence attempts.[5] *Influencing outcome* attempts include commitment, compliance, and resistance.

Commitment. Commitment occurs when the follower internally agrees with the leader and makes a great effort to carry out the leader's requested behavior. When leaders are implementing complex changes, follower commitment is often critical to the success of implementing the change. Internalization and identification are forms of commitment to being influenced. Commitment is more likely when the leader request is important and enjoyable to implement, and when other influencing tactics are used,[6] which you will learn about later in this section.

Compliance. Compliance occurs when the follower is willing to do what the leader asks, but is apathetic rather than enthusiastic about the change, and is willing to make only a minimal effort. The follower is not convinced that the change is desirable. For simple, routine requests, compliance may be all that is necessary for the leader to influence the follower to accomplish task objectives.

Resistance. Resistance occurs when the follower is opposed to the leader's influence for changed behavior, and the follower tries to avoid the change. The follower will respond in one or more ways: (1) make excuses about why the change cannot be implemented, (2) try to persuade the leader to withdraw or change the request, (3) ask higher managers to overrule the supervising leader, (4) delay acting in hopes that the leader will forget or not follow up to ensure compliance, (5) make a pretense of complying while trying to sabotage the change, or (6) refuse to make the change.

The influencing process is successful when the outcomes are commitment and compliance; it is unsuccessful when the outcome is resistance. This is illustrated in Figure 9-1.

Influencing Process	Outcome
Instrumental compliance	Compliance
Internalization	Commitment
Identification	Commitment
Unsuccessful influencing process	Resistance

Figure 9-1 *Influencing process and outcomes.*

Ross Perot and the Reform party have had some success at influencing voters to elect their political candidates to public office. For example, Jesse Ventura was elected governor of Minnesota. However, other candidates were unsuccessful in the influencing process and were not elected. The voters of the traditional Republican and Democratic two-party system have been resistant to accepting a third political party. And the Reform party has also been split.

Influencing Tactics

In recent years, specific types of behavior used to exercise influence have been separated from power and politics. A number of researchers have iden-

Leader Has an Objective	Leader Selects Influencing Tactic(s)	Influencing Outcome
	1. Rational persuasion	Objective achieved:
	2. Inspirational appeals	Commitment or
	3. Consultation	Compliance
	4. Ingratiation	Objective not achieved:
	5. Personal appeals	May be due to resistance
	6. Exchange	
	7. Coalitions	
	8. Legitimization	
	9. Pressure	

Figure 9-2 *Influencing.*

rational persuasion tactic: the leader presents logical arguments with factual evidence to persuade the follower that the behavior will result in meeting the objectives.

tified categories of proactive influence behavior that are called "influence tactics."[7] Gary Yukl and his colleagues built on and extended earlier work, identifying nine proactive influencing tactics that are relevant for managers; they are shown in Figure 9-2.[8] The goal of each tactic is to successfully complete the influencing process, with the outcome of commitment or compliance, in order to accomplish an objective. The tactics are used to influence—to overcome resistance. We present here the nine influencing tactics, their appropriate use, and guidelines for using them.[9]

Rational Persuasion.   *With the **rational persuasion tactic,** the leader presents logical arguments with factual evidence to persuade the follower that the behavior will result in meeting the objective.* The leader's knowledge is the source of facts used to build a persuasive case. However, the leader may also include some opinions or inferences when facts are not available, making credibility (trust and confidence in the leader) important in such cases. Researchers have shown that leaders who are viewed as credible are more successful at using rational persuasion.[10] When you use rational persuasion, you need to develop a persuasive case based on the followers' needs. What seems logical and reasonable to you may not be logical to others. With multiple followers, a different logical argument may have to be made to meet individual needs.

Appropriate Use of Rational Persuasion.   Researchers found that leaders who use a strong form of rational persuasion were effective at influencing followers.[11] Logical arguments generally work well with people whose behavior is more influenced by thinking than emotions. They work well when the leader and follower share the same objective, but not when the follower disagrees that the leader's plan is the best way to achieve the objective, or when the follower would rather achieve the objective in a different way. Thus, it is usually a good idea to check agreement, first on objectives and then on the plan, to determine what the disagreement is.

Using Rational Persuasion.   When you develop a rational persuasion, follow these guidelines.

1. *Explain why the objective needs to be met.*   To get a commitment to meet an objective, people want to know why it needs to be met; is it important?

2. *Explain how the follower will benefit by meeting the objective.* Try to think of the other party's often-unasked question—what's in it for me? Sell the benefits to the followers, rather than focusing on how you and the organization benefit by achieving the objective. Note that you are not offering something extra; that is exchange. For example, when delegating an assignment, tell your followers it is an opportunity to make work more interesting and challenging, to learn new things and develop new skills, to get a better performance review, to advance in their career, and to earn more money. Suggest that the task may be interesting and enjoyable; don't take the approach that this is a lousy job, but someone has to do it.

3. *Provide evidence that the objective can be met.* Remember the importance of expectancy motivation theory (Chapter 3). When possible, demonstrate how to do a task—seeing is believing. Give examples of how others have met the objective. Offer a detailed, step-by-step plan. Be supportive and encouraging, showing your confidence in the followers' ability to meet the objective.

4. *Explain how potential problems and concerns will be handled.* Know the potential problems and concerns and deal with them in the rational persuasion. If others bring up some issues that you have not anticipated, which is likely, be sure to address them. Do not ignore people's concerns or make simple statements like, "that won't happen," or "we don't have to worry about that." Get the followers' input on how to resolve any possible problems as they come up. This will help gain their commitment.

5. *If there are competing plans to meet the objective, explain why your proposal is better than the others.* Do your homework. You need to be well versed about the competition. To simply say that your idea is better than theirs won't cut it. Be sure to state how your plan is superior to the others, and point out the weaknesses and problems with the other plans.

Inspirational Appeals. With the **inspirational appeals tactic,** the *leader attempts to arouse follower enthusiasm through internalization to meet the objective.* The leader appeals to the followers' values, ideals, and aspirations or increases followers' self-confidence by displaying his or her feelings to appeal to followers' emotions and enthusiasm.[12] As with rational persuasion, no tangible rewards are promised, only the positive feelings of accomplishment in meeting the objective.

Appropriate Use of Inspirational Appeals. Researchers found that leaders who use inspirational appeals were effective at gaining the commitment of followers.[13] Inspirational appeals generally work well with people whose behavior is more influenced by emotions than by logical thinking. To be inspirational, you need to understand the values, hopes, fears and goals of followers.

Great sports coaches, such as Vince Lombardy, are well respected for their inspirational appeals to get the team to win the game. Have you heard the "win one for the Gipper," saying from Notre Dame? The U.S. Steel (a division of USX) Gary Works plant was threatened with being closed down. Thomas Usher, president of U.S. Steel, made an emotional appeal to the steelworkers, asking how long they were going to put up with being insulted

inspirational appeals tactic: the leader attempts to arouse follower enthusiasm through internalization to meet the objective.

for their shoddy quality, their high costs, and their smug attitude toward customers. Usher's emotionally charged appeal helped start a process of constructive change that brought success back to its Gary Works plant.

Using Inspirational Appeal. When you develop an inspirational appeal, follow these guidelines.

1. *Appeal to the followers' ideals and values.* Leaders appeal to the desire to be important, to be useful, to develop skills, to accomplish something worthwhile, to perform an exceptional feast, or to be the best. When you use inspirational appeals, you need to develop emotions and enthusiasm based on the followers' values. When dealing with multiple followers, you may have to make different inspirational appeals to meet individual values.

2. *Link the appeal to the followers' self-concept.* Appeal to the self-image as a professional or as the member of a team, department, or organization. Accomplishing the objective will help the followers to feel good about themselves, which enhances self-concept.

3. *Link the request to a clear, appealing vision.* Create a vision of how things will be when the objective is achieved. You will learn more about creating a vision in Chapter 10.

4. *Be positive and optimistic.* Make your confidence and optimism about meeting the objective contagious. This is especially important when giving difficult, complex tasks to followers who lack self-confidence. Again, know the followers. For example, say *when* we accomplish the objective, not *if, could,* or *might.*

5. *Use nonverbal communication to bring emotions to the verbal message.* Your communication skills will have a direct impact on how inspirational your appeal will be. Use nonverbal communications, such as raising and lowering voice tone and pausing to intensify key points, showing moist eyes or a few tears, and maintaining eye contact. Use facial expressions and body movement; gestures like pounding a table have effectively reinforced verbal messages with emotions.

Consultation. The leader uses the consultative leadership style (Chapter 5). *With the **consultation tactic**, the leader seeks the follower's input, and the leader is willing to modify the objective and plans.* The leader uses high task behavior to achieve the objective, as well as high relationship behavior. Thus, consultation is a leadership style, and it has been found to be an effective influencing tactic.[14]

Appropriate Use of Consultation. When using consultation as an influencing tactic, the leader's primary concern is to gain a commitment from the followers. Followers are more committed to implementing a change when they give input.

Using Consultation. When you use consultation, follow these guidelines.

1. *Present a tentative proposal, and be willing to modify it.* The leader commonly presents a proposed change and asks the group that will implement it to suggest ideas for improvement. Knowing that the idea is a proposal, followers are more apt to give honest ideas and state concerns,

consultation tactic: the leader seeks the follower's input, and the leader is willing to modify the objective and plans.

which can be overcome with their help. It is important to respond to follower concerns and to implement their suggestions.

2. *State your objective, and ask the followers how they can help.* If you don't expect the followers to want to change, make a rational persuasion and ask how they can help you attain it. This approach works best for people you have a good relationship with. Once a person has agreed to help, it is easier to ask for additional things as you progress toward the objective.

3. *State the objective, but let the followers develop the implementation plan.* When followers are capable and committed to the objective, implementation of the objective is often left to the followers.

Ingratiation. *With the* **ingratiation tactic,** *the leader is friendly and praises his or her followers to get them in a good mood before being asked to meet the objective.*

Appropriate Use of Ingratiation. Ingratiation works best as a long-term influencing strategy to improve relationships with followers.[15] The ingratiation must also be sincere to be effective. If you usually don't complement followers, and one day you suddenly compliment them and then ask for a favor, they will think you are manipulating them. Thus, this technique can backfire on you.

Using Ingratiation. When using ingratiation, follow these guidelines.

1. *Be sensitive to the follower's moods.* Ingratiation works well with people who are moody, but asking them at the wrong time can lead to resistance to the change. With moody followers, start out with some complements to determine their mood. If it's good, make the request; if not, wait for a more opportune time, if possible.

2. *Compliment the follower's past related achievements.* Begin by talking about how well the follower handled some earlier task. Be specific about what they did well; use the giving praise model in Chapter 3. Then move into the request. If you start with the request first, but find resistance and give compliments, the compliments may be seen as insincere manipulation to get what you want.

3. *State why the follower was selected for the task.* Compliment the follower by saying how uniquely qualified he or she is to do the task. When followers believe the task is important and they are well qualified, it is tough to refuse an assignment.

4. *Acknowledge inconvenience of your request.* Apologize for adding to a busy workload and inconvenience that will result in doing the task. Praise the follower as you show your appreciation for the follower's willingness to be inconvenienced with your request.

Personal Appeals. *With the* **personal appeal tactic,** *the leader requests the followers to meet the objective based on loyalty and friendship.* Present your request as a favor to you: "Please do it for me," not "this is an order."

Appropriate Use of Personal Appeals. Personal appeals are especially important when you have weak power over the followers, such as when assigning a task to people who work in other departments. Personal appeals are more commonly used with peers and outsiders than with employees or

ingratiation tactic: the leader is friendly and praises his or her followers to get them in a good mood before being asked to meet the objectives.

personal appeal tactic: the leader requests the followers to meet the objective based on loyalty and friendship.

managers. It is also important to have a good relationship with the follower. If you ask a personal favor of a person who doesn't like you, the request may end in resistance.

Using Personal Appeals.   When using personal appeals, follow these guidelines.

1. *Begin by stating that you need a favor and explaining why it is important.* Then ask for the favor. In effect, you are hoping for a positive commitment before giving the details. When a person understands why the request is important to you and agrees to do you a favor, it's tough for them to say no. But be sure not to be viewed as manipulative and hurt the relationship.

2. *Appeal to your friendship.*   When you have a very strong relationship, a friendship appeal is usually not needed, and it generally does not work with people you don't know. It is usually most effective with individuals you work with, but do not have a close personal relationship with. This type of appeal might be successful with customers, suppliers, or people in other departments. For example, begin by saying, "We have been friends for a long time and I've asked very little of you, would you please . . . "

3. *Tell the followers that you are counting on them.*   This helps the followers realize the importance of the request to you and your friendship. This statement lets the follower know that you don't want the request ignored, and that failure to help you could hurt your relationship. Again, friendship is needed for full effect.

exchange tactic: the leader offers a reward for helping to meet the objective.

Exchange.   With the **exchange tactic,** *the leader offers a reward for helping to meet the objective.* The actual reward may be explicitly stated, or it may be some type of implied reward. The leader may agree to share the benefits of achieving the objective with the follower, or to do something else for the follower for helping. You could also be calling in a favor you have done for the person.

Appropriate Use of Exchange.   People who associate with each other over time can help each other. The incentive for exchange can be anything of value, such as scarce resources, information, advice or assistance on another task, or career and political support.

Using Exchange.   When using exchange, follow these guidelines.

1. *Offer to share the benefits.*   For example, in exchange for their help, you could put the person's name on a report. You could say that the next time the person does a report, you will help them.

2. *Offer an unrelated reward.*   With manager-employee relationships, a pay raise, promotion, extra time off, additional funds or resources, and equipment may be the exchange.

3. *Offer to help the follower.*   When a follower lacks confidence, helping them can often overcome resistance, or an unpleasant task can be more fun when done with others.

4. *Offer to do some of the follower's regular work.*   If the follower already has too much to do, you can do some of their work in exchange for the new task that requires their special talent.

5. *Offer to reciprocate later.* You may have heard the expression, "I owe you one." If you have nothing to exchange now, you can offer a future favor in return for help today. Although not explicitly stated, this exchange is often implied.

Coalitions. Sometimes it is difficult to influence others by yourself. There is power and safety in numbers. The more people you can get on your side, the more influence you can have on followers. *With the* **coalitions tactic,** *the leader uses others' help to persuade the follower to meet the objective.* The leader gets others to directly influence the follower, or the leader uses others' names as agreeing with him or her as a further reason for meeting the objective.

Appropriate Use of Coalitions. Coalitions are used when the leader can't get the followers to meet the objective alone. Superiors, peers, subordinates, and outsiders can help to influence the followers. Coalitions are often used with other influencing methods. For example, at a meeting one person may make a personal or inspirational appeal, followed by coalition members speaking up in support of the idea.

Using Coalitions. When using coalitions, follow these guidelines.

1. *Tell the followers who supports your idea.* Try to get one or more people who are highly respected to say that they support your idea. Then when you talk to others, mention that these people support your idea. If you are dealing with multiple followers, you can start with those who are most likely to be influenced by your idea. Then as you get to the followers who may be resistant, you can mention all the people who support the idea, influencing them to go along too.

2. *Have a supporter with you when you make your request.* Rather than simply stating the names of your supporters, have one or more with you to help you. This is especially helpful when you know you will meet resistance.

3. *Have supporters follow up.* If your influence alone fails, you can have a supporter talk to the follower to try to change resistance into compliance for you.

4. *Ask a higher authority for help.* Have a higher-level manager tell a peer within the organization to comply with your request. For example, say you made a sale with a very short delivery date. You talk to the manager in production and are told that the order will not be filled on time. If you went to a higher manager with authority over production, you could get the order done. However, it is risky to go over a person's head to a higher manager. The production manager could still try to delay meeting the order deadline, and/or intentionally miss some other future order to get even with you. Use this tactic only as a last resort for influence attempts with peers or a manager who refuses to comply with a request that is clearly legitimate and very important to you.

Legitimization. *With the* **legitimization tactic,** *the leader relies on organizational authority that a reasonable request is being made, and that the follower should meet the objective.*

coalitions tactic: the leader uses others' help to persuade the follower to meet the objective.

legitimization tactic: the leader relies on organizational authority that a reasonable request is being made, and that the follower should meet the objective.

Appropriate Use of Legitimization. You must indicate that you have legitimate authority or right to make a particular type of request. Legitimacy is more likely to be questioned when you make a request that is unusual, when the request clearly exceeds your authority, or when the follower does not know who you are or what authority you have. Thus, you have to deal with the issue of being viewed as legitimate.

Using Legitimization. When using legitimization, follow these guidelines.

1. *Refer to organizational policies, procedures, rules, and other documentation.* Explain how the request is verified within the organization structure.

2. *Refer to written documents.* If the followers don't believe your reference to documents, show them the policy manual, contract, letter of agreement, blueprint, work order, or other documents that make your request legitimate.

3. *Refer to precedent.* If some other person has made the same request, refer to it in support of your request.

4. *Give the name of the person who gave you authority.* For example, a manager may tell an employee to get information from another employee. If the person does not want to cooperate, the employee making the request should state that his or her manager authorized the request, and suggest the person can check with that manager.

Pressure. The leader uses an autocratic leadership style to force the follower to meet the objective. *With the **pressure tactic**, the leader issues threats and warnings of discipline, and uses assertive behavior such as repeated demands and frequent checking on the follower, to ensure the objective is met.*

Appropriate Use of Pressure. Effective leaders generally do not use pressure.[16] However, when the follower is low in maturity and capability level due to being unwilling to cooperate, pressure is needed to gain compliance—although commitment is usually not obtained. Hard pressure (threats and punishment) may also hurt relationships, whereas soft pressure (continually checking) may not. Pressure is sometimes needed to enforce rules and get the job done, and on time.

Using Pressure. When using soft pressure, follow these guidelines.

1. *Be persistent.* If you request that followers do something, and you don't follow up to make sure it is done, followers will take advantage of the situation and ignore your request. The next two guidelines will help. Put the deadline and progress checks on your calendar to make sure you persistently follow up.

2. *Set specific deadlines for task completion.* You may include some input from the follower to get an agreement to meet the deadline.

3. *Frequently check progress.* Checking can help ensure that the task will be completed by the deadline. However, if there are circumstances beyond the follower's control, the deadline may need to be pushed back. But at least you will be aware of why the deadline will not be met ahead of time.

Now that you are familiar with the nine influencing tactics, it is inter-

pressure tactic: the leader issues threats and warnings of discipline, and uses assertive behavior such as repeated demands and frequent checking on the follower, to ensure the objective is met.

esting to see how they fit with the various personality traits. Complete Self-Assessment Exercise 9-1 to explore how your personality affects your approaches to influencing other people.

Self-Assessment Exercise 9-1

Influencing Tactics, Power, and Personality Traits

Review the nine influencing tactics. Which ones do you tend to use most often to help you get what you want? Also review your personality profile self-assessment exercises in Chapter 2.

Surgency/High Need for Power

If you have n Pow, you are apt to try to influence others, and you enjoy it. You tend to hate to lose, and when you don't get what you want, it bothers you. Thus, you are more likely to use harder methods of influence and power, such as pressure, exchange, coalitions, and legitimization than other personality types. You probably also like to use rational persuasion and don't understand why people don't think or see things the way you do. Be careful to use socialized rather than personalized power to influence others.

Agreeableness/High Need for Affiliation

If you have a high n Aff, you are apt to be less concerned about influencing others and gaining power than getting along with them. Thus, you are more likely to use softer methods of influence, such as personal and inspirational appeals and ingratiation, as well as rational appeals. You may tend not to seek power, and even avoid it.

Conscientiousness/High Need for Achievement

If you have a high n Ach, you tend to be between the other two approaches to influencing others. You tend to have clear goals and work hard to get what you want, which often requires influencing others to help you. So you don't want power for its own sake, only to get what you want. But you like to play by the rules and may tend to use rational persuasion frequently.

Based on the preceding information, briefly describe how your personality affects the ways you attempt to influence others.

_____

_____

_____

_____

_____

Research on Influencing Tactics

Researchers have found that leaders take a contingency approach to selecting which influencing tactic to use in a given situation. For example, leaders typically use hard tactics (legitimization or pressure) when they have the upper hand, anticipate resistance, or when the follower's behavior violates important norms. Leaders typically use softer tactics (ingratiation) when they are at a disadvantage, anticipate resistance, or when they will personally benefit from achieving the objective. Leaders typically use a rational approach (rational appeal and exchange) when others have equal power, when resistance is not anticipated, and when the benefits of meeting the objective help the organization and leader.[17] Researchers have found contingency approaches to influencing tactics based on direction, sequencing, and effectiveness.

Directional Differences in Use of Influencing Tactics. Rational persuasion is by far the most commonly used influencing tactic. However, researchers have found that leaders use different tactics when attempting to influence in upward (superiors), lateral (peers), and downward (subordinates) directions. Thus, although rational persuasion is used most often, it is more commonly used in an upward direction. Differences are as follows.[18]

- *Upward tactics.* Rational persuasion is the most commonly used influencing tactic with superiors. Coalitions are also used.
- *Lateral tactics.* Personal appeal and coalitions are more commonly used with peers. Ingratiaton, exchange, and legitimization are also used.
- *Downward tactics.* Consultation, exchange, inspirational appeal, ingratiation, legitimization, and pressure are more commonly used with subordinates.

Sequential Differences in Use of Influencing Tactics. The influencing process may take days or weeks, possibly longer. Therefore, when selecting an influencing tactic, leaders also consider which tactic to use as an initial request and which to use as a follow-up. As a general guide, begin with the softer, more positive tactics that take less effort and cost. You could begin with a simple rational persuasion; if you don't think it will work, try personal appeals, ingratiation, consultation, or inspirational appeals. These tactics can be used alone, in various combinations with each other, or with rational persuasion. If your influence objective is not met, you can give up or go on to harder tactics using pressure, exchange, and coalitions as follow-up attempts. The general sequence is as follows.[19] Note that since inspirational appeal and consultation can be used at either step, they are not listed.

1. *Initial requests.* Rational persuasion, ingratiation, and personal appeal are commonly used as initial requests, which may be in sequence before going on to follow-up requests.
2. *Follow-up requests.* Exchange and legitimization are commonly used as immediate follow-up requests. Coalition and pressure are commonly used as delayed follow-up requests.

Effectiveness of Influencing Tactics. The effectiveness of influencing tactics at gaining commitment to achieve the objective can be approached from two levels: when used individually and when used in combination.

Individual Tactic Effectiveness. Researchers found consultation and inspirational appeals were relatively effective tactics for gaining task commitment regardless of direction, although they were used most often with downward and lateral directions and usually in combination with another tactic.[20]

Rational appeals were more effective when they were strong (detailed proposal, elaborate documentation, convincing reply to concerns raised by followers) than weak, and when used in combination with other soft tactics (consultation, inspirational appeals, or ingratiation) than when used alone or with hard tactics (pressure, coalitions, legitimization).

Ingratiation and exchange were moderately effective for influencing subordinates and peers, but seldom effective with superiors. Personal appeals were also moderately effective for influencing subordinates and peers, but have limited use.

The hard tactics of pressure, coalition, and legitimization are the least effective at gaining commitment to the task. However, they were useful at gaining compliance to meet the objective, especially when combined with rational appeals, which is sometimes all that is needed. Thus, consistent with contingency leadership theory, all influencing tactics can be effective based on the given situation. We have covered the appropriate use of each tactic. However, when people don't get results with soft tactics, they tend to revert to hard tactics.[21] Be careful to use hard tactics only when appropriate and as a last resort, so that you don't hurt relationships and long-term performance.

Combined Tactic Effectiveness. It is often more effective to use a combination of tactics at the same time rather than just one or a sequence of individual tactics if the first one does not work. A study found that using two or more tactics at the same time was more effective than using a single tactic. However, some combinations are more effective than others. Whether a combination or single tactic was more effective depends on which tactics are combined. Some tactics are more compatible with others and work well together, while others don't work well in combination. For example, pressure and personal appeal or ingratiation will weaken feelings of friendship. Rational persuasion is very flexible and is compatible with the others.[22]

Combinations of soft tactics (consultation, ingratiation, and inspirational appeals) were usually more effective than when used alone. A combination of soft tactics with rational persuasion also works well. However, when a soft tactic was mixed with a hard tactic (pressure, coalitions, or legitimization), the influence attempt was usually less successful than when a soft tactic was used alone. Likewise, combining a hard tactic with rational persuasion was not more effective than using rational persuasion alone. And combining two hard tactics was no more effective than using one alone.

Effective leaders use the appropriate tactic or combination to meet the situation. If the combined tactics don't work, you can try sequencing individual tactics or using a different combination. In summary, combine soft tactics; don't mix soft and hard; and use hard tactics individually and only when necessary. See Figure 9-3 for a review of research findings.

As indicated in the opening case, Ross Perot is willing to use hard influencing tactics when he is not getting what he wants. When members of the Reform party wanted to split from him, Perot used pressure to try to keep them. After the split, he spoke negatively to the media about the new party. Ross developed the Reform political party, which is a form of coalition. Over the years, Perot has used all nine influencing tactics.

Tactic	Directional Use	Sequence of Request	Type of Tactic—Combine or Use Alone
1. Rational persuasion	Superiors	Initial	Soft—either
2. Inspirational appeals	Subordinates	Either	Soft—combine
3. Consultation	Subordinates	Either	Soft—combine
4. Ingratiation	Subordinates	Initial	Soft—combine
5. Personal appeals	Lateral	Initial	Soft—either
6. Exchange	Subordinates	Follow-up, immediate	Soft—either
7. Coalitions	Lateral	Follow-up, delay	Hard—use alone
8. Legitimization	Subordinates	Follow-up, immediate	Hard—use alone
9. Pressure	Subordinates	Follow-up, delay	Hard—use alone

Figure 9-3 *Influencing tactics research findings.*

POWER

Power may be the single most important concept in all of social science. Scholars have emphasized the need to conceptualize leadership as a power phenomenon. However, there is more confusion about influence and power than any other leadership concept. Various authors have used the terms influence, power, and politics interchangeably and without definitions.[23] We will not. We defined *influencing* as the process of affecting others' attitudes and behavior in order to achieve an objective. Power is also about influencing others. However, **power** *is the leader's potential influence over followers*. Because power is the *potential* to influence, you do not actually have to use power to influence others. Often it is the perception of power, rather than the actual use of power, that influences others. In this section we discuss sources of power, types of power and ways to increase your power, and how power is acquired and lost.

power: the leader's potential influence over followers.

Sources of Power

There are two sources of power: position power and personal power.[24]

Position Power. *Position power* is derived from top management, and it is delegated down the chain of command. Thus, a person who is in a management position has more potential influence (power) than an employee who is not a manager. Likewise, the higher the level of management, the greater potential to influence more people. Power is used to get people to do something they otherwise would not have done. Some people view power as the ability to make people do what they want them to do, or the ability to do something to people or for people. These definitions may be true, but they tend to give power a manipulative, negative connotation, as does the old saying by Lord Acton, "Power corrupts. Absolute power corrupts absolutely."

Within an organization, power should be viewed in a positive sense. Without power, managers could not achieve organizational objectives. Leadership and power go hand in hand. Employees are not influenced without a reason, and the reason is often the power a manager has over them. Managers rely on position power to get the job done.[25]

Applying the Concept 9-1

Influencing Tactics

Select the most appropiate individual tactic for each situation. Write the appropriate letter in the blank before each item.

a. rational persuasion
b. inspirational appeals
c. consultation

d. ingratiation
e. personal appeals
f. exchange

g. coalition
h. legitimization
i. pressure

_____ **1.** You are in sales and want some information about a new product that has not yet been produced, nor has it been announced inside or outside the company. You know a person in the production department who has been working on the new product, so you decide to contact that person.

_____ **2.** Two of your five crew workers did not come in to work today. You have a large order that should be shipped out at the end of the day. It will be tough for the small crew to meet the deadline.

_____ **3.** Although the crew members in situation 2 have agreed to push to meet the deadline, you would like to give them some help. You have an employee whose job is to perform routine maintenance and cleaning. He is not one of your five crew workers. However, you realize that he could be of some help filling in for the two missing workers. You decide to talk to this nonunion employee about working with the crew for two hours today.

_____ **4.** The nonunion employee in situation 3 is resisting helping the other workers. He is basically asking, "What's in it for me?"

_____ **5.** You have an employee who is very moody at times. You want this employee, who has a big ego, to complete an assignment before the established due date.

_____ **6.** You believe you deserve a pay raise, so you decide to talk to your manager about it.

_____ **7.** You serve on a committee, and next week the committee members will elect officers. Nominations and elections will be done at the same time. You are interested in being the president, but don't want to nominate yourself and lose.

_____ **8.** You have an employee who regularly passes in assignments late. The assignment you are giving the person now is very important to have done on time.

_____ **9.** You have an idea about how to increase performance of your department. You are not too sure if it will work, or if the employees will like the idea.

_____ **10.** The production person from situation 1 has given you the information you were looking for. She calls a week later to ask you for some information.

Personal Power. *Personal power* is derived from the follower based on the leader's behavior. Charismatic leaders have personal power. Again, followers do have some power over leaders. Followers must consent to the governing influence of managers for the organization to be successful.[26] Unions are often the result of follower dissatisfaction with management behavior and the desire to balance power. Followers in units or departments also have personal power to influence their manager's evaluation, especially when 360-degree feedback is used. Followers can restrict performance, sabotage operations, initiate grievances, hold demonstrations, make complaints to higher managers, and hurt the leader's reputation. Friendship also gives personal power, and personal power can be gained or lost—we will discuss how later.

The two sources of power are relatively independent, yet they have some overlap.[27] For example, a manager can have only position power or both position and personal power, but a nonmanager can have only personal power. The trend is for managers to give more power (empowerment) to employees. Today's effective leaders are relying less on position power and more on personal power to influence others, and they are open to being influenced by followers with personal power. Therefore, as a manager, it is best to have both position power and personal power.

Types of Power and Ways to Increase Your Power

Some of the influencing tactics are related closely to types of power. Seven types of power are illustrated, along with their source of power and influencing tactics, in Figure 9-4. In the late 1950s, French and Raven distinguished five types of power (reward, coercive, legitimate, expert, and referent).[28] Connection (politics) and information power have been added to update the important types of power. In this section we discuss these seven types of power, and explore ways to increase each type. You can acquire power, and you do not have to take power away from others to increase your power.[29] Generally, power is given to those who get results and have good human relations skills.

legitimate power: based on the user's position pwer, given by the organization.

Legitimate Power. *Legitimate power* *is based on the user's position power, given by the organization.* Managers assign work, coaches decide who plays, and teachers award grades. These three positions have formal authority from the organization. Without this authority, they could not influence followers in the same way. Notice that legitimate power and the legitimization influencing tactic are essentially the same. Employees tend to feel that they ought to do what their manager says within the scope of the job. However, recall from Chapter 1 that a person can be a manager but not be a leader, and vice versa.

Appropriate Use of Legitimate Power. Employees agree to comply with management authority in return for the benefits of membership.[30] The use of legitimate power is appropriate when asking people to do something that is within the scope of their job. Most day-to-day manager-employee interactions at EDS, Perot Systems, the Reform party, and other organizations are based on legitimate power.

Increasing Legitimate Power. To increase your legitimate power, follow these guidelines.

1. To have legitimate power, you need to get a management job. This could also be part of your current job, for example, being in charge of some team project with your peers. Work at gaining people's perception that you do have power. Remember that people's perception that you have power gives you power.

Figure 9-4 *Sources and types of power with equivalent influencing tactics.*

Position Power ——————————————→ ←—————————————— **Personal Power**

Legitimate	Reward	Coercive	Connection	Information	Expert	Referent
Legitimization	Exchange	Pressure	Coalitions	No equivalent	No equivalent	Personal appeal

2. Exercise your authority regularly. Follow up to make sure your objective was achieved.

3. Follow the guidelines for the legitimization influencing tactic if your authority is questioned.

4. Back up your authority with rewards and punishment. These are our next two types of power, which are primarily based on having legitimate power.

Reward Power. **Reward power** *is based on the user's ability to influence others with something of value to them.* Notice that the exchange tactic uses rewards. Reward power affects performance expectations and achievement.[31] In a management position, use positive reinforcements to influence behavior, with incentives such as praise, recognition (with pins, badges, hats, or jackets), special assignments or desirable activities, pay raises, bonuses, and promotions. Many organizations, including Kentucky Fried Chicken, have employee-of-the-month awards. Tupperware holds rallies for its salespeople, and almost everyone gets something—ranging from pins to lucrative prizes for top performers. Recall from contingency leadership theory (Chapter 5) that a leader's power is strong or weak based on his or her ability to punish and reward followers. The more power, the more favorable the situation for the leader.

An important part of reward power is having control over resources, such as allocating expense and budget funds. This is especially true for scarce resources. Upper- and middle-level managers usually have more discretion in giving rewards (including scarce resources) than do lower-level managers.[32] Employees at EDS and Perot Systems get a variety of rewards for doing a good job.

Appropriate Use of Reward Power. You can exchange favors as a reward; this is especially important with peers.[33] Let people know what's in it for them. If you have something attractive to others, use it. For example, when Professor Jones is recruiting a student aide, he tells candidates that if they are selected and do a good job, he will recommend them for an MBA fellowship at Suffolk University, where he has connection power. As a result he gets good, qualified help, at minimum wages, while helping both his student aide and his alma mater.

Increasing Reward Power. To increase your reward power, follow these guidelines.

1. Gain and maintain control over evaluating your employees' performance and determining their raises, promotions, and other rewards.

2. Find out what others value, and try to reward people in that way. Using praise can help increase your power. Employees who feel they are appreciated rather than used will give the manager more power.

3. Let people know you control rewards, and state your criteria for giving rewards. However, don't promise more than you can deliver. Reward as promised, and don't use rewards to manipulate or for personal benefit.

4. Follow the guidelines for using the exchange influencing tactic.

reward power: based on the user's ability to influence others with something of value to them.

coercive power: involves punishment and withholding of rewards to influence compliance.

Coercive Power. *The use of* **coercive power** *involves punishment and withholding of rewards to influence compliance.* Notice the similarity in the definitions of coercive power and the pressure influencing tactic. From fear of reprimands, probation, suspension, or dismissal, employees often do as their manager requests. The fear of lost valued outcomes or rewards—such as receiving poor performance evaluations, losing raises and benefits, being assigned to less desirable jobs, and hurting a relationship—employees do as requested. Other examples of coercive power include verbal abuse, humiliation, and ostracism. Group members also use coercive power to enforce norms.

Appropriate Use of Coercive Power. Coercive power is appropriate to use in maintaining discipline and enforcing rules. When employees are not willing to do as requested, coercive power may be the only way to gain compliance. In fact, without it, employees may not take you seriously and ignore your requests. Coercion is effective when applied to a small percentage of followers under conditions considered legitimate by most of them. When leaders use coercion on a large scale against followers, it undermines their authority and creates a hostile opposition that may seek to restrict their power or to remove them from office. Employees tend to resent managers' use of coercive power. There has been a general decline in use of coercion by all types of leaders. So keep your use of coercive power to a minimum by using it only as a last resort.[34]

Increasing Coercive Power. To increase your coercive power, follow these guidelines.

1. Gain authority to use punishment and withhold rewards. However, make sure employees know the rules and penalties, give prior warnings, understand the situation, remain calm and helpful, encourage improvement, use legitimate punishments (withhold rewards) that fit the infraction, and administer punishment in private.

2. Don't make rash threats; do not use coercion to manipulate others or to gain personal benefits.

3. Follow the guidelines for using the pressure influencing tactic.

referent power: based on the user's personal relationship with others.

Referent Power. **Referent power** *is based on the user's personal relationship with others.* Notice that referent power is essentially the same as personal appeal. Power stems primarily from friendship, or the employee's attractiveness to the person using power. The personal feelings of "liking" or the desire to be liked by the leaders also gives referent power. Today's managers are relying more on referent power than position power to get the job done.[35]

Appropriate Use of Referent Power. The use of referent power is particularly appropriate for people with weak, or no, position power, such as with peers. Referent power is needed in self-managed teams because leadership should be shared.

Increasing Referent Power. To increase your referent power, follow these guidelines.

1. Develop your people skills, which are covered in all preceding chapters. Remember that you don't have to be a manager to have referent power.

The better you get along with (good working relationships) more people, the more referent power you will have.

2. Work at your relationship with your manager and peers.   Your relationship with your manager will have a direct effect on your job satisfaction.[36] Gain your manager's confidence in order to get more power. Remember that the success of your manager and peers depends to some extent on you and your performance.

3. Use personal appeals and ingratiation influencing tactics.

Expert Power. *Expert power* is based on the user's skill and knowledge. Being an expert makes other people dependent on you. Employees with expert power have personal power and are often promoted to management positions. People often respect an expert, and the fewer the people who possess an expertise, the more power the individual has. For example, because so few people have the ability to become top athletes like basketball star Michael Jordan, these athletes can command multimillion-dollar contracts. The more people come to you for advice, the greater is your expert power. In the changing global economy, expert power is becoming more important.[37] It's wise to be sure that your expertise does not become unimportant or obsolete.

Appropriate Use of Expert Power.   Managers, particularly at lower levels, are often—but not always—experts within their departments. New managers frequently depend on employees who have expertise in how the organization runs and know how to get things done politically. Thus, followers can have considerable influence over the leader.[38] Expert power is essential to employees who are working with people from other departments and organizations. Because such employees have no direct position power to use, being seen as an expert gives them credibility and power. EDS and Perot Systems obtain clients based on their expertise, which is needed by clients.

Increasing Expert Power.   To increase your expert power, follow these guidelines.

1. To become an expert, take all the training and educational programs your organization provides.

2. Attend meetings of your trade or professional associations, and read their publications (magazines and journals) to keep up with current trends in your field. Write articles to be published. Become an officer in the organization.

3. Keep up with the latest technology. Volunteer to be the first to learn something new.

4. Project a positive self-concept (Chapter 2), let people know about your expertise by developing a reputation for having expertise. You have no expert power unless others perceive that you have an expertise and come to you for advice. You may want to display diplomas, licenses, publications, and awards.

Information Power. *Information power* is based on the user's data desired by others. Information power involves access to vital information and

expert power: based on the user's skill and knowledge.

information power: based on the user's data that is desired by others.

control over its distribution to others.[39] Managers often have access to information that is not available to peers and subordinates. Thus, they have the opportunity to distort information to influence others to meet their objective. Distortion of information includes selective editing to promote only your position, giving a biased interpretation of data, and even presenting false information. Managers also rely on employees for information, so followers sometimes have the opportunity to distort information that influences management decisions. Distortion of information is an ethical issue. Some secretaries have more information and are more helpful in answering questions than the managers they work for.

Appropriate Use of Information Power. An important part of the manager's job is to convey information. Employees often come to managers for information on what to do and how to do it. As a consulting firm, EDS obtains its clients because of the information the company has about how to set up computer information systems for client organizations and help them solve business problems. EDS gives organizational members information power, as information flows freely through informal channels.

Increasing Information Power. To increase your information power, follow these guidelines.

1. Have information flow through you. For example, if customer leads come in to the company and all sales representatives have direct access to them, the sales manager has weak information power. However, if all sales leads go directly to the manager, who then assigns the leads to sales representatives, the manager has strong information power. Having control of information makes it easier to cover up failures and mistakes, and to let others know of your accomplishments, which can also increase expertise.[40]

2. Know what is going on in the organization. Provide service and information to other departments. Serve on committees, because it gives you both information and a chance to increase connection power.

3. Develop a network of information sources, and gather information from them.

connection power: based on the user's relationship with influential people.

Connection Power. *Connection power is based on the user's relationship with influential people.* Notice that coalitions are a form of connection power. Connection power is also a form of politics, the topic of our next major section, but first we discuss how power is acquired and lost. You rely on the use of contacts or friends who can influence the person you are dealing with. The right connections can give power, or at least the perception of having power. If people know you are friendly with people in power, they are more apt to do as you request. For example, if the owner's son has no position power but wants something done, he may gain compliance by making a comment about speaking to his father or mother about the lack of cooperation. When Ross Perot entered politics, he realized how important connection power can be.

Appropriate Use of Connection Power. When you are looking for a job or promotions, connections can help. There is a lot of truth in the statement, "It's not what you know, it's who you know." Connection power can also help you to get resources you need and increased business.

Increasing Connection Power. To increase connection power, follow these guidelines.

1. Expand your network of contacts with important managers who have power.
2. Join the "in crowd" and the "right" associations and clubs. Participating in sports like golf may help you meet influential people.
3. Follow the guidelines for using the coalition influencing tactic. When you want something, identify the people who can help you attain it, make coalitions, and win them over to your side.
4. Get people to know your name. Get all the publicity you can. Have your accomplishments known by the people in power; send them notices.

Research on Power

Research has been conducted to determine whether effective leaders have or use different types of power than ineffective leaders, and to determine how much a leader uses each type of power. Overall, the results suggest that effective leaders rely more on expert and referent power to influence subordinates. The most common reason for compliance by followers is legitimate power, and backing up legitimate power with reward and coercive power is likely to produce results for the leader. Referent power was also shown to result in the strongest commitment by followers to achieve the leader's objective. However, in keeping with contingency leadership theory, effective leaders use a mix of different types of power.[41] Now that you have learned the appropriate use of seven types of power and how to increase your power, keep in mind the importance of using the appropriate type of power for the situation.

Acquiring and Losing Power

Power can change over time. There are two major theories of how power is acquired, maintained, or lost in organizations: social exchange theory (individual power level of analysis) and strategic contingencies theory (organizational-unit power level of analysis). Personal power is more easily gained and lost than position power. Having strong power can lead to temptation to act in ways that misuse power and may eventually lead to failure.[42] Although President Clinton was impeached, he did keep his job; but he lost personal power because his integrity was damaged for many people.

Social Exchange Theory. *Social exchange theory* explains how power is gained and lost as reciprocal influence processes occur over time between leaders and followers in small groups.[43] Social interaction is an exchange of benefits or favors, which include material benefits such as expression of approval, respect, esteem, and affection. Friendship is a social exchange, and some people place a higher value on the friendships they have at work

Applying the Concept 9-2

Using Power

Identify the relevant type of power to use in each situation. Write the appropriate letter in the blank before each item.

a. coercive
b. connection
c. reward or legitimate
d. referent
e. information or expert

_____ **1.** One of your best workers needs little direction from you. However, recently her performance has slumped. You're quite sure that a personal problem is affecting her work.

_____ **2.** You want a new personal computer to help you do a better job. PCs are allocated by a committee, which is very political in nature.

_____ **3.** One of your best workers wants a promotion. He has talked to you about getting ahead and has asked you to help prepare him for when the opportunity comes.

_____ **4.** One of your worst employees has ignored one of your directives again.

_____ **5.** An employee who needs some direction and encouragement from you to maintain production is not working to standard today. As occasionally happens, she claims that she does not feel well but cannot afford to take time off. You have to get an important customer order shipped today.

than on the work itself. Each member of a small work group has a status position. Members with expertise and loyalty to the group tend to have higher-level status, which can change over time. Group members especially watch the manager, because they each have expectations of the leader. If the leader meets follower expectations, power is acquired and maintained. If not, the leader loses status and expert power with followers, and they may undermine the leader's legitimate authority as well.[44] However, we cannot offer you any guidelines for gaining power or exercising it effectively, because social exchange theory provides none.

Strategic Contingencies Theory. *Strategic contingencies theory* explains how organizational units gain and lose power over influencing strategic decisions for the organization.[45] Power of organizational units depends on three things: (1) expertise in coping with important problems, (2) central-ity of the unit within the work flow, and (3) the extent to which the unit expertise is unique rather than substitutable. The changing environment, including technology and competitors, creates problems for the organization. The unit that can best help the organization adapt to the environment tends to get power in strategic decisions. The more powerful unit often gets one of its members selected as the CEO, which helps it to perpetuate its strategic power. However, the strategic contingencies theory fails to explain how units sometimes keep their power when the unit's expertise is no longer critical to the organization. This is where our next topic, politics, comes in.

ORGANIZATIONAL POLITICS

You need to be able to navigate through tricky organizational politics, because politics are essential to the very fabric of organizational life. Politics are necessary to achieve organizational objectives.[46] In this section we discuss the nature of politics, political behavior, and guidelines to develop political skills. But first, determine your own use of political behavior, complete Self-Assessment Exercise 9-2.

Self-Assessment Exercise 9-2

Use of Political Behavior

Select the response that best describes your actual or planned use of the following behavior on the job. Place a number from 1 to 5 on the line before each statement.

1 — 2 — 3 — 4 — 5
Rarely   *Occasionally*   *Usually*

_____ 1. I use my personal contacts to get a job and promotions.

_____ 2. I try to find out what is going on in all the organizational departments.

_____ 3. I dress the same way as the people in power and take on the same interests (watch or play sports, join the same clubs, and so forth).

_____ 4. I purposely seek contacts and network with higher-level managers.

_____ 5. If upper management offered me a raise and promotion requiring me to move to a new location, I'd say yes even if I did not want to move.

_____ 6. I get along with everyone, even those considered to be difficult to get along with.

_____ 7. I try to make people feel important by complimenting them.

_____ 8. I do favors for others and use their favors in return, and I thank people and send them thank-you notes.

_____ 9. I work at developing a good working relationship with my manager.

_____ 10. I ask my manager and other people for their advice.

_____ 11. When a person opposes me, I still work to maintain a positive working relationship with that person.

_____ 12. I'm courteous, pleasant, and positive with others.

_____ 13. When my manager makes a mistake, I never publicly point out the error.

_____ 14. I am more cooperative (I compromise) than competitive (I seek to get my own way).

_____ 15. I tell the truth.

_____ 16. I avoid saying negative things about my manager and others behind their back.

_____ 17. I work at getting people to know me by name and face by continually introducing myself.

_____ 18. I ask some satisfied customers and people who know my work to let my manager know how good a job I'm doing.

_____ 19. I try to win contests and get prizes, pins, and other awards.

_____ 20. I send notices of my accomplishments to higher-level managers and company newsletters.

To determine your overall political behavior, add the 20 numbers you selected as your answers. The number will range from 20 to 100. The higher your score, the more political behavior you use. Place your score here _____ and on the continuum below.

20 — 30 — 40 — 50 — 60 — 70 — 80 — 90 — 100
Nonpolitical   *Political*

To determine your use of political behavior in four areas, add the numbers for the following questions and divide by the number of questions to get the average score in each area.

A. *Learning the organizational culture and power players*

Questions 1–5 total: _____ divided by 5 = _____

B. *Developing good working relationships, especially with your boss*

Questions 6–12 total: _____ divided by 7 = _____

C. *Being a loyal, honest team player*

Questions 13–16 total: _____ divided by 4 = _____

D. *Gaining recognition*

Questions 17–20 total _____ divided by 4 = _____

The higher the average score of items A–D, the more you use this type of political behavior. Do you tend to use them all equally, or do you use some more than others?

The Nature of Organizational Politics

politics: the process of gaining and using power.

Because political skills are a part of power, you need to understand politics in terms of power. Managers use their existing position power and politics to increase their power.[47] *Politics is the process of gaining and using power.* Politics is a reality of organizational life. All the current business trends such as globalization, diversity, total quality management, teams, and so on have not eliminated politics. The amount and importance of politics varies from organization to organization. However, larger organizations tend to be more political; and the higher the level of management, the more important politics becomes. A survey of executives revealed that 20 percent of their time is spent on politics.[48]

Politics is a Medium of Exchange. Like power, politics often has a negative connotation due to people who abuse political power. A positive way to view politics is to realize that it is simply a medium of exchange. Like money, politics in and of itself is inherently neither good nor bad.[49] Politics is simply a means of getting what we want. In our economy, money is the medium of exchange (tangible currency); in an organization, politics is the medium of exchange (political behavior). Leaders in organizations use political behavior, our next topic.

Political Behavior

Politics and support are related to job satisfaction, commitment, and turnover intentions.[50] Thus, how well you play politics directly affects you in these areas. Networking, reciprocity, and coalitions are common organizational political behaviors.

networking: the process of developing relationships for the purpose of socializing and politicking.

Networking. *Networking is the process of developing relationships for the purpose of socializing and politicking.* The activities managers engage in and the time spent on each area have been studied. The activities have been categorized into four areas: traditional management, communication, human resource management, and networking. Of these four activities, networking has the most relative contribution to successful management advancement. Successful managers spend around twice as much time networking than average managers, so reach out to establish an ongoing network of contacts.[51]

Keys to Networking Success. Follow these seven guidelines to networking.[52]

1. *Become a participant.* Go where the action is. Your network should include people within and outside your organization. Again, join committees, trade, or professional associations—and attend meetings.

2. *Develop a plan.* Don't network haphazardly. Decide who you want to meet, and develop a plan for doing so. But you also have to be realistic. If you are a new employee in a large organization, don't start with the president.

3. *Do your homework.* As part of your plan, learn about the person you want to meet. When you meet them, say something insightful to them that shows you are aware of their achievements; the more specific, the better.

4. *Be generous in giving.* Remember to answer the usually unasked question, "What's in it for me?" When developing your plan, don't focus on what the other person can do for you. Try to come up with ideas about what you can do for them.

5. *Make the first move.* Don't wait for people to come to you. Most people consider it a compliment when someone seeks them out, so walk right up and introduce yourself. Make that insightful comment, and during the communication, say what you can do for the other person (or call or write first). Try not to sound like a salesperson during these interactions.

6. *Nurture relationships with your contact.* Personal visits and phone calls are good for close contacts, but writing is great for more distant contacts. E-mail makes the job quick and easy, but a handwritten note is more personal.

7. *Don't give up easily.* Go to reasonable lengths to meet the people who can be beneficial to your network.

Reciprocity. Using **reciprocity** involves *creating obligations and developing alliances, and using them to accomplish objectives.* Notice that the exchange influencing tactic is similar to reciprocity. When people do something for you, you incur an obligation that they may expect to be repaid. When you do something for people, you create a debt that you may be able to collect at a later date when you need a favor. You should work at developing a network of alliances that you can call on for help in meeting your objectives.

reciprocity: creating obligations and developing alliances, and using them to accomplish objectives.

Coalitions. Using coalitions as an influencing tactic is political behavior. Each party helps the others get what they want.[53] Reciprocity is used to achieve ongoing objectives, whereas coalitions are developed for achieving a specific objective. A political tactic when developing coalitions is to use co-optation. *Co-optation* is the process of getting a person whose support you need to join your coalition rather than compete. Management has been known to make strong union leaders managers. Presidential candidates have taken competitors as their vice presidential running mates.

Except for networking, we have not listed appropriate use of political behavior and how to increase your political skills with each type of political behavior, because all three may be used at the same time. As you'll see, our upcoming guidelines can be used with any of the three political behaviors. Before considering how to develop political skills, review Figure 9-5 for a list of political behaviors and guidelines.

Figure 9-5 *Political behavior and guidelines for developing political skills.*

Reciprocity | Guidelines | Coalitions

- Learn the organization culture and power players.
- Develop good working realationships, especially with your manager.
- Be a loyal, honest team player.
- Gain recognition.

Networking

Guidelines for Developing Political Skills

People who make it to the top are those who understand the reward system, power relationships, and how to play organizational politics.[54] If you want to climb the corporate ladder, or at least avoid getting thrown off it, you should develop your political skills. Successfully implementing the behavior guidelines presented here can result in increased political skills. However, if you don't agree with any political behavior, don't use it. You do not have to use all of the political behaviors to be successful. Learn what it takes in the organization where you work as you follow the guidelines.

Learn the Organizational Culture and Power Players. Develop your connection power through politicking. It is natural, especially for young people, to take a purely rational approach to a job without considering politics. But many business decisions are not very rational; they are based on power and politics.[55] For example, a common reason for choosing the location of a new business facility is simply because it's convenient to where the person in power wants to live.

Learn the cultural (Chapter 11) shared values and beliefs, and how business and politics operate where you work. Learn to read between the lines. For example, a manager asked a new employee to select one of two project teams to work on. The employee selected one and told the manager his selection. The manager asked him to rethink the decision. In talking to others, the new employee found out that the manager of the team he wanted to join was disliked by the new CEO. No matter how good the project or how well the team did, the team was doomed to fail, and so would the employee.

In all organizations, there are some powerful key players. Your manager is a key player to you. Don't just find out who the managers are; gain an understanding of what makes each of them tick. By understanding them, you can tailor the presentation of your ideas and style to fit each person's needs. For example, some managers want to see detailed financial numbers and statistics, while others don't. Some managers expect you to continually follow up with them, while others will think you are bugging them.

Review Self-Assessment Exercise 9-2, questions 1–5; you can use these tactics to increase your political skills. Network with power players. Try to do favors for power players. When developing coalitions, get key players on your side. When selecting a mentor, try to get one who is good at organizational politics. Your mentor can help you learn how to play politics. Also try to observe people who are good at politics, and copy their behavior. Ross Perot was successful—but too heavy-handed—in playing politics at General Motors, so they got rid of him.

Develop Good Working Relationships, Especially with Your Manager. The ability to work well with others is critical to your career success, and it's an important foundation of politics.[56] The more people like and respect you, the more power you will gain. Good human relations give you personal power and a basis for using the influencing tactic of personal appeal. You've already learned about relationships with higher-level managers and with peers who have influence and power, so in this section we focus on the relationship with your manager.

Politics and support are related to supervisor ratings.[57] If you want to get ahead, you need to have a good working relationship with your manager. Your manager usually gives you the formal performance appraisals, which are the primary bases for raises and promotions. Fair or not, many evaluations are influenced by the manager's relationship with the employee. If your manager likes you, you have a better chance of getting a good review, raises, and promotions. Also, most important decisions are made outside of formal meetings. Leaders consult others outside of a meeting (influencing tactic) when making decisions. You want to be one of the in-group that can influence the manager.

Supervisors also give higher ratings to employees who share their goals (goal congruence) and priorities than they give to those who don't.[58] Thus, get to know what your manager expects from you, and do it. Beat or at least meet deadlines, and don't miss them. It's common to put off telling the manager bad news. But if you are having a job problem, don't put off letting your manager know about it. Most managers, and peers, like to be asked for advice. If you are behind schedule to meet an important deadline and your manager finds out about it from others, it is embarrassing, especially if your manager finds out from his or her manager. Also avoid showing up your manager in public, such as during a meeting. If you do, don't be surprised if the next time you open your mouth at a meeting, your manager embarrasses you.

If you cannot get along with your manager and are in conflict, avoid going to his or her manager to resolve the conflict. There are two dangers with going over the manager's head. First, chances are your manager has a good working relationship with his or her manager, who will side with them. Even if the higher-level manager agrees with you, you will most likely hurt your relationship with your manager. He or she may consciously or unconsciously take some form of retaliation, such as giving you a lower performance review, which can hurt you in the long run. You need all the friends and allies you can get, so try to resolve important conflicts; use the conflict model (Chapter 4) with everyone you work with.

Review Self-Assessment Exercise 9-2, questions 6–12; you can use these tactics to increase your political skills. Include your manager in your network, try to do favors for your manager, and include your manager in your coalitions. Use the ingratiation tactic with everyone. When was the last time you gave anyone, including your manager, a compliment? When was the last time you sent a thank-you or congratulations note? Ross Perot was ultimately not successful in playing politics at General Motors, because he did not develop good relationships, he publicly criticized GM managers, he did not resolve conflicts, and he attempted to go over his manager's head. Perot did similar things within his Reform party. Are you surprised that GM bought him out, and that members of the Reform party split from him?

Be a Loyal, Honest Team Player.   Ethical behavior is important in organizational politics.[59] The Indian leader Mahatma Gandhi called business without morality and politics without principle a sin. Some backstabbing gossips may get short-term benefits from such behavior, but in the long run they are generally unsuccessful because others gun them down in return. In any organization you must earn others' respect, confidence, and trust. Once you are caught in a lie, it's difficult to regain trust. There are very few, if any, jobs in which organizational objectives can be achieved without the support of a group or team of individuals. Even lone-wolf salespeople are subject to the systems effect, and they need the help of production to make the product, transportation to deliver it, and service to maintain it. The trend is toward teamwork, so if you're not a team player, work at it.

Review Self-Assessment Exercise 9-2, questions 13–16; you can use these tactics to increase your political skills. Be a loyal, honest team player in your network, in your reciprocity, and with your coalition members. Members of the American Reform party accused Ross Perot of making false, negative public statements about the party split and about the new party. Perot has also been accused of being a team player only when he gets his own way. The power-based personality of Perot is illustrated in his motto, which he quotes from Winston Churchill, "Never give in. Never." This belief shows Perot's unwillingness to compromise for the team. When one of his business facilities in California voted to organize a union, Perot shut the facility down rather than tolerate a union.

Gain Recognition.   Doing a great job does not help you to get ahead in an organization if no one knows about it, or who you are. Recognition and knowing the power players go hand in hand; you want the power players to know who you are and what you can do. You want people higher in the organization to know your expertise and the contributions you are making to the organization.

Review Self-Assessment Exercise 9-2, questions 17–20; you can use these tactics to increase your political skills. Let people in your network and coalitions, and people you reciprocate with, know of your accomplishments. You can also serve on committees and try to become an officer, which gives you name recognition. A committee job many people tend to avoid is that of secretary. But when the meeting minutes are sent to higher management and throughout the organization with your name on it as secretary, you increase your name recognition. Ross Perot has been recognized by different organizations for his contributions. Read his biography at his personal website (**www.perot.org**) for details.

NEGOTIATION

In this section, we focus on getting what you want through negotiation. Influence tactics, power, and politics can all be used during the negotiation process. Also recall (Chapter 4) that negotiation is one of the five conflict management styles. **Negotiating** *is a process in which two or more parties are in conflict and attempt to come to an agreement.*

negotiating: a process in which two or more parties are in conflict and attempt to come to an agreement.

Negotiating

At certain times, negotiations are appropriate, such as when conducting management-union collective bargaining, buying and selling goods and services, accepting a new job compensation offer, or getting a raise—all situations without a fixed price or deal. If there's a set, take-it-or-leave-it deal, there is no negotiation. For example, in almost all U.S. retail stores, you must buy the product for the price listed; you don't negotiate price. Some car dealers have also stopped negotiating, in favor of a set sticker price.

All Parties Should Believe They Got a Good Deal.

Negotiation is often a zero-sum game in which one party's gain is the other party's loss. For example, every dollar less that you pay for a car is your gain and the seller's loss. Therefore, you don't have a true collaboration (win-win situation). Negotiating is about getting what you want, but at the same time it is about developing ongoing relationships. To get what you want, you have to sell your ideas and convince the other party to give you what you want. However, negotiation should be viewed by all parties as an opportunity for everyone to win some, rather than as a win-lose situation. In other words, all parties should believe they got a good deal.[60] If union employees believe they lost and management won, employees may experience job dissatisfaction, resulting in lower performance in the long run. If customers believe they got a bad deal, they may not give repeat business.

Negotiation Skills Can Be Developed.
Not everyone is born a great negotiator. In fact, most people don't have a clue about how to get what they want, other than making demands and digging in their heels. Taking the time to learn how to negotiate before entering a deal is the best way to arrive at a successful conclusion. Although negotiators are not born, they can be made.[61] Following the steps in the negotiation process can help you develop your negotiation skills.

Applying the Concept 9-3

Political Behavior

Identify the behavior in each situation as effective or ineffective political behavior. Write the appropriate letter in the blank before each item.

a. effective   b. ineffective

____ **1.** Julio is taking golf lessons so he can join the Saturday golf group, which includes some higher-level managers.

____ **2.** Paul tells his manager's manger about mistakes his manager makes.

____ **3.** Sally avoids spending time socializing, so that she can be more productive on the job.

____ **4.** John sent a very positive performance report to three higher-level managers to whom he does not report. They did not request copies.

____ **5.** Carlos has to drop off a daily report by noon. He delivers the report at around 10:00 A.M. on Tuesday and Thursday, so that he can run into some higher-level managers who meet at that time near the office where the report goes. On the other days, Carlos drops the report off at around noon on his way to lunch.

The Negotiation Process

The negotiation process has three, and possibly four, steps: plan, negotiations, possibly a postponement, and an agreement or no agreement. These steps are summarized in Model 9-1 and discussed in this section. Like the other models in this book, Model 9-1 is meant to give you step-by-step guidelines. However, in making it apply to varying types of negotiation, you may have to make slight adjustments.

Plan. Success or failure in negotiating is often based on preparation.[62] Be clear about what it is you are negotiating over. Is it price, options, delivery time, sales quantity, or all four? Planning has four steps:

step 1 ▪ Research the other party(s). As discussed, know the key power players. Try to find out what the other parties want, and what they will and will not be willing to give up, before you negotiate. Find out their personality traits and negotiation style by networking with people who have negotiated with the other party before. The more you know about the other party, the better your chances of getting an agreement. If possible, establish a personal relationship before the negotiation.[63] If you have experience working with the other party (for example, your manager or a potential customer), what worked and did not work in the past? How can you use that experience in your negotiations (in getting a raise or making a sale)?

step 2 ▪ Set objectives. Based on your research, what can you expect? You have to identify the one thing you must come away with.[64] Set a lower limit, a target objective, and an opening objective. In many negotiations the objective will be a price, but it could be working conditions, longer vacation, job security, and so on. (a) Set a specific lower limit and be willing to walk away; do not come to an agreement unless you get it. You need to be willing to walk away from a bad deal.[65] (b) Set a target objective of what you believe is a fair deal. (c) Set an opening objective offer that is higher than you expect; you might get it. Remember that the other

Model 9-1 *The negotiation process.*

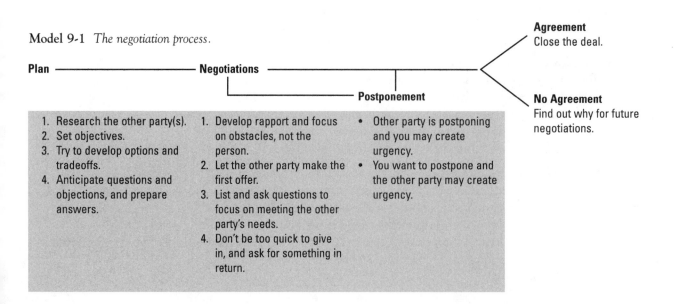

party is probably also setting three objectives. So don't view their opening offer as final. The key to successful negotiations is for all parties to get between their minimum and target objective. This creates a win-win situation.

step 3 ▪ Try to develop options and tradeoffs. In purchasing something as well as in looking for a job, if you have multiple sellers and job offers, you are in a stronger power position to get your target price. It is common practice to quote other offers and to ask if the other party can beat them.

If you have to give up something, or cannot get exactly what you want, be prepared to ask for something else in return. If you cannot get the size raise you want, maybe you can get more days off, more in your retirement account, a nicer office, an assistant, and so on. When Eastern Airlines was having financial difficulty, it asked employees to take a pay cut. Rather than simply accept a cut, they asked for a tradeoff and got company stock. Based on your research, what tradeoffs do you expect from the other party?

step 4 ▪ Anticipate questions and objections, and prepare answers. The other party may want to know why you are selling something, looking for a job, how the product or service works, or what are the features and benefits. You need to be prepared to answer the unasked question, "what's in it for me?" Don't focus on what you want, but on how your deal will benefit the other party. Talk in *you* and *we*, not *I* terms, unless you are telling others what you will do for them.

There is a good chance that you will face some objection—reasons why the negotiations will not result in agreement or sale. When a union asks for a raise, management typically says the organization can't afford it. However, the union has done its research and quotes the specific profits for a set period of time to overcome the objection. Unfortunately for you, not everyone comes out and tells you their real objections. So you need to listen and ask questions to find out what is preventing the agreement.

You need to fully understand your product or deal, and project positive self-esteem, enthusiasm, and confidence. If the other party does not trust you, and believes the deal is not a good one, you will not reach an agreement. To use our examples, during the selection process, you must convince the manager that you can do the job, or that your product will benefit the customer. When you are in sales, you should have some closing-the-sale statements prepared, such as, "Will you take the white one or the blue one?"

Negotiations. After you have planned, you are now ready to negotiate the deal. Face-to-face negotiations are generally preferred because you can see the other person's nonverbal behavior (Chapter 4) and better understand objections. However, telephone and written negotiations work too. Again, know the other party's preference.

step 1 ▪ Develop rapport and focus on obstacles, not the person. Smile and call the other party by name as you greet them. A smile tells people you like them, are interested in them, and enjoy them.[66] Open with some small talk, like the weather. Deciding on how much time to wait until you get down to business depends on the other party's style. Some people like to get right down to business; others, like the Japanese, want to get to know you first. However, you want the other party to make the first offer, so don't wait too long or you may lose your chance.

"Focus on the obstacle, not the person" means never to attack the other's personality or put others down with negative statements like, "You are being unfair to ask for such a price cut." If you do so, the other party will become defensive, you may end up arguing, and it will be harder to reach an agreement. So even if the other person starts it, refuse to fight on a name-calling level.[67] Make statements like, "You think my price is too high?" Not saying negative things about others includes your competitors; just state your competitive advantage in a positive way. People look for four things: inclusion, control, safety, and respect. Most people, if they perceive that you are trying to push them into something, threaten them in some way, or belittle them, will not trust you and make an agreement.

step 2 ▪ Let the other party make the first offer. This gives you the advantage, because if the other party offers you more than your target objective, you can close the agreement. For example, if you are expecting to be paid $25,000 a year (your target objective) and the other party offers you $30,000, are you going to reject it? On the other hand, if you are offered $20,000 you can realize that it may be low and work at increasing the compensation. Ask questions like, "What is the salary range?" or "What do you expect to pay for a such a fine product?"

Try to avoid negotiating simply on price.[68] When others pressure you to make the first offer with a common question like, "Give us your best price, and we'll tell you whether we'll take it," try asking them a question such as, "What do you expect to pay?" or "What is a reasonable price?" When this does not work, say something like, "Our usual (or list) price is *xxx*. However, if you make me a proposal, I'll see what I can do for you."

If things go well during steps 1 and 2, you may skip to closing the agreement. If you are not ready to agree, proceed to the next step or two.

step 3 ▪ Listen and ask questions to focus on meeting the other party's needs. Create opportunity for the other party to disclose reservations and objections. When you speak you give out information, but when you ask questions and listen, you receive information that will help you to overcome the other party's objections. If you go on and on about the features you have to offer, without finding out what features the other party is really interested in, you may be killing the deal. Ask questions such as, "Is the price out of the ballpark?" or "Is it fast enough for you?" or "Is any feature you wanted missing?" If the objection is a "want" criteria, such as two years of work experience and you have only one, play up the features you know they want and that you do have, and you may reach an agreement.[69] If the objection is something you cannot meet, at least you found out and don't waste time chasing a deal that will not happen. However, be sure the objection is really a "must" criteria: What if the employer gets no applicants with two year's experience and you apply? He or she may offer you the job.

step 4 ▪ Don't be too quick to give in, and ask for something in return. Those who ask for more get more. Don't give up whatever it takes to get the agreement. If your competitive advantage is service, and during negotiation you quickly give in for a lower price, you lose all the value in a minute. You want to satisfy the other party without giving up too much during the negotiation.[70] Remember not to go below your minimum objective. If it is realistic, be prepared to walk away. When you are not getting what you want, having other planned options can help give you bargaining power. If you do walk away, you may be called back; and if not, you may be able to come back for the same low price—but not always. If the other party knows you are desperate, or just weak and will accept a low agreement, they will likely take advantage of you. Have you ever seen a sign on a product saying, "must sell—need cash?" What type of price do you think that seller gets? You also need to avoid being intimidated by comments such as this said in a loud voice: "Are you kidding me, that's too much." Many people will quickly drop the price, but you don't have to let it happen.

However, when you are dealing with a complex deal, such as a management-union contract negotiation with tradeoffs, be willing to be the first to make a concession. The other party tends to feel obligated, and then you can come back with a counter-tradeoff that is larger than the one you gave up.

Avoid giving unilateral concessions. Recall your planned tradeoffs. If the other party asks for a lower price, ask for a concession such as a large-volume sale to get it, or a longer delivery time, a less popular color, and so on. You need to send the message that you don't just give things away.[71]

Postponement.   When there doesn't seem to be any progress, it may be wise to postpone the negotiations.[72]

Other Party Is Postponing, and You May Create Urgency.   The other party says, "I'll get back to you." When you are not getting what you want, you may try to create urgency. For example, "This product is on sale, and the sale ends today." However, honesty is the best policy. The primary reason people will negotiate with you is that they trust and respect you. Establishing a relationship of trust is the necessary first step in closing a deal. Honesty and integrity are the most important assets a negotiator can possess.[73] If you do have other options, you can use them to create urgency, such as saying, "I have another job offer pending; when will you let me know if you want to offer me the job?"

But what if urgency does not apply—or does not work—and the other party says, "I'll think about it?" You might say, "That's a good idea." Then at least review the major features the other party liked about your proposed deal and ask if it meets their needs. The other party may decide to come to an agreement or sale.[74] If not, and they don't tell you when they will get back to you, ask, for example, "When can I expect to hear if I got the job?" Try to pin the other party down for a specific time; tell the person that if you don't hear from them by then, you will call them. If you are really interested, follow up with a letter (mail, e-mail, or fax) of thanks for their time, and again highlight the features you think they liked. If you forgot to include any specific points during the negotiation, add them in the letter.

One thing to remember when the other party becomes resistant to making the agreement is that the hard sell will not work. Take off the pressure.[75] Ask something like, "Where do you want to go from here?" (to a client). If you press for an answer, it may be no agreement; however, if you wait you may have a better chance. To your manager, you might say, "Why don't we think about it and discuss it some more later?" (then pick an advantageous time to meet with your manager).

You also need to learn to read between the lines, especially when working with people from different cultures. Some people will not come right out and tell you there is no deal. For example, it is common for the Japanese to say something like, "It will be difficult to do business." Americans tend to think this means they can keep trying to close the deal; however, the Japanese businessperson actually means stop trying, but will not say so directly because it is impolite.

You Want to Postpone, and the Other Party May Create Urgency. If you are not satisfied with the deal, or want to shop around, tell the other party you want to think about it. You may also need to check with your manager, or someone else, which simply may be for advice, before you can finalize the deal.[76] If the other party is creating urgency, be sure it really is urgent. In many cases, you can get the same deal at a later date; don't be pressured into making a deal you are not satisfied with or may regret later. If you do want to postpone, give the other party a specific time that you will get back to them, and do so with more prepared negotiations or simply to tell them you cannot make an agreement.

Agreement. Once the agreement has been made, restate it and/or put it in writing when appropriate. It is common to follow up an agreement with a letter of thanks, restating the agreement to ensure the other parties have not changed their mind about what they agreed to. Also, after the deal is made, stop selling it. Change the subject to a personal one and/or leave, depending on the other person's preferred negotiations. If they want a personal relationship, stick around; if not, leave.

No Agreement. Rejection, refusal, and failure happen to us all, even the superstars. The difference between the also-rans and the superstars lies in how they respond to the failure.[77] The successful people keep trying, learn from their mistakes, and continue to work hard; failures usually don't persevere. If you cannot come to an agreement, analyze the situation and try to determine where you went wrong, so that you can improve in the future. You may also ask the other party for advice, such as, "I realize I did not get the job; thanks for your time. Can you offer me any suggestions for improving my resume and interview skills, or other ideas to help me to get a job in this field?"

Ross Perot is viewed as a tough negotiator who uses his power to get what he wants. Few will not agree that he is a successful businessperson. However, you don't have to be like Ross Perot, or anyone else. You need to be you, and to be the best that you can be. In this chapter we have covered many ideas that can help you to get what you want by using influencing tactics, power, politics, and negotiation.

10 Organizational Leadership and Change

Kenneth Chenault, the first African American in line to become the next CEO of American Express, has said, "What I want to do is make a difference." Currently chief operating officer of American Express—a company that ranks 65th on the Fortune 500 list, has 70,000 employees worldwide, and earns $16.2 billion in annual revenues—Kenneth Chenault is set to become the company's new chairman and chief executive officer by the year 2004. It will be historic if it happens, because Chenault will be the first African American to lead a Fortune 500 company. Chenault has been on the fast track since joining American Express in 1981 as the director of strategic planning. The qualities that have enabled Chenault to come this far have less to do with affirmative action and more to do with his drive, ambition, confidence, and vision. In many ways, those who know him say he is a master strategist, visionary, and charismatic leader who has what it takes to lead American Express in the 21st century.

Kenneth Chenault clearly understands his company's mission statement and articulates it very well. Asked to talk about the future of American Express, Chenault said, "Against our vision of being the world's most respected service brand, I'd like to be one of the most admired companies in the world"[1] He stresses that he wants American Express to be one of the fastest-growing companies in the world, but not at any cost. To hear Mr. Chenault being described by his friends and coworkers removes any doubt that they consider him a charismatic leader.

When Harvey Golub, current chairman and CEO of American Express, officially confirmed Chenault as his choice for successor, it is said that employees cheered. There was a feeling of relief and confidence that the future of the company was in good hands. It is reported that Chenault's office was flooded with congratulatory e-mails and messages from corporate and political leaders. He has been described as having unmatchable "people power." A warm, caring individual, he knows how to inspire and motivate people through respect rather than fear, how to criticize without humiliating, and how to get people to do what they thought was impossible.

Mitch Kurz, President of Y & R Advertising, describes him as the most human of all chief executives with whom he has worked. "He has extraordinary listening skills; he actively wants to hear your opinions. A senior executive can spend 15 minutes with Ken and be motivated for the next month without any more contact. Ken engenders a kind of loyalty which money can't buy." Chenault, according to Kurz, is one of the few leaders who can make the painful bearable. Kurz explains that when American Express had to reduce company expenses by $1.4 billion, which included letting 12,000 people go between 1991 and 1994, Chenault was chosen for the job. He would talk to the employees and share their pain, but convince them that the cuts were necessary and unavoidable. Said Chenault, terminating employees is very difficult work if you have a conscience. Those who know him believe he surely has a conscience.

If Chenault has a weakness, some might say it is his tendency to make himself too accountable. According to David Kenny, a former employee of American Express, "Ken will share the credit when it goes well, but when it doesn't he takes it on himself." In his push to do the best, Chenault doesn't stop long enough to be satisfied. "He declares victory for an hour and then he's off to how to make it better," Kenny said. "He really wants things to always be perfect. It's propelled him to excellence."

Concluding an interview session with *Ebony* magazine, Chenault said all he wants to do is to make a difference. Beyond the corporate board, Chenault sees his role as that of public service to society. He is a true transformational leader who believes that his career has offered him a platform and opportunity to bring about fundamental change.[2] Kenneth Chenault is a multi-talented individual. He exhibits all the traits of a charismatic, transformational, and strategic leader—all key topics to be discussed in this chapter.

■ *Go to the Internet:* For more information on Kenneth Chenault and American Express, Inc., and to update the information provided in this case, do a name search on the Internet and visit the American Express website at **www.americanexpress.com**.

The term *charismatic leadership* is sometimes considered synonymous with transformational and/or strategic leadership and thus used interchangeably by some writers. In this chapter we discuss major theories and research findings on charismatic, transformational, and strategic leadership and describe the contributions of each toward organizational success. Distinguishing characteristics and similarities between these three constructs of leadership are also discussed. From a different perspective of leadership, we then explore the topic of stewardship and servant leadership, which is a shift in leadership toward serving the followers that many view as a model for successful leadership in any field or profession. We conclude by examining the concept of change, described by some as the most important and difficult leadership responsibility in today's dynamic business environment. We conclude the chapter by examining the concept of change, described by some as the most important and difficult leadership responsibility in today's dynamic business environment.

CHARISMATIC LEADERSHIP

The Greek word *charisma* means "divinely inspired gift." Like the term *leadership* itself, charisma has been defined from various organizational perspectives by researchers studying political leadership, social movements, and religious cults. Nevertheless, there is enough consistency among these definitions to create a unifying theme. In this section, we examine Max Weber's early conceptualization of charismatic leadership and its influence on later theories, the characteristics of charismatic leadership, the question of whether charismatic qualities can be acquired, the positive and negative aspects of charisma, and finally, the implications of charismatic leadership for organizational success.

Weber's Conceptualization of Charismatic Leadership

Of the early theories of charismatic leadership, probably the single most important contribution was written by the German sociologist Max Weber. In 1947, Weber used the term *charisma* to explain a form of influence based not on traditional or legal-rational authority systems, but rather on follower perceptions that the leader is endowed with the gift of divine inspiration or supernatural qualities.[3] Charisma has been called "a fire that ignites followers' energy and commitment, producing results above and beyond the call of duty."[4] Therefore, **charisma** is defined as *the process of influencing major changes in the attitudes and assumptions of organization members, and building commitment for the organization's objectives*.[5] Charismatic leaders are thought to possess exceptional qualities and to inspire and motivate people to do more than they would under normal circumstances. Charismatic leaders are more likely to emerge as leaders during times of great social crisis, and they are instrumental in directing society's attention to the problems it faces and to a radical vision that provides a solution to the crisis.

charisma: the process of influencing major changes in the attitudes and assumptions of organization members, and building commitment for the organization's objectives.

Locus of Charismatic Leadership

Over the years, scholars from different fields have commented on Weber's conceptualization of charismatic leadership. Probably the biggest controversy concerns the locus of charismatic leadership. Is charisma primarily the result of (1) the situation or social climate facing the leader, (2) the leader's extraordinary qualities, or (3) an interaction of the situation and the leader's qualities? Proponents of the view that charismatic leadership could not take place unless the society was in a crisis argue that before an individual with extraordinary qualities would be perceived as a charismatic leader, the social situation must be such that followers would recognize the need for the leader's qualities.[6] Proponents of this view would argue that neither Martin Luther King, Jr., nor Gandhi would have emerged as charismatic leaders to lead their followers without the prevailing social crisis in their respective countries.

Others have argued that charismatic leadership is primarily the result of leader attributes, not the situation alone. These attributes include a strong sense of vision, exceptional communication skills, trustworthiness, high self-confidence and intelligence, and high energy and action orientation. Proponents of this view would argue that Martin Luther King, Jr., and Gandhi possessed these qualities and without them, would never have emerged as leaders of their respective followers, regardless of the situation.[7]

Finally, there are those who believe that charismatic leadership does not depend on the leader's qualities or the presence of a crisis alone, but rather that it is an interactional concept. There is increasing acceptance of this view. Most theorists now view charisma as the result of follower perceptions and reactions, influenced not only by actual leader characteristics and behavior but also by the context of the situation.[8]

Characteristics of Charismatic Leaders

A number of studies have identified characteristics that differentiate between charismatic and uncharismatic leaders and have described the behaviors that help charismatic leaders achieve remarkable results. These characteristics are attributions by followers based on several types of leader behaviors. These behaviors are not assumed to be present to the same extent in every leader. Attributional theorists have thus used these behaviors as distinguishing characteristics for charismatic and uncharismatic leaders.[9] Many of these characteristics also apply to transformational leaders, because charisma is a key component of transformational leadership. Transformational leadership is covered in the next section of this chapter. Figure 10-1 lists some distinguishing characteristics of charismatic leaders, followed by an explanation of each.

a. **Visionary**
b. **Superb communication skills**
c. **Self-confidence and moral conviction**
d. **Ability to inspire trust**
e. **High risk orientation**
f. **High energy and action orientation**
g. **Relational power base**
h. **Minimum of internal conflict**
i. **Empowering others**
j. **Self-promoting personality**

Figure 10-1 *Characteristics of charismatic leaders.*

Visionary. Charismatic leaders are future oriented. They have the ability to articulate an idealized vision of a future that is significantly better than the present. They quickly recognize fundamental discrepancies

vision: the ability to imagine different and better conditions and the ways to achieve them.

between the status quo and the way things can (or should) be. **Vision** is defined as *the ability to imagine different and better conditions and the ways to achieve them.*[10] A vision uplifts and attracts others. For this to happen, the leader's vision must result from a collaborative effort. Charismatic leaders formulate their vision by synthesizing seemingly disparate issues, values, and problems from many sources of the organization or work unit. They have a compelling picture of the future and are very passionate about it. Kenneth Chenault's vision for American Express is to make it one of the most respected brands in the world.

Superb Communication Skills. In addition to having a vision, charismatic leaders have an ability to communicate complex ideas and goals in clear, compelling ways, so that everyone from the top-management level to the bottom level of the organization can understand and identify with their message. Their eloquent, imaginative, and expressive manner heightens followers' emotional levels and inspires them to embrace the leader's vision. Charismatic leaders use their superior rhetorical skills to stir dissatisfaction with the status quo while they build support for their vision of a new future. Researchers have identified some of the rhetorical techniques used by charismatic leaders.[11]

Charismatic leaders make extensive use of metaphors, analogies, and stories rather than abstract rational discourse to make their points. While metaphors and analogies are inspiring, charismatic leaders are also adept at tailoring their language to particular groups, thereby better engaging them mentally and emotionally. For example, a CEO attempting to inspire vice presidents may use an elevated language style, but that same CEO attempting to inspire first-line employees to keep working hard may speak on a colloquial level. Another significant aspect of the communication style of charismatic leaders is that they make extensive use of anecdotes to get their message across. Communicating through anecdotes can result in inspiring stories. Chenault is such an effective communicator that he was able to convey bad news in a positive way and make it less painful when he had to fire 12,000 employees.

Self-Confidence and Moral Conviction. Charismatic leaders build trust in their leadership through unshakable self-confidence, an abiding faith, strong moral conviction, and sacrifice.[12] Martin Luther King's "I Have a Dream" speech is an example of how a leader's self-confidence, faith, and strong moral conviction can inspire hope and faith in a better future. In the opening case, Chenault describes his moral conviction as his conscience.

Ability to Inspire Trust. Constituents believe so strongly in the integrity of charismatic leaders that they will risk their careers to pursue the leader's visions. Charismatic leaders build support and trust by showing commitment to followers' needs over self-interest. This quality inspires followers and engenders mutual trust between a leader and his or her followers. Described in the opening case as people power, it is Kenneth Chenault's greatest strength.

High Risk Orientation. Charismatic leaders earn followers' trust by being willing to incur great personal risk. It is said that charismatic leaders romanticize risk.[13] People admire the courage of those who take high risk. Putting themselves on the line is one way charismatic leaders affirm self-advocacy for their vision and thus gain the admiration and respect of their followers. It has been reported that Martin Luther King, Jr., received death threats against himself and his family almost every day during the civil rights movement. Yet, he persisted with his mission until his assassination. In addition to assuming great risk, charismatic leaders use unconventional strategies to achieve success. Herb Kelleher, chairman and CEO of Southwest Airlines, is a leader who is well known for inspiring employees with his unconventional approach, thus helping to make the airline consistently profitable. Kelleher encourages employees to break the rules, maintain their individuality, and have fun—a style he calls "management by fooling around." It is a style that has made Southwest Airlines' employees the most productive in the industry.

High Energy and Action Orientation. Charismatic leaders are energetic and serve as role models for getting things done on time. They engage their emotions in everyday work life, which makes them energetic, enthusiastic, and attractive to others. Charismatic leaders tend to be emotionally expressive, especially through nonverbal emotional expressiveness, such as warm gestures, movement, tone of voice, eye contact, and facial expressions.[14] It is partly through their nonverbal behaviors that charismatic leaders are perceived to have a magnetic personality.

Relational Power Base. A key dimension of charismatic leadership is that it involves a relationship or interaction between the leader and the followers. However, unlike other types of leadership, it is intensely relational and based almost entirely upon referent and expert power (Chapter 9), even when the leader occupies a formal organizational role. Charismatic leadership involves an emotionalized relationship in which a follower's response to the leader is characterized by the following outcomes: awe, trust, identification with and emulation of the leader, devotion, similarity of beliefs, and unquestioning acceptance of and affection for the leader.

Minimum of Internal Conflict. Typically, charismatic leaders are convinced they are right in their vision and strategies, which explains why they persist and stay the course, even through setbacks. Because of this conviction, they experience less guilt and discomfort in pushing followers to stay the course even when faced with threats.

Empowering Others. Charismatic leaders understand that they cannot make the vision come true alone: They need help and support of their followers. Charismatic leaders empower followers by building their self-efficacy. They do this by assigning followers tasks that lead to successively greater positive experiences and heightened self-confidence, thus persuading followers of their capabilities and creating an environment of positive emotions and heightened excitement. Charismatic leaders also empower followers by role-modeling and coaching, providing feedback and encouragement, and persuading followers to take on more responsibilities as their skills and self-confidence grow.

Applying the Concept 10-1

Characteristics of Charismatic Leaders

Referring to the characteristics listed in Figure 10-1, identify each statement by its characteristic using the letters a–j.

____ 1. We don't need a committee to evaluate the plan. I'm ready to implement it next week. Let's get going before we miss the opportunity.

____ 2. Last month our department had the highest level of productivity in the organization.

____ 3. The odds of hitting a sales goal that high are maybe 70 percent. Are you sure you want to set this goal?

____ 4. Cutting our plant pollution is the right thing to do. I'm sure we can exceed the new EPA standards, not just meet the minimum requirements.

____ 5. Will you do me a favor an ... for me right away?

Self-Promoting Personality. Even if no one will take up their cause, charismatic leaders are frequently out promoting themselves and their vision. Richard Branson, chairman and CEO of the Virgin Group (the British corporation that owns Virgin Airlines, Virgin Records, and other strategic business units), has relied on self-promotion to help build his empire. Charismatic leaders are not afraid "to blow their own horn."

How a Person Acquires Charismatic Qualities

Given the potential benefits of charismatic leadership, it is reasonable to wonder whether some of the traits, characteristics, and behaviors of charismatic people can be developed or enhanced.

Research Results. While some research supports the possibility of training leaders to be more charismatic, others don't believe that research results are conclusive enough to support such a position. In one laboratory experiment, several actors were coached to display people-oriented, autocratic, or charismatic behaviors as leaders of four-person work groups.[15] In one instance, actors exhibiting charismatic behaviors acted confidently and expressed high confidence in followers, set high performance targets, empowered followers, and empathized with the needs of followers. The results revealed that the four-person work groups of charismatic leaders had higher performance and satisfaction levels than the four-person work groups having an autocratic or people-oriented leader who did not exhibit the same leadership traits. While some researchers have used these findings to argue that it is possible to train leaders to be more charismatic, others think it is still too early to make such a claim. They point out the weaknesses in the study. Because the actors playing leaders in the study were not trained to exhibit both high-task and high-relationship behaviors, it is uncertain whether the followers of charismatic leaders would have higher performance or satisfaction levels than followers of people-oriented or autocratic leaders.[16] However, the very fact that it is possible for actors to exhibit certain charismatic leadership behaviors through training and coaching lends support to the notion that these are trainable behaviors.

Developing Charismatic Qualities. Several of the characteristics of charismatic leaders described in this chapter are capable of being enhanced. For example, it is possible through training for people to enhance their communication skills, build their self-confidence, and learn techniques to inspire and empower others. There are suggested strategies for acquiring or enhancing charismatic qualities.

- Through practice and self-discipline, you can develop your visionary skills by practicing the act of creating a vision in a college course like this one. This would be a key factor in being perceived as charismatic.

- You can practice being candid. Although not insensitive, the charismatic person is typically forthright in giving his or her assessment of a situation, whether the assessment is positive or negative. Charismatic people are direct rather than indirect in their approach, so that there is no ambiguity about their position on issues.

- You can develop a warm, positive, and humanistic attitude toward people, rather than a negative, cool, and impersonal attitude. Charisma, as mentioned earlier, is a relational and emotional concept that ultimately results from the perception of the followers.

- You can develop an enthusiastic, optimistic, and energetic personality. A major behavior pattern of charismatic people is their combination of enthusiasm, optimism, and a high energy level. This is the pattern that was revealed in the opening case about Kenneth Chenault. He celebrates his victories briefly, and then moves on to the next challenge.

Charisma: A Double-Edged Sword

Most people agree that charisma can be a double-edged sword capable of producing both positive and negative outcomes. It is possible in reading about the personal magnetism, vision, self-confidence, masterful rhetorical skills, and empowering style of charismatic leaders to conclude that they are the best leaders, and that others should emulate them. It is important to remind ourselves that not all charismatic leaders are necessarily good leaders. Leaders such as Gandhi, Martin Luther King, Jr., John F. Kennedy, and Winston Churchill exhibited tremendous charisma. So did leaders such as Charles Manson, David Koresh, Adolph Hitler, and the Reverend Jim Jones of the People's Temple. Charisma can cut both ways; it is not always used to benefit others.

One method for differentiating between positive and negative charisma is by the values and personality of the leader. The key question for determining classification is whether the leaders are primarily oriented toward their own needs or the needs of followers and the organization. Researchers acknowledge that all charismatic leaders intentionally seek to instill commitment to their ideological goals and, either consciously or unconsciously, they seek follower devotion and dependency.[17] Negative charismatic leaders emphasize devotion to themselves more than to ideals. Decisions of these leaders are often self-serving. Group accomplishments are used for self-glorification. In their affect, negative charismatic leaders emphasize personal identification rather than internalization. Personal identification is leader-centered, while internalization is follower-centered. Ideological appeals are only a ploy to gain power, after which the ideology is ignored or arbitrarily changed to serve the leader's self-interest. In contrast, positive charismatic leaders seek to instill devotion to ideology more than devotion to them-

selves. In affect, they emphasize internalization rather than personal identification. Therefore, outcomes of their leadership are more likely to be beneficial to followers and society.

Consistent with this notion of positive and negative charisma are the
views and findings of some leadership scholars who propose that negative
charismatic leaders have a personalized power orientation, whereas positive
charismatic leaders have a socialized power orientation (Chapter 2).[18]
Personalized charismatic leaders *pursue leader-driven goals and promote feel-*
ings of obedience, dependency, and submission in followers. ***Socialized charis-***
matic leaders *pursue organization-driven goals and promote feelings of*
empowerment, personal growth, and equal participation in followers. In the former, rewards and punishment are used to manipulate and control followers,
and information is restricted and used to preserve the image of leader infal-
libility or to exaggerate external threats to the organization. In the latter,
rewards are used to reinforce behavior that is consistent with the vision and
mission of the organization.

personalized charismatic leaders:
pursue leader-driven goals and promote
feelings of obedience, dependency, and
submission in followers.

socialized charismatic leaders:
pursue organization-driven goals and
promote feelings of empowerment,
personal growth, and equal participation in
followers.

Evaluation and Implications of Charismatic Leadership for Organizational Success

It is evident from the discussion in this section that charismatic theory has
contributed to our understanding of the exceptional influence some leaders
have on followers—from a viewpoint not adequately revealed by existing
theories of leadership. Charismatic theory has highlighted the importance of
feelings and emotional reactions by followers toward leaders; earlier theories
emphasized quantitative, rational aspects of leader-to-follower relationships.
The bond between charismatic leaders and their followers is not always
explained by rational-predictive processes, but by collective social processes,
as acknowledged in some of the charismatic theories (for example, attribution, self-concept, and social contagion theories).[19] Regardless of a leader's
measurable accomplishment, he or she may not be considered a charismatic
leader by followers. Ultimately, it is the followers' subjective evaluations of
their affection, love, confidence, trust, and respect for the leader that determines charismatic or uncharismatic status. Thus, the comment that "charisma is in the eye of the beholder" is true. Also, while earlier theories saw leadership as a direct influencing activity between a leader and a follower
(dyadic relationship), charismatic theories offer an alternative explanation
of how leaders are able to influence people indirectly without face-to-face
interaction (social identification and social contagion theories).[20]

Despite the contributions by charismatic theorists to the field of leadership, charisma is not without its limitations. Charismatic leadership theories emphasize the role of an individual leader who takes the initiative for
developing and articulating a vision to followers. However, in an organization facing threatening environmental challenges or serious internal conflicts rooted in conflicting values, aspirations, and ideals, successful
transformation is more likely to come from a shared leadership process than
a lonely individualistic approach. Most of the descriptive research on effective leaders suggests that charisma in its individualized form is not necessary
to achieve major changes in an organization and improve its performance.

In fact, positive organizational change is usually the result of transformational leadership by individuals not perceived as charismatic. Thus, charismatic theories that emphasize "lone star" leadership by extraordinary individuals may be most appropriate for describing a visionary entrepreneur who establishes a new organization. Examples include Richard Branson of the Virgin Group, Stephen Case of America Online, Jeff Bezos of Amazon.com, and the exceptional "turnaround manager" Al Dunlap of Sunbeam Corporation. All of these leaders rescued an organization about to collapse. However, lone-star leadership is not a panacea for the problems of every organization.

TRANSFORMATIONAL LEADERSHIP

Transformational leadership focuses on what leaders accomplish, rather than on a leader's personal characteristics and followers' reactions. As organizations continue to face global challenges, the need for leaders who can successfully craft and implement bold strategies that will transform or align the organization with the level of environmental turbulence is ever greater. We will examine the similarities and differences between charismatic, transactional, and transformational leadership; the transformation process; and the attributes of transformational leaders.

Charismatic versus Transformational Leadership

Much of the early research on characteristics of charismatic leaders did not differentiate between charismatic and transformational leadership. The two terms have been used interchangeably. However, there have always been research efforts to distinguish between the two concepts. A leading researcher on this topic has argued successfully that charisma is a necessary requirement of transformational leadership, but by itself it is not sufficient to account for the transformational process. In other words, all transformational leaders are charismatic, but not all charismatic leaders are transformational.[21] *Transformational leadership serves to change the status quo by articulating to followers the problems in the current system and a compelling vision of what a new organization could be.* Transformational leaders take charisma one step further, in that they are more likely to go beyond the visionary stage into the action stage in an attempt to transform their organizations. Charismatic leaders can convey a vision and form strong emotional bonds with followers; but in some cases, as we have seen with negative charismatics, they do so for their own self-interest. Many individuals are described as charismatic (for example, celebrities), but they seldom motivate their followers to transcend self-interest for the benefit of a higher ideal or societal need. Transformational leaders are similar to charismatic leaders; they can articulate a compelling vision of the future and influence followers by arousing strong emotions in support of the vision. This vision and the leader-follower relationship must be in line with followers' value systems in order to connect the followers' needs with those of the organization.

transformational leadership: serves to change the status quo by articulating to followers the problems in the current system and a compelling vision of what a new organization could be.

Transformational leaders can emerge from different levels of the organization. Therefore, an organization may have many transformational leaders. In contrast, charismatic leaders are few in number. Charismatic leaders are most likely to emerge in the throes of a crisis, when an organization is in turmoil because of conflicting value and belief systems. People's responses to a charismatic or transformational leader are often highly polarized: Those with the most to lose from abandoning the old system will put up the most resistance to any change initiative. Additionally, it would appear that the emotional levels of resistance toward charismatic leaders are more extreme than those toward transformational leaders. This may be the underlying cause for the violent deaths of some charismatic leaders like Martin Luther King, Jr., John F. Kennedy, and Mahatma Gandhi.[22] Both charismatic and transformational leadership always involve conflict and change, and both types of leaders must be willing to embrace conflict, create enemies, make unusual allowances for self-sacrifice, and be extraordinarily focused in order to achieve and institutionalize their vision.

Attributes of Transformational Leaders

Although much remains to be learned about transformational leadership, there is enough convergence from the many years of research to suggest some attributes that are common to transformational leaders. Many of the characteristics of charismatic leaders listed in Figure 10-1 are equally applicable to transformational leaders, thus there are similarities between these attributes and the characteristics of charismatic leaders.

Effective transformational leaders are said to possess certain attributes:

- They see themselves as change agents.
- They are visionaries who have a high level of trust for their intuition.
- They are risk takers, but not reckless.
- They are capable of articulating a set of core values that tend to guide their own behavior.
- They possess exceptional cognitive skills and believe in careful deliberation before taking action.
- They believe in people and show sensitivity to their needs.
- They are flexible and open to learning from experience.

All of these attributes are applicable to Kenneth Chenault in the opening case. He is not afraid of challenges. His objective to make American Express one of the fastest-growing companies in the world is not going to be an easy task: American Express has only 16 percent of the United States credit card market, compared to Visa's 49 percent and MasterCard's 27 percent. His determination and commitment are unquestionable, and many financial analysts are optimistic that he can accomplish his objectives. Even when faced with imminent crisis, Chenault refuses to accept defeat. He is quick to turn a setback into a lesson, a lesson into an action plan, and an action plan into an advantage. These qualities may help explain his phenomenal rise at American Express and his pending promotion to CEO. American

Express operates in a highly turbulent business environment, in which maintaining the status quo is not an option. The selection of Chenault as its next CEO is an indication that the board of directors has faith in his ability to transform the company as future changes and needs demand.

Transformational versus Transactional Leadership

To begin this section, complete Self-Assessment Exercise 10-1 to determine if you are a more transactional or transformational leader.

Transformational leadership is best understood when compared to transactional leadership. Transactional and transformational leadership are unique but not mutually exclusive processes; the same leader may use both types of leadership at different times and under different circumstances.[23] This new vision of the organization is closely linked to both the leaders' and followers' values; it is the basis of the exchange relationship between leaders and followers, rather than tangible incentives. ***Transactional leadership** seeks to maintain stability rather than promoting change within an organization, through regular economic and social exchanges that achieve specific goals for both the leaders and their followers.*[24] The transactional leader goes into specific contractual arrangements with followers: In exchange for meeting specified objectives or performing certain duties, the leader provides benefits that satisfy followers' needs and desires. An example of transactional leadership occurs when managers give monthly bonuses to salespeople for meeting and exceeding their monthly sales quotas, or to production people for exceeding quality standards. The exchanges involve specific goods that are tangible, not the intangible incentives (inspiring vision, shared values, or emotional bonding) associated with transformational exchange relationships.

transactional leadership: seeks to maintain stability rather than promoting change within an organization, through regular economic and social exchanges that achieve specific goals for both the leaders and their followers.

Self-Assessment Exercise 10-1

Are You More a Transactional or a Transformational Leader?

Complete the following questions based on how you will act (or have acted) in a typical work or school situation. Using the following scale, write the appropriate number in the blank before each item.

1 — 2 — 3 — 4 — 5
Disagree   *Agree*

_____ 1. I enjoy change and see myself as a change agent.

_____ 2. I am better at inspiring employees toward a new future than motivating them to perform in their current jobs.

_____ 3. I have (or had) a vision of how an organization can change for the better.

_____ 4. I see myself as someone who is comfortable encouraging people to express ideas and opinions that differ from my own.

_____ 5. I enjoy taking risks, but am not reckless.

_____ 6. I enjoy spending time developing new solutions to old problems rather than implementing existing solutions.

_____ 7. I deliberate carefully before acting; I'm not impulsive.

____ 8. I like to support change initiatives, even when the idea may not work.

____ 9. I learn from my experience; I don't repeat the same mistakes.

____ 10. I believe the effort to change something for the better should be rewarded, even if the final outcome is disappointing.

Add up the numbers on lines 1–10, and place your total score here ____ and on the continuum.

10 — 20 — 30 — 40 — 50
Transactional leader   *Transformational leader*

The higher the score, generally, the more you exhibit transformational leader qualities. However, transformational leaders also perform transactional behaviors. It is also generally easier to be transformational at higher levels of management than at lower levels.

Transactional leadership tends to be transitory in that once a transaction is completed, the relationship between the parties may end or be redefined. Transformational leadership is more enduring, especially when the change process is well designed and implemented. Transactional leaders promote stability, while transformational leaders create significant change in both followers and organizations. Transformational leadership inspires followers to go beyond their own self-interest for the good of the group. Transactional leadership seeks to satisfy followers' individual needs as a reward for completing a given transaction. Despite these differences, it is worth mentioning that effective leaders exhibit both transactional and transformational leadership skills in appropriate situations.

Applying the Concept 10-2

Transformational or Transactional Leadership

Identify each statement as being more characteristic of:

a. transformational leadership   b. transactional leadership

____ **1.** We don't need a committee to work on a plan. Let's get going on this now..

____ **2.** I'd say we have a 75 percent chance of being successful with the new product. Let's market it.

____ **3.** The current inventory system is working fine. Let's not mess with success.

____ **4.** That is a good idea, but we have no money in the budget to implement it.

____ **5.** We need to monitor the demographics to make sure our products satisfy our customers.

The Transformation Process

Transformational leaders are usually brought into an organization experiencing a crisis or approaching total collapse to institute turnaround strategies that can rescue the organization. The process of successfully accomplishing such a challenging task is best undertaken through a sequence of phases, beginning with recognizing the need for change and followed by

Key Phrases	Suggested Activities
1. Recognizing Need for Change	Increase sensitivity to environmental changes and threats. Respond to subtle and/or radical changes in the environment. Employ alternative strategies for monitoring environment.
2. Creating a New Vision	Encourage everyone to think with a future orientation. Involve others. Express in ideological, not just economic terms.
3. Managing Transition	Instill in managers a sense of urgency for the change. Raise followers' awareness and expectations. Help followers understand need for change. Increase followers' self-confidence and optimism Avoid the temptation of a "quick fit." Recognize and deal openly with emotional component of resisting change.
4. Institutionalizing the Change	Enable and strengthen followers with a "greatness attitude." Help followers find self-fulfillment with new vision. Help followers look beyond self-interest. Change reward systems and appraisal procedures. Implement team-building interventions and personnel changes. Appoint a special task force to monitor progress.

Figure 10-2 *The transformation process.*

creating the new vision, managing the transition, and then institutionalizing the change.[25] Figure 10-2 lists these key phases, with suggested activities to ensure effective and efficient execution of each phase.

STRATEGIC LEADERSHIP

Achieving organizational success is not a chance occurrence. It is determined largely by the decisions leaders make. It is the responsibility of top managers like Kenneth Chenault to monitor the organization's internal and external environments, project or anticipate what its configuration in five to ten years will be, and develop a vision for the future that followers can believe in. This series of activities constitutes what researchers describe as strategic leadership, considered by some to be synonymous with transformational leadership.

Strategic leadership *is the process of providing the direction and inspiration necessary to create and implement a vision, mission, and strategies to achieve and sustain organizational objectives.*[26]

In today's rapidly changing global world, leaders are bombarded with so much information, often conflicting, that no two leaders will see things the same way or make the same choices. The complexity of the environment and the uncertainty of the future make the task of strategic leadership more difficult. Effective strategic leaders will be those who constantly monitor

strategic leadership: the process of providing the direction and inspiration necessary to create and implement a vision, mission, and strategies to achieve and sustain organizational objectives.

strategic management: the set of decisions and actions used to formulate and implement specific strategies that will achieve a competitively superior fit between the organization and its environment so as to achieve organizational goals.

the environment to ensure a competitive fit between their strategies and the environment. *Strategic management is the set of decisions and actions used to formulate and implement specific strategies that will achieve a competitively superior fit between the organization and its environment so as to achieve organizational goals.*[27] Though closely related in meaning, the role of strategic leadership is to effectively carry out the task of strategic management.

As a strategist, Kenneth Chenault has shown that he can lead. His analytical and cognitive skills, which allow him to see relationships among variables that lead to long-term opportunities, are exceptional. These skills proved useful when he made the risky decision to allow the American Express card to be used at discount outlets like Sears and Wal-Mart. It was viewed as a step down for a card that prided itself on symbolizing prestige and a certain exclusivity. Chenault believed he could succeed with this strategy without losing the company's qualitative difference and exercised his leadership responsibility by going against popular opinion. So far the strategy is working successfully. Another instance when Chenault's strategic leadership skills were tested occurred in 1991. There was a boycott by merchants who were protesting American Express's high fees. Chenault knew there had been dissatisfaction with the rate, compared to lower rates charged by Visa and MasterCard, but he was shocked by the level of emotion captured in a newspaper headline, "Boston Tea Party." A restaurant manager in Boston had cut up an American Express card in front of the customers, prompting a citywide reaction. Chenault described the sessions designed to seek a solution to the crisis as very contentious and emotional. Reacting to the moment, many top managers wanted an across-the-board lowering of the company's rate. Once again, Chenault stepped in and provided leadership. He believed in the value of the company's product relative to competitors and wanted the price to reflect it. Chenault's intuition and conviction was not to lower rates to bankcard levels, but to lower the rate selectively. Ultimately, Chenault's lonely stance and strategic thinking prevailed, and the company weathered the storm without major losses.

This section focuses on the strategic management process shown in Figure 10-3, and at each level of the framework, it describes certain associated characteristics, behaviors, and practices of strategic leaders like Chenault.

Figure 10-3 starts with the analysis of internal and external environments to identify organizational strengths and weaknesses and environmental threats and opportunities. Next is a vision of where the organization wants and needs to be in the future, given the outcomes of environmental analysis. The vision leads to the development of a mission statement that reflects

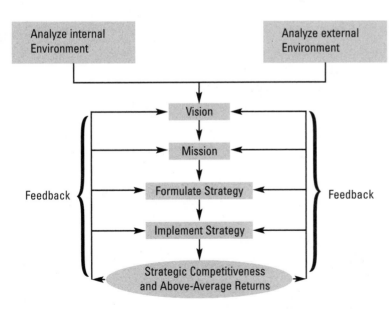

Figure 10-3 *Strategic management framework.*

the organization's core values, beliefs, culture, and purpose. Strategy formulation provides direction for translating the mission into action or initiatives that help the organization achieve its goals. The final phase, strategy implementation, takes place through the basic organizational architecture (structure, systems, incentives, and governance) that makes things happen. Each part of this framework is briefly discussed.

Analyzing the Environment

One of the most important activities of leadership is direction setting, which involves anticipating and creating a future for the organization. To set the right direction for the future, the leader must accurately forecast or anticipate the future. This takes constantly monitoring the environment and the organization. It is essential to learn and understand the concerns of customers, the availability and bargaining power of suppliers and vendors, the actions of competitors, market trends, economic conditions, government policies, and technological advances.[28] Analyzing the internal environment focuses on assessing the organization's position in the market, financial status, capabilities, core competencies, and structure.

Accurate interpretation of both types of environments requires considerable analytical and cognitive skills such as the ability to think critically, to identify and make sense of several complex trends, and to streamline all this information into a concise plan of action. The amount of change and turbulence in the external environment will determine how much external monitoring is necessary. When the environment is rapidly changing and the organization faces severe competition or serious threats, more external monitoring is needed. Effective strategic leaders are those who can create the future under rapidly changing conditions rather than anticipate the future under these conditions. Using multiple sources of information, a leader can create a future that many people will not believe in. He or she must foresee a future that will evolve in a way that is advantageous to the company, and be sure the company takes the necessary steps to achieve the future they have created. Furthermore, the leader must recognize the skills and capabilities that must be developed or acquired now for the company to have a competitive advantage over rivals in the future.[29] Monitoring the environment through an internal and external analysis is referred to as a SWOT analysis—identification of strengths, weaknesses, opportunities, and threats.

Strategic Vision

When the outcome of a SWOT analysis reveals the need for a major overhaul or transformation of the organization, it becomes imperative to create a new vision that conveys an intuitive, appealing picture of what the organization can be in the future. Therefore, a *strategic vision is an ambitious view of the future that everyone in the organization can believe in and that is not readily attainable, yet offers a future that is better in important ways than what now exists.*[30] To be motivating, a vision must be expressed in ideological terms,

strategic vision: an ambitious view of the future that everyone in the organization can believe in and that is not readily attainable, yet offers a future that is better in important ways than what now exists.

not just in economic terms, to help people develop a personal connection with the organization.

A clear and inspiring vision serves a number of important functions:

- Facilitates decision making in that it helps people determine what is good or bad, important or trivial
- Inspires followers by appealing to their fundamental human need to feel important, useful, and to be a part of something great
- Links the present to the past by rationalizing the need for changing old ways of doing work
- Gives meaning to work by explaining not just what people do, but why they do it
- Establishes a standard of excellence

To be widely accepted, vision creation should be a shared exercise. To make a difference, a vision must be based on the input and values of followers and other key stakeholders. An effective vision is one that is the result of teamwork, simple enough to be understood, appealing enough to energize and garner commitment, and credible enough to be accepted as realistic and attainable.[31]

Here are some examples of companies with simple, yet inspiring visions:

- Komatsu: "Encircle caterpillar."
- Coca-Cola: "A Coke within arm's reach of everyone on the planet."
- Microsoft: "A personal computer on every desk in every home."
- Citibank: "To be the most powerful, the most serviceable, the most far reaching world financial institution that has ever been."
- Nike: "To crush the enemy."
- American Express: "To be the world's most respected service brand."

Mission Statement

At the core of the vision is the organization's mission statement, which describes the general purpose of the organization. *The **mission statement** is the organization's core broad purpose and reason for existence.* The two components that are often featured in a mission statement are the core values and the core purpose. The core values outline the guiding principles and ethical standards by which the company will conduct itself, no matter the circumstance.

The core purpose doesn't just describe goods and services, it describes the broad needs (immediate and anticipated) of the people served by the organization. For Discovery Toys, the mission is "to be a parent educator"; for 3M, it is "To solve unsolved problems innovatively"; for Merck, it is "To preserve and improve human life"; for the Army, it is "To be all you can be"; and for Ford, it is to make "Quality job one." In these and many other examples, there is no mention of the specific products or services these organizations manufacture or serve. Examples abound of organizations that have been adversely affected by poorly crafted mission statements. The railroad industry almost brought about its own demise by defining its mission as

mission statement: the organization's core broad purpose and reason for existence.

being in the railroad business rather than the transportation business. The March of Dimes' original mission was "to cure polio," until a cure was discovered and the organization found itself without a purpose. Today, its mission is to advance human health. Motorola and Zenith were once successful competitors in the manufacture and sale of televisions. Yet, while Zenith has lost ground, Motorola has continued to grow and expand. The difference, according to one source, is that Motorola, unlike Zenith, defined its mission as "applying technology to benefit the public," not as "making television sets."[32]

Visions are for the future and should change and adapt with the changing environment, whereas the mission statement represents the enduring character, values, and purpose of the organization. The job of strategic leadership is to ensure this pattern.

Strategy Formation

Armed with a strong mission and a guiding vision, an organization must formulate a strategy or plan of action for carrying out the mission and achieving strategic objectives. *Strategy is the general plan of action that describes resource allocation and other activities for exploiting environmental opportunities and helping the organization attain its goals.*[33] Research supports the proposition that effective strategy formulation has a positive effect on organizational performance.[34] However, to achieve this result, strategic leaders must put forth relevant strategies. A relevant strategy necessarily changes over time to fit environmental conditions, and it is realistic in light of the organization's strengths and weaknesses. Also, a relevant strategy must reflect the core mission and objectives of the organization. To maintain a competitive edge over rivals, effective strategic leaders develop strategies that:

- Enhance value to the customers.
- Create synergistic opportunities.
- Build on the company's core competence.

Delivering value to the customer should be central to any strategy. *Value is the ratio of benefits received to the cost incurred by the customer.* A strategy without this quality is sure to fail. Synergy occurs when a chosen strategy (such as in related diversification) calls for organizational units or systems to interact and produce a joint result that is greater than the sum of the parts acting independently—the "2 + 2 = 5" phenomenon. Synergistic benefits include lower cost, greater market power, or superior employee skills and capabilities. Finally, strategies that are based on a company's core competencies have a better chance of improving an organization's performance. *A core competence is a capability an organization performs extremely well in comparison to competitors.* A strategic leader's job is to identify the organization's unique strengths—what differentiates the organization from its competitors in the industry. Unlike physical resources, which are depleted when used, core competencies increase (assuming their efficient application) as they are used. They represent the source of a company's competitive advantage over its rivals.

strategy: the general plan of action that describes resource allocation and other activities for exploiting environmental opportunities and helping the organization attain its goal.

value: the ratio of benefits received to the cost incurred by the customer.

core competence: a capability an organization performs extremely well in comparison to competitors.

Examples of competitive strategies include niche strategies, low cost, differentiation, diversification, alliances or partnerships, and benchmarking. The ultimate purpose of any organization is to identify and satisfy its customers' needs. Strategy is just the means to this end, and although every leader is aware of this, many business failures can still be attributed to companies paying too much attention to the means and ignoring the customer, or ignoring both. Strategic leadership is about ensuring that this doesn't happen.

Strategy Implementation

Strategy implementation has been described as the most important and most difficult part of the strategic management process. An excellent strategy that is poorly executed will yield the same poor results as a bad strategy.[35] Strong leadership is considered one of the most important tools for strategy implementation. The difficulty of strategy implementation is related to the many components and tools that need to be integrated in order to put a chosen strategy into action. Leadership decisions on key issues such as structural design, pay or reward systems, budget allocation, and organizational rules, policies, and procedures will determine the success or failure of strategy implementation. Decisions in these areas must match the requirements of the chosen strategy and the mission of the company. A mismatch such as a company pursuing a strategy of differentiation through innovation in a bureaucratic, hierarchical structure will result in poor performance and objectives not met. However, a company pursuing a strategy of internal efficiency and stability to offer customers lower prices than competitors will succeed with this type of centralized structure.

Achieving strategic competitiveness and earning above-average returns for a company is not a matter of luck. It is determined by the decisions and actions of leaders throughout the strategic management process.

STEWARDSHIP AND SERVANT LEADERSHIP

Stewardship and servant leadership represent the shift in the leadership paradigm toward followers. The thesis of this shift is that leadership has less to do with directing other people and more to do with serving other people. Stewardship and servant leadership are about placing others ahead of one-self, and together are viewed as a model for successful leadership in any field or profession. In this section, we discuss the nature and importance of stewardship and servant leadership and the framework for establishing both.

The Nature of Stewardship and Servant Leadership

Stewardship is an employee-focused form of leadership that empowers followers to make decisions and have control over their jobs. Servant leadership is leadership that transcends self-interest to serve the needs of others, by helping them grow professionally and emotionally. The fulfillment of others' needs is said to be the servant leader's ultimate goal.[36] Though some may view these two con-

stewardship: an employee-focused form of leadership that empowers followers to make decisions and have control over their jobs.

servant leadership: transcends self-interest to serve the needs of others, by helping them grow professionally and emotionally.

cepts of leadership as synonymous and use the terms interchangeably, there do exist subtle, yet significant differences between the two concepts. While both shine the spotlight on those who actually perform the day-to-day tasks of producing goods and services for an organization's customers, servant leadership takes stewardship assumptions about leaders and followers one step further. Servant leadership calls for the highest level of selflessness—a level some doubt exists in the real world. The leader completely assumes the role of follower at the lowest rung of the ladder and serves others in the accomplishment of organizational goals.[37]

Both stewardship and servant leadership are related to the self-managed team concept (Chapter 8) because of their focus on empowering followers, not leaders, to exercise leadership in accomplishing the organization's goals. Traditional leadership theory emphasized the leader-follower structure, in which the follower accepted responsibility from the leader and was accountable to the leader. However, the nontraditional view of leadership views the leader as a steward and servant of the people and the organization. It is less about directing or controlling and more about focusing on helping followers do their jobs, rather than to have followers help the managers do their jobs.

Framework for Stewardship

Leadership thinking based on stewardship prescribes a relationship between leaders and followers in which leaders lead without dominating or controlling followers. Leaders and followers work together in a mutually supportive environment to achieve organizational goals. The key to stewardship is based on four supporting values, illustrated in Figure 10-4.

- *Strong teamwork orientation.* Stewardship works best in situations where self-managed teams of core employees and the leader work together to formulate goals and strategies for a changing environment and marketplace. Here, the leader's role is less dominant and more supportive of the process. Where a strong team spirit is absent,

---

Applying the Concept 10-3

Strategic Leadership

Identify for each statement whether you think the view expressed reflects that of a strategic or non-strategic thinker. Write the appropriate letter in the blank before each item.

a. strategic thinker   b. non-strategic thinker

___ 1. It makes good sense for top management to frequently ask themselves the question, "What will the future of this industry look like?"
___ 2. I spend my time focusing on solving the day-to-day problems.
___ 3. We are not concerned about developing skills or capabilities that cannot help us perform the present job.
___ 4. A company cannot reach its full potential without an inspiring vision.
___ 5. In our business the environment changes very quickly. Therefore, we generally take thinks one week at a time.

Figure 10-4 *Values of stewardship.*

a leader must play a dominant role to push individuals in the right direction. However, this defeats the purpose of stewardship.

- *Decentralized decision making and power.* Stewardship is realized when authority and decision making are decentralized down to where work gets done and employees interact with customers. In this environment, stewardship has a great chance to succeed given the empowered status of employees and the closer relationship between managers and followers. The absence of this principle makes stewardship inoperable.

- *Equality assumption.* Stewardship works best when there is perceived equality between leaders and followers. It is a partnership of equals rather than a leader-follower command structure. The applicability of stewardship is enhanced as leaders find opportunities to serve rather than manage. Honesty, respect, and mutual trust prevail when there is equality, and these are values that enhance the success of stewardship.

- *Reward assumption.* Stewardship puts greater responsibility in the hands of employees. Therefore, to realize successful stewardship, the organization must redesign the compensation system to match rewards to actual performance. Employees with more responsibility and authority who are compensated accordingly flourish under stewardship, because they are motivated and committed to the organization's mission. Without this value, it is hard to sustain stewardship.

Stewardship leaders are known not for their great deeds, but for empowering others to achieve great deeds. Stewardship leaders offer the best chance for organizations to succeed and grow in today's dynamic environment because these leaders don't just lead, they coach (Chapter 4) followers to do the leading. This focus on people is what encourages followers to be more creative, energetic, and committed to their jobs.

Framework for Servant Leadership

Servant leaders approach leadership from a strong moral standpoint. The servant leader operates from the viewpoint that we all have a moral duty to one another.[38] Leadership is seen as an opportunity to serve at the ground level, not to lead from the top. An individual like Mother Theresa—through her humble and ordinary nature, strong moral values, and dedicated service to the poor and the afflicted—inspired hundreds of followers to join her order and emulate her example. The framework for servant leadership consists of the following basic guidelines,[39] as shown in Figure 10-5.

- *Helping others discover their inner spirit.* The servant leader's role is to help followers discover the strength of their inner spirit and their potential to make a difference. This requires servant leaders to be empathetic to the circumstances of others. Servant leaders are not afraid to show their vulnerabilities.

- *Earning and keeping others' trust.* Servant leaders earn followers' trust by being honest and true to their word. They have no hidden

Figure 10-5 *Guidelines to servant leadership.*

agendas, and they are willing to give up power, rewards, recognition, and control.

- *Service over self-interest.* The hallmark of servant leadership is the desire to help others, rather than the desire to attain power and control over others. Doing what's right for others takes precedence over protecting personal position. Servant leaders make decisions to further the good of the group rather than promote their own interests.

- *Effective listening.* Servant leaders do not impose their will on the group; rather, they listen carefully to the problems others are facing and then engage the group to find the best course of action. Servant leaders affirm their confidence in others.

This discussion so far has emphasized leadership approaches (charismatic, transformational, strategic, stewardship and servant leadership) that operate under the premise that change is inevitable. However, not every leader is capable of managing change successfully. Thus, we have identified the different leadership tools and guidelines that equip leaders to deal with change effectively. In the last section of this chapter, we examine the concept of change itself.

LEADING CHANGE

Recall that change is part of our definition of leadership (Chapter 1); leadership is the process of influencing followers to achieve organizational objectives through change. As the discussion on charismatic, transformational, and strategic leadership revealed, the outcome of each of these three leadership disciplines is change—not stability. In this last section we discuss the need for change, the change process, why people resist change, and guidelines for overcoming resistance to change.

The Need for Change

Rapid environmental changes are causing fundamental transformations that are having a dramatic impact on organizations and presenting new opportunities and threats for leadership.[40] Every organization is facing an environment characterized by rapid technological changes, a globalized economy, changing market requirements, and intense domestic and international competition. These changes have created opportunities such as larger, under-served markets in developing economies, as well as falling trade barriers. Threats in the form of more domestic competition, increased speed in innovations, shortened product life cycles, and global competition are also evident in this type of environment. Change-oriented leaders are responding by initiating strategies that match the requirements of these turbulent environments. For instance, many organizations are responding to these challenges by reengineering business processes; negotiating new partnerships, mergers, and acquisitions; and developing quality products and new technologies.[41]

The Change Process

Despite the growing consensus that change is imperative if organizations are to grow and thrive in the current and future environment, effecting change, especially major change, is still not an easy undertaking. The role of the leader is to facilitate change that results in better organizational performance; however, the question has always been how to do it effectively and successfully, given the stress, discomfort, and dislocation associated with change. One solution has been to view change as a process, not a product. The change process is the means of transforming an organization, a way to realize the new vision for the organization. Change process theories describe a typical pattern of events that occurs from the time a problem is identified to when it is resolved. It is important for leaders to recognize that each stage is important and requires different actions and commitments from the leader. Ignoring stages or committing critical errors at any stage can cause the change process to fail.

One of the earliest and most widely used change process theories is the force-field model.[42] This model proposed that the change process can be divided into three phases: unfreezing, changing, and refreezing (see Figure 10-6). A more recent theory is the eight-stage model of planned organizational change.[43] This model is also shown in Figure 10-6, which is an adaptation of the force-field model. The difference between the two models is the expansion of the second phase of the force-field model into six stages on the eight-stage model. We incorporate both models in explaining the change process.

The similarities between the two models do not warrant separate discussions; thus we will describe the characteristics and proposed actions required at each phase of the change process from the base point of the force-field model, incorporating the eight-stage model into it for comparison.

Unfreezing Phase. Instigated by the actions of a charismatic, strategic, or transformational leader, people in an organization may become aware of the need for change. In other words, a leader may inspire people with a vision of a better future that is sufficiently attractive to convince them that the old ways of doing business are no longer adequate. This recognition may occur as a result of an immediate crisis, proposed earlier as a precursor to charismatic leadership; or it may result from the efforts of a transformation or strategic leader to describe threats and opportunities not yet evident to most people in the organization. Awareness of the need for change, and a leader's ability to inspire followers to transcend their own immediate interests for the sake of the organization's mission, set the stage for the second phase of the change process to begin. The first step, according to the eight-

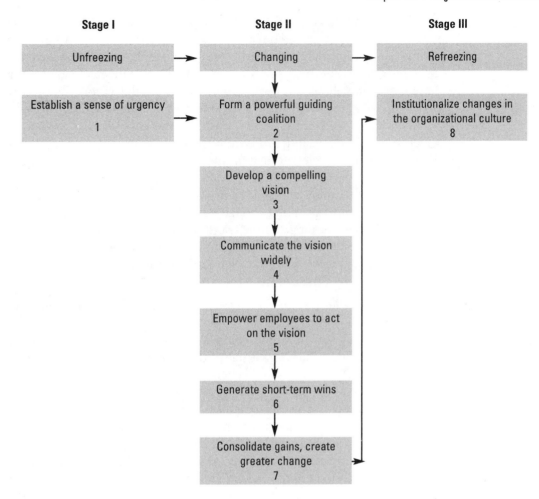

Stage I	Stage II	Stage III
Unfreezing	Changing	Refreezing
Establish a sense of urgency 1	Form a powerful guiding coalition 2	Institutionalize changes in the organizational culture 8
	Develop a compelling vision 3	
	Communicate the vision widely 4	
	Empower employees to act on the vision 5	
	Generate short-term wins 6	
	Consolidate gains, create greater change 7	

Figure 10-6 *Stages in the change process: A comparison of the force-field model and the eight-stage model.*

stage model, is to establish a sense of urgency. People need to know that change is needed—now—and why.

Changing Phase. This is the stage where the actual change takes place. It is the implementation phase. Here people look for leadership in finding new ways of doing things. Lack of a carefully designed plan of action at this stage will result in an uninspiring outcome. The difference between the force-field model and the eight-stage model occurs during this stage. The eight-stage model prescribes six systematic steps for the leader to follow in implementing change.

The second step, according to the eight-stage model, is for the leader to form a powerful guiding coalition (Chapter 9) by establishing a cross-functional team with enough power to guide the change process and develop a sense of teamwork among the group. In the third step, the leader must develop and articulate a compelling vision that will guide the change effort, and formulate the strategies for achieving that vision. To be committed to the change process, people need to have a vision of a promising future that is significantly better than the present to justify the costs and hardships the transformation will bring. The fourth step is active communication of the new vision and strategies. The leader's excellent communication skills and ability to mobilize widespread participation in the change process are critical for success. The fifth step describes the importance of empowering employees throughout the organization to act on the vision. The leader must empower people with resources, information, and discretion to make decisions. Empowerment must also include removing obstacles to change, which may include adapting the infrastructure (systems, structure, procedures, policies, and rules) to match the requirements of the change effort. The sixth and seventh steps require the leader to organize the change activities in ways that allow for short-term accomplishments, and to celebrate such accomplishments. Major change takes time to complete, and without some visible signs of progress, the transformation effort may lose momentum. Confidence, enthusiasm, and pride gained via short-term wins will create the drive and motivation to tackle bigger challenges and bring about a faster completion of the change.

Refreezing Phase. In this phase, the change process has been completed. However, this phase also involves institutionalizing the new approach in the organizational culture—the last step in the eight-stage model. Old habits, values, traditions, attitudes, and mindsets are permanently replaced. New values and beliefs are instilled in the culture in other to avoid a reversal to the old ways after implementation.

Though stages in the change process generally overlap, each phase is critical for success. An attempt to start implementing change without first unfreezing old attitudes is likely to meet with strong resistance. Not refreezing new attitudes and behaviors may result in the change being reversed soon after implementation. Understanding these phases is important for change-oriented leaders, who must exercise good judgment throughout the process.

Why People Resist Change

Change disrupts the status quo and often leads to stress, discomfort, and for some even dislocation. These conditions motivate people to resist change. For managers and employees, change is often perceived as a win-lose proposition: Managers see it as a positive way to strengthen the organization, and employees view it as a threat to their status and livelihood. Attempts to implement change are more likely to be successful if leaders understand the reasons behind employees' resistance to change. Resistance is a natural response by employees who want to protect their self-interest in the organization. Effective leaders do not downplay resistance or perceive it like managers—as a discipline problem to be dealt with through punishment or coercion. Rather, leaders view resistance as energy that can be redirected to support change. Figure 10-7 summarizes research findings on the most common reasons why people resist change.[44]

a. **Threat to one's self interest**

b. **Uncertainty**

c. **Lack of confidence that change will succeed**

d. **Lack of conviction that change is necessary**

e. **Distrust of leadership**

f. **Threat to personal values**

g. **Fear of being manipulated**

Figure 10-7 *Reasons for resisting change.*

• *Threat to one's self-interest.* An employee's self-interest in protecting his or her power, position, prestige, pay, and company benefits is a major reason for opposing change. When an organization embarks on a major change such as pursuing a new strategy, it often results in a shift in the relative power structure and status of individuals and units within the organization. For example, changes in job design or technology may require knowledge and skills not possessed by current employees. For these employees, the fear of losing their jobs or status is a major impetus for resisting change, regardless of the benefits to the organization.

- *Uncertainty.* Uncertainty represents a fear of the unknown. Lack of information about a change initiative creates a sense of uncertainty. When employees don't have full knowledge of how a proposed change will affect them, they may worry that replacing skills they have mastered over the years with new ones may prove too difficult to achieve. Therefore, a proposed change may have a better chance of acceptance if it includes a generous provision for helping employees learn new skills required by the change.

- *Lack of confidence that change will succeed.* A proposed change may require such a radical transformation from the old ways of doing business that employees will question its likelihood of succeeding. In this case, even though there may be a general acknowledgment of problems and the need for change, the lack of confidence that the change will succeed creates resistance. Also, if there have been instances of past failures, this may create cynicism and doubt in future change proposals.

- *Lack of conviction that change is necessary.* People may resist change if the leader has failed to articulate a real need for change and urgency. This is especially true in cases where employees believe that the current strategy has been successful and there is no clear evidence of serious problems in the near future.

- *Distrust of leadership.* Trust between parties is the basic requirement for sustaining any relationship. The absence of trust will cause people to resist change, even if there are no obvious threats. Change is resisted if people suspect that there are hidden consequences that management is not revealing. Trust is a valuable currency for leaders to have, because it is the basis upon which the benefits of a proposed change can be sold to employees who may suffer personal losses from such action.

- *Threat to personal values.* When a proposed change threatens a person's values, it ignites powerful feelings that fuel resistance to change. Any proposed change must take into account its impact on the values of those who are affected by the change; especially values that are closely aligned with an entrenched organizational culture. If threatened, values that are aligned with an entrenched organizational culture will ignite resistance that is organization-wide rather than isolated.

- *Fear of being manipulated.* When people perceive change as an attempt by others to control them, they will resist. However, when people understand and accept the need for change and believe that they have a voice in determining how to implement the change, resistance is lessened.

In the end, leaders who regard resistance as a distraction rather than a real and legitimate concern will find it hard to move beyond the first stage of the change model (Figure 10-6). Effective leaders will not only follow the steps in the model, but also employ the best implementation techniques or guidelines to overcome employee resistance.

Applying the Concept 10-4

Resistance to Change

Referring to Figure 10-7, use the letters a–g to identify which reason for resisting change explains each employee statement

_____**1.** I'm not too sure about this new program. Is it going to be another fad?

_____**2.** If we get these new machines, we will need fewer operators.

_____**3.** How can management ask us to take a pay cut when they are the ones who are making all the money? We shouldn't let them take advantage of us.

_____**4.** Why should our company get bought out? What do we know about that foreign company anyway?

_____**5.** Why do we have to put in a new system when the current one is only a year old and is working fine?

Guidelines for Overcoming Resistance to Change

There are guidelines that if followed can significantly reduce the level of resistance encountered during the change implementation process. These guidelines or actions can be grouped into two separate but overlapping categories—people-oriented actions and task-oriented actions.

People-Oriented Actions. These are the various techniques or guidelines that leaders can exercise to keep employees informed, supportive, and motivated about a change. Effective communication before, during, and after the change implementation process will prevent misunderstandings, false rumors, and conflict. It is important that those responsible for implementing change not learn about it from second-hand sources. Also, because major

---

To reduce or eliminate resistance to change, effective leaders:

- Show relentless support and unquestionable commitment to the change process.
- Communicate a strong message about the urgency for change.
- Maintain ongoing communication about the progress of change.
- Avoid micromanaging and empower people to implement the change.
- Help people deal with the trauma of change.
- Anticipate and prepare people for the necessary adjustments that change will trigger, such as career counseling and/or retraining.

Figure 10-8 *Guidelines for overcoming resistence to people-oriented change.*

To reduce or eliminate resistance to change, effective leaders:
- Assemble a coalition of supporters inside and outside the organization.
- Align the organizational structure with new strategy for consistency.
- Survey the organizational landscape for likely supporters and opponents..
- Recruit and fill key positions with competent and committed supporters.
- Know when and how to use ad hoc committees or task forces to shape implementation activities.
- Know when a full-scale or limited-scale approach to implementation is needed.

Figure 10-9
Guidlines for overcoming resistance to task-oriented change.

change involves adjustments, disruptions, and even dislocation, training and guidance is needed to help employees acquire skills and capabilities for their role in the implementation process or for their new responsibilities. Through research and case studies, several techniques for overcoming resistance have been identified.[45] They are listed in Figure 10-8.

Task-Oriented Actions. These are task-focused activities dealing with power and structural issues of implementing major change. Focusing on key tasks needed to accomplish implementation enables leaders to apply appropriate techniques that can simplify and facilitate successful completion of each task. Also, the approach used in designing tasks will affect the level of resistance encountered. Although it is time-consuming, getting employees involved in designing change activities does pay off by giving people a sense of control. Specific techniques for designing appropriate task and power structures are identified in the literature and summarized in Figure 10-9.[46]

Now that you have learned about the various styles of leadership described in this chapter, you may find it interesting to see how your own personality traits match up with each style. Complete Self-Assessment Exercise 10-2.

Self-Assessment Exercise 10-2

Personality, Leadership, and Change

Charismatic leaders have charisma based on personality and other personal traits that cut across all of the Big Five personality types. Review the ten characteristics of charismatic leaders in Figure 10-1. Which traits do you have?

_____

_____

_____

If you have a high *surgency* Big Five personality style (high need for power), you need to focus on using socialized rather than personalized charismatic leadership.

Transformational leaders tend to be charismatic as well. In Self-Assessment Exercise 10-1, you determined whether you were more transformational or transactional. How does your personality affect your transformational and transactional leadership styles?

_____

_____

_____

Strategic leadership is less based on personality than are charismatic and transformational leadership. Management level also has a lot to do with strategic planning and leadership, because it is primarily a function of top-level managers. Are you a strategic thinker with a focus on long-term planning? Do you have any business or personal plans for three to five years from now, or do you take things as they come without planning for the future?

_____

_____

Change leadership is based on the Big Five personality type _openness to experience_. Charismatic, transformational, and strategic leadership all require being receptive to change and influencing others to change. Are you open to trying new things and change, or do you tend to like the status quo and resist change? Do

you attempt to influence others to try new things?

_____

_____

Stewardship and servant leadership are more about changing management behavior and leadership style than follower behavior. Both are influenced by personality. If you have a high _agreeableness_ (high need for affiliation) Big Five personality type, you will tend to be more of a steward and servant than if you have a high _surgency_ (high need for power) personality type. Based on cultural roles, women possess these leadership characteristics more frequently than men. Do you focus on empowering others and putting their needs ahead of your own? Would you describe yourself as being a steward or servant leader? Explain.

_____

_____

_____

_____

_____

_____

11

Leadership of Culture, Diversity, and the Learning Organization

When Jim Adamson accepted the job of CEO of Advantica, the parent company of Denny's, the restaurant chain's image and reputation were being ripped to shreds by public opinion and in the legal court for its discriminatory practices. Today, Denny's is a model of equal opportunity employment in its industry, and prides itself on a diverse workforce that is committed to the company and devoted to serving all customers regardless of their race or ethnic background. The Denny's restaurant chain has been actively trying to repair its tarnished image after a racial discrimination lawsuit filed by Black customers six years ago resulted in the company paying $45.7 million to settle the case.

The restaurant chain's transformation to a leader in workplace diversity is largely credited to its tenacious and principled leader, Jim Adamson. Adamson began his tenure at Denny's with several bold initiatives that revealed the extent to which he believed in the company and his commitment to change its culture for the better. Denny's transformation began with the policy, "If you discriminate, we will fire you." Adamson continued with a series of actions that showed he was accessible to all, willing to discuss ideas with any member of the company, and open to suggestions. Using these tactics, Adamson set out to transform Denny's into a company that values diversity and promotes the efforts of minority-owned businesses by doing business with them.

The evidence supports the transformation that has taken place at Denny's. Today, nearly 40 percent of Denny's franchise restaurants are owned and operated by African Americans, and 36 percent of its board members are African Americans. Each year, Denny's does in excess of $125 million in business with minority suppliers, a collaborative effort that is mutually beneficial to both parties. To reinforce and promote its new culture, every person employed by Denny's receives training that emphasizes respect for racial and cultural differences, and each employee is encouraged to value and celebrate those differences. The company now spends more than $2 million annually on antiracism commercials trying to educate the public on the need for greater diversity in society. Denny's efforts and successes have not gone unnoticed by the same media that made it the butt of jokes in national headlines. Denny's is now ranked among *Fortune* magazine's top 10 companies in the United States for minorities. *Working Woman* magazine has ranked Denny's parent company, Advantica, eighth in its Year 2000 survey of the top 25 companies for women executives. There is no doubt that these changes would never have taken place without the leadership of Jim Adamson. Thanks to him, Denny's is now a visionary example of equal opportunity and anti-discrimination business practices.

■ *Go to the Internet:* For more information on Jim Adamson and Advantica Group, Inc. and to update the information provided in this case, do a name search on the Internet and visit Denny's website at **www.advanticadine.com.**

In this chapter we examine issues about organizational culture, values, and diversity—and the leader's role in shaping them. The final section of the chapter explores elements of organizational design that support efficient operations, comparing them with a new organizational form that emphasizes creativity and innovation. This new organizational form is called the learning organization.

CREATING A HIGH-PERFORMANCE CULTURE

culture: the set of key values, assumptions, understandings, and ways of thinking shared by members of an organization and taught to new members.

Culture is defined as the set of key values, assumptions, understandings, and ways of thinking that is shared by members of an organization and taught to new members.[1] Every organization has its own unique culture, distinguished by its own beliefs and philosophy about how it approaches problems and makes decisions. An organization's culture is manifested in the values and principles that leaders preach and practice, in its employees' attitudes and behavior, in ethical standards and policies, in the "chemistry" that permeates its work environment, and in the stories people repeat about events in the organization. An organization's position on diversity and multiculturalism is determined by its culture. It would appear from the opening case that organizational culture at Denny's prior to the class-action lawsuit and the ascension of Jim Adamson to the CEO position was largely responsible for the employees' treatment of Black customers. The broad scope of the problem across Denny's restaurants is evidence that the organization's culture supported or reinforced the negative beliefs of the employees about Black customers. An organization's culture determines the way that it responds to problems of survival in its external and internal environments. The responses to problems in the external environment are in the organization's vision, strategic intent, objectives, core strategies, and ways in which success is measured. The responses to internal problems include the basis for determining power and status, the criteria and procedure for allocating resources, the criteria for determining membership, and the prevailing mentality on how to interpret and respond to unpredictable and uncontrollable forces in the external environment. The beliefs that develop around these issues serve as the basis for role expectations that guide behavior, become embedded in how the organization conducts its business, are shared by managers and employees, and then persist as new employees are encouraged to embrace them.[2] As solutions are developed through experience, they become shared assumptions that are passed to new members. Over time, assumptions may become so deeply rooted in a culture that organizational members are no longer consciously aware of them. These basic underlying assumptions (whatever they are) become the core essence of the culture. Many components of culture are associated with the statements, values, philosophies, or policies articulated by a founder or other pioneering leaders. These principles are often incorporated in the leader's vision, mission statement, and core components of the organization's strategy. An example of this would be Wal-Mart. The essence of Wal-Mart's culture is dedication to customer satisfaction, zealous pursuit of low costs, and strong work ethic.

In addition to that are the ritualistic Saturday morning executive meetings at headquarters to exchange ideas and review problems and the company executives' commitment to visit stores, talk to customers, and solicit suggestions from employees. Creating a high-performance culture such as Wal-Mart's is a critical element of organizational success.

In this section, we will examine the power of culture, weak versus strong cultures, characteristics of low- and high-performance cultures, leadership actions for shaping culture, and different types of organizational cultures.

The Power of Culture

When an organization's culture fits the needs of its external environment and strategy, employees usually find it easy to implement the strategy successfully.[3] A culture grounded in values, practices, and behavioral norms that match the requirements for good strategy implementation helps energize people to do their jobs in an effective and efficient manner. For example, a strategy of product innovation and technological leadership will thrive in a culture where creativity, embracing change, risk taking, and challenging the status quo are popular themes. When an organization's culture is out of sync with what is needed for successful strategy implementation, it creates a strategy-culture gap that must be closed either by changing the strategy to fit the culture or changing the culture to fit the strategy. The narrower the strategy-culture gap, the more successful the organization's employees can be in creating a competitive advantage that is hard to beat.[4] Therefore, a deeply rooted culture that is well matched to strategy is a strong recipe for successful strategy execution. In this context, culture serves two important functions in organizations: (1) it creates internal unity, and (2) it helps the organization adapt to the external environment.

Internal Unity. A supportive culture provides a system of informal rules and peer pressures, which can be very powerful in determining behavior, thus affecting organizational performance.[5] It is culture that provides a value system in which to operate; and it promotes strong employee identification with the organization's vision, mission, goals, and strategy. Culturally approved behavior thrives and is rewarded, while culturally disapproved behavior is discouraged and even punished. The right culture makes employees feel genuinely better about their jobs, work environment, and the mission of the organization; employees are self-motivated to take on the challenge of realizing the organization's objectives and to work together as a team. Discrimination at Denny's thrived because the old culture supported it.

External Adaptation. Culture determines how the organization responds to changes in its external environment. The appropriate cultural values can ensure that an organization responds quickly to rapidly changing customer needs or to the offensive actions of a competitor. For example, if the competitive environment requires a strategy of superior customer service, the organizational culture should encourage such principles as listening to customers, empowering employees to make decisions, and rewarding employees for outstanding customer service deeds. The power of culture is in its potential to bring employees together, creating a team rather than a collection of isolated individuals. However, to ensure long-term survival and profitability, the organization's culture should also encourage adaptation to the external environment. Despite the importance of culture to strategy execution, not every organization can boast of a strong culture. Strong cultures are a contributing factor to attaining a competitive advantage, and a weak culture does the reverse. Therefore, understanding the differences between strong and weak cultures is critical to the culture creation process.

Weak versus Strong Cultures

Organizational cultures vary widely in the extent to which they are woven into the fabric of the organization's practices and behavioral norms. Therefore, the strength of any culture represents the degree of agreement among its people about the importance of specific values and ways of doing things. A weak culture symbolizes a lack of agreement on key values and norms, and a strong culture symbolizes widespread consensus.[6]

Weak Culture. An organization's culture is considered weak when there is little agreement on the values and norms governing member behavior.[7] This could be because the leader has not articulated a clear vision for the organization, or because members have not bought into the leader's vision for the organization. With no knowledge of what the organization stands for or allegiance to any common vision, weak cultures work against or hinder strategy implementation. Members of the organization typically show no deeply felt sense of identity with the organization's vision and strategy.

Strong Culture. An organization's culture is considered strong and cohesive when it conducts its business according to a clear and explicit set of principles and values. In this culture, management commits considerable time to communicating these principles and values and explaining how they relate to its mission and strategies. These values are shared widely across the organization, from top management to rank-and-file employees.[8] Organizations that have a strong culture typically feature public displays of creeds or values statements, and employees are urged to use these values and principles as the basis for decision making and other actions taken throughout the organization. In strong cultures, values and behavioral norms are so deeply ingrained that they do not change much even when a new leader takes over.

Factors that contribute significantly to strong cultures include (1) a strong leader or founder who develops principles, practices, and behavioral norms that are aligned with customer needs, strategic requirements, and competitive conditions; (2) total organizational commitment to operating the business according to these established traditions; and (3) unwavering commitment and support from the organization's key stakeholders—employees, customers, and shareholders.[9]

A strong culture is a valuable ally when it matches the requirements of a good strategy execution and a formidable enemy when it doesn't. Therefore, a strong culture by itself is not a guarantee of success unless it also encourages adaptation to a new strategy and the external environment.[10] A strong culture that does not encourage adaptation can, according to some, be more destructive to an organization than having a weak culture.[11] For example, Denny's rigid culture of close-mindedness and intolerance became a formidable enemy to the organization's efforts to change at a time of major demographic shifts in our racial mix.[12] IBM's strong bureaucratic and mainframe culture clashed with the shift to a PC-dominated world. Apple's culture clash stemmed from strong company sentiment to continue with the internally developed Macintosh technology (incompatible with all other brands of computers) despite growing preferences for Windows and Intel-compatible equipment and software.

Applying the Concept 11-1

Strong or Weak Culture

Identify each statement by its culture, writing the appropriate letter in the blank before each item.

a. weak   b. strong

_____ 1. I think we spend too much time in meetings hearing about our mission.

_____ 2. One thing I like about this place is that I can say and do whatever I want, and no one says anything about my behavior.

_____ 3. I think every department in the company has a copy of the mission statement on the wall somewhere.

_____ 4. I know that Jean Claude started the company, but he died 10 years ago. Do I have to keep hearing all these stories about him?

_____ 5. I find it a bit frustrating because top management seems to change its mind about our priorities whenever it suits them.

Characteristics of a Low-Performance Culture

Weak cultures are more likely to be associated with low performance. Low-performance cultures have a number of unhealthy characteristics that can undermine an organization's attempt to achieve its objectives. Figure 11-1 lists these characteristics.

- Insular thinking
- Resistance to change
- Politicized internal environment
- Unhealthy promotion practices

Figure 11-1 *Characteristics of low-performance cultures.*

Insular Thinking. In a low-performance culture, there is a tendency to avoid looking outside the organization for superior practices and approaches. Sometimes a company's past successes and status as an industry leader may lead to complacency. People within these organizations believe they have all the answers. Managerial arrogance and inward thinking often prevent the organization from making the necessary culture adaptation as external conditions change, thus leading to a decline in company performance. This was clearly the case at Denny's: Until the lawsuit and Jim Adamson's arrival, the organization refused to adapt to a changing external environment.

Resistance to Change. A second characteristic of low-performance cultures is one that can plague companies suddenly confronted with fast-changing domestic and global business conditions; it is resistance to change. The lack of leadership in encouraging and supporting employees with initiative or new ideas destroys creativity. Low-performance cultures want to maintain the status quo, so avoiding risk and not making mistakes becomes more important to a person's career advancement than entrepreneurial successes and innovative accomplishments. Companies such as Ford, General

Motors, Kmart, Sears, and Xerox enjoyed considerable success in years past, but when their business environments underwent significant change, they were burdened by a stifling bureaucracy and an inward-thinking mentality that rejected change.[13] Today, these companies and many others like them are struggling to reinvent themselves and rediscover what caused them to succeed in the first place.

Politicized Internal Environment. An environment that allows influential managers to operate their units autonomously—like personal kingdoms—is more likely to resist needed change. In a politically charged culture, many issues or problems get resolved along the lines of power. Vocal support or opposition by powerful executives, as well as personal lobbying by key leaders and coalitions among individuals or departments with vested interests in a particular outcome, may stifle important change. This culture has low performance because what's best for the organization is secondary to the self-interests of individual players.

Unhealthy Promotion Practices. Low-performance cultures tend to promote managers into higher leadership positions without serious consideration of a match between the job demands and the skills and capabilities of the appointee. To reward a hard-working manager or a long-time employee, an organization may promote a manager who is good at managing day-to-day operations, but lacking in strategic leadership skills such as crafting vision, strategies, and competitive capabilities or inspiring and developing the appropriate culture. This example represents a case of promoting a transaction-type manager to a senior executive position requiring transformation skills. While the former is adept at managing day-to-day operations, if he or she ascends to a senior executive position, the organization can find itself without a long-term vision and lack of leadership in forging new strategies, building new competitive capabilities, and creating a new culture—a condition that is ultimately harmful to long-term performance.[14]

Characteristics of High-Performance Cultures

Strong cultures are more likely to be associated with high performance. In a high-performance culture, there are a number of healthy cultural characteristics that enhance the organization's performance. High-performance cultures are results oriented and tend to create an atmosphere in which there is constructive pressure to perform. Figure 11-2 lists the key characteristics of high-performance cultures.

Culture Reinforcement Tools. Some of these tools include ceremonies, symbols, stories, language, and policies. High-performance cultures pull together these mechanisms to produce extraordinary results with ordinary people. High-performance organizations have ceremonies that highlight dramatic examples of what the company values. Ceremonies recognize and celebrate high-performing employees and help create an emotional bond among all employees.[15] Also, in high-performance cultures, leaders tell stories to new employees to illustrate the company's primary values and provide a shared understanding among workers. They also use symbols and

- Culture reinforcement tools
- Intensely people oriented
- Results oriented
- Emphasis on achievement and excellence

Figure 11-2 *Characteristics of high-performance cultures.*

specialized language like slogans to convey meaning and values. In high-performance cultures, policies on recruitment, selection, and training of new employees are different from those in low-performing cultures. For example, companies with strong, healthy cultures, such as W. L. Gore and Associates, 3M, Southwest Airlines, and Nordstrom often employ careful and vigorous hiring practices. At W. L. Gore and Associates, new employees go through an extensive interviewing process; when hired, a new employee is assigned a sponsor from within the company. The sponsor, who is usually an experienced veteran of the company, will ensure that the new associate fully understands the company's culture and approach to things. Southwest Airlines looks first and foremost for a sense of humor in the prospective employee; at 3M, creativity and team spirit are critical; and at Nordstrom, "niceness" is an important cultural value.[16]

Intensely People Oriented. Organizations with high-performance cultures reinforce their concern for individual employees in many different ways. They treat employees with dignity and respect, grant employees enough autonomy to excel and contribute, hold managers at every level responsible for the growth and development of the people who report to them, use the full range of rewards and punishment to enforce high performance standards, encourage employees to use their own initiative and creativity in performing their jobs, and set reasonable and clear performance standards for all employees.[17] An organization that treats its employees this way will generally benefit from increased teamwork, higher morale, and greater employee loyalty.

Applying the Concept 11-2

Low- or High-Performance Culture

Identify each statement as characteristic of a low- or high-performance culture. Write the appropriate letter in the blank before each item.

a. low   b. high

____ **1.** I wonder how many of the executives here ever climbed so high up the corporate ladder.

____ **2.** I enjoy being treated like a person, not like a number or a piece of equipment.

____ **3.** We get together regularly to celebrate one thing or another.

____ **4.** Why do I hear it's not in the budget so often around here?

____ **5.** I like the way management just tells us what it wants done. They let us do the job our way, so long as we meet the goals.

Results Oriented. High-performance cultures invest more time and resources to ensure that employees who excel or achieve performance targets are identified and rewarded. Control systems are developed to collect, analyze, and interpret employee performance data. Quantitative measures of success are used to identify employees who turn in winning performances. At General Electric and 3M, top executives make a point of honoring individuals who take it upon themselves to champion a new idea from conception to finished product or service. In these companies, "product champions" are given high visibility and room to push their ideas, with strong backing from managers. In high-performance cultures, every one and every task counts. Companies seek out reasons and opportunities to give out pins, buttons, badges, certificates, and medals to those in ordinary or routine jobs who stand out in their performance.

While a discussion of a results-oriented culture tends to emphasize the positive, there are negative reinforcers too. In high-performance cultures, managers whose units consistently perform poorly are quickly replaced or reassigned. In addition, weak-performing employees who reject the cultural emphasis on high performance and results are weeded out. To lessen the use of negative reinforcers, high-performance organizations aim at hiring only motivated, ambitious applicants whose attitudes and work ethic mesh well with a results-oriented work culture.

Emphasis on Achievement and Excellence. High-performance cultures create an atmosphere in which there is constructive pressure to be the best. Management pursues policies and practices that inspire people to do their best. When an organization performs consistently at or near peak capability, the outcome is not only more success but also a culture permeated with a spirit of high performance.[18]

Leaders as Culture Creators

Changing a company's culture and aligning it with strategy are among the most challenging responsibilities of management. There are many options leaders can exercise to create and maintain strong, high-performance cultures that facilitate internal unity as well as enable the organization to adapt to the needs of the external environment. First, the leader must diagnose which aspects of the existing culture are strategy supportive and which are not. Second, the leader must communicate openly and honestly to all employees about those aspects of the culture that have to be changed or the need for a whole new culture. Third, the leader has to follow swiftly with visible actions to modify the culture or implant a new one. Jim Adamson followed these three steps when he became the CEO of Denny's, and the results have been impressive.

To create strong, high-performance cultures, leaders can initiate many different types of actions. Some of these actions are substantive, while others are primarily symbolic—one scholar used the terms *primary* and *secondary mechanisms* to make the distinction.[19] Symbolic actions are valuable for the signals they send about the kinds of behavior and performance leaders wish to encourage and promote. The meaning is implied in the action taken. Substantive actions are explicit and highly visible, and they indicate management's commitment to new strategic initiatives and the associated cultural changes. These are actions that everyone will understand are intended to establish a new culture more in tune with the organization's strategy. Figure 11-3 summarizes the key managerial actions that offer the greatest potential for shaping organizational culture. These are divided into symbolic and substantive actions.

Symbolic Actions
- Leaders serving as role models
- Ceremonial events for high achievers
- Special appearances by leaders
- Organizational structure

Substantive Actions
- Replacing old-culture members with new members
- Changing dysfunctional policies and operating practices
- Creating a strategy-culture fit
- Realigning rewards/incentives and resource allocation
- Facilities design
- Developing a written values statement

Figure 11-3 *Leadership actions for shaping culture.*

Leaders Serving as Role Models. Employees learn what is valued most in an organization by watching what attitudes and behaviors leaders pay attention to and reward, and whether the leaders' own behavior matches the espoused values. For example, top executives set good examples when they lead a cost reduction effort by curtailing executive perks, and when they emphasize the importance of responding to customers' needs by requiring all managers and executives to spend a portion of each week talking with customers and understanding their needs. The message employees get when a leader institutes a policy or procedure but fails to act in accordance with it is that the policy is really not important or necessary.

Ceremonial Events for High Achievers. Leaders can schedule ceremonies to designate and honor people whose actions and performance exemplify what is called for in the new culture. Ceremonies reinforce specific values and create emotional bonds by allowing employees to share in important moments.[20] A ceremony often includes the presentation of an award. Mary Kay Cosmetics awards an array of prizes—from ribbons to pink automobiles—to its beauty consultants for reaching various sales targets.[21]

Special Appearances by Leaders. Leaders who are serious about their role in creating a high-performance culture make a habit of appearing at ceremonial functions to praise individuals and groups who symbolize the values and practices of the new culture. Effective leaders will also make special appearances at non-ceremonial events such as employee training programs to stress strategic priorities, values, cultural norms, and ethical principles. They understand the symbolic value of their presence at group gatherings and use the opportunity to reinforce the key aspects of the culture. To organization members, the mere appearance of the executive—and the things he or she chooses to emphasize—clearly communicate management's commitment to the new culture.

Organizational Structure. Organizational structure can symbolize culture. A decentralized structure reflects a belief in individual initiative and shared responsibility, whereas a centralized structure reflects the belief that only the leader knows what is best for the organization.

In addition to symbolic actions that leaders can employ in communicating their organization's culture, substantive actions must be used to complement the symbolic actions. Substantive actions have to be credible, highly visible, and indicative of management's commitment to new strategic initiatives and cultural changes. Figure 11-3 lists six substantive actions that leaders can initiate to shape culture.

Replace Old-Culture Members with New Members. The strongest sign that management is truly committed to creating a new culture is replacing old-culture members who are unwilling to change with a "new breed" of employees. Beyond immediate actions to replace old-culture employees, leaders can influence culture by establishing new criteria for recruiting, selecting, promoting, and firing employees. These new criteria should be consistent with the new culture of the organization. At Denny's, Jim Adamson's first executive action was to introduce a new policy that said, "If you discriminate, we will fire you."

Changing Dysfunctional Policies and Operating Practices. Existing policies and practices that impede the execution of new strategies must be changed. Policies on budgets, planning, reports, and performance reviews can be used to emphasize aspects of the organization's culture. Through these actions, leaders let other members know what is important. Wal-Mart executives have had a long-standing practice of spending two to three days every week visiting Wal-Mart's stores and talking with store managers and employees. Sam Walton, Wal-Mart's founder, insisted, "The key is to get out into the store and listen to what the associates have to say. Our best ideas come from clerks and stock persons."[22] This practice instituted by the founder himself has over the years become part of Wal-Mart's culture.

Creating a Strategy-Culture Fit. It is the leader's responsibility to select a strategy that is compatible with the prevailing culture or to change the culture to fit the chosen strategy. The lack of a fit will hinder or constrain strategy execution. In rapidly changing business environments, the capacity to introduce new strategies is a necessity if a company is to perform well over long periods of time. Strategic agility and fast organizational response to new conditions requires a culture that quickly accepts and supports company efforts to adapt to environmental change rather than a culture that resists change. A strategy-culture fit allows for easy adaptation, while a strategy-culture mismatch makes for a difficult adaptation. Even during periods of stability and economic growth, it is still critical for the leader to pay attention to the existing culture. The culture of an organization naturally evolves over time, and without strong leadership, it can change in the wrong direction. Key values or practices in a culture may gradually erode if no attention is paid to the culture.[23] For example, incompatible subcultures may develop in various departments of the organization, leading to a culture of isolation rather than teamwork and cooperation.

Realigning Rewards/Incentives and Resource Allocation. Tying compensation incentives directly to new measures of strategic performance is a culture-shaping undertaking, because it gives the leader leverage to reward only those performances that are supportive of the strategy and culture. Shifting resources from old-strategy projects and programs to new-strategy projects and programs also communicates management's commitment to a new strategy and culture, assuming there is a strategy-culture fit.

Facilities Design. Leaders can design the work environment to reflect the values they want to promote within the organization. For example, having common eating facilities for all employees, no special parking areas, and similar offices is consistent with a value of equality. An open office layout with fewer walls separating employees is consistent with a value for open communication.

Developing a Written Values Statement. Many leaders today set forth their organization's values and codes of ethics in written documents. Written statements have the advantage of explicitly stating the company's position on ethical and moral issues, and they serve as benchmarks for judging company policies and actions as well as individual conduct. Value statements serve as a building block in the task of culture creation and maintenance.[24] Figure 11-4 presents Starbucks' mission statement as it appears on the company's website. The mission is followed by six guiding value statements that symbolize the company culture.

Once values and ethical norms have been formally set forth, they must be ingrained in the company's policies, practices, and daily operations. Value statements have no credibility unless all employees at every level of the organization put them into action.

Cultural Value Types

Rather than looking at culture as either good or bad, some scholars view it as a construct that varies according to an organization's external environment and its strategic focus. Therefore, organizations that operate under similar environments will tend to reveal similar cultural values.[25] The emerging consensus is that an appropriate match between cultural values, organizational strategy, and the external environment can enhance organizational performance.[26]

Research on organizational effectiveness and culture suggests that the match between environment, strategy, and values is associated with four types of cultures. The makeup of the culture types is based on two dimensions: (1) the degree of environmental turbulence (stable versus dynamic environment) and (2) the organization's leadership focus or orientation (internal versus external focus). As shown in Figure 11-5, together the dimensions reveal four types of culture with emphasis on specific values.[27] The extent to which an organization's external environment is stable or changing will influence its culture. Also, top management's philosophy may be to focus on internal or external requirements as imperatives for achieving organizational objectives. This too would influence the organization's culture. The interaction of these two variables—degree of environmental turbulence and management's strategic focus—creates four types of organizational cultures.

The four types of organizational cultures are competitive, bureaucratic, adaptive, and cooperative. These cultural types are not mutually exclusive; an organization may have cultural values that fall into more than one group,

Establish Starbucks as the premier purveyor of the finest coffee in the world while maintaining our uncompromising principles as we grow. The following six guiding principles will help us measure the appropriateness of our decisions.

Treat each other with respect and dignity.

Embrace diversity as an essential component in the way we do business.

Apply the highest standards of excellence to the purchasing, roasting, and fresh delivery of our coffee.

Develop enthusiastically satisfied customers all of the time.

Contribute positively to our communities and our environment.

Recognize that profitability is essential to our future success.

Source: www.starbucks.com

Figure 11-4 *Starbucks' mission statement.*

Figure 11-5 *Types of organizational culture.*

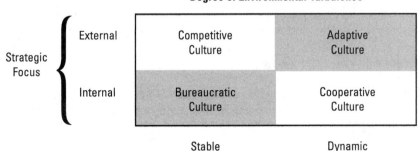

Degree of Environmental Turbulence

Strategic Focus		Stable	Dynamic
	External	Competitive Culture	Adaptive Culture
	Internal	Bureaucratic Culture	Cooperative Culture

or even into all groups. However, high-performance cultures with strong values tend to emphasize or lean more toward one particular culture type. The four cultural value types are discussed in the following sections.

Cooperative Culture. In a period of change and uncertainty, the cooperative culture is seen by some leaders as the key to superior performance. The *cooperative culture* has an *internal focus on empowering employees to respond quickly to changing expectations from the external environment.* This culture emphasizes the value of satisfying employee needs above all others. In organizations with cooperative cultures, leaders emphasize teamwork, cooperation, and consideration for employees and customers as well as social equality. These organizations are generally friendly places to work in, and the atmosphere is more like a family than the "cut and dried" task-oriented cultures found in some organizations. For example, Starbucks is a very aggressive, innovative company that could be considered to have a competitive or adaptive culture; however, its overall set of values (as revealed in its mission statement) places it more closely in the cooperative culture group because of its focus on employees. Howard Schultz, Starbucks' CEO, believed that the company's success was heavily dependent on customers having a positive experience in its stores. According to Schultz, this meant having store employees who were knowledgeable, dedicated, and passionate and who have the skills and personality to deliver consistently pleasing customer service. Consequently, Schultz set out to create a people-oriented, cooperative culture to achieve that goal.[28]

Adaptive Culture. The *adaptive culture* is *characterized by a fast-changing business environment and an external strategic focus.* This culture encourages values that support the organization's ability to introduce new strategies and practices in response to changing environmental conditions. In adaptive cultures, members are receptive to risk taking, experimentation, and innovation. There is a spirit of doing what is necessary to ensure long-term organizational success, provided that core values and business principles are upheld in the process. Members have the autonomy to make decisions and act freely to meet new customer needs, and responsiveness to customers is highly valued and rewarded. There is a sense of equality in the adaptive culture; each member is valued and encouraged to develop to their full potential. The adaptive culture is generally referred to as the culture of innovation.

The leaders of adaptive cultures are skilled at changing the right things in the right ways, not changing for the sake of change and not compromising core values or principles. Rewarding employees for experimenting and taking risks is a big factor in gaining their support for change. Leaders consciously seek to train and promote individuals who display initiative, creativity, and risk taking. A company like 3M, where experimentation and risk taking are a way of life, is a perfect example of the adaptive culture at work.[29]

Competitive Culture. A *competitive culture* is *characterized by a stable business environment and an external strategic leadership focus.* An organization with a competitive culture operates in a stable external environment and as

cooperative culture: internal focus on empowering employees to respond quickly to changing expectations from the external environment.

adaptive culture: characterized by a fast-changing business environment and an external strategic focus.

competitive culture: characterized by a stable business environment and an external strategic leadership focus.

such is less concerned about rapid environmental changes. Leaders of competitive cultures focus on achieving specific targets such as market share, revenue growth, or profitability. This is a results-oriented culture that values competitiveness, personal initiative, aggressiveness, and the willingness to work long and hard to achieve results. The drive to win is what holds the organization together. Pepsi-Cola and Coca-Cola are two companies that exemplify the competitive culture. Both have the vision to be the best in the world. Each company socializes its members to view the other's employees as enemies and to do whatever is necessary to defeat them in the marketplace. High performance standards and tough reviews are used to weed out the weak and reward the strong. At Pepsi-Cola for example, former CEO Wayne Calloway was known to set back-breaking standards and then systematically raise them each year. Executives who met his standards were generously rewarded—stock options, bonuses, rapid promotions, and first-class air travel—and those who did not would feel the pressure to produce or risk negative consequences such as demotions, transfers, or losing their jobs.[30]

Bureaucratic Culture. *The **bureaucratic culture** has an internal focus and operates in a stable environment.* The bureaucratic culture emphasizes strict adherence to set rules and procedures, which ensure an orderly way of doing business. Organizations with bureaucratic cultures are highly structured and efficiency driven. The bureaucratic culture is becoming increasingly difficult to maintain because of the growing level of environmental turbulence facing most organizations. Few organizations operate in a stable environment, forcing their leaders to make the shift away from bureaucratic cultures because of the need for greater flexibility and responsiveness.

bureaucratic culture: has an internal focus and operates in a stable environment.

The four cultural value types can be successful under different environmental conditions and organizational orientations. The relative emphasis on various cultural values depends on the organization's strategic focus and on the needs of the external environment. It is the responsibility of strategic leaders to create the fit between strategy and culture by ensuring that organizations do not persist in cultural values that worked in the past but are no longer relevant.

Applying the Concept 11-3

Type of Organizational Culture

Identify each statement as characteristic of one of the types of organizational cultures. Write the appropriate letter in the blank before each item.

a. competitive
b. adaptive
c. bureaucratic
d. cooperative

_____ **1.** Things don't change much around here. We just focus on doing our functional tasks to standards.

_____ **2.** In the airline industry, we keep a close eye on ticket prices to make sure we are not under-priced.

_____ **3.** At Toyota, we focus on teamwork with much input into decision making to satisfy customers.

_____ **4.** Being a young Internet company, we go with the flow.

VALUE-BASED LEADERSHIP

values: generalized beliefs or behaviors that are considered by an individual or a group to be important.

Values are generalized beliefs or behaviors that are considered by an individual or a group to be important.[31] Relationships between leaders and members of an organization are based on shared values. How leaders' ethical values influence organizational behavior and performance is the subject of value-based leadership. Employees learn about values by watching leaders. In this section we will examine the following topics: the leader's role in advocating and enforcing ethical behavior, stages of moral development and how they affect an individual's ability to translate values into behavior, a framework for understanding global cultural value differences, and finally, the implications for leadership practice. However, before we begin, complete Self-Assessment Exercise 11-1 to determine your personal values in eight areas.

Self-Assessment Exercise 11-1

Personal Values

Following are 16 items. Rate how important each one is to you on a scale of 0 (not important) to 100 (very important). Write a number from 0 to 100 on the line to the left of each item.

0—10—20—30—40—50—60—70—80—90—100
Not important   *Somewhat important*   *Very important*

_____ 1. An enjoyable, satisfying job

_____ 2. A high-paying job

_____ 3. A good marriage

_____ 4. Meeting new people, social events

_____ 5. Involvement in community activities

_____ 6. My relationship with God/my religion

_____ 7. Exercising, playing sports

_____ 8. Intellectual development

_____ 9. A career with challenging opportunities

_____ 10. Nice cars, clothes, home, etc.

_____ 11. Spending time with family

_____ 12. Having several close friends

_____ 13. Volunteer work for not-for-profit organizations like the cancer society

_____ 14. Meditation, quiet time to think, pray, etc.

_____ 15. A healthy, balanced diet

_____ 16. Educational reading, TV, self-improvement programs, etc.

Next, transfer your rating numbers for each of the 16 items to the appropriate columns. Then add the two numbers in each column.

	Professional	Financial	Family	Social
	1. _____	2. _____	3. _____	4. _____
	9. _____	10. _____	11. _____	12. _____
Totals:	_____	_____	_____	_____

	Community	Spiritual	Physical	Intellectual
	5. _____	6. _____	7. _____	8. _____
	13. _____	14. _____	15. _____	16. _____
Totals:	_____	_____	_____	_____

The higher the total in any area, the higher the value you place on that particular area. The closer the numbers are in all eight areas, the better rounded you are.

Think about the time and effort you put forth in your top three values. Is it sufficient to allow you to achieve the level of success you want in each area? If not, what can you do to change? Is there any area in which you feel you should have a higher value total? If yes, which, and what can you do to change?

Advocating Ethical Behavior

Many values make up an organization's culture, but the one that is considered most critical for leaders is ethics.[32] Recall from Chapter 2 that ethics are the standards of right and wrong that influence behavior; in Self-Assessment Exercise 2-6, you determined how ethical your behavior is. Ethics provide guidelines for judging conduct and decision making.[33] However, for an organization to display consistently high ethical standards, top leadership must model ethical and moral conduct. Value-based leaders cultivate a high level of trust and respect from members, based not just on stated values but on their willingness to make personal sacrifices for the sake of upholding values. A leader's ethics reflect the contributions of diverse inputs, including personal beliefs, family, peers, religion, and the broader society. The family and religious upbringing of leaders often influence the principles by which they conduct business. A leader's personal beliefs may enable him or her to pursue an ethical choice even if the decision is unpopular. It is evident from the opening case that Jim Adamson's personal beliefs and ethnics were influential factors in his decision to change the discriminatory practices of Denny's. His open-door policy and willingness to discuss ideas with any and every member of the organization set the example for other managers. Given the widespread nature of discrimination at Denny's, it is safe to assume that Adamson's push for a different set of values and ethics was not a popular move from the start.

In organizations that strive hard to make high ethical standards a reality, top management communicates its commitment through formal policies and programs such as codes of ethics, ethics committees, training programs, and disclosure mechanisms. These structures are discussed in the following sections.

Code of Ethics. A code of ethics is usually a formal statement of an organization's ethical values. Leaders must consistently communicate to members the value of not only observing ethical codes but also reporting ethical violations. "Gray areas" must be identified and openly discussed with members, and procedures created to offer guidance when issues in these areas arise. A growing number of organizations have added to their list of formal statements and public pronouncements a code of ethics. According to a study by the Center for Business Ethics, 90 percent of *Fortune* 500 companies now have codes of ethics.[34] The lesson from these companies is that it is never enough to assume that activities are being conducted ethically, nor can it be assumed that employees understand they are expected to act with integrity.

Some organizations include ethics as part of their mission. Such mission statements generally define ethical values as well as corporate culture and contain language about company responsibility, quality of product, and treatment of employees. For example, Figure 11-4 featuring Starbucks Corporation's mission statement contains a set of six guiding principles that illustrates how the company's mission and core values translate into ethical business practices.

Ethics Committees. To encourage ethical behavior, some organizations are setting up ethics committees charged with overseeing ethical issues.

ombudsperson: a single person entrusted with the responsibility of acting as the organization's conscience.

In other organizations the responsibility is given to an ombudsperson. *An ethics **ombudsperson** is a single person entrusted with the responsibility of acting as the organization's conscience.* He or she hears and investigates complaints and points out potential ethics failures to top management. In many large corporations, there are ethics departments with full-time staff charged with helping employees deal with day-to-day ethical problems or questions.

Training Programs. Training provides the opportunity for everyone in the organization to be informed and educated on key aspects of the code of ethics. Training teaches employees how to incorporate ethics into daily behavior. Starbucks Corporation uses new employee training to ingrain values such as embracing diversity, taking personal responsibility, and treating everyone with respect.[35]

Disclosure Mechanism. As part of enforcing ethical conduct, employees are encouraged to report any knowledge of ethical violations. *Whistle blowing is employee disclosure of illegal or unethical practices on the part of the organization.* Whistle blowing can be risky for those who choose to do it—they have been known to suffer consequences including being ostracized by coworkers, demoted or transferred to less desirable jobs, and even losing their jobs. Policies that protect employees from going through these setbacks will signal management's genuine commitment to enforce ethical behavior. Some organizations have done this by setting up hotlines to give employees a confidential way to report unethical or illegal actions.

whistle blowing: employee disclosure of illegal or unethical practices on the part of the organization.

Levels of Moral Reasoning

moral reasoning: the process leaders use to make decisions about ethical and unethical behaviors.

Here the focus of our discussion shifts to the question of how one thinks about value-laden issues or ethical dilemmas—what others refer to as moral reasoning. *Moral reasoning refers to the process leaders use to make decisions about ethical and unethical behaviors.* According to research findings, people progress through a series of developmental stages in their moral reasoning. The sequence of these stages is fixed, moving through progressively more complex constructs of analyzing moral solutions. A leader's stage of moral development will affect his or her ability to translate values into behavior. Therefore, moral reasoning is instrumental in shaping ethical values.[36]

pre-conventional level: a person's criteria for moral behavior are based primarily on satisfying their self-interest.

The focus of moral reasoning is on the reasoning process rather than on the decision per se. The first stage of moral reasoning is called the *pre-conventional level, in which a person's criteria for moral behavior are based primarily on satisfying their self-interest.* For example, some people make decisions and act primarily to obtain rewards or to avoid punishment for themselves. The second stage of moral reasoning is the *conventional level, in which the criteria for moral behavior are based primarily on gaining others' approval and behaving according to societal standards.* This means acting not just from self-interest but beyond that to include willingly conforming to the law and responding to the expectations of others. Ethical violations lead to feelings of guilt or dishonor. The final stage of moral reasoning is the *post-conventional level, in which the criteria for moral behavior are based on universal, abstract principles, which may even transcend the laws of a particular*

conventional level: the criteria for moral behavior are based primarily on gaining others' approval and behaving according to societal standards.

post-conventional level: the criteria for moral behavior are based on universal, abstract principles, which may even transcend the laws of a particular society.

society. These are self-imposed ethical principles that do not change with reward or punishment. Individuals strive to develop higher moral principles that maintain their self-respect and the respect of others.

Because people's level of moral reasoning shapes their values, leaders can strive to develop higher moral principles so that their actions reflect appropriate ethical values. When faced with difficult decisions, value-based leaders know what they stand for, and they have the courage to act on their principles regardless of external pressures. A manager's values are also shaped by differences in national or societal culture. The following section describes a framework for understanding the bases of broad societal cultural differences.

Applying the Concept 11-4

Levels of Moral Reasoning

Identify each statement by its level of moral reasoning. Write the appropriate letter in the blank before each item.

a. pre-conventional level   c. post-conventional level
b. conventional level

_____ **1.** The boss is really committed to being politically correct; why is he so concerned about making sure everyone likes him?

_____ **2.** When are you going to learn that our managers are only concerned about getting their stock options?

_____ **3.** The boss is committed to ethics and leads in this area by example.

A Framework of Value Dimensions for Understanding Cultural Differences

Whether organizational or national, culture is a product of values and norms that people use to guide and control their behavior. Recall from section two that values are generalized beliefs or behaviors that are considered by an individual or group to be important. Values determine what people think are the right, good, or appropriate ways to behave. Values therefore specify the norms that prescribe the appropriate behaviors for reaching desired goals. On a national level, a country's values and norms determine what kinds of attitudes and behaviors are acceptable or appropriate. The people of a particular culture are socialized into these values as they grow up, and norms and social guidelines prescribe the way they should behave toward one another.

The growing diversity of the workforce and the increasing globalization of the marketplace create the need for multicultural leaders. Multicultural leaders possess skills and attitudes that enable them to relate effectively to and motivate people across race, gender, age, social strata, and nationality. Each unique culture has overt and subtle differences that influence how its members behave and interact with others. In this section we explore how national cultures differ by examining their values. Seven key dimensions of differences in cultural values and the implications for leadership practice are discussed.

Researchers have developed a conceptual framework for analyzing cultural differences. This framework examines seven different value dimensions and how selected nationalities relate to them. Each value dimension represents a continuum. The first five dimensions came from Geert Hofstede's research, spanning 18 years and involving over 160,000 people from over sixty countries.[37] The last two value dimensions are the result of recent qualitative research.[38] Figure 11-6 summarizes these values, which are briefly discussed in the following sections.

Individualism–Collectivism. This dimension involves a person's source of identity in society. Some societies value individualism more than collectivism, and vice versa. **Individualism** *is a psychological state in which people see themselves first as individuals and believe their own interest and values are primary.* **Collectivism,** at the other end of the continuum, *is the state of mind wherein the values and goals of the group whether extended family, ethnic group, or company are primary.* In a company or business setting, members of a society who value individualism are more concerned with individual accomplishments than with group or team accomplishments. They are more highly motivated by individual-based incentives than by group-based incentives. Members of a society who value collectivism, on the other hand, are typically more concerned with the group or organization than with themselves. The United States, Great Britain, and Canada have been described as individualistic cultures, while Greece, Japan, and Mexico are said to have collectivistic cultures.

High–Low Uncertainty Avoidance. *A society with* **high uncertainty avoidance** *is a culture in which most people do not tolerate risk, avoid the unknown, and are comfortable when the future is relatively predictable and certain.* The other end of the continuum is a society whose people have **low uncertainty avoidance;** *most people in this culture are comfortable and accepting of the unknown, and tolerate risk and unpredictability.* This dimension is about a person's response to ambiguity. From an organizational context, the culture of a company with high uncertainty avoidance will emphasize tight controls and a rigid structure to ensure a certain outcome. The culture of a company with low uncertainty avoidance will emphasize greater tolerance for ambiguity and uncertainty, evident in its loose controls and a dynamic

individualism: a psychological state in which people see themselves first as individuals and believe their own interest and values are primary.

collectivism: state of mind wherein values and goals of the group, whether extended family, ethnic group, or company, are primary.

high uncertainty avoidance: refers to a culture in which most people do not tolerate risk, avoid the unknown, and are comfortable when the future is relatively predictable and certain.

low uncertainty avoidance: refers to a culture in which most people are comfortable and accepting of the unknown, and tolerate risk and unpredictability.

Figure 11-6 *A framework of value dimensions for understanding cultural differences.*

Individualism	High Uncertainty Avoidance	High Power Distance	Long-term Orientation	Masculinity	Informality	Scarce Time Orientation
↕	↕	↕	↕	↕	↕	↕
Collectivism	Low Uncertainty Avoidance	Low Power Distance	Short-term Orientation	Femininity	Formality	Abundant Time Orientation

structure. The United States, Australia, and Canada are associated with cultures having low uncertainty avoidance; Argentina, Italy, Japan, and Israel have cultures displaying high uncertainty avoidance.

High–Low Power Distance. This dimension deals with society's orientation to authority. The extent to which people of different status, power, or authority should behave toward each other as equals or unequals is referred to as *power distance. In a **high-power-distance culture,** the leaders and followers rarely interact as equals; while in a **low-power-distance culture,** leaders and their followers interact on several levels as equals.* In an organization with a high-power-distance culture, the leader makes many decisions simply because he or she is the leader, and the group members readily comply. On the other end of the continuum, an organization with a low-power-distance culture will have employees who do not readily recognize a power hierarchy. Decision making is a group-oriented and participative activity. Members will accept directions from their leaders only when they think the leader is right. High-power-distance cultures include Mexico, Japan, Spain, and France. Low-power-distance cultures include Germany, the United States, and Ireland.

high-power-distance culture: society in which the leaders and followers rarely interact as equals.

low-power-distance culture: society in which leaders and their followers interact on several levels as equals.

Long-term–Short-term Orientation. This dimension refers to a society's long- or short-term orientation toward life and work. People from a culture with a long-term orientation have a futuristic view of life and thus are thrifty (saving) and persistent in achieving goals. They do not demand immediate returns on their investments. A short-term orientation derives from values that express a concern for maintaining personal stability or happiness and for living for the present. Pacific Rim countries, known for their long-term orientation, are also known for their high rate of per capita savings. France and the United States, two countries that tend to spend more and save less, have a more short-term orientation.

Masculinity–Femininity. This value dimension was used by Hofstede to make the distinction between the quest for material assets and the quest for social connections with people. In this context, *masculinity describes a culture that emphasizes assertiveness and a competitive drive for money and material objects.* At the other end of the continuum is *femininity, which describes a culture that emphasizes developing and nurturing personal relationships and a high quality of life.* Countries with masculine cultures include Japan and Italy; feminine cultures include Sweden and Denmark.

masculinity: describes a culture that emphasizes assertiveness and a competitive drive for money and material objects.

femininity: describes a culture that emphasizes developing and nurturing personal relationships and a high quality of life.

Informality–Formality. This dimension refers to a society's attitude toward rules, traditions, rank, and customs. A society that values formality emphasizes strict adherence to customs, social rules, rank, and ceremonial protocol. In contrast, a society that values informality displays a casual attitude toward customs, social rules, rank, and ceremonial protocol. From an organizational context, a company with a culture of formality will enforce strict rules and order and maintain a very rigid organizational structure, whereas a company with a culture of informality is more likely to possess a flexible, organic structure. Latin American countries value formality, while the United States and Canada value informality.

Scarce Time–Abundant Time Orientation. This value dimension is about a society's perspective on time; it is the sense that time is a scarce—or abundant—resource. Cultures with a scarce time orientation focus on short-term planning and investment. There is a sense of urgency and impatience associated with people who have a scarce time orientation. People with an abundant time orientation view time as an unlimited resource and tend to show more patience. They have a long-term focus on planning and investment. People in the United States are noted for their scarce time orientation. Everything runs on deadlines and strict time schedules. Asians and Middle Easterners, in contrast, are patient negotiators whose sense of time is more casual or laid back.

Implications for Leadership Practice. To successfully manage in the global environment, organizations and their leaders have to learn to deal with the different values, norms, and attitudes that characterize different national cultures. Leaders have to recognize, for example, that although organizations in the United States may reward and encourage individual accountability, a different norm applies in industrialized Japan, where the group makes important decisions. In the United States, competition between work-group members for career advancement is desirable. In some other cultures, however, members resist competing with peers for rewards or promotions to avoid disrupting the harmony of the group or appearing self-interested. A leader, for example, who wants to improve quality and has adopted total quality management (TQM) as his technique must hire people who value collectivism rather than individualism.

Value differences can be a source of interpersonal conflict. Often, people on different sides of an issue see only their side as morally justifiable. Nonetheless, in today's global economy, people holding contrasting values will need to work together. Dealing with diverse and divergent values will be an increasingly common challenge for leaders. Both leaders and followers will have to learn to minimize the conflict and tension often associated with value differences. Strategies for effectively managing multicultural work-groups with value differences are discussed in the next section on diversity.

CHANGING DEMOGRAPHICS AND DIVERSITY

In the United States and many other societies of the industrialized world, multiculturalism is a fact of life. The United States has been described as the "melting pot" of cultures. The thinking not long ago was that to make it in this society, one had to blend in with the mainstream culture. Individuals from different cultures responded to this pressure by trying to lose or disguise their identity—adopting new names, changing accents, and abandoning old customs, traditions, and values. The prevailing belief was that to get ahead, one had to assimilate into mainstream culture. Job opportunities favored those who blended in.

In the recent past, however, it would appear that the melting-pot mentality has been replaced by the "salad bowl" mentality. Rather than assimilation, the emphasis has shifted toward cultural integration without necessarily losing one's identity. Diversity in the workplace, brought on by a multicultural society, is no longer viewed as a liability but an asset. Many organizations have found that tapping into diversity reveals new and innovative ways of viewing traditional problems, and that diversity provides a rich mix of talents for today's globally competitive marketplace. Valuing and effectively managing diversity is an imperative for competitive success in many industries.[39] In this section, we explore the current state of diversity in the U.S. workforce, reasons for embracing diversity, and strategies organizations are employing to achieve full diversity. These strategies include removing obstacles to achieving diversity, creating a culture that supports diversity, and conducting diversity training and leadership education programs.

Current State of Workforce Diversity

Diversity describes differences resulting from age, gender, race, ethnicity, religion, and sexual orientation. In the last twenty-five years, attitudes toward diversity have changed, for obvious reasons:— increasing diversity of the workforce and globalization. Demographic changes as well as minority representation in the workforce have accounted for the most significant increase in workforce diversity. These two trends have made it imperative for U.S. companies to pay attention to issues of diversity. The demographic makeup of employees entering the workforce has been changing rapidly. By the year 2005, African American and Hispanic employees are expected to make up over 25 percent of the workforce, and the percentage of White males is expected to decrease from 51 percent to 44 percent. If the estimates hold true, through the year 2000, approximately 45 percent of all net additions to the workforce will be non-Caucasian, with half of them first-generation immigrants and almost two-thirds female.[40]

The other factor that has led to companies valuing and managing diversity is globalization. Globalization has led to firms originating, producing, and marketing their products and services worldwide. The emergence of a largely borderless economic world has created a new reality for organizations of all shapes and sizes. The dollar value of world trade has more than doubled in the past decade and will exceed $8 trillion in 2002. U.S.-based companies like Pepsi-Cola, Coca-Cola, Procter & Gamble, AT&T, Ford, Nike, General Mills, Boeing, McDonald's, and many others have established a significant presence in Europe, Asia, and South America. They face competition from European companies such as Daimler-Chrysler, Nestlé of Switzerland, Canada's Northern Telecom, Siemens of Germany, Sweden's Ericsson, and many others who also have a significant presence in the United States.

Collaboration between companies has become a common way to meet the demands of global competition. Global strategic alliances between independent firms for the purpose of achieving common goals are becoming quite prevalent. General Mills and Nestlé of Switzerland created Cereal Partners Worldwide for the purpose of fine-tuning Nestlé's European cereal, and for marketing and distributing General Mills' cereals worldwide.[41] In this global environment, most manufactured goods contain components from more than one country. Also, the number of foreign-born managers being appointed to lead U.S. companies is increasing. U.S. companies such as Ford, Gerber, Heinz, and NCR are led by CEOs from other countries. Almost every employee in the workforce today is dealing with a wider range of cultures than ever before. The challenge for organizational leaders is to recognize that each person can bring value and strengths to the workplace based on his or her own unique combination of characteristics.

Reasons for Embracing Diversity

Some may ask, "Is diversity really an important issue?" We've already discussed globalization. But even if we focus only on the United States, by the year 2030 it has been estimated that, although Caucasians will still be the majority race, less than 50 percent of Americans will be Caucasian. The obvious reason for embracing diversity is that shifting demographics and increasing globalization have significantly changed the composition of the workforce. Thus, organizations are forced to change their views and approach to diversity in order to reflect this new reality. However, there are other pertinent reasons that organizations need to embrace diversity.

- Embracing diversity can offer a company a marketing advantage. A diversified workforce may offer insight into understanding and meeting the needs of diverse customers. A representative workforce facilitates selling goods and services, because employees who share similar cultural traits with the customers may be able to develop better, longer-lasting customer relationships.

- Embracing diversity can help a company to develop and retain talented people. When an organization has a reputation for valuing diversity, it tends to attract the best job candidates among women and other culturally diverse groups.

- Embracing diversity can be cost effective. As organizations become more diversified, some are experiencing higher levels of job dissatisfaction and turnover among minority groups, who are finding it hard to fit in with the old, Caucasian-male culture. This has been the case with organizations that have not shown a total commitment and support for diversity. Organizations that wholeheartedly embrace diversity and make everyone feel valued for what they can contribute may increase the job satisfaction of diverse groups, thus decreasing turnover and absenteeism and their associated costs.

- Embracing diversity may provide a broader and deeper base of creative problem solving and decision making. Creative solutions to problems are more likely to be reached in diverse work groups than homogeneous groups. In diverse groups, people bring different perspectives to problems—and the result is a better solution. A study of organizational innovation suggested that innovative companies had more diversity in their workforce than less innovative companies.[42]

In innovative companies, leaders are challenged to create organizational environments that nurture and support creative thinking and the sharing of diverse viewpoints.

Some have described diversity as a double-edged sword.[43] This is because, despite the benefits of diversity just described, it can also bring about negative outcomes if not effectively managed. The greater the amount of diversity within an organization, the greater the potential for conflict. This may occur because, in general, people feel more comfortable dealing with others who are like themselves. To some extent, society has played a role in creating the gap that often exists among ethnic groups. In many communities, ethnic groups still do not interact socially, and this custom carries over into the workplace. Rather than a unified team, competition with, and even distrust between groups may characterize a diverse work environment. A leader in a diverse work unit may spend more of his or her time and energy dealing with interpersonal issues than in trying to achieve organizational objectives. Therefore, effective management of a diverse workforce is necessary for an organization to perform at a high level and gain a competitive advantage.

Leadership Initiatives for Achieving Full Diversity

For organizations to embrace and value diversity, the concept itself must be embedded in the organizational strategy. When diversity is part and parcel of the organizational strategy, all employees are given equal opportunities to contribute their talents, skills, and expertise toward achieving organizational objectives, independent of their race, gender, ethnic background, or any other definable characteristic. Achieving full diversity requires top management to show its commitment to diversity by (1) removing personal and organizational obstacles to achieving diversity, (2) implanting a diversity-supportive culture, and (3) engaging employees in diversity awareness training and leadership education.

Removing Obstacles to Achieving Diversity. To increase performance, organizations have to unleash and take advantage of the potential of a diverse workforce; however, leaders often face a number of personal and organizational obstacles to realizing the full potential of diverse employees. Figure 11-7 lists five obstacles to achieving diversity. Each is briefly discussed.

Stereotypes and Prejudice. This is perhaps the most prevalent obstacle to achieving diversity in many organizations. **Prejudice** *is the tendency to form an adverse opinion, without just cause, about people who are different from the mainstream in terms of their gender, race, ethnicity, or any other definable characteristic.* It is an assumption, without evidence, that people who are not part of the mainstream culture (women and other minorities) are inherently inferior, less competent at their jobs, and less suitable for leadership positions. Leadership commitment toward eradicating stereotypes and prejudice of this kind will pave the way for a diverse workforce to thrive.[44]

Ethnocentrism. **Ethnocentrism** *is the belief that one's own group or subculture is naturally superior to other groups and cultures.* Ethnocentrism is an obstacle to diversity because it tends to produce a homogeneous culture, a

- Stereotypes and prejudice
- Ethnocentrism
- Policies and practices
- The glass ceiling
- Unfriendly work environment

Figure 11-7 *Obstacles to achieving diversity.*

prejudice: the tendency to form an adverse opinion, without just cause, about people who are different from the mainstream in their gender, race, ethnicity, or any other definable characteristic.

ethnocentrism: the belief that one's own group or subculture is naturally superior to other groups and cultures.

314 / Chapter 11 • Leadership of Culture, Diversity, and the Learning Organization

culture where everyone looks and acts the same and shares the same set of values and beliefs. Removing ethnocentrism and replacing it with a belief that all groups, cultures, and subcultures are inherently equal will greatly enhance the achievement of a diverse workforce's full potential.

Policies and Practices. A third obstacle to diversity is embedded in organizational policies and practices that work against maintaining a diverse workforce. The leader must perform an audit of the organization to determine if existing policies, rules, procedures, and practices work against minorities, for example, uncovering and removing barriers to the selection of women and minorities, such as job requirements that may not be valid or relevant to the job. Policies regarding human resource management issues such as hiring, training, promotion, compensation, and retirement or layoffs must be examined to make sure that minorities are not unfairly treated by actions taken in these areas. Xerox Corporation, for example, has undertaken major initiatives to increase diversity by adopting practices that increase the proportion of women and minorities it recruits and promotes. Xerox has also established a sophisticated support network for minority employees. The Xerox Hispanic Professional Association is an example of such a support network.

Glass Ceiling. The fourth obstacle to diversity is the presence of the glass ceiling, or what others have described as the "White male" club. *The glass ceiling is an invisible barrier that separates women and minorities from top leadership positions.* Evidence of the glass ceiling is seen in the concentration of women and minorities at the lower rungs of the corporate ladder, where the skills and talents of women and minorities are not being fully utilized because older White males steadfastly refuse to recognize them. White men hold more than 50 percent of all administrative and managerial positions, while Black and Hispanic representation is in the single digits.[45]

Unfriendly Work Environment. The work environment for many minorities is a lonely, unfriendly, and stressful place, particularly in executive-level positions where Caucasian men outnumber women and minorities. Minorities and women may be excluded from social activities in or out of the office, which often leads to a feeling of alienation and despair. This often leads to job dissatisfaction and high turnover among minority groups. Removing this obstacle can go a long way toward alleviating the problem of high turnover and thus preserve diversity initiatives.

Creating a Culture That Supports Diversity. Removing obstacles to diversity creates the environment for diversity initiatives to begin to take root. But to institutionalize the concept, leaders are encouraged to create a whole new culture of multiculturalism. A culture of multiculturalism is one that continuously values diversity, so that it has become a way of life in the organization. Developing a multicultural organization helps achieve the benefits of embracing diversity described earlier. To achieve full diversity, leaders are challenged to work to ensure that women and other minorities have opportunities to move up the corporate ladder into leadership positions. In today's organizational culture, there is a mismatch between the Caucasian-male-dominated leadership structure and the growing employee population of minorities, and this has led to the under-utilization of the tal-

glass ceiling: an invisible barrier that separates women and minorities from top leadership positions.

ents and skills of minorities. To achieve full diversity, top leaders must actively pursue the objective of changing the organization culture to one that values diversity at every level of the organization—from the top to the bottom.

Studies have identified certain key characteristics of cultures that support diversity.[46] Figure 11-8 highlights these characteristics, followed by a brief discussion of each.

Low Levels of Conflict.   As mentioned earlier, diversity can be a double-edged sword. While it can lead to improved decision-making quality and creativity, it also has the potential to create conflict and distrust. If diversity produces conflict and distrust among organizational members, individual, group, and organizational performance suffers. To minimize conflict, many organizations have instituted cultural diversity training programs to improve personal and group relationships, to promote cultural sensitivity and acceptance of differences between people, and to teach skills for working in multicultural environments. Diversity training and education is the third leadership initiative for effectively managing diversity; it will be discussed later.

Bias-free Environment.   Another characteristic of a diversity-supportive culture is leadership effectiveness in creating a bias-free environment. Ethnocentrism and prejudice often lead to bias, which then leads to discrimination. To effectively manage diversity, successful companies create task forces that monitor organizational policies and practices for evidence of bias. The result is an organizational culture where everyone is treated equally and fairly regardless of race, gender, ethnicity, or age. Denny's zero tolerance of discriminatory behavior is intended to create such a bias-free environment.

Diverse Leadership Structure.   A diversity-supportive culture is also characterized by management's effectiveness in creating a diverse leadership structure. A diversity-supportive culture has mechanisms in place to ensure that there is an equal distribution of women and minorities throughout the organizational hierarchy or structure. In organizations where this is true, there is zero correlation between culture-group identity and job status. Investing in the education and training of minority group members will provide the skills and talents they need to function successfully at higher levels

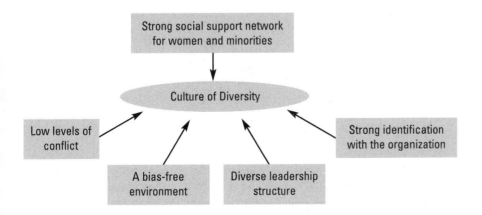

Figure 11-8   *Characteristics of cultures that support diversity.*

of the organization. The firm's performance appraisal and compensation systems can be used as an influencing mechanism to ensure broad representation of women and minorities throughout the leadership structure. In one company, for example, managers' salaries and bonuses were based on four criteria: financial performance, customer satisfaction, environmental and safety improvement, and workforce diversity. Because having and maintaining a diverse workforce was on equal footing with traditional performance criteria, managers were quick to see that diversity was not only an important organizational goal but also of benefit to them personally.[47] It would appear from the opening case that Jim Adamson has achieved this characteristic at Denny's.

Strong Identification with the Organization. Members of a diversity-supportive culture display strong identification with the organization. In a fully integrated organization, there is a strong feeling of identification with the company by all members of the workforce, not just a select few. This would mean, for example, that African Americans would identify as strongly with the organization as would Caucasian males. All members of the workforce—regardless of gender, race, or ethnicity—share the same sense of membership, ownership, and loyalty to the organization. The strength of identification with the organization is determined by the degree to which both majority and minority group members are influential in creating behavioral norms, policies, and values.

A Strong Social Support Network for Women and Minorities. A diversity-supportive culture is characterized by management's effectiveness in creating a strong social support network for women and minorities. As mentioned earlier, women and minorities are often excluded from social functions, lunches, and even regular office conversation, making it hard for them to network and achieve career advancement. Women and minorities often find themselves in a "no-win" situation. If they try to fit in the dominant culture's social circles, they are rejected; yet if they keep their distance, they are perceived as unsociable or aloof. Companies that are doing a good job of managing diversity have found effective ways to integrate women and minorities into social networks. These include company-sponsored social events that encourage minorities to attend and company-sponsored mentoring programs that target minorities.

Diversity Awareness Training and Leadership Education. The benefits of diversity as we have demonstrated are enormous, but without a well-trained workforce that values diversity awareness and leadership commitment, increased cultural diversity may actually lead to decreased productivity and lower financial and strategic performance. As mentioned in the introduction to this section, the notion that culturally diverse individuals coming into the workforce have to assimilate into the mainstream culture is a thing of the past. The challenge now is for organizations to make the necessary adjustments such as removing obstacles to achieving diversity and creating a diversity-supportive culture. As revealed in the preceding discussions, strong leadership commitment is needed to make these adjustments. Many of today's leaders belong to the baby-boom generation, most of them grew up in segregated communities with homogeneous cultures. Some have little experience with managing and leading diverse work groups. For example, some leaders are uncertain how to handle the challenge of communicating with employees whose cultural backgrounds result in assumptions, values, and even language skills that differ from the leaders'. Various racial or ethnic groups may respond differently to the demands of their job responsibilities or to the approaches that leaders are using to manage relationships in the workplace. Similarly, some men still find it difficult to report to or be evaluated by women. These are some of the challenges that come with the growing diversity of the workforce, and that many leaders are still unprepared to deal with effectively. We will explore the role of diversity training and education in fostering a deeper cultural awareness among leaders and employees and helping organizations effectively manage diversity.

Diversity Training. Diversity training can facilitate the management of a diverse workforce. The purpose of diversity training is to develop organizations as integrated communities in which every employee feels respected, accepted, and valued regardless of gender, race, ethnicity, or other distinguishing characteristic. Training sessions are aimed at increasing people's awareness of and empathy for people from different cultures and backgrounds. To reinforce and promote its diversity policy, each person employed by Denny's receives training that emphasizes these values. There are many diversity-training programs with many different objectives. Diversity training can include but is not limited to:

- Role-playing, in which participants act out appropriate and inappropriate ways to deal with diverse employees
- Self-awareness activities, in which participants discover how their own hidden and overt biases direct their thinking about specific individuals and groups
- Awareness activities, in which participants learn about others who differ from them in race, gender, culture, and so on

Diversity training programs can last hours or days. They can be conducted by outside experts on diversity, or by existing members of an organization with expertise in diversity. Small organizations are more likely to rely on outside assistance; larger organizations often have their own in-house staff. More than half of *Fortune* 500 companies have diversity managers on staff.[48] Leaders in these companies understand the value of effectively managing diversity to ensure their future competitiveness. The primary objectives of diversity training programs include one or more of the following:

- Helping employees of varying backgrounds communicate effectively with one another
- Showing members how to deal effectively with diversity-related conflicts and tensions
- Exploring how differences might be viewed as strengths, not weaknesses, in the workplace
- Improving members' understanding of each other and their work relations

Not all diversity training programs are successful. Diversity training is most likely to be successful when it is not a one-time event, but an ongoing or repeated activity; and when there are follow-up activities to see whether the training objectives were accomplished.

Education. Sometimes effectively managing diversity requires that leaders of an organization receive additional education to make them better able to communicate and work with diverse employees. Through training and education, leaders develop personal characteristics that support diversity. Through education, leaders are taught to see diversity in the larger context of the organization's long-term vision. Managers should have long-term plans to include employees of different cultures at all levels of the organization. They should be educated on the strategic significance of linking diversity to the organization's competitiveness, rather than simply told to do it.

To develop and implement diversity programs, leaders must first examine and change themselves. Through education, leaders learn how to communicate effectively and encourage feedback from all employees regardless of background, how to accept criticism, and how to adjust their behavior when appropriate. A broad knowledge base on multiculturalism and diversity issues helps.

Also through education, leaders learn how to mentor and empower employees of diverse cultures. They learn to appreciate their role in creating opportunities for all employees to use their unique abilities.

Without an educated and committed leadership team, the task of creating and managing a diverse workforce is unlikely to yield positive results. Everyone must be involved, including employees and managers at all levels, and top management commitment must be visible for the benefits of diversity to be realized. In the last section of this chapter, we describe and explore the emerging concept of the learning organization. The learning organization concept is predicated on the assumption of equality and community where people are able to communicate openly and honestly with one another and also maintain their unique differences. The culture of a learning organization is therefore one of accepting the principles and beliefs embedded in multiculturalism and diversity.

THE LEARNING ORGANIZATION AND ITS CULTURE

By all accounts, most organizations operate in environments characterized by continuous change. But for some—like the high-tech industry—the level of change is discontinuous. ***Discontinuous change*** *is when anticipated or expected changes bear no resemblance to the present or the past.* The emergence of better and cheaper technologies, rivals' introduction of new or better products and services, competition from lower-cost foreign competitors, and demographic shifts represent major threats to the profitability and even survival of many organizations. To succeed in this dynamic environment, leaders are challenged to transform their organizations into flexible systems capable of continuous learning and adaptation. In this section we examine what a learning organization represents, how a learning organization differs

discontinuous change: occurs when anticipated or expected changes bear no resemblance to the present or the past.

from a traditional organization, and the role of leadership in creating a learning organization.

What Is a Learning Organization?

In a stable environment, change is slow and incremental. Organizations have time to react and still retain their competitive positions. However in rapidly changing environments, change is frequent and discontinuous; reacting is not the best approach to staying competitive. To succeed, organizations must be proactive or anticipatory, which requires an orientation toward learning and continuous improvement. A *learning organization is one that is skilled at creating, acquiring, and transferring knowledge; and at modifying behavior to reflect new knowledge and insights.*[49] The following are characteristics of a learning organization:

- Embedded in the organization's culture and included in the reward and appraisal systems are values of experimentation, initiative, innovation, and flexibility.

- There is visible and strong top-management support.

- There are mechanisms and structures in place to support and nurture ideas generated by people at lower levels in the organization.

- Knowledge and information are disseminated or made accessible to anyone who needs them, and people are encouraged to apply them to their work.

- Resources are committed to fostering learning at all levels (such as at 3M, where employees are allowed to spend 15 percent of the work day experimenting or doing whatever they please—called the 15 percent rule).

- Employees are empowered to resolve problems as they arise and to find better ways of doing work.

- There is equal emphasis on the short- and long-term performance of the organization.

- There is a deep desire throughout the organization to develop and refine knowledge on how things work, how to adapt to the environment, and how to achieve organizational objectives.

- People are not afraid to fail.

In stable environments, organizations focus on being efficient and on achieving this objective by developing highly structured command systems with strong vertical hierarchies and specialized jobs. Today, however, this traditional organization form is being replaced with the learning organization form.

The Traditional versus the Learning Organization

The traditional organization is based on a rational model that emphasizes a command and control structure, centralized decision making, highly formalized systems, specialized tasks, competitive strategy, and a rigid, closed

learning organization: one that is skilled at creating, acquiring, and transferring knowledge; and at modifying behavior to reflect new knowledge and insights.

culture. The learning organization represents a shift in paradigm that is less structured, decentralized, and informal: Its strategy is more collaborative, and its culture is more open and adaptable. Figure 11-9 compares the two organization types, and a brief discussion follows.

As indicated in Figure 11-9, the traditional, efficiency-driven organization's structure is vertical (a tall pyramid), starting with the CEO at the top and everyone else functionally organized in layers down below. These vertical structures are effective under stable environmental conditions. The organization's vision, mission, and strategy are formulated at the top and disseminated through the layers of authority and responsibility. There is little or no input from the lower ranks of the organization. Decision making is centralized at the top of the hierarchy, which controls and coordinates all functional units throughout the organization. To ensure reliable and predictable results, tasks are rigidly defined and broken down into specialized jobs. Strict formal rules and procedures on performing each task are enforced. Though repetitive, boring and unchallenging, it is an efficient way of keeping the production line running smoothly. The culture of the organization is fixed on values, practices, beliefs, and principles that have helped it attain success in the past and the present. The traditional organization often becomes a victim of its own success by aligning with an outdated culture that does not promote adaptability and change. Finally, the traditional organization is characterized by an elaborate formal system of reporting that allows leaders to closely monitor work operations and maintain efficient, steady performance. This formal system is a powerful tool for controlling information and often acts as a filter in determining what information leaders decide to pass down to lower-level employees.

By contrast, in learning-driven organizations, the vertical structure is abandoned for a flat, horizontal structure. The horizontal structure is constituted around workflows or processes rather than functional specialties. The learning organization recognizes that work processes and procedures are the means to satisfying customer needs rather than an end in themselves. The self-managed team concept discussed in Chapter 8 is characteristic of the learning organization and functions best under the horizontal

Traditional (efficiency driven)	Learning (learning driven)
• Stable environment	• Changing environment
• Vertical structure	• Flat, horizontal structure
• Strategy is formulated from the top and passed down	• Strategy is a collaborative effort within the organization and with other companies
• Centralized decision making	• Decentralized decision making
• Rigidly defined and specialized tasks	• Loose, flexible, and adaptive roles
• Rigid culture that is not responsive to change	• Adaptive culture that encourages continuous improvement and change
• Formal systems of communication tied to the vertical hierarchy with lots of filters	• Personal and group networks of free, open exchanges with no filters

Figure 11-9 *The traditional versus the learning organization.*

structure. The horizontal structure is appropriate in today's rapidly changing business environment, where competitive pressures, technological innovations, global market changes, and evolving customer needs are more intense than ever before. To encourage innovation and creativity in meeting current challenges, learning organizations are designing tasks that are much looser, free flowing, and adaptive. There are few strict rules and procedures prescribing how things should be done. Some have used the term *organic* to describe this type of organization.[50] Responsibility and authority are decentralized to lower-level workers, empowering them to think, experiment, create, learn, and solve problems at their level. Teamwork is highly valued, and there are network systems to facilitate open communication and exchange throughout the organization and with other companies. A shared vision and mission are the basis for the emergence of strategy in a learning organization. Employee input and active participation in strategy formulation are highly valued, because employees are at the front line making daily contact with customers, suppliers, competitors, and other stakeholders.[51] Thus, strategy formulation is a collaborative process, not a restricted activity for top executives. In the end, one of the most important qualities for a learning organization to have is a strong, adaptive culture. An adaptive culture encourages teamwork, openness, equality, relationships, creativity, and innovation.

Examples of learning organizations today include Intel, Microsoft, Starbucks, W. L. Gore and Associates, Lucent Technologies, Motorola, Xerox, 3M, Johnson and Johnson, and many recently created Internet-based companies—America Online, Amazon.com, Ebay, and Yahoo.

Applying the Concept 11-5

Traditional or Learning Organization

Identify each statement by its type of organization. Write the appropriate letter in the blank before each item.

a. traditional   b. learning

_____ **1.** Top-level managers make all the important decisions around here.
_____ **2.** There aren't many levels of management in our company.
_____ **3.** With a union, we have clearly defined jobs and are not allowed to do other work.

The Role of Leaders in Creating a Learning Organization

Leaders in learning organizations face a dual challenge to maintain efficient operations and create an adaptive organization at the same time. Efficient performance often requires incorporation of the characteristics of the traditional vertical organization, which can conflict with the requirements for creating a learning organization. This potential conflict poses a major challenge in creating a successful learning organization. Here we identify important leadership initiatives that enhance a learning environment. The following guidelines (see Figure 11-10) are ways in which leaders can create conditions conducive to learning and continuous improvement. Theses guidelines are supported by research findings, theory, and practitioner contributions.[52]

Encourage Creative Thinking. Leaders can enhance learning by encouraging members to "think outside the box." In other words, consider possibilities that do not already exist. Rather than responding to known challenges, employees are encouraged to create the future. Therefore, people with maverick ideas or out-of-the-ordinary proposals have to be welcomed and given room to operate in a learning organization. People who advocate radical or different ideas must not be looked on as disruptive or troublesome. Another approach to enhance creative thinking is to encourage employees to research and learn from some of the best competitors in the industry. This process, known as benchmarking, allows a company to imitate the best practices of others. However, mere imitation does not yield a competitive advantage; it is a follower strategy. An organization must improve upon the best practices of competitors and launch innovations ahead of its competitors.

Create a Climate Where Experimentation Is Encouraged. Learning is more likely to take place in an organization where experimentation on a small scale is encouraged and permitted. The purpose of an experiment is to learn by trial in a controlled environment. The costs of failure are not as significant as in a real attempt. People who are afraid of failing and risking their reputation or careers may be more likely to try something new or creative on a small scale. Also, the leader must create a culture that nurtures and even celebrates experimentation and innovation. Everybody must be expected to contribute ideas, show initiative, and pursue continuous improvement. One way to do this is to create a sense of urgency in the organization, so that people see change and innovation as a necessity. Another way is to sometimes reward those who fail, because it symbolizes the importance of taking risks.

Provide Incentives for Learning and Innovation. The use of incentives and rewards is a powerful tool that leaders can apply to encourage learning and innovation. Rewards for successful ideas and innovations must be large and visible for others to notice. Rewards and incentives reinforce positive learning and innovation in the organization.

Build Confidence in Followers' Capacity to Learn and Adapt. The environment of the learning organization is one of rapid change, wherein survival depends on a timely response to threats and opportunities. Providing opportunities for employees to solve problems within the group or unit will increase their confidence and pride in the process. With each celebrated

- Encourage creative thinking.
- Create a climate where experimentation is encouraged.
- Provide incentives for learning and innovation.
- Build confidence in followers' capacity to learn and adapt.
- Encourage systems thinking.
- Create a culture conducive to individual and team learning.
- Institute mechanisms for channeling and nurturing creative ideas for innovation.
- Create a shared vision for learning.
- Broaden employees' frame of reference.
- Create an environment where people can learn from their mistakes.

Figure 11-10 *Guidelines for enhancing organizational learning.*

success comes greater confidence in dealing with change. Over time, familiarity with the change process will create an appreciation for flexibility and learning.

Encourage Systems Thinking. To enhance learning, the leader should help members regard the organization as a system in which everybody's work affects the work of everybody else. Therefore, everyone in the organization considers how their actions affect other elements of the organization. The emphasis on the whole system reduces boundaries both within the organization and with other companies, which allows for collaboration and continuous learning.[53] Members begin to see how relationships with other companies can lower cost, increase sales, or bring in new competencies.

Create a Culture Conducive to Individual and Team Learning. Personal development and a lifetime of learning must be strong cultural values in learning organizations. Leaders must create a culture in which each person is valued, and the organization promotes and supports people to develop to their full potential. To facilitate learning by teams, learning organizations have created self-managed teams, made up of employees with different skills who rotate jobs to produce an entire product or service. In self-managed teams, formal leaders are nonexistent; team members have the authority to make decisions about new and creative ways of doing things. This facilitates a learning environment for teams. The self-managed team concept was covered in Chapter 8.

Institute Mechanism for Channeling and Nurturing Creative Ideas for Innovation. Knowledge that is shared can help an employee with a difficult problem or provide an opportunity for employees from different parts of the organization to interact with each other in getting advice and support about common problems. Also, ideas generated within an organization may become the source of new products or innovations. Therefore, ensuring that all employees' ideas are properly channeled and evaluated is critical. Most ideas do not pan out, but the individual and the organization learn from a good attempt even when it fails. Leaders should use organizational mechanisms such as venture teams, task forces, information systems networks, seminars, and workshops to diffuse knowledge and to channel creative ideas to the appropriate locations for evaluation.

Create a Shared Vision for Learning. Creating a shared vision enhances learning as organization members develop a common purpose and commitment to make learning an ongoing part of the organization. If employees all believe that the organization is headed toward greatness, they will be motivated to be part of it by learning and contributing their best ideas and solutions.

Broaden Employees' Frame of Reference. People's frame of reference determines how they see the world. The way we gather, analyze, and interpret information—and how we make decisions based on such information—are affected by our personal frames of reference. A frame of reference determines what implicit assumptions people hold, and those assumptions, consciously or unconsciously, affect how people interpret events. To enhance employees' ability to learn, it is helpful for leaders to broaden the frames employees use to see the organization and its external environment. Learning is constrained when leaders and their followers fail to see the world from a different perspective and therefore are unable to help the organization adapt to a changing environment. Broadening employees' frames of reference or perspective provides for a greater variety of approaches to solving problems and thus facilitates learning and continuous improvement.[54]

Create an Environment Where People Can Learn from Their Mistakes. Some of the most important inventions or scientific breakthroughs have resulted from investigating failed outcomes. Unfortunately, in many organizations, when experiments or full-scale ventures fail, the tendency is to immediately abandon the activity to save face or avoid negative consequences. This is often the wrong approach, because more learning takes place when things go wrong rather than when they go right. After all, when things turn out as expected, it just confirms existing theories or assumptions. New insights are more likely when there is an investigation into why expected outcomes were not realized. Therefore, to encourage learning, leaders must communicate the view that failure is tolerated. Then, they must provide opportunities for people to engage in post-activity reviews regardless of outcome. Creating a culture that rewards those who succeed, as well as occasionally rewarding those who fail, sends a message that the organization encourages risk taking.

Learning is a never-ending exercise. Leaders must communicate the message that learning and continuous improvements are imperative in a highly turbulent environment. Leaders must take the lead in challenging the status quo and creating organizational conditions that are conducive to learning and continuous innovation.

Now that you have learned about the culture, diversity, and learning organizations described in this chapter, you may find it interesting to see how your own personality traits match up. Complete Self-Assessment Exercise 11-2.

Self-Assessment Exercise 11-2

Personality and Culture, Values, Diversity, and the Learning Organization

Culture and Values

If you scored high on the Big Five personality dimension of conscientiousness (high need for achievement), you tend to be a conformist and will most likely feel comfortable in an organization with a strong culture. If you have a high agreeableness (high need for affiliation) personality, you tend to get along well with people, can fit into a strong culture, and would do well in a cooperative type of culture that values collectivism, low power distance, and femininity. If you have surgency (high need for power), you like to dominate and may not like to fit into a strong culture that does not reflect the values you have. You would tend to do well in a competitive culture that values individualism, high power distance (if you have it), and masculinity. On the Big Five, if you are open to new experience you will do well in an adaptive culture that values low uncertainty avoidance: if you are closed to new experience, you will tend to do well in a bureaucratic culture that values high uncertainty avoidance. Would you like to work in an organization with a weak or strong culture? What types of culture and values interest you?

_____

_____

_____

Diversity

If you have a Big Five agreeableness personality type (high need for affiliation), openness to experience, and are well adjusted, you will tend to embrace diversity and get along well with people who are different from you. However, if you have a surgency personality type (high need for power), are closed to experience, and are not well adjusted, you will tend to want to have things done your way (melting pot vs. salad bowl) and may

have problems with a diverse group of people who don't want to give you the power. If you have a conscientiousness personality type (high need for achievement), openness to experience, and are well adjusted, you will tend to work with those who share your achievement values regardless of other differences. Do you enjoy working with a diverse group of people?

_____

_____

Learning Organization

The key personality trait that differs between the traditional and learning organization is openness to new experience. If you are closed to new experience, you will tend to like a traditional organization in which change is slow and top management makes the decisions. If you are open to new experience, you will tend to enjoy a learning organization in which you are encouraged and valued for implementing change and making many of your own decisions. Would you be more comfortable in a traditional or learning organization?

_____

_____

Appendix

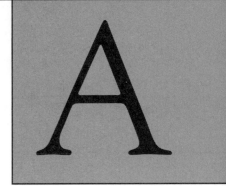

Leadership and Spirituality in the Workplace

Judith A. Neal, Ph.D.

The purpose of this appendix is threefold. (1) It explains what the concept of spirituality in the workplace entails. (2) It presents spiritual principles that have been useful to many leaders in their personal and professional development. (3) It provides a list of some of the resources that are available to people who are interested in learning more about the relationship between leadership and spirituality.

SPIRITUALITY IN THE WORKPLACE

Tom Aageson, Director of Aid to Artisans, takes an annual retreat where he contemplates questions about the purpose of his life and evaluates how well he is living in alignment with his values. Angel Martinez, former CEO of Rockport Shoes, invited all his top executives to a retreat that included exploring the integration of each person's spiritual journey with his or her work journey. At Integrated Project Systems (IPS) in San Francisco, CEO Bill Kern has created a document called "The Corporate Stand" that is very explicit about "The Integrity of the Human Spirit." These are key principles that employees live by at IPS. Rodale Press, publisher of such well-known magazines as *Prevention, Men's Health, Runner's World,* and *Organic Gardening,* has a "kiva room" at corporate headquarters where employees may go to meditate, pray, or just spend quiet time when things get too stressful.

Appendix A written by Judith A. Neal, Ph.D., Professor of Management, University of New Haven; and editor, Spirit At Work website. ©2000 by Judith Neal, University of New Haven; used by permission of the author.

Stories like these are becoming more and more common in all kinds of workplaces. Academic and professional conferences are offering an increasing number of sessions that have words such as *Spirituality* or *Soul* in the title. There is a new openness in management education to recognition of our spiritual nature. This recognition can be on a personal level, such as when a person explores his or her own spiritual journey and struggles with what this means for their work. It is also on a conceptual level, as both academics and practitioners explore the role that spirituality might have in bringing meaning, purpose and increased performance to organizational life. There is a major change going on in the personal and professional lives of leaders as many of them more deeply integrate their spirituality and their work. And most would agree that this integration is leading to very positive changes in their relationships and their effectiveness.

Defining Spirituality in the Workplace

Spirituality is difficult to define, and many of the people writing on spirituality in the workplace don't even try. However, here are some definitions. The Latin origin of the word *spirit* is *spirare*, meaning "to breathe." At its most basic, then, spirit is what inhabits us when we are alive and breathing; it is the life force. Spirituality has been defined as, "That which is traditionally believed to be the vital principle or animating force within living beings; that which constitutes one's unseen intangible being; the real sense or significance of something"[1] A fairly comprehensive definition, part of which is provided here, is as follows:

> One's spirituality is the essence of who he or she is. It defines the inner self, separate from the body, but including the physical and intellectual self. ... Spirituality also is the quality of being spiritual, of recognizing the intangible, life-affirming force in self and all human beings. It is a state of intimate relationship with the inner self of higher values and morality. It is a recognition of the truth of the inner nature of people. ... Spirituality does not apply to particular religions, although the values of some religions may be a part of a person's spiritual focus. Said another way, spirituality is the song we all sing. Each religion has its own singer.[2]

Perhaps the difficulty people have had in defining spirituality is that they are trying to objectify and categorize an experience and way of being that is at its core very subjective and beyond categorizing. For this reason, some have resorted to poetry as a way of trying to capture the essence of the experience of spirituality. Lee Bolman did this very effectively in his keynote presentation on spirituality in the workplace to the Eastern Academy of Management in May 1995, by quoting the Persian poet Rumi:[3]

> All day I think about it, then at night I say it
>
> Where did I come from and what am I supposed to be doing?
>
> I have no idea
>
> My soul is elsewhere, I'm sure of that
>
> And I intend to end up there.

James Autry, a successful Fortune 500 executive, wrote a poem called "Threads." This is an excerpt from that poem:[4]

> Listen.
>
> In every office
>
> You hear the threads
>
> of love and joy and fear and guilt,
>
> the cries for celebration and reassurance,
>
> and somehow you know that connecting those threads
>
> is what you are supposed to do
>
> and business takes care of itself.

Spirituality in the workplace is about people seeing their work as a spiritual path, as an opportunity to grow personally and to contribute to society in a meaningful way. It is about learning to be more caring and compassionate with fellow employees, with bosses, with subordinates and customers. It is about integrity, being true to oneself, and telling the truth to others. Spirituality in the workplace can refer to an individual's attempts to live his or her values more fully in the workplace. Or it can refer to the ways in which organizations structure themselves to support the spiritual growth of employees.

In the final analysis, the understanding of spirit and of spirituality in the workplace is a very individual and personal matter. There are as many expressions of these concepts as there are people who talk or write about them. The interpretations of spirituality as it is applied to management education are just as varied. They can range from quietly practicing one's own spiritual principles in the teaching process without ever mentioning the word *spirituality* to actually offering courses on spirituality in the workplace. It is hoped that the resources listed here will provide useful information and inspiration to management educators, whatever the form of their expression of spirituality in their workplace.

GUIDELINES FOR LEADING FROM A SPIRITUAL PERSPECTIVE

I now present five spiritual principles that have been useful to many leaders in their personal and professional development.

Know Thyself

All spiritual growth processes incorporate the principle of self-awareness. Leading provides a great opportunity to become more self-aware. Examine why you respond to situations the way you do. Take a moment in the morning to reflect on the kind of leader you would like to be today. At the end of the day, take quiet time to assess how well you did, and to what extent you were able to live in alignment with your deepest held core values.

Act with Authenticity and Congruency

I believe that followers learn a lot more from who we are and how we behave than from what we say. Authenticity means being oneself, being fully congruent, and not playing a role. Many managers really get into the role of "leader" and see managing as a place to assert their superiority and control. They would never want employees to see the more human, softer parts of them. Yet we are finding that managers who are more authentic and congruent tend to be more effective.

It is a real challenge to be authentic and congruent in the workplace. Most people feel that if they are truly themselves and if they say what they are really thinking, it will be the end of their careers. But I believe that if we don't do this, we sell a little bit of our souls everytime we are inauthentic, and that saps our creative energy and our emotional intelligence. It also reduces our sense of commitment to the work we do, and we cannot perform at our highest level. Experiment with greater authenticity and with showing more of your humanness. You will be surprised at how positively people will respond.

It is also important to create a climate where employees are encouraged to behave authentically and congruently. This means that they should be comfortable expressing feelings as well as thoughts and ideas.

Respect and Honor the Beliefs of Others

It can be very risky and maybe even inappropriate to talk about your own spirituality in the workplace. Yet if spirituality is a guiding force in your life and your leading, and if you follow the guideline of authenticity and congruency, you cannot hide that part of yourself. It is a fine line to walk.

What seems to work best is to build a climate of trust and openness first and to model an acceptance of opinions and ideas that are different from yours. Then, if an appropriate opportunity comes up where you can mention something about your spiritual beliefs, you should emphasize that they are yours alone. Explain that many people have different beliefs and that you respect those differences. It is extremely important that employees do not feel that you are imposing your belief system (spiritual, religious, or otherwise) on them.

Be as Trusting as You Can Be

This guideline operates on many levels. On the personal level, this guideline of "being as trusting as you can be" applies to trusting yourself, your inner voice, or your source of spiritual guidance. This means trusting that there is a Higher Power in your life, and that when you ask you will receive guidance on important issues.

Maintain a Spiritual Practice

In a research study on people who integrate their spirituality and their work, the most frequently mentioned spiritual practice is spending time in nature.

Examples of other practices are meditation, prayer, reading inspirational literature, hatha yoga, shamanistic practices, writing in a journal, and walking a labyrinth. These people report that it is very important for them to consistently commit to whatever individual spiritual practice they have chosen. The regular involvement in a chosen practice appears to be the best way to deepen spirituality.[5]

When leaders faithfully commit to a particular spiritual practice, they are calmer, more creative, more in tune with employees and customers, and more compassionate.[6]

ANNOTATED BIBLIOGRAPHY ON SPIRITUALITY IN THE WORKPLACE

The materials provided here were selected for their ability to inform the leader about issues related to spirituality in the workplace. This list is not exhaustive, and suggestions are provided on where to find more in-depth information on resources related to spirituality in the workplace. There are 31 books categorized in eight sections in this review. Because of space limitations, because the book reviews are available online, and because the list continues to grow, there are no book reviews provided in this appendix. However, you can go to the Spirit at Work website to read the book reviews of the 31 books listed here, in addition to new ones. Spirit at Work Internet Exercise A-2 provides directions for getting to and reading these book reviews. Let's begin by describing the Spirit at Work website, and follow that by explaining the eight categories of books with the list of 31 references.

Spirit at Work Website

http://www.spiritatwork.com

I have created a comprehensive website on spirituality in the workplace that is a free resource to people interested in this field. It consists of an online journal called "The Spirit at Work Newsletter," which features articles written by leaders, academics, consultants, and everyday working people. There are also editorials, poetry, and book reviews. An extensive bibliography of hundreds of references on the topic can be found at the site. There is also information on all the conferences worldwide that are being held on spirituality and business. One of the most useful tools is a "supersite" of websites that allows the visitor to connect to the websites of consultants, authors, conference websites, websites of similar organizations, online newsletters and discussion groups, and online articles. New features are constantly being added.

Overview of Spirituality in the Workplace

The books described in this section are edited books that offer a wide array of perspectives on spirituality in the workplace and provide a good overview for someone who is just beginning to explore this field.

1. *The New Paradigm in Business: Emerging Strategies for Leadership and Organizational Change*, edited by Michael Ray and Alan Rinzler (New York: Jeremy Tarcher, 1993).

2. *New Traditions in Business: Spirit and Leadership in the 21st Century*, edited by John Renesch. (San Francisco: Berrett-Koehler, 1992).

Leadership from a Spiritual Perspective

Perhaps more has been written about leadership and spirituality than any other topic related to spirituality in the workplace. The books highlighted here are only a small sampling of what is available, but they are among the best on the topic. The offerings here include two parables, a book that explores what the new sciences have to teach us about leadership, a book of essays, a workbook, and three books that offer leading-edge concepts on leadership that incorporate body, mind, heart, and spirit.

3. *Managing from the Heart*, by Hyler Bracey, Jack Rosenblum, Aubrey Sanford, and Roy Trueblood (New York: Dell, 1990).

4. *Leading with Soul: An Uncommon Journey of Spirit*, by Lee Bolman and Terrence Deal (San Francisco: Jossey-Bass, 1995).

5. *Leadership and the New Science: Learning about Organizations from an Orderly Universe*, by Margaret Wheatley (San Francisco: Berrett-Koehler, 1992).

6. *Invisible Leadership: Igniting the Soul at Work*, by Robert Rabbin (Lakewood, CO: Acropolis Books, 1998).

7. *Leadership from the Inside Out: Seven Pathways to Mastery*, by Kevin Cashman (San Francisco: Berrett-Koehler, 1998).

8. *Fusion Leadership: Unlocking the Subtle Forces That Change People and Organizations*, by Richard Daft and Robert Lengel (San Francisco: Berrett-Koehler, 1998).

9. *Learning as a Way of Being: Strategies for Survival in a World of Permanent White Water*, by Peter Vaill (San Francisco: Jossey-Bass, 1996).

10. *Leading Consciously: A Pilgrimage towards Self-Mastery*, by Debashis Chatterjee (Boston: Butterworth-Heinemann, 1998).

Case Studies of Leaders Who Have Applied Spiritual Principles to Their Work

This section reviews three books that provide concrete examples of leaders who are integrating spirituality and work. The first book is a collection of interviews with business leaders, and the last two books are written by CEOs who applied spiritual principles and practices to their organizations.

11. *Merchants of Vision: People Bringing New Purpose and Values to Business*, by James E. Liebig (San Francisco: Berrett-Koehler 1994).

12. *The Soul of a Business: Managing for Profit and the Common Good*, by Tom Chappell (New York: Bantam Books, 1993).

13. *Love and Profit: The Art of Caring Leadership*, by James Autry (New York: Avon Books, 1991).

Creativity and Spirituality in the Workplace

Poetry, music, and other forms of art are shortcuts to the human soul. Enlightened leaders are beginning to recognize this and to build artistic approaches into their leadership style and into their organizational transformation processes.

14. *The Heart Aroused: Poetry and Preservation of the Soul in Corporate America*, by David Whyte (New York: Currency Doubleday, 1994).
15. *Small Decencies: Reflections and Meditations on Being Human at Work*, by John Cowan (New York: HarperBusiness, 1992).
16. *The Common Table: Reflections and Meditations on Community and Spirituality in the Workplace*, by John Cowan (New York: HarperBusiness, 1993).
17. *Artful Work: Awakening Joy, Meaning, and Commitment in the Workplace*, by Dick Richards (San Francisco: Berrett-Koehler, 1995).
18. *Creating an Imaginative Life*, by Michael Jones (Berkeley, CA: Conari Press, 1995).

Spiritual Principles for Career Development

The most important management principle of all is "know thyself." And it certainly is the most important principle to keep in mind when making career decisions. These three books each take a slightly different approach to self-knowledge, but the goal is the same in each—to choose work that is in alignment with your soul's path.

19. *Do What You Love, the Money Will Follow: Discovering Your Right Livelihood*, by Marsha Sinetar (New York: Dell Publishing, 1987).
20. *Find Your Calling, Love Your Life: Paths to Your Truest Self in Life and Work*, by Martha Finney and Deborah Dasch (New York: Simon & Schuster, 1998).
21. *The Path: Creating Your Mission Statement for Work and for Life*, by Laurie Beth Jones (New York: Hyperion, 1996).

Spirituality at the Team Level

As far as I know, there is only one book on teams and spirituality; it is based on a very successful training program that is used in organizations.

22. *Building Team Spirit: Activities for Inspiring and Energizing Teams*, by Barry Heerman (New York: McGraw Hill, 1997).

Systemic Approaches

The concept of spirituality in the workplace can be looked at on the individual level, the team level, the organizational level, and the societal level. At the organizational level the main concern is with how to incorporate attention to spirit in organizational transformation approaches. Three books are offered here that have very different, but compatible approaches.

23. *Managing with the Wisdom of Love: Uncovering Virtue in People and Organizations*, by Dorothy Marcic (San Francisco: Jossey-Bass, 1997).

24. *The Living Organization: Spirituality in the Workplace*, by William Guillory (Salt Lake City, UT: Innovations International, Inc., 1997).

25. *Liberating the Corporate Soul: Building a Visionary Organization*, by Richard Barrett (Boston: Butterworth-Heinemann, 1998).

The Role of Business in a Changing World

These six books take a very macro view of the issue of spirituality and business. Each of them postulates that we are entering a new era where it can no longer be "business as usual," and the authors each offer their vision of what the world can be like and their prescriptions for how we can get there.

26. *Creative Work: The Constructive Role of Business in Transforming Society*, by Willis Harman and John Hormann (Indianapolis: Knowledge Systems, 1990).

27. *The Global Brain Awakens: Our Next Evolutionary Leap*, by Peter Russell (Palo Alto, CA: Global Brain Inc., 1995).

28. *Waking Up in Time: Finding Inner Peace in Times of Accelerating Change*, by Peter Russell (Novato, CA: Origin Press Inc., 1998).

29. *Conscious Evolution: Awakening the Power of Our Social Potential*, by Barbara Marx Hubbard (Novato, CA: New World Library, 1998).

30. *Building a Win-Win World: Life beyond Global Economic Warfare*, by Hazel Henderson (San Francisco: Berrett-Koehler, 1996).

31. *The Reinvention of Work: A New Vision of Livelihood for Our Time*, by Matthew Fox (San Francisco: HarperCollins, 1994).

SUMMARY

There is a growing trend the past few years for people to talk more openly about their spirituality and to want to integrate spiritual principles into all aspects of life—relationships, community, and work. This appendix has presented some resources for leaders who are interested in more fully integrating their spirituality and their leadership. Living more congruently with deeply held spiritual principles is never easy, but it is extremely rewarding and meaningful. I hope that some of the resources provided here will help to make the journey a little easier.

Appendix

B

The Management General Website

This appendix is designed to give the Internet novice some basic information about the Net and some of the basic software features to use. If you have self-training experience with the Internet, you may get a better understanding of what you are doing and hopefully a new idea or two to improve your efficiency on the Web. We also provide you with more details about how to use the Management General (MG) website. The novice will particularly benefit from the step-by-step instructions provided for using each subsite of the MG website.

This supplement was designed as a learning aid, with the idea that a picture is worth a thousand words. You can refer to it while using your browser and when visiting the MG website. For best results, read this supplement in front of the computer, so that you can see what is being talked about on your computer screen.

B.1 WELCOME TO THE MG "NEW IDEAS" WEBSITE! FROM EDITOR TOM BROWN

Today, managers and leaders live in a wired world. They communicate via dozens of personal voice mails and e-mails—and then track their daily goals, meetings, and other tasks via a handheld computer. Their computers—many times more powerful than the huge mainframes developed in the mid-1900s—provide them with the ability not only to calculate financial problems with deft ease but also to manipulate complex engineering matters with awesome rapidity and precision. E-commerce now allows people to buy and sell anywhere, anytime, anyplace. One source estimates that 2.8 billion e-mails are sent daily—and that's just the ones related to business!

Somewhere on the planet—right now—those who are guiding organizations large and small, global and local, are doing so with electronic assistance that is so much a part of their daily lives that to proceed without such help seems unthinkable, if not impossible.

The "central nervous system" for all the interconnectedness we now enjoy is, of course, the Internet. A countless number of computers are interconnected by modems and other high-speed access lines, so that the world of management and the *world* are one and the same. Through the wonders of hypertext, people with so-called "browsers" can log onto a seemingly endless bounty of electronic information pages. As the *London Times* recently reported, "there are some 800 million pages, amounting to six terabytes of data, held on three million servers, or central computers," the number was growing rapidly and, as they say, exponentially. Just three years ago, the Internet contained less than half the data that exists today.

In January 1997, the Management General website (**http://www. mgeneral.com**) was started. The mission of the site then was quite simple: to provide pertinent information to friends and associates about new books, trends, or concepts in managerial leadership. Now, this public service, noncommercial website (you can't buy anything on our website even if you want to) has grown vastly. Our mission today is to provide free and easily accessible information about management and leadership to the world. We are now MG—The "New Ideas" website, with known readers in more than 50 countries who, combined, log onto our hundreds of Web pages at the rate of two million or more hits per year.

MG is a *webzine*, or "magazine" published on the World Wide Web. Each month, we publish new material about management and leadership in four distinct ways in separate subsites of the MG website: E-Books, Leader-Lines, Leaders, and Top 10. Your author, with input from me, will explain all subsites of the MG website in detail later.

In Beverly Goldberg's well-written book, *Overcoming High-Tech Anxiety* (Jossey-Bass, 1999), she notes: "On a personal level, there is time for each of us to decide how much a part of the electronically connected world we want to be." She goes on to note that this vast, interconnected world has forced all of us to adapt: "We must adapt—but adaptation and even mastery of this high-tech world that is constantly developing is not all that frightening if approached in the right way."

What the MG website offers you, we hope, is the "right way" to think about the exciting field of management and leadership. There are few certainties in the world today. One of them is that organizations will continue to face new challenges as leaders strive to mesh people, productivity, and profits into harmonious enterprises. Another verity is that we will become more wired, not less. MG—The "New Ideas" website—is all about managerial leadership and being interconnected.

We eagerly welcome you as a new reader of our website. If you see ways we can serve you better, I hope you'll send me an e-mail without delay. The Internet is a way to connect millions of people simultaneously. It is probably *the* technological breakthrough of the 1900s, with vast potential for a new century. Yet, for all its scope and breadth, The Internet offers the opportunity for one person on one computer to link to another person living and working right around the block—or halfway around the globe. Yes, leaders today live in a wired world; and the beauty of that is simply this: they can connect to their profession and the thinkers who are shaping it in ways that are faster, more personal, and perhaps even a lot more fun.

Tom Brown (mail@mgeneral.com)
Editor, MG—The "New Ideas" website

B.2 THE MANAGEMENT GENERAL (MG) WEBSITE AND ITS HOME PAGE

The MG mission is to define, establish, and promote managerial leadership. We believe this is the best website in the world for cutting-edge leadership information: It features current information from the top leadership thinkers in the world, along with links to over 1,000 other good sites. The site has regular readers from over 48 countries and was visited over 1 million times in 1998, its second year on the Web. MG estimates over 2 million visits in 1999. These numbers will continue to skyrocket as the site continues to get more hits every month. Use of the MG website is free of charge as a public service.

We thank the MG founder and editor, Tom Brown, for reviewing our material and giving his input into using the MG website, to ensure a seamless integration of this book with the website. In this appendix, we now present step-by-step instructions for going to all subsites of the MG website. By visiting the MG "New Ideas" website at **http://www.mgeneral.com**, you will be kept on the cutting edge of leadership. The MG website is updated monthly, and you can have a monthly e-mail (MG ALERT) sent to your address to find out what's new each month. Signing up for MG ALERT can be done at any of the eight subsites. One of the subsites is devoted to contacting MG.

Getting to the MG Home Page

All you need to do to get to the MG home page is to get on the Web and type in **http://www.mgeneral.com**. The first time you get to the home page, set up a favorites for a quick return.

The MG Home Page

The top of the MG home page tells you what is new at the website. At the bottom of the home page, you may need to scroll (click the arrows ⇧ ⇩ in the right margin up or down) down to it; there are eight unique subsites or sections to visit by clicking on the word link at the bottom of the screen with your mouse. *We refer to each area or section of the website as a **subsite**, because that is what it is.* The eight subsites to visit are presented in Figure B-1. Each of the following subsites in this appendix discusses each of the subsites of the MG Website.

Figure B-1 *The MG Website Home Page*

E-BOOKS	LEADER-LINES	LEADERS	TOP 10
ABOUT MG	CONTACT US	SEARCH	SUPERSITE

Monthly Table of Contents and MG ALERT.   Getting hold of all the new material MG publishes each month is actually quite easy. First, when you come to the MG home page, you can simply click anywhere in the middle of the page and hop directly to the Table of Contents for the current month. There, you will find the specific new offerings under each of the four major categories for the website. An even easier way to keep up on the progress of the website is to sign up for the MG ALERT: This is a monthly *e*-letter that is e-mailed to hundreds of readers who want a quick snapshot of each issue of the webzine. You can begin receiving MG ALERT today. Simply send an e-mail with the single word *Alert* in the subject or message subsite to **response@mgeneral.com**. Signing up for MG ALERT is part of MG Internet Exercise 1-1.

B.3   ABOUT MG—INFORMATION

The "About MG—Information" subsite of the website provides background information about the Editor Tom Brown and the MG website. This is a useful place to go to during your first visit to the MG website. The first MG Internet Exercise in Chapter 1 includes a visit to this subsite.

B.4   CONTACT US—E-MAIL MG

The MG website is designed to be interactive; you are encouraged to contact MG. All you do is click the "Contact Us," type your message and your name, and click the Send icon in your browser. Your e-mail message to MG could even be published on the website. MG does include some information that came from college students using the website as part of a managerial leadership course. You can find out how you can get published (it is very competitive) by reading on in this appendix and by and visiting some of the website subsites.

Contacting MG is encouraged not just by going to a specific subsite designed for the purpose. Other subsites give you the opportunity to contact MG and its authors, as described later in this appendix.

B.5   E-BOOKS—BOOKS ONLINE

E-books are complete books (some short, some long) about leadership that are different not only because they are on the Web and are free; they are also different in that they openly challenge the prevailing wisdom about the norms in management. As such, don't be surprised to find e-paintings, color photos, and even sound files in the webzine. At this subsite, you will find *The Anatomy of Fire*, the first e-book about leadership to be written with the direct input of readers who gave suggestions about how to improve the book *while it was being written*. You'll also find *Fiscal Fairy Tales*, the first e-book about managing and working to become a printed publication after being published on the World Wide Web. Our e-books are being used as textbooks in colleges today.

From the home page, click "E-Books," and read the full description about the E-Books subsite. When reading an evolving e-book, you can give the author your response: Submit your own input, ideas, reactions, and suggestions for improvements about the material presented by contacting the author directly with a message in 50 words or less by clicking the "Your Response" link, as discussed later. As a leader, here's your chance to influence the content of a book to be published in the future.

Fiscal Fairy Tales

Fiscal Fairy Tales is a completed e-book containing 12 traditional folk tales rewritten by Tom Brown with a humorous spin to stimulate your thinking and discussion about today's real work world. You can read the original tale by clicking the "Fiscal Fairy Tales" link. The tales are called *chaplets*, because they are short chapters of around four textbook pages for the actual tale. They are independent tales, so they can be read in any sequence and/or some can be skipped. Average to slow readers can finish most of them in 10 minutes or so.

The tales have been successfully used in college leadership classes. Students rated them high in value, liked their originality and the style, and praised them for their accuracy in pointing out what appears to be a daily reality for many at work. You become more aware of what is "really" taking place at work, because you can often see yourself, managers, and coworkers in the stories: They hit a nerve, and have led to lively debate about what is taking place at work, how it affects employees, and what should be taking place at work.

The best responses from anyone visiting the site from anywhere in the world are printed following the tale, so here's a shot at being published online. Just scroll down past the printed responses, and after *What do you think?—Your Response*, click "Your Response," and you will go into an e-mail addressed to the author, MG Editor Tom Brown.

B.6   LEADERS—EZZAYS

"Leaders" is the subsite that contains "ezzays" by leaders we admire and whom we invite to answer a core question: "What should a leader be thinking about—now?" Ezzays simply take the idea of a personal essay (a literary form invented hundreds of years ago) and bring the genre into the 21st century. Though MG might not always agree with the avant garde positions taken by our guest writers, we feel that it's important to offer the current opinions of others. You'll find hundreds of compelling voices arguing for new priorities in managerial leadership; some ezzayists are well known (for examples, Warren Bennis, Peter Senge, or Meg Wheatley), and some are completely unknown to the general public. It's the mix of voices that makes this one of the most popular offerings on MG.

The Leaders—Ezzays are around 2–3 text pages and can be read by most people in 10 minutes or less. Go to the home page and click "Leaders," and then read the full description about Ezzays to get a better understanding of what they are. You can respond directly to the authors if you want to. Scroll down to the bottom of the page to the "Contact . . ." box, and click "E-Mail." Type your response and name, and click "Send," and your e-mail goes to the author's e-mail box.

Ezzay Clickdex (Index) Topics

Ezzays are organized by series number and year they were written. There are 15 topics in the Clickdex (index).

Steps to Getting to Read an Ezzay

1. Go to the MG home page at **http://www.mgeneral.com** using Favorites.
2. Click "Leaders" at the bottom of the page. Scroll down to the boxed Ezzay year you are interested in; you will see the names of all the authors in that year's series.
3. (a) Click the "author's name" if you know a specific Ezzay you want to read by the author's name. Or (b) Click the word "Series" (between the year and Ezzay) that you want to see the Clickdex for.
4. If you selected an author (a), click the "title" of the Ezzay you want to read. If you selected (b), click the Clickdex "category"—there are 15.
5. If you selected (a), read the Ezzay. For (b), click the Ezzay "title" you want to read. You can read it online and/or make a copy of it using the print function.

Search. One strong feature of the MG website is that it has a search engine (Search), so that you can type in a chapter topic and a list of Ezzays, with other subsite material, appears on screen. You can then go to any topic by simply clicking the title on screen. We will talk more about Search in the next section.

B.7 SEARCH—SITE MAP

Once something is published on the MG website, it remains online. We archive everything we publish, simply because much that appears on MG is timeless. That's why our high-speed internal search engine makes it easy to find any person or concept presented on MG. More than that, as the MG website grows, it becomes a unique tool for taking any dimension in management and finding out what's new; MG also allows a reader to probe for comparative approaches to the same issue in order to see how different thinkers handle major questions in our profession. You can access our MG Search engine right from the bottom of our home page.

The Search—Site Map enables you to find information at all subsites of the MG website by name of a person or organization, or by word(s) describing a concept. Links to search About, AltaVista, Excite, HotBot, and Northern Light Internet search engine sites for additional information outside of MG are also provided here. These other search engines are discussed in Appendix C.

Searching All of MG

As you read this book, you may be interested in finding out more about a specific concept discussed. You have two major options:

- You can go to the endnotes at the end of the book and find the references for these journal articles and books. A few of them are taken from the MG site. So to search for any reference that is not citing the MG website, you should use a different search engine, and you can get to others from MG Search by clicking on the search logo. See Appendix C for details on using other search engines, related to cases, without using the MG website.

- With MG Search, you can search for almost any of the major concepts in the textbook and find an E-Book, Ezzay, News & Notes, or Top 10 resource that has more information about the concept. In many ways, this is possibly the strongest feature of the site. You'll use Search for doing Internet exercises that use other parts of the site for the information.

Steps to Finding Information Using Search

1. Go to the MG home page at **http://www.mgeneral.com** using Favorites.
2. Click "Search" at the bottom of the page.
3. Find the word "Enter."

   (a) If you want to find out if a specific person (say, Judith Neal, author of the text Appendix A) has written anything in MG, or another author talks about her, place the cursor in the box and type the name. If you want to know if there is information on a specific organization (say, GE from Chapter 1), type its name in the box.

   (b) If you want to find out if the MG website has information on a specific concept from the text, click the circle next to the word "Enter." The dot will now be in the lower circle next to "word(s)." Now type in the concept(s), say, motivation. Most exercises require a concept search, so you will be using option (b).

4. Click "Start Search."
5. *No matches.*

   (a) If you don't find any information on your topic, you have no *match*, and you may have "mistyped" the information in the box; check it. If it is spelled correctly, and there is no information, click "New Search" and try typing in other words that basically mean the same thing.

   (b) Or broaden your search, as discussed under step 7, because you may not need to use that step.

(c) You can also try rearranging the order of words, which sometimes results in matches or some different document matches.

(d) If these ideas don't work, there may not be any information in the MG website; try another search engine (such as Excite). You can go directly to *another search engine* by simply clicking its link. When you go to another website, you should return to MG by clicking the close **X** icon in the SuperSite window.

6. *Order of appearance of matches.*

(a) *Confidence.* When you find a match, there may be up to 20 sources (not documents) for you to choose from; they are presented in "grouped by confidence" mode. Understand that the same document can be listed multiple times, such as different pages of the same E-Book. So you will be linked to different pages/parts of the same document. You need to click the "*summary*" link to get the title of the document/article, and it helps to determine which one(s) you want to read. Usually the highest percentages of confidence (top) are the best, but not always, so do look at multiple summaries. You may want to work your way down through the documents. Use the browser Back icon to return to your listing of documents. You may want to click *summary* to determine if you want to go on, and click the "*title*" link to read the full document. After determining which document(s) you want to read, click the *title* to read it.

Although you normally select the best document to get the information you are searching for, some exercises will ask you to select a document based on which subsite of the site it comes from (which is listed after Management General—"*subsite listed*"). This may be your last step. However, you can go on to rearrange your matches (see step 6b) and/or to fine-tune your search (step 7).

(b) *Subject.* You can rearrange your matches, before and/or after reading any of the summaries or documents, by clicking "Subject" at the top of the page to the right of "Grouped by." When I typed in "motivation," 20 documents appeared under the confidence mode. I clicked Subject and had 5 groups with 26 total documents. However, you lose the confidence percentage in how good a match you have in the subject mode.

7. *Broadening and narrowing a search.*

(a) If there are not enough matches, you may be able to *broaden* your search by cutting down the words you type in to search. Conduct a new search (click "New Search" near the top of the screen) and try typing in fewer words, if possible. When I typed in "motivation in banking," I received 7 matches. When I did a new search with just "motivation," I received 20 matches (which means there were probably many more with a lower level of confidence).

(b) If there are too many matches, or the confidence percentage is low, you may *narrow* your search by adding more descriptive words to limit the number compare motivation—20+ matches vs. motivation in banking—7 matches). You can continue to fine-tune your search until you are satisfied with your results.

Most beginners need to narrow their searches. You will find that narrow searches usually result in higher confidence that you have a good match. So start narrow, be as specific as you can, and broaden if you need to. For example, use one selection before and after motivation— "Hierarchy of needs/two-factor/expectancy/reinforcement" *motivation* "your job/organization/industry."

When you do find information you want, read it online and/or make a copy of it using the print function. Your instructor may require you to copy it and to bring it to class to facilitate class use of the exercise. Copying the information also makes it easier to cite the reference to verify your information sources.

B.8   LEADER-LINES—NEWS & NOTES

"Lines" are pages that provide information about new thinking in any field of management. Whether in personal column format (in which I provide my own observations) or in question-and-answer format, the purpose of this subsite is to provide observations about managerial leadership with enthusiasm and verve. This part of MG tries to go behind the faces of management thinkers found on book covers: What are they like personally? What shaped their points of view? Do they see things differently today than when they first wrote their book? Look also for the popular "QQ&A" series, which has four management thinkers addressing one issue at the same time. It really is a "Quintessential Question & Answer" feature. Our major links to other websites MG admires are also found in "Lines": the MG SuperSite now has more than 1,000 links.

There are well over 100 leadership insight and tip documents. From the home page, click "Leader-Lines" and read the full description of News & Notes to get a better understanding of their value. Documents are around 2–3 text pages in MG and can be read by most people in 10 minutes or less—if you don't go to find more information at other SuperSite links, that is. We talk more about this shortly, under steps with SuperSite. This subsite includes all of the MG SuperSite links, discussed further in section B.10.

No Categories of Information

Leader-Lines does not categorize information. We are discussing it after MG Search because we recommend that you search by author/organization or concept that you want to learn more about. If you don't have specific information you are looking for, it's a great place to surf to find hidden treasures. But be careful, you could lose track of time. So tell someone to come and find you at the computer online at the MG website if you don't show up in a day or so.

Steps to Finding Information at News & Notes and SuperSites

1. Go to the MG home page at **http://www.mgeneral.com** using Favorites.

2. Click "Leader-Lines" at the bottom of the page. Scroll down to access by year.

3. Click "Lines Year" or "Here" and surf around and select a document to view.

4. Click the "Title" and scroll down to read the information in the MG document.

5. Click the underlined, colored words to get more information on the specific concept of interest to you. You will be taken to one of over 1,000 websites through the MG SuperSite.

6. Click Back to return to the MG Leader-Line document to continue reading, surfing this subsite, or to go to another MG subsite.

Steps to Finding Leader-Lines
Information from the MG Search Subsite

You guessed it, follow the steps from MG Search. However, don't get confused. Be sure to click documents with Management General— "Lead.NOW" (from Leader-Lines) rather than "Leaders.NOW" (from leaders—Ezzays) before (summary). The end-of-chapter MG Internet Exercises for Leader-Lines will use MG Search.

Steps to Getting to Use the MG SuperSite Subsite

Just click "SuperSite" anywhere in Leader-Lines, and you will go to it. Stay tuned; this is our next topic.

B.9   SUPERSITE—LEADERLINKS

There are over 1,000 links to other Internet web sites that provide leadership information worthy of a "site cite" by MG. Go to the home page and click "SuperSite" and read the full description about these links to get a better understanding of this subsite. The sites are grouped under 10 Clickdex category topics: (1) associations, (2) authors, (3) book worlds, (4) careers, (5) consultants, (6) journals/special, (7) News, (8) video-webcasts, (9) websources, and (10) 'zines/mega.

There is information at all these websites that relates to leadership. If you are looking for specific information from outside of MG, I'd suggest using a search engine link from the MG Search subsite. If you are not looking for specific information, this is another great place to surf to find more hidden treasures at other websites. If you are considering a new job, click [Careers l "Jumpstart"] and check it out.

Steps to Get to SuperSite Subsite

1. Go to the MG home page at **http://www.mgeneral.com** using Favorites.

2. Click "SuperSite" at the bottom of the page. Scroll down to the Clickdex of 10 categories.

3. (a) Click [*category name* 1 "Jumpstart"] to read a description of the SuperSite grouped under this category. You can surf (scroll up or down) to see all the 10 descriptions.

   (b) Click [*category name* 1 "Jumpstart"] to bypass the category descriptions and go right to the list of available websites under this category.

4. If you selected option 3a, Click "one of 10 categories names" to see all the available links for this category. If you selected option 3b, you are on this step.

5. Click "the name/title" of the website you want to go to.

6. When you are finished at the SuperSite, you should close the window (click X) to return to MG. You may be able to return by clicking the Back icon too; but you may have open windows behind the MG page.

B.10 TOP 10—BEST BOOKS

"Top 10" contains book reviews. With literally thousands of books published each year, it's impossible for anyone to read them all. MG receives hundreds of books each year, and we scour them to find the ones that stand out because they contain provocative new ideas, or because they treat an established subsite of management in a whole new way. Each year we profile about 50 books, which are then considered as nominees for our final "Top 10 Books of the Year." Needless to say, MG has no business arrangement with any writer or publisher; and we do not consider volume of sales in our opinion about what's best in management books.

MG's selection of the top 10 resources of the year also includes some videos, CD-ROMS, or other enduring resources. Go to the home page and click "Top 10" and read the full description about what the Top 10 includes and how MG picks the winners.

However, the Top 10 gives only a review of the books/resources (and sometimes excerpts and interviews with authors), so it is very helpful in understanding what the latest books are about—or to find out what's hot and what's not. Also, when you search for information at the MG Search subsite, you will most likely get matches from the Top 10.

Top 10 Categories

The Top 10 are categorized simply by year, with the most current year listed first in the Clickdex.

Steps to Finding Top 10 Information from the MG Search Subsite

You guessed it, follow the steps from MG Search. Be sure to click documents with Management General—"Tops Year" before (*summary*).

Steps to Getting to Read about Top 10 Resources

1. Go to the MG home page at *http://www.mgeneral.com* using Favorites.

2. Click "SuperSite" at the bottom of the page. Scroll down to the Clickdex by year.

3. Click the "Year" you want to surf.

4. Depending on what year you are in, you have Click "link" options to choose from, including "Nominees," "Best of Year" (for past years only), "How we pick Top 10," "Interviews," and so on.

5. Within nominees and best of year (and others), you also have click options to choose, from including SuperSite link to the publisher for more information about the book and to buy it online. (Click the "*publisher name*" link to go to its website, and return to MG clicking the close X icon in the SuperSite window. Many of the authors have written Ezzays, and you can click where it tells you to go and read the Ezzay, returning with the Back icon. Some years will show you a brief statement about the book, and you can click the link to read the full *review* of the book, with more links.

Appendix

MG—The Anatomy of Fire: Sparking a New Spirit Of Enterprise

Gerald L. Pepper, Ph.D.

*T*he *Anatomy of Fire: Sparking a New Spirit of Enterprise,* by Tom Brown, Editor of Management General webzine (photographs by Tom Brown; original e-paintings by Mac Thornton).

Anatomy of Fire is an e-book—a book written exclusively online and available only online. In the book, author Tom Brown presents his beliefs about the current status of leadership in our organizations, and in society in general. It is a very personal statement, written in a way that pulls readers in and challenges them at the same time.

The book grew out of Brown's despair with what he was observing in the many organizations in which he had worked, and had visited while a journalist. In days of unheard-of profits and unmatched output, incomprehensible revenue and growth, Brown found disillusioned and scared workers, motivated by fear, defined more by fatigue than pride. Why the disconnect between the paper versus real daily experiences?

Brown argues that it's leadership—or the lack thereof, rather—that is to blame. The soul of a corporation, of civilization, lies with its leaders. But, when searching for them, Brown found placeholders instead. This book is his response, his call for leaders to step forward and take their necessary and rightful place at the front of society. For in leaders and genuine leadership lie the possibility of a tomorrow that respects and nourishes each of our souls.

Appendix D written by Gerald L. Pepper, Ph.D., Associate professor, Department of Communications, University of Minnesota Duluth; © 1999 by Jerry Pepper; used by permission of the author.

The Anatomy of Fire e-book is divided into six chapters, which comprise twenty-two "chaplets." A chaplet is a chapter segment, written to accommodate a central thought, while at the same time meeting the needs of the reader to not be forced to read too much text on a computer screen for too long. The following is a chaplet-by-chaplet summary to give you an overview of the entire book, and a sense for its flow and rhythm. After reading these summaries, I think you'll want to read the book. I warn you, though, brief summaries cannot do justice to the book as a whole. How do you summarize poetry (yes, Brown uses a poem or two)? How do you summarize original art, created specifically for a book written online? How do you summarize examples and personal stories, both of which abound throughout the text? And, how do you summarize an author's treatment of personal disbelief, as well as personal joy and exuberance? I'll do my best, but I encourage you to get out of this appendix and get into the e-book. That's where the fun is.

One last thing before you get to the text summary. You'll not find descriptions here of the original art by Mac Thornton. The art is placed into each chapter and very much deserves a long, thoughtful look. To say that it highlights the points made in the text is to do it serious mistreatment. The art is original and wonderful, and stands alone as Thornton's own statement about leadership. Read the text, and don't pass over the art. Use it to help your understanding, and enjoy it in its own right.

USING ANATOMY OF FIRE

It is recommended that you first read the text summary from this appendix material assigned. Then go and read the e-book.

Steps to Getting to Read *Anatomy of Fire*

Option A.

1. Go to the MG home page at **http://www.mgeneral.com**
2. Click "E-Books" at the bottom of the page.
3. Click "Anatomy of Fire."
4. Click "Table of Contents."
5. Click the "chaplet title" you want to read.

Option B.

Go to **http://www.mgeneral.com/4-ebook/97-ebook/firetitl.htm**

SUMMARY OF *THE ANATOMY OF FIRE: SPARKING A NEW SPIRIT OF ENTERPRISE*

Brief Chaplet Overviews
Foreword by Jim Collins (Chaplet 0.1)

Foreword

In the foreword, Collins raises the point that what the e-book really does is move us ever closer to the ideal of democratizing knowledge. It is an interactive book in which the reader can watch the author think and work, which is exactly how this book was created and posted.

The book offers a picture of leadership in a wholistic sense: in organizations, society, and in our personal lives. Ultimately the book is an example of Brown's own message: Not settling for placeholding. Leaders must contribute in order to make an impact.

Author's Preface

The preface poses the question, "What is your inner fire?" What burns, for you? What is wrong with organizations? Where have the leaders gone? What is the connection between social progress and leadership?

In the preface, Brown tells the story of a college student—a newspaper reporter in Florida—who stumbles onto an airplane crash and experiences the deaths of others, without realizing the peril into which he has actually placed himself. That newspaper reporter was Tom Brown, and it was there at that crash that he found a fire within himself—to report, to understand—that eventually merged with the equally strong fire to understand management, organizations, and learning.

But one day the realization hit: Everywhere he looked Brown found apathy, minimalism, and the willingness to settle for less than anyone deserves. And with it, he found a lack of respect for leadership. Indeed, he found himself asking, "where are the leaders?" Managers abounded, but leaders were nowhere to be found. Brown was lost. It was from this starting place that he found himself in Yellowstone National Park.

CHAPTER 1.   FORWARD

Chaplet 1.1: Journeys

Chaplet 1.1 is about the difficulty of beginning, of starting a journey (such as writing an e-book). This is a journey of ideas, and like any journey, this one has beginnings. The chaplet is the beginning of this e-book journey—this "e-journey." The excursion will evolve (chaplets were posted as they were in progress), electrify (electronic enhancements will make the journey richer and fuller), and embrace (the author will bond with the reader through this new technology and way of writing).

This journey of ideas will be most appreciated by a reader who is willing to adopt a posture of curiosity and willing to travel, explore, and learn. The territory will be leadership, and the terrain is rough. Ideas are like that. Keep in mind, though, that the view at the end of the trip is worth the effort.

Chaplet 1.2: Yellowstone

Travel and journeys can often leave the traveler better and healthier upon the return than before the trip. Yellowstone continually represents such an opportunity for Brown. He and his family have "adopted" the park, and it has adopted them. The chaplet presents the metaphor of Yellowstone as a challenge, an idea, rather than a place.

Yellowstone is awesome, beautiful, and challenging. In it, answers as well as questions hide. On the face of it, the park seems to be the opposite of the unnatural world of business. But people in business have perhaps the most reason to visit the park, for upon a closer look you're able to see differently, to understand the world of business and organizations and leadership differently. Experiencing Yellowstone, Brown realized that after 20 years of living in the world of corporations, he hadn't seen many radical or significant changes. The same lack of resources, the same apathy, the same leadership vacuums, the same hollow sounds emerged. The promised quality of life was not there, and it seemed to correspond with the lack of quality leadership.

Wealth, technology, and growing resources were not adding up to wisdom, love, and enrichment of people. Brown's search for answers led to Yellowstone. What he found was less a destination than an idea. The world of business seemed not to change. Technology wasn't solving problems, it was creating different ones. People weren't happier, they were busier. Wealth wasn't buying satisfaction, it was becoming an objective.

And people were much more interested than ever before in escaping their workplaces. Where was the love, where was the concern for people, and without it, what actually mattered?

Chaplet 1.3: Beginnings

We tend to begin journeys with the sense that we'll arrive at a place and, with speed and skill, consume it. Such were Brown's original efforts at Yellowstone. Pictures took the place of understanding. Capturing images and covering ground substituted for asking questions and finding answers.

Eventually, though, Yellowstone as *place* became replaced by Yellowstone as *idea*. The idea has a power to connect us to the past as well as the future. We can consider questions of proportion, such as "is there something bigger than me, and what I've made and what I've done?" Only with such questions can we return to our beginnings, to recapture the trip. The idea of Yellowstone, what the experience can symbolize, is the focus of this chaplet.

The idea of Yellowstone, in the forests, the wildlife, and the water, confronts you with a slap in the face, making you slightly embarrassed at your own sense of self-importance. At that point we're ready to begin our relearning, both from where we are and simultaneously from the real beginning—the idea. The pre-industrial, natural beginning from which we all came.

For Brown, the realization emerged that what he was seeing most were managers bent on mastering places. But they were not building ideas: they were not embracing the future. Quality, excitement, and growth were held in check by the objective of "winning the race," "moving product," and "increasing revenue." The past was seen as done; the future as not yet a problem. And the present too often was viewed as something to get through.

So, we've allowed ourselves, our workplaces, our communities to degenerate into minimum expectations. We've forsaken ideas and excitement, questions, and quality. We have forsaken leadership.

CHAPTER 2. INERTIA

Chaplet 2.1: Placeholders

Chaplet 2.1 is about the difference between placeholders and leaders, and the dilemma of being over-managed and under-led. It is the difference between seeing only boundaries versus larger purposes; between being transfixed by products versus defining new mandates; between sucking out wealth versus cultivating resources; between exploiting versus enhancing; between doing versus dreaming; between seeing workers versus seeking learners. Placeholders are preoccupied by dollar signs, not ideas.

Leaders have the courage to shape the future. The blur of time doesn't give us the option of stopping and considering what we're doing, what matters, what counts, and what we should do. Yet, this is exactly what the thoughtful leader needs to do, and does.

History has always presented us with dual options: peace versus war, oppression versus freedom, poverty versus wealth, ignorance versus education, and so forth. And in organizations we're confronted too often with the false dichotomy of profit versus failure. Too often the choice is profit, leading to over-management and under-leadership. The result is an infatuation with placeholders—those skilled at maintaining—and an under-appreciation and even a disdain for leaders—those with fire, drive, passion, and respect.

The differences between placeholders and leaders are glaring. They include seeing boundaries versus purpose; focusing on proven products rather than future mandates; a philosophy of "using it up" rather than renewal and reinvestment; doing rather than dreaming; and providing employment instead of stimulating enterprise. The result of this misdirected focus is that we've created a world preoccupied by dollar signs, in which we've come to believe that money precedes ideas. The reality is the opposite. Leaders know this; placeholders do not. We are experiencing global inertia, ruled by placeholders who have become leader substitutes.

Chaplet 2.2: Doubt

Those who lead have to reconcile economic achievement with human aspirations. Placeholding amounts to little more than running fast in place. Profits go up, but progress is an illusion. The placeholder tends to adopt the position of "if the organization is happy, then we must all be happy." So, if profit is up, if revenue is up, then employee dissatisfaction must be artificial—the result of rabble-rousers. Interestingly, when times are bad, the placeholder views employee dissatisfaction as a possible cause of downturns in revenue. The employee can't win because she or he isn't taken seriously.

But the success of today is very different from the possibilities of tomorrow. History always confirms this. "Lean and mean" resulted in fatigue, dissatisfaction, and burnout more than riches, progress, and success. Restructuring increased workload and distanced more workers from their product. It retired generations of workers who believed in the company and made cynics of the entering generations. And, technology did not bring people together. It allowed us to work farther apart, and to take our work wherever we go, to home, on vacation, to the movies. We keep in touch, but we don't actually touch.

The placeholder mentality tries to control our bodies; but the human spirit will prevail.

Chaplet 2.3: Churn

Placeholding does not account for "churn," the constant change and turmoil that defines the workplace and the world. To regard this dramatic amount of churn and upheaval as simple change is to devalue the significant impact it has on the human spirit. It is new ideas that agitate the churn, shake up the status quo, hit us in the gut and challenge our sense of perspective and place.

History suggests that it has always been this way. Social growth is a series of ideas that served to disrupt the way things were, and move society, usually against its will, to a new understanding of itself and its possibilities. Social order is shaken, religion recoils, education gasps, medicine reconsiders, and organizations retool. And individuals shake their heads, oftentimes lost in a catch-up world where just when they think they knew the rules, the whole game changed.

Today, the one sure thing is change, speed, movement, catch-up. And stress. This is the world of the placeholder. The placeholder substitutes this running in place for actual growth and progress. We need leaders to help us out of the despair of upheaval, to define the questions and possibilities of the 21st century. Because churn dislocates, we need leaders to show us five things:

1. We don't know what to learn.
2. We don't know what to believe.

3. We don't know what to esteem.
4. We don't know who to trust.
5. We don't know where to go.

CHAPTER 3. POSSIBILITIES

Chaplet 3.1: Engines

Placeholders view churn with anger and fear. Churn is movement and change, and these things cause stress and anxiety. Churn is steady, never-ending, inexorable "permanent white water." Leaders need to be the engines of change, while placeholders become the victims of churn. Leaders seek the new ideas and embrace them, rather than turning away in the hope that they will go away. They know that the downfall of any entity "is first a failure of an idea followed by a failure of place."

Churn is about the nonstoppable movement of the world. It is our journey into the future, and the cause of no small amount of fear, resentment, distress, anger, and for some, shutdown. For a few, churn means increased revenue at the expense of others. And for a lucky some, effective leadership transforms churn into growth, development, and a genuinely better existence. For organizations ruled by placeholders, churn disrupts and is seen as a never-ending series of shifts, changes, and crises to be addressed.

Embracing the future, moving forward, takes some audacity. "Success is always an if; but failure is never an accident." While the placeholder works harder, lowering prices, slashing the workforce, revising the mission statement, change leaders work differently. They *think* the new ideas that will define the churn of tomorrow, just as they've already leapfrogged the churn of yesterday. So, while placeholders are victims of churn, leaders are excited by the opportunities. The leader wants to be the engine, not the track.

Chaplet 3.2: Taproots

Roots matter. Human survival, any survival, is dependent on roots. From them we derive our foundation and nourishment. Our roots give us the strength to change and grow. Growth, development, evolution—churn—is based on the essential taproot of change. It is foundational. To ignore it is to deny an inevitability.

Yet, placeholders choose to do just this. They live in the now. Profit now, maximize now, use now. Now is low risk, high yield, and a known quantity. Leaders have little use for now. The leader knows that now is the beginning of tomorrow's discontent. The leader's concern is in rallying now as an opportunity for tomorrow. Now is the start of a new idea.

And this is not only what people need; it is what they want. People do not want sluggishness. They don't prize crisis management. They don't value exploitation. People want positive movement. They want progress. Churn is inevitable because it grows from the basic, causative taproots of humankind. We need to understand them, or we will fall prey to their force.

These seven taproots are at the bottom of historical churn, on both large and small scales:

1. The demand to be free.
2. The demand to be healthy.
3. The demand to be intelligent.
4. The demand to be prolific.
5. The demand to be connected.
6. The demand to be happy.
7. The demand to be harmonious.

Chaplet 3.3: Quietus

Life expectancy, be it personal or organizational, is defined by our ability to confront churn. Unfortunately, the "good life" can easily become complacency and a myopia whereby the owner spends all of his or her time protecting what they've got, maximizing its value, and squeezing every dime out of it. This mindless exploitation distorts the original idea, and greed takes the place of building, and then often results in demise, ruin, less of place and profit.

Even the essential taproots of change are distorted as governments and companies limit citizen choices, mislead consumers, distort education, produce low-quality products, sanction divisiveness, allow frustration, fear, and insecurity to dominate our workplaces, and allow cultural and social bankruptcy. All of this usually for the sake of short-term profit, increased revenues and stock prices, vanity, and paternalism. In essence, we've taken the basic, essential taproots of churn, and supported their opposites. We've substituted enslavement for freedom; illness for health; idiocy for intelligence; consumer satisfaction for profligacy; divisiveness for connections; sweatshops for happiness; and mammon (greed) for harmony.

One need only read the past carefully to understand the present; and read the present carefully to understand the future. The signs are there. But, placeholders don't want us to see the signs. They block and overlook the markers that point at new directions, at change, at churn. And the price of this misdirection? Extinction. Placeholders will fall, ultimately, because churn will push them out of the way. To get, to accumulate, without understanding is a sure path to oblivion. And at the end, the placeholder is left asking, "What else might I have done?"

Chaplet 3.4: Invincible

Churn, change, actually equates with stability in the long run. The mantra of the placeholder is: Control the now! Placeholders are blinded by the "right now!" Their focus, effort, and agenda revolve around preserving and exhausting the present. The churn of ideas becomes replaced by the complacency of success, followed by the failure of place.

Though placeholding abounds in all walks of life, it is easiest to examine in business. The data defy the attitude of the placeholder. New companies define the marketplace, because older companies die off. Why? Why do so many successful companies die out?

The answer is that at some point they used up their good idea(s), and nobody came forward with new ones. Ideas are the taproot of growth, and new ideas are the source of organizational renewal, as well as personal renewal. The apparent invincibility of today is only one competitor's good idea away from vulnerability, failure, and corporate death. Arrogance leads to people becoming nothing more than the means to secure greater security and a firmer place. Leaders reject this. People are valued as the only growth mechanism that matters.

CHAPTER 4. *FIRE*

Chaplet 4.1: Glow

"Glow" is an original poem by Tom Brown. Read it and understand the loss of glow, and the need to regain it. Brown writes that we're "born to glow." To do otherwise is to relinquish our potential and our possibilities. Glow depends on our willingness and ability to create, to shine, to bring into being. Every new age brings the new challenges that spark the mind and spirit to renew and push.

Chaplet 4.2: Flickers

To merely exist is unnatural. It contradicts what we are as humans, what we're about, what we're born to do and be. Our glow comes from five flickers, or human tendencies, which when ignited flame into the fire of leadership. Those flickers are:

1. *Exploration*—the human drive to see beyond the immediate and present. You can't quell this desire in infants, yet so many adults lose it altogether. We're simply not meant to run in place. To do so is unnatural.

2. *Enthusiasm*—the exuberance of a new idea, the excitement in a new challenge, the courage to overcome. This is the dedication to follow through.

3. *Resourcefulness*—the ability to move projects forward. It is internal motivation, knowledge, and commitment, coupled with political and interpersonal savvy.

4. *Resolve*—resiliency. This is the ability to face adversity and come back; to find lessons, growth, and learning in temporary setbacks.

5. *Contribution*—the innate desire to contribute and make a difference. Leaders have this—they seek a higher ground.

Chaplet 4.3: Kindling

Being in charge is not being a leader. Leadership is not corporacy, or the manipulation of money and assets, or greed, or the destructive use of raw power, or relying on fads. Leadership is about fire, dreams, and ideas. And when we get too close—ignition happens and leadership works. To lead is to kindle. The leader influences and liberates.

Accept no substitutes. We have to find real, true leaders. Too often we're misled by false leadership, promises, image, and the appearance of sincerity and true belief. Find the passion, for it is the passion which defines the person. It is our natural desire to be ignited, and leaders are that kindling. Leadership ignites; false leaders smother. Leaders offer dreams that inspire or motivate ideas, which lead to actions, which then spark others.

Chaplet 4.4: Phlogiston

Phlogiston. For hundreds of years it was an accepted explanation for what lay at the heart of fire. It was the mysterious source of flame. The merger of science and belief often lead to unquestioned assumptions in the form of answers that, when viewed in hindsight, appear childish. What do we assume about leaders, and what happens when we look closer? In the twisted logic of false premises, we too often create imaginary leaders who do not stand up under the scrutiny of a closer look.

Leaders don't simply have followers. True leaders measure up to a standard. Put simply, the world is better off for them being there. Hitler and his like were not leaders. What we need to do is focus our search for leadership, rather than leaders. Then we're less likely to be misled by the false prophets whose charisma may cloud our understanding. Leaders leave the world better than they found it. The source of leadership is not charisma. Look for the source.

Chaplet 4.5: Sparks

True leadership does not lie in power or titles or rank or symbols or income. True leadership comes from the heart. In a time of churn, are there enough leaders? Are there enough people of heart, to see the way clearly through the stress and change, to move us to a better future? We have generations of managers, task masters, data organizers. To change this, we need a new definition of leadership with new ways to facilitate its growth. As Brown says in the chaplet: "Leadership can be schooled, but it cannot be taught." To know leadership, one must experience and observe five passions:

1. Leaders are discoverers.

2. Leaders are cheerleaders.

3. Leaders are synthesizers.

4. Leaders are soldiers.

5. Leaders are givers.

CHAPTER 5. *ILLUMINATION*

Chaplet 5.1: Embers

Chaplet 5.1 is an original poem by Tom Brown, about the difference between doing work and being driven by the fire. And the sense of loss when we're reduced to being nothing more than an ember. What will it take to light the fire again?

Chaplet 5.2: Leaders

Momentary fame, the ability to capitalize on a fad, blips in status—these are not leadership or leaders. They're singular moments with minimal or no lasting impact that improves the lot of humankind. The world does not get better for them.

The true leader is not diverted by these things. And although it is easy for us to gravitate toward false promise and the illusion of progress, we'll find true progress only in the passion of compelling ideas. Leadership is about ideas that leave an imprint on the world.

It is the idea, championed by the leader, that breathes life into the ember, producing the spark that grows into the fire. Brown writes: "Leaders are society's vessels for progressive ideas; they are the unrelenting, unyielding, unremitting force for a new idea with the promise of positive changes." And, interestingly, where leaders come from is an ongoing mystery. Their appearance is as unpredictable as a cat's mood. But don't look for them in the established order of things. Leaders will be found on the fringe, testing the boundaries for kinks and holes and cracks.

Chaplet 5.3: Greatness

Using as his springboard the proposition that in a moneyless world, success could not be measured by numbers but rather by great achievements, Brown argues that leaders focus on doing great things. And great things are born in ideas. Leaders dwell in the world of possibilities. And leaders give the same answers to these five questions:

1. Do you want to explore or exploit?
2. Do you want to rally or to rule?
3. Do you want to imagine or to inventory?
4. Do you want to achieve or to comply?
5. Do you want to give or to take?

CHAPTER 6. *ENTERPRISE*

Chaplet 6.1: Dawn

Chaplet 6.1 is an original poem by Tom Brown. We're born with the fire, deep within us. Each day brings us an opportunity. What we do with it is up to us.

Chaplet 6.2: Apothecary

Are there no frontiers left to conquer? Is leadership only about corporate giants? Of course not. Leadership begins where each person is. The need and the opportunity confront the person each day, looking only for the right idea to emerge. The need is there. The leader finds the boundary and then expands it. He or she asks, "What could this be?" And "What might happen if...?"

In the chaplet, Yellowstone Apothecary is a case study of leadership, about a visionary who saw what a drugstore could be among the embers of a school slated for demolition. It is a drugstore that nurtures the soul, with a waterfall, bright lighting, cheer and warmth, friendly greetings, and even art. The process of building this business is a case study in resourcefulness, resolve, exploration, enthusiasm, and contribution.

Chaplet 6.3: Inversia

Standing still is not leading. Leading is precipitated by movement. Successful movement, though, oftentimes results in growth and heaviness that eventually chokes off the life that it once supported. Trends and false progress will eventually cover and smother us under their weight. We lose track of genuineness, of the things that actually count. This leads to a depletion of the soul, to false promise. And against that effect stands the leader. Brown writes: "Which is why we suffer today from inversia: The larger and more successful the organization, the less any one human being within it feels of consequence. Revenues soar; people sour. Production swells; pride shrinks. Profits skyrocket; spirits sink."

And against the weight of this choking stands the leader with a new idea, ready to redefine, renew, and redo.

Chaplet 6.4: Frontiers

Let the leaders come forward. We need them. We're not looking for idols to worship. Rather, we're looking for our roots, for what we are, for who we can be. Leaders are the opportunity to move forward. They supply the ideas to help us find ourselves and our purpose. We need leaders to help us become what we're capable of being. Actual, real progress and growth and development are leadership stories. They are testaments to the relationship between passion, ideas, inspiration, and ultimately the empowerment and actions of others.

Leaders convey urgency, they inaugurate aspiration, they invoke spirit; and, leaders provide purpose. Finally, as Brown writes: "Only if leadership fails us can tomorrow possibly scare us."

Endnotes

Preface

1 *Journal of Management Education* 17 (3), 1993: 399–415.

2 Robert N. Lussier, *Human Relations in Organizations: Applications and Skill Building* (Trwin/McGraw-Hill, 1999), 4.

Chapter 1: Who Is a Leader?

1 T. Stevens, "Follow the Leader: Under CEO Jack Welch, Leadership Development is Priority No. 1 at GE," *Industry Week*, 18 November 1996, 16–18.

2 Taken from GE's website: **http://www.ge.com**.

3 A.J. DuBrin, *Leadership: Research Findings, Practice, and Skills* (Boston: Houghton Mifflin, 1998).

4 H.S. Austin and A.W. Austin, *A Social Change Model of Leadership Development Guidebook* (Los Angeles: Higher Education Research Institute).

5 R.E. Kelley, "In Praise of Followers," *Harvard Business Review*, November-December 1998, 142–148.

6 R.J. House and R.N. Aditya, "The Social Scientific Study of Leadership: Quo Vadis?" *Journal of Management* 23 (May-June 1997): 409–474.

7 See note 6 above.

8 D.G. Bowers and S.E. Seashore, "Predicting Organizational Effectiveness with a Four-Factor Theory of Leadership," *Administrative Science Quarterly* 11 (1966): 238–263; G. Eagleson, *Notes from the workshop on leadership development*. Unpublished manuscript, Australian Graduate School of Management, Sidney, Australia.

9 D.A. Heenan and W. Bennis, *Co-Leaders: The Power of Great Partnerships* (New York: Wiley, 1999).

10 D. Cullen, "Developing Managers: Motivation and Leadership Make the Management Team thrive over the long haul," *Fleet Owner*, April 1999, 53–56.

11 R. Purser, "The Self Managing Organization," *MG Alert*, 12 May 1999, p. 1; C. Hymowitz, "In the Lead," *Wall Street Journal*, 16 March 1999, p. 1.

12 H. Klein and J. Kim, "A field study of the influence of situations constraints, leader-member exchange, and goal commitment on performance," *Academy of Management Journal* 41 (February 1998): 8–9

13 D. Ellerman, "Global Institutions," *Academy of Management Executive* 13 (1999): 25–27.

14 G. Vasilash, "Leading from the Front," *Automotive Manufacturing & Production*, September 1998, 8–9.

15 See note 10 above; M. Barrier, "Leadership Skills," *Nation's Business*, January 1999, 28–29; M. Maccoby, "Find Young Leaders or Lose Them," *Research-Technology Management*, January-February 1999, 58–60; J.A. Petrick, R.F. Scherer, J.D. Brodzinski, J.F. Quinn, and M.F. Ainina, "Global Leadership Skills and Reputational Capital: Intangible Resources for Sustainable Competitive Advantage," *Academy of Management Executive* 13 (1999): 58–69; D. Mitchell and M. Winkleman, "Eighth Annual CE Growth 100 Index," *Chief Executive*, May 1999, 40–45.

16 R.E. de Vries, R.A. Roe, and T.C.B. Taillien, "Need for Supervision: Its Impact on Leadership Effectiveness," *Journal of Applied Behavioral Science* 34 (December 1998): 486–487; "Gallup Poll Report," WFCR Radio Broadcast, 17 May 1999.

17 L. Bassi, "Point, Counterpoint," *Training & Development*, April 1999, 26–31; F. Luthans and A.D. Stajkovic, "Reinforce for Performance: The Need to Go Beyond Pay and Even rewards," *Academy of Management Executive* 13 (May 1999): 37–48.

18 M. McGue and T.J. Bouchard, "Genetic and Environmental Determinants of Information Processing and Special Mental Abilities: A Twin Analysis," In *Advances in the Psychology of Human Intelligence*, ed. R.J. Sternberg (Hillsdale, NJ: Erlbaum, 1989), pp. 7–45; R.R. McCrae and P.T. Costa, "The Stability of Personality: Observations and Evaluation," *Current Directions in Psychological Science* 3 (1994): 173–175.

19 G. Capowski, "Anatomy of a Leader: Where are the Leaders of Tomorrow?" *Management Review*, March 1994, 10–17.

20 J. Barker, "Leadershift," *MG Alert*, 28 April 1999, p. 1; see note 4 above; Staff, "Hard Wired Leadership: Unleashing the Power of Personality to Become a New Millenium Leader," *HR Magazine*, January 1999, 113–114.

21 S. Zahra, "The Changing Rules of Global Competitiveness in the 21st Century," *Academy of Management Executive* 13 (1999): 36.

22 A. Thomson, C. Mabey, and J. Storey, "The Determinants of Management Development: Choice or Circumstance?" *International Studies of Management & Organization* 28 (Spring 1998): 91–104.

23 See note 1.

24 K. Melymuka, "Kraft's 5% Solution," *Computerworld*, 2 November 1998, 69.

25 H. Mintzberg, *The Nature of Managerial Work* (New York: Harper & Row, 1973).

26 L. Kurke and H. Aldrich, "Mintzberg Was Right! A Replication and Extension of the Nature of Managerial Work," *Management Science* 29 (1983): 975–984; C Pavett and A. Lau, "Managerial Work: The Influence of Hierarchical Level and Functional Specialty," *Academy of Management Journal* 26 (1983): 170–177; C. Hales, "What Do Managers Do? A Critical Review of the Evidence," *Journal of Management Studies* 23 (1986): 88–115.

27 See note 6.

28 G. Yukl, *Leadership in Organizations*, 4th ed. (Upper Saddle River, NJ: Prentice Hall, 1998).

29 See note 28.

30 R. Mendonsa, "Keeping Who You Want to Keep: Retaining the Best People," *Supervision*, January 1998, 10–12.

31 See note 28.

32 See note 6.

33 D. Walman and F. Yammarino, "CEO Charismatic Leadership: Levels-of-Management and Levels-of-Analysis Effects," *Academy of Management Review* 24 (April 1999): 266–267.

34 R. Williams, "Summarize the Transactions," *MG Alert*, 14 April 1999, p. 1.

35 See note 28.

36 R.L. Ackoff and J. Gharajedaghi, "Reflections on Systems and Their Models," *Systems Research*, 13 (1996): 13–23.

37 See note 6.

38 See note 6.

39 See note 6.

40 See note 6.

41 N. Nicholson, "Personality and Entrepreneurial Leadership: A Study of the Heads of the UK's Most Successful Independent Companies," *European Management Journal* 16 (October 1998): 529–539; A. Zaleznik, "Managers and Leaders: Are They Different?" *Harvard Business Review*, May-June 1977, 67–78.

42 P. Pittard, "The Evolving Role of the Chief Executive Officer," *Corporate Board*, January-February 1999, 23–25; J. Connolly, "Leaders Must Stand for Something," *MG Alert*, 17 March 1999, p. 1.

43 C.D. Herring, "Dedicated to a Service Orientation," *MG Alert*, 3 March 1999, p. 1.

44 See note 28.

45 See note 13.

46 M. Sorcher and A.P. Goldstein, "A Behavior Modeling Approach in Training," *Personnel Administration*, 1972, Vol. 35, pp. 5–41.

47 See note 28.

48 See note 19.

Chapter 2: Leadership Traits and Ethics

1 Information from the opening case was taken from C. Wheller, "She Thinks Like a CEO (because she is one)" *Executive Female*, 19 (5), 1996, 32–35.

2 R.R. Perman, "Hard Wired Leadership: Unleashing the Power of Personality to Become a New Millennium Leader," *HRMagazine*, January 1999, 113–114.

3 R.J. House and R.N. Aditya, "The Social Scientific Study of Leadership: Quo Vadis?" *Journal of Management*, 23 (May-June 1997), 409–474.

4 S.H. Chiang and M. Gort, "Personality Attributes and Optimal Hierarchical Compensation Gradients," *Journal of Economic Behavior & Organization* 33 (January 1998): 227–241; D.F. Caldwell and J.M. Burger, "Personality Characteristics of Job Applicants and Success in Screening Interviews," *Personnel Psychology* 51 (Spring 1998): 119–137.

5 J. Madeleine Nash, "The Personality Genes," *Time*, 27 April 1998, 60–62.

6 See note 2.

7 See note 2.

8 D.F. Caldwell and J.M. Burger, "Personality Characteristics of Job Applicants and Success in Screening Interviews," *Personnel Psychology* 51 (Spring 1998): 119–137.

9 T.W. Smith, "Punt, Pass, and Ponder the Questions: In the NFL, Personality Tests Help Teams Judge the Draftees," *New York Times*, 20 April 1997, pp. 13–19; A.M. Ryan, R.E. Ployhart, and L.A. Friedel, "Using Personality Testing to Reduce Adverse Impact: A Cautionary Note," *Journal of Applied Psychology* 83 (April 1998): 298–308.

10 R.J. Heckman and B.W. Roberts, "Personality Profiles of Effective Managers Across Functions," Personality Application in the Workplace, *1997 Proceedings of the Society of Industrial and Organizational Psychology*, 1997, pp. 123–134.

11 J.F. Salgado, "The Five-Factor Model of Personality and Job Performance in the European Community," *Journal of Applied Psychology* 82 (1997): 30–43.

12 M.W. Morgan and M.M. Lombardo, "Off the Track: Why and How Successful Executives Get Derailed," (Greensboro, NC: Center for Creative Leadership, January 1988), Technical Report no. 21 & 34.

13 See note 3 above.

14 P. Lowe, "9 Secrets of Superstar Salespeople," *Success 1998 Yearbook*, 1998, pp. 38–39; 15 D. Vitale, "Winning the Game of Life," *Success 1998 Yearbook*, 1998, p. 49; V. Parachin, "Ten Essential Leadership Skills," *Supervision*, February 1999, pp. 13–16; J. McCann, "How to Grow a Thriving Business," *Success 1998 Yearbook*, 1998, p. 18; P. Lowe, "The Seven Essentials for Success," *Success 1998 Yearbook*, 1998, p. 70; M. Maccoby, "Find Young Leaders or Lose Them," *Research & Technology Management*, January-February 1999), 58–60.

15 B. O'Neill, "Investigating Equity Sensitivity as a Moderator of Relations between Self-Efficacy and Workplace Attitudes," *Journal of Applied Psychology* 83 (June 1998): 392–402; A. Howard and D.W. Bray, *Managerial Lives in Transition: Advancing Age and Changing Times* (New York: Gullford Press, 1988).

16 See note 1.

17 B. Tracy, "Welcome to the Golden Age," *Success 1998 Yearbook*, 1998, p. 19.

18 A. Howard and D.W. Bray, *Managerial Lives in Transition: Advancing Age and Changing Times* (New York: Gullford Press, 1988); N.D. Tichy and M.A. Devanna, *The Transformational Leader* (New York: Wiley, 1986).

19 P. Lowe, "9 Secrets of Superstar Salespeople," *Success 1998 Yearbook*, 1998, pp. 38–39; D. Mitchell and M. Winkleman, "Eighth Annual CE Growth 100 Index," *Chief Executive*, May 1999, pp. 40–46; A. Svendsen, "Trust Is Critical to Business Success," *MG Alert*, 5 May 1999, p. 1; S. Puffer, "CompUSA's CEO James Halpin on Technology, Rewards, and Commitment," *Academy of Management Executive* 13 (May 1999): 29–36.

20 M. Barrier, "Leadership Skills Employees Respect," *Nation's Business*, January 1999, p. 28; J.M. Kouzes and B.Z. Posner, *Credibility: How Leaders Gain and Lose It, Why People Demand It* (San Francisco: Jossey-Bass, 1993), p. 14.

21 S. Zahra, "The Changing Rules of Global Competitiveness in the 21st Century," *Academy of Management Executive* 13 (1999): 36; S. Weintraub, "Hidden Intelligence," *MG Alert*, 19 May 1999, p. 1; H. Gardner, *Leading Minds: An Anatomy of Leadership* (New York: Basic Books, 1995).

22 J. Schutz, "E-cards Can Pull the World Together," *MG Alert*, 5 May 1999, p. 1; P. Pittard, "The Evolving Role of the Chief Executive Officer," *Corporate Board*, January-February 1999, pp. 23–26; C. Hymowitz, "In the Lead," *Wall Street Journal*, 16 March 1999, p. 1.

23 J. Pfeffer, *Managing with Power: Politics and Influence in Organizations* (Boston: Harvard Business School Press, 1992), p. 172; I. Wylie, "Is Management a Dead Duck?" *Guardian*, 1 March 1997, p. 2; J. Pfeffer and J.F. Viega, "Putting People First for Organizational Success," *Academy of Management Executive* 13 (May 1999): 37–48.

24 L. King, "The Business of Communication," *Success 1998 Yearbook*, 1998, p. 27; C. Reeve, "A Message from Christopher Reeve," *Success 1998 Yearbook*, 1998, p. 77.

25 See note 3.

26 D. McClelland, *The Achieving Society* (New York: Van Nostrand Reinhold, 1961); D. McClelland and D.H. Burnham, "Power Is the Great Motivator," *Harvard Business Review*, March-April 1978, p. 103.

27 R.J. House, D. Spangler, and J. Woycke, "Personality and Charisma in the U.S. Presidency: A Psychological Theory of Leadership Effectiveness," *Administrative Science Quarterly 36*, (1991): 364–396.

28 N. Nicholson, "Personality and entrepreneurial leadership: a study of the heads of the UK's most successful independent companies," *European Management Journal 16*, (October 1998): 529–540.

29 D.C. McClelland and R.E. Boyatzis, "Leadership Motive Pattern and Long Term Success in Management," *Journal of Applied Psychology 67*, (1982): 737–743.

30 D.C. McClelland, *Human Motivation* (Glenview, IL: Scott Foresman, 1985).

31 D.I. Jung and B.J. Avolio, "Effects of Leadership Style and Follower's Cultural Orientation on Performance in Individual Task Conditions," *Academy of Management Journal 41*, (February 1998): 88–96; M. Maccoby, "Find Young Leaders or Lose Them," *Research & Technology Management*, January-February 1999, pp. 58–60.

32 L. King, "The Business of Communication," *Success 1998 Yearbook*, 1998, p. 27; L. Holtz, "Setting a Higher Standard," *Success 1998 Yearbook*, 1998, p. 74.

33 D. McGregor, *Leadership and Motivation* (Cambridge, MA: MIT Press, 1966).

34 M. Tietjen and R. Myers, "Motivation and Job Satisfaction," *Management Decisions*, May-June 1998, pp. 226–232.

35 J. Hall and S.M. Donnell, "Managerial Achievement: The Personal Side of Behavioral Theory," *Human Relations*, 1979, Vol. 32, pp. 77–101.

36 J.S. Livingston, "Pygmalion in Management," *Harvard Business Review on Human Relations* (New York: Harper & Row, 1979), p. 181; G. Baxter and J. Bower, "Beyond Self-Actualization: The Persuasion of Pygmalion," *Training and Development Journal*, August 1985, p. 69; J. Kouzes and B. Posner, *Encouraging the Heart: A Leader's Guide to Rewarding and Recognizing Others* (Jossey-Bass, 1999).

37 L. Holtz, "Setting a Higher Standard," *Success 1998 Yearbook*, 1998, p. 74.

38 L. DiDio, "Crashing the Glass Ceiling," *Computerworld*, 26 January 1998, pp. 72–75; K. Klenke, "Think Contextually, Metaphorically, Futuristically!" Lead Now Ezzay, *Management General*, June 1999; S.B. Nuland, "Human Spirit Is the Source of Will to Live," *MG Alert*, 12 May 1999, p. 1.

39 P. Lowe, "9 Secrets of Superstar Salespeople," *Success 1998 Yearbook*, 1998, pp. 38–39; see note 37.

40 P. Lowe, "9 Secrets of Superstar Salespeople," *Success 1998 Yearbook*, 1998, pp. 38–39.

41 L. Holtz, "Setting a Higher Standard," *Success 1998 Yearbook*, 1998, p. 74.

42 C. Reeve, "A Message from Christopher Reeve," *Success 1998 Yearbook*, 1998, p. 77.

43 R.L. Hughes, R.C. Ginnett, and G.J. Curphy, *Leadership: Enhancing the Lessons of Experience*, 3rd ed. (Burr Ridge, IL: Irwin/McGraw-Hill, 1999), p. 184.

44 K. Brown, "Using Role Play to Integrate Ethics into the Business Curriculum," *Journal of Business Ethics 13* (February 1994): 105; T. Donaldson and T.W. Dunfee, *Ties That Bind: A Social Contracts Approach to Business Ethics* (Boston: Harvard Business School Press, 1999); A. Mahoney, "Giving Values a Voice, and How Technology Raises Uncharted Issues," *Association Management*, April 1999, pp. 49–50; G. McDonald, "Business Ethics: Practical Proposals for Organizations," *Journal of Business Ethics 19* (April 1999): 143–144.

45 P. Primeaux and J. Stieber, "Profit Maximization: The Ethical Mandate of Business," *Journal of Business Ethics 13* (April 1994): 287–294; F. Daly, "The Ethics Dynamic," *Business & Social Review*, Spring 1999, pp. 37–38.

46 "The '90s May Tame the Savage M.B.A.," *Wall Street Journal*, 14 June 1991, p. B1; T. Donaldson and T.W. Dunfee, *Ties That Bind: A Social Contracts Approach to Business Ethics* (Boston: Harvard Business School Press, 1999).

47 R. Mendonsa, "Keeping Who You Want to Keep: Retaining the Best People," *Supervision*, January 1998, pp. 10–13; see note 3 above; T. Jones and A. Wicks, "Convergent Stakeholder Theory," *Academy of Management Review 24* (April 1999): 206–207.

48 M. Jennings, "Ethics: Why It Matters and How You Do It," *Government Accountant Journal 47* (Winter 1998): 12–13.

49 D.M. Anderson and M. Warshaw, "The Number One Entrepreneur in America," *Success*, March 1995, pp. 32–43.

50 M.B. Monagham, "Respond to the Light Within!" Lead Now Ezzay, *Management General*, May 1999; V. Parachin, "Ten Essential Leadership Skills," *Supervision*, February 1999, pp. 13–16.

51 D.P. Campbell, *Campbell Leadership Index Manual* (Minneapolis: National Computer Systems, 1991).

52 For more information on training materials, contact the Zig Ziglar Corporation, 3330 Earhart, Carrollton, TX 75006, 972–233–9191.

Chapter 3: Leadership Behavior and Motivation

1 E. Pooley, "One Good Apple," *Time*, 19 January 1996, 54–56; NYPD website, **http://www.ci.nyc.ny.html/nypd/home.html.**

2 L.L. Larson, J.G. Hunt, and R.N. Osborn, "Correlates of Leadership and Demographic Variables in Three Organizational Settings," *Journal of Business Research 2* (1974): 335–347.

3 D.P. Skarlicki, R. Folger, and P. Tesluk, "Personality as a Moderator in the Relationship between Fairness and Retaliation," *Academy of Management Journal 42* (February 1999): 100–108; J.A. Petrick, R.F. Scherer, J.D. Brodzinski, J.F. Quinn, and M.F. Ainina, "Global Leadership Skills and Reputational Capital: Intangible Resources for Sustainable Competitive Advantage," *Academy of Management Executive 13* (1999): 58–69; D.J. Jung and B.J. Avolio, "Effects of Leadership Style and Followers' Cultural Orientation on Performance in Individual Task Conditions," *Academy of Management Journal 41* (February 1998): 208–218.

4 "Gallup Poll Report," WFCR Radio Broadcast, 17 May 1999; D. Konst, R. Vonk, and R. Van der Vlist, "Inferences about Causes and Consequences of Behavior of Leaders and Subordinates," *Journal of Organizational Behavior 20* (March 1999): 261–262.

5 P. Lowe, "Maximized Management," *Success 1998 Yearbook*, 1998, p. 16.

6 K. Lewin, R. Lippett, and R.K. White, "Patterns of Aggressive Behavior in Experimentally Created Social Climates," *Journal of Social Psychology 10*, (1939): 271–301.

7 P. Pittard, "The Evolving Role of the Chief Executive Officer," *Corporate Board*, (January-February 1999): 23–26.

8 R. Likert, *New Patterns of Management* (New York: McGraw-Hill, 1961).

9 R.M. Stogdill and A.E. Coons (eds.), *Leader Behavior: Its Description and Measurement* (Columbus: The Ohio State University Bureau of Business Research, 1957).

10 J. Monoky, "What's Your Management Style?" *Industrial Distribution*, June 1998, 142–143.

11 B.M. Bass, *Handbook of Leadership: A Survey of Theory and Research* (New York: Free Press, 1990).

12 R.J. House and R.N. Aditya, "The Social Scientific Study of Leadership: Quo Vadis?" *Journal of Management 23* (May-June 1997): 409–474.

13 See note 11 above.

14 D.G. Bowers and S.E. Seashore, "Predicting Organizational Effectiveness with a Four-Factor Theory of Leadership," *Administrative Science Quarterly 11* (1966): 238–263.

15 R. Likert, *The Human Organization: Its Management and Value* (New York: McGraw-Hill, 1967).

16 R. Blake and J. Mouton, *The Managerial Grid* (Houston: Gulf Publishing, 1964); R. Blake and J. Mouton, *The New Managerial Grid* (Houston: Gulf Publishing, 1978); R. Blake and J. Mouton, *The Managerial Grid III: Key to Leadership Excellence* (Houston: Gulf Publishing, 1985); R. Blake and A.A. McCanse, *Leadership Dilemmas —Grid Solutions* (Houston: Gulf Publishing, 1991).

17 D.J. Jung and B.J. Avolio, "Effects of Leadership Style and Followers' Cultural Orientation on Performance in Individual Task Conditions," *Academy of Management Journal 42* (April 1999): 208–218; L. Pheng and B. Lee, "Managerial Grid" and Zhuge Liang's 'Art of Management': Integration for Effective Project Management," *Management Decision 35* (May-June 1997): 382–392.

18 R. Blake and J. Mouton, *The Managerial Grid* (Houston: Gulf Publishing, 1964).

19 R. Blake and J. Mouton, *The New Managerial Grid* (Houston: Gulf Publishing, 1978).

20 P. Nystrom, "Managers and the Hi-Hi Leader Myth," *Academy of Management Journal 21* (June 1978): 325–331.

21 B.M. Fisher and J.E. Edwards, "Consideration and Initiating Structure and Their Relationship with Leader Effectiveness: A Meta-analysis," *Proceeding of the Academy of Management*, August 1988, pp. 201–205.

22 See note 21.

23 J. Misumi, *The Behavioral Science of Leadership: An Interdisciplinary Japanese Research Program* (Ann Arbor, MI: University of Michigan Press); R.J. House and R.N. Aditya, "The Social Scientific Study of Leadership: Quo Vadis?" *Journal of Management 23* (May-June 1997): 409–474.

24 R.F. Bales, "In Conference," *Harvard Business Review*, (March-April, 1954): 44–50.

25 C. Hymowtiz and M. Murray, "Raises and Praise or Out the Door," *Wall Street Journal*, 21 June 1999, p. B1.

26 D.J. Jung and B.J. Avolio, "Effects of Leadership Style and Followers' Cultural Orientation on Performance in Individual Task Conditions," *Academy of Management Journal 42* (April 1999): 208–218; D. Cullen, "Developing Managers: Motivation and Leadership Make the Management Team Thrive over the Long Haul," *Fleet Owner*, April 1999, 53–56; C. Hymowitz and M. Murray, "Raises and Praise or Out the Door," *Wall Street Journal*, 21 June 1999, p. B1; K. Wreed, "Identifying Natural Talents Lets Company Make Right Choice," *HR Focus*, April 1999, 6.

27 K. Down and L. Liedtka, "What Corporations Seek in MBA Hires: A Survey," *Selections*, Winter 1994, 34–39; R. Mendosa, "Keeping Who You Want to Keep: Retaining the Best People," *Supervision*, January 1998, 10–13.

28 A. Maslow, "A Theory of Human Motivation," *Psychological Review 50* (1943): 370–396; A. Maslow, *Motivation and Personality* (New York: Harper & Row, 1954).

29 A. Maslow, *Maslow on Management* (New York: Wiley, 1998); T. Petzinger, "The Front Line: Radical Work by Guru Leader (Maslow) Takes 30 Years to Flower," *Wall Street Journal*, 25 April 1997, p. 1; R. Zemke, "Maslow for a New Millennium," *Training*, December 1998, 54–59.

30 F. Herzberg, "The Motivation-Hygiene

Concept and Problems of Manpower," *Personnel Administrator*, (1964): 3–7; F. Herzberg, "One More Time: How Do You Motivate Employees?" *Harvard Business Review*, January-February 1968, 53–62.

31 D.A. Heenan and W. Bennis, *Co-Leadership: The Power of Great Partnerships* (New York: Wiley, 1999); D. Ellerman, "Global Institutions: Transforming International Development Agencies into Learning Organizations," *Academy of Management Executive 13* (February 1999): 109–111.

32 A. Kohn, "Challenging Behaviorist Dogma: Myths about Money and Motivation," *Compensation and Benefits Review*, March/April 1998, 27–33.

33 C. Hymowitz and M. Murray, "Raises and Praises or Out the Door," *Wall Street Journal*, 21 June 1999, p. B1; J Pfeffer and J.F. Viega, "Putting People First for Organizational Success," *Academy of Management Executive 13* (February 1999): 109–111.

34 M. Tietjen and R. Myers, "Motivation and Job Satisfaction," *Management Decisions 36* (May-June 1998): 226–232; I. Adigun, "Generalizability of a Theory of Job Attitudes: A Cross-Cultural View," Research note, *Journal of Public Administration 21* (November 1998): 1629–1637.

35 H. Murray, *Explorations in Personality* (New York: Oxford Press, 1938); J. Atkinson, *An Introduction to Motivation* (New York: Van Nostrand Reinhold, 1964).

36 D. McNees-Smith, "The Relationship between Managerial Motivation, Leadership, Nurse Outcomes, and Patient Satisfaction," *Journal of Organizational Behavior 20* (March 1999): 243–244.

37 T. Brown, "Tim Soldier," *Chaplet 10, Fiscal Fairy Tales E-Book*, 1998, website **http://www.mgeneral.com.**

38 See note 3 (Skarlicki et al.).

39 J. Stacy Adams, "Toward an Understanding of Inequity," *Journal of Abnormal and Social Psychology 67* (1963): 422–36.

40 D. van Dierendonck, W.B. Schaufeli, and B.P. Buunk, "The Evaluation of an Individual Burnout Intervention Program: The Role of Inequity and Social Support," *Journal of Applied Psychology 83* (June 1998): 392–408.

41 M. Bloom, "The Performance Effects of Pay Dispersion on Individuals And Organizations," *Academy of Management Journal 42* (February 1999): 25–40.

42 B. O'Neill and M. Mone, "Investigating Equity Sensitivity as a Moderator of Relations between Self-Efficacy and Workplace Attitudes," *Journal of Applied Psychology 83* (October 1998): 805.

43 V. Vroom, *Work and Motivation* (New York: John Wiley & Sons, 1964).

44 D. Ilgen, D. Nebeker, and R. Pritchard, "Expectancy Theory Measures: An Empirical Comparison in an Experimental Simulation," *Organizational Behavior and Human Performance 28* (1981): 189–223; W. Van Eerde and H. Tierry, "Vroom's Expectancy Model and Work-Related Criteria: A Meta-Analysis," *Journal of Applied Psychology 81* (October 1996): 548–556; R. Fudge and J. Schlacter, "Motivating Employees to Act Ethically: An Expectancy Theory Approach," *Journal of Business Ethics 18* (February 1999): 295–296.

45 E.A. Locke, K.N. Shaw, L.M. Saari, and G.P. Latham, "Goal Setting and Task Performance," *Psychological Bulletin 90* (August 1981): 125–152; R.J. House and R.N. Aditya, "The Social Scientific Study of Leadership: Quo Vadis?" *Journal of Management 23* (May-June 1997): 409–474.

46 H. Klein and J. Kim, "A Field Study in the Influence of Situation Constraints, Leader-Member Exchange, and Goal Commitment on Performance," *Academy of Management Journal 41* (February 1998): 88–95.

47 See note 46; D. Frink and G. Ferris, "Accountability, Impression Management, and Goal Setting in the Performance Evaluation Process," *Human Relations 51* (October 1998): 1259–1274.

48 B.F. Skinner, *Beyond Freedom and Dignity* (New York: Alfred A. Knopf, 1971).

49 F. Luthans and A.D. Stajkovic, "Reinforce for Performance: The Need to Go Beyond Pay and Even Rewards," *Academy of Management Executive 13* (May 1999): p. 49.

50 See note 49.

51 S. Kerr, "On the Folly of Rewarding A, While Hoping for B," *Academy of Management Executive 9* (February 1995): 32–40.

52 See note 51.

53 See note 51.

54 See note 49.

55 L. Leland, "Fire 'em up," *American Printer*, March 1999, 30–34.

56 F. Luthans and A.D. Stajkovic, "Reinforce for Performance: The Need to Go Beyond Pay and Even Rewards," *Academy of Management Executive 13* (May 1999), 49; "A Pat on the Back," *Wall Street Journal*, 3 January 1989, p. 1; "Odds and Ends," *Wall Street Journal*, 18 April 1989, p. B1.

57 J. Kouzes and B. Posner, *Encouraging the Heart: A Leader's Guide to Rewarding and Recognizing Others* (Jossey-Bass, 1999).

58 Kenneth Blanchard and Spencer Johnson, *The One-Minute Manager* (New York: Wm. Morrow & Co., 1982).

59 This statement is based on Robert N. Lussier's consulting experience.

60 See note 59.

Chapter 4: Communication, Coaching, and Conflict Skills

1 Information for the opening case is taken from the *Wall Street Journal*, the *New York Times*, and the Coca-Cola Company website **www.cocacola.com** from June to December 1999.

2 L. King, "The Business of Communication," *Success Yearbook*, 1998, p. 27; P. Lowe, "How to Boost Your Market Value," *Success Yearbook*, 1998, p. 22; C. Pettifor, "Match Points," *The Guardian*, April 24, 1999, p. R3–4; D. Luse, "Incorporating Business Communication in an Integrative Business Seminar," *Business Communications Quarterly 62* (March 1999): 96–111.

3 S. Hirst, "Verbal Remedy," *People Management*, 11 March 1999, 50–53; L. Pheng and B. Lee, "'Managerial Grid' and Zhuge Liang's 'Art of Management': Integration for Effective Project Management," *Management Decision 35* (May-June 1997): 382–392; B.M. Bass, *Bass & Stogdill's Handbook of Leadership: Theory, Research, & Managerial Applications*, 3rd ed. (New York: The Free Press, 1990), p. 111.

4 D. Cullen, "Developing Managers: Motivation and Leadership Make the Management Team Thrive over the Long Haul," *Fleet Owner*, April 1999, 53–56; D. Mitchell and M. Winkleman, "Eighth Annual CE Growth 100 Index," *Chief Executive*, May 1999, 40–46.

5 Staff, "Only Communicate," *The Economist*, 24 June 1995, pp. S18–S19; M. Barrier, "Leadership Skills Employees Respect," *Nation's Business*, January 1999, 28–29; P. Lowy and B. Reimus, "Ready, Aim, Communicate!" *Management Review*, July 1996, 40–43.; Lee Iacocca, *Iacocca* (New York: Bantam Books, 1985), p. 15; Staff, "Send & Receive 201 Messages a Day," *Wall Street Journal*, 22 June 1999, p. 1.

6 R.J. Klimoski and N.J. Hayes, "Leaders' Behavior and Subordinate Motivation," *Personnel Psychology* (Autumn 1980): 543–555.

7 R. Walker, "Where the Rubber Meets the Road," *Workforce*, January 1999, pp. G14–16.

8 Staff, "Talking Too Fast and Giving Too Much Detail Are the Main Mannerisms Hindering Career Advancement," *Wall Street Journal*, 3 August 1999, Commentary Insert, p. 1.

9 See note 8 above.

10 N. Woodward, "Do You Speak Internet?" *HR Magazine*, April 1999, pp. S12–17.

11 G. Blake, "It Is Recommended That You Write Clearly," *Wall Street Journal*, 2 April 1995, p.14.

12 V. Parachin, "Ten Essential Leadership Skills," *Supervision*, February 1999, 13–16.

13 J. Gitomer, "One of the Skills We Need Most Is Listening," *Dallas Business Journal*, 4 November 1994, pp. 1B–2B; E. Wycoff, "The Language of Listening," *Internal Auditor*, April 1994, 26–28; Staff, "Communicating: Face-to-Face," *Agency Sales Magazine*, January 1994, 22–23.

14 H. Lawrence and A. Wiswell, "Feedback Is a Two-Way Street," *Training & Development*, July 1995, pp. 49–52; S. Caudron, "The Top 20 Ways to Motivate Employees," *Industry Week*, 3 April 1995, pp. 12–16; T. Heinselman, "Executive

Coaching Defined," *Training & Development*, March 1999, 34–40; J.C. Kunich and R.I. Lester, "Leadership and the Art of Feedback: Feeding the Hands That Back Us," *Journal of Leadership Studies 3* (1996): 3–22.

15 W. Kaydos, *Operational Performance Measurement: Increasing Total Productivity* (St. Lucie Press, 1999); R.J. House and R.N. Aditya, "The Social Scientific Study of Leadership: Quo Vadis?" *Journal of Management 23* (May-June 1997): 409–474; K. Melymuks, "Kraft's 5% Solution," *Computerworld*, 2 November 1998, 69–70.; J. Kouzes and B. Posner, *Encouraging the Heart: A Leader's Guide to Rewarding and Recognizing Others* (Jossey-Bass, 1999).

16 K.W. Bunker and A.D. Webb, *Learning How to Learn from Experience: Impact of Stress and Coping*, Technical Report 154 (Greensboro, NC: Center for Creative Leadership, 1992); M.B. Monagham, "Respond to the Light Within," *Leaders—Ezzay*, MG website **www.mgeneral. com**, August 20, 1999.

17 L. Leland, "Fire 'em Up," *American Printer*, March 1999, 30–34.

18 S. Shellenbarger, "Work & Family," *Wall Street Journal*, 9 June 1999, p. 4.

19 See note 18.

20 K. Morical, "A Product Review: 360 Assessments," *Training & Development*, April 1999, 43–48; R. Lepsinger and A.D. Lucia, *The Art and Science of 360 Degree Feedback* (San Francisco: Pfeiffer, 1997); M.N Tichy and E. Cohen, *The Leadership Engine: How Winning Companies Build Leaders at Every Level* (New York: HarperCollins, 1997).

21 Staff, "Strategic Coaching," *HR Focus*, February 1999, 7–8.

22 See note 12; L. Gigilo, T. Diamante, and J.M. Urban, "Coaching a Leader: Leveraging Change at the Top," *Journal of Management Development 17* (February-March 1998): 93–116; S. Shellenbarger, "Are Saner Workloads the Unexpected Key to More Productivity?" *Wall Street Journal*, 10 March 1999, p. B1; L. McDermott, *World Class Teams* (New York: Wiley, 1999); See note 21; K. Rancourt, "Real-Time Coaching Boosts Performance," *Training & Development 49* (April 1995): 53–57; Staff, "Buddy System," *Wall Street Journal*, 12 December 1995, p. 1.

23 P. Calabria, "Top Execs Should Take a Few Cues from the Coach," *LI Business News*, 8 January 1999, pp. 27–28A.

24 "Gallup Poll Report," *WFCR Radio Broadcast*, 17 May 1999; J. Kotter, "In Findfire! #9," *MG Alert*, 3 March 1999; see note 22, Giglio et al.

25 T. Peters and N. Austin, *A Passion for Excellence* (New York: Random House, 1985), 378–392.

26 See note 24, Kotter.

27 V. Parachin, "Ten Essential Leadership Skills," *Supervision*, February 1999, 13–16; S. Shellenbarger, "Work & Family," *Wall Street Journal*, 9 June 1999, p. 4.

28 S. Brown, "Failing to Train and Coach New Hires is Failing to Manage," *Supervision*, March 1999, 18–20; see note 28, Shellenbarger.

29 See note 28, Shellenbarger.

30 I. Cunningham and L. Honold, "Everyone Can Be a Coach," *HR Magazine*, July 1998, 63–67.

31 J. Falvey, "To Raise Productivity, Try Saying Thank You," *Wall Street Journal*, 6 December 1982.

32 R.G. Lord and K.J. Maher, *Leadership and Information Processing: Linking Perceptions and Performance* (Boston: Unwin-Hyman, 1991); see note 29, Brown; see note 28, Parachin.

33 S.G. Green and T.R. Mitchell, "Attributional Processes of Leadership in Leader-Member Exchanges," *Organizational Behavior and Human Performance 23* (1979): 429–458.

34 P.F. Duarte, J.R. Goodson, and N.R. Klich, "Effects of Dyadic Quality and Duration on Performance Appraisal," *Academy of Management Journal 37* (1994): 499–521.

35 D.B. Turban and T.W. Dougherty, "Role of Protégé Personality in Receipt of Mentoring and Career Success," *Academy of Management Journal 37* (1994): 688–702.

36 C. Powell, "Sharing in the American Dream," *Success Yearbook*, 1998, p. 69.

37 T. Brown, "How to Cut the Costs of Conflict," Leader-Lines, MG website **www. mgeneral.com**, 9 June 1999; T. Petzinger, "A Humanist Executive Leads by Thinking in Broader Terms," *Wall Street Journal*, 16 April 1999, p. B1.

38 G.H. Johnson, T. Means, and J. Pullis, "Managing Conflict," *Internal Auditor*, December 1998, 54–59.; J. Olson-Buchanan, F. Drasgow, P.J. Moberg, A.D. Mead, P.A. Keenan, and M.A. Donovan, "Interactive Video Assessment of Conflict Resolution Skills," *Personnel Psychology 51* (Spring 1998): 1–25; J. Clarke, "Just When You Thought It Was Safe . . . Dare You Swim in the Shark-infested Waters of Office Politics?" *The Guardian*, 24 April 1999, p. R3; see note 28, Parachin; O. Janssen, "How Task and Person Conflict Shape the Role of Positive Interdependence in Management Teams," *Journal of Management 25* (March-April 1999): 117–119; S. Adams, "Settling Cross-cultural Disagreements Begins with "Where" not "How," *Academy of Management Executive 13* (February 1999): 109–111.

39 J. Olson-Buchanan, F. Drasgow, P.J. Moberg, A.D. Mead, P.A. Keenan, and M.A. Donovan, "Interactive Video Assessment of Conflict Resolution Skills," *Personnel Psychology 51* (Spring 1998): 1–25; I. Innami, "The Quality of Group Decision, Group Verbal Behavior, and Intervention," *Organizational Behavior and Human Decision Process 60* (December 1994): 409–430.

40 M.A. Rahim, *Managing Conflict in Organizations* (Westport, CT: Praeger, 1992.)

41 See note 39, Olson-Buchanan et al.

42 See note 3, Pheng and Lee.

43 Staff, "Keeping Hot Buttons from Taking Control," *Supervisory Management*, April 1995, 1.

44 E. Niemyer, "The Case for Case Studies," *Training and Development*, January 1995, 50–52.

45 See note 37, Brown; J. Denny, "The Keys of Conflict Resolution: Proven Methods of Settling Disputes Voluntarily," *Library Journal 124* (May 1, 1999): 96; see note 39, Olson-Buchanan et al.

46 D.H. Gobeli, H.F. Koenig, and I. Bechinger, "Managing Conflict in Software Development Teams: A Multilevel Analysis," *Journal of Product Innovation Management 15* (September 1998): 423–436.

47 S. Weide and G. Abbott, "Management on the Hot Seat: In an Increasingly Violent Workplace, How to Deliver Bad News," *Employment Relations Today 21* (Spring 1994): 23–34.

48 See note 37, Brown.

49 E. Anderson, "Communication Patterns: A Tool for Memorable Leadership Training," *Training*, January 1984, 55–57.

50 See note 49.

Chapter 5: Contingency Leadership Theories

1 Information for the opening case taken from the *Wall Street Journal*, 20 July 1999, p. 1; and the HP website **www.ph.com** on 2 September 1999.

2 R. Gordon, "Substitutes for Leadership," *Supervision*, July 1994, 17–20.

3 R.J. Hughes, R.C. Ginnett, and G.J. Curphy, *Leadership: Enhancing the Lessons of Experience*, 3rd ed. (Burr Ridge, IL: Irwin/McGraw-Hill, 1999), p. 26.

4 R. Mendosa, "Keeping What You Want to Keep: Retaining the Best People," *Supervision*, January 1998, 10–13; "Gallup Poll Report," *WFCR Radio Broadcast*, 17 May 1999; D.J. Jung and B.J. Avolio, "Effects of Leadership Style and Followers' Cultural Orientation and Performance in Individual Task Conditions," *Academy of Management Journal 42* (April 1999): 208–209; N. Nicholson, "Personality and Entrepreneurial Leadership: A Study of the Heads of the UK's Most Successful Independent Companies," *European Management Journal 16*, (October 1998): 529–541; K. Klenke, "Think Contextually, Metaphorically, Futuristically!" Leaders-Ezzay, MG website **www.mgeneral.com**, 1999.

5 Staff, "Global Companies Reexamine Corporate Culture," *Personnel Journal 73*, (August 1994): S12–13; B. Duffer, "Dealing with Diversity: Management Education in Europe," *Selections*, Winter 1994, 7–15.

6 W. Ouchi, *Theory Z—How American Business Can Meet the Japanese Challenge* (Reading, MA: Addison-Wesley, 1981).

7 R.N. House and R.J. Aditya, "The Social Scientific Study of Leadership: Quo Vadis?" *Journal of Management* 23 (May-June 1997): 409–474; F.E. Fiedler, A *Theory of Leadership Effectiveness* (New York: McGraw-Hill, 1967).

8 F.E. Fiedler, "The Contingency Model and the Dynamics of the Leadership Process." In *Advances in Experimental Social Psychology*, ed. L. Breakouts (New York: Academic Press, 1978); see note 7, House and Aditya.

9 F.E. Fiedler and M.M. Chemers, *Improving Leadership Effectiveness: The Leader Match Concept*, 2nd ed. (New York: Wiley, 1982).

10 C. Schriesheim and S. Kerr, "Theories and Measures of Leadership: A Critical Appraisal of Present and Future Directions." In J.C. Hunt and L.L. Larson (eds.), *Leadership: The Cutting Edge* (Carbondale, IL: Southern Illinois University Press, 1977), 9–44; A.S. Ashour, "Further Discussion of Fiedler's Contingency Model of Leadership Effectiveness: An Evaluation," *Organizational Behavior and Human Performance* 9 (1973): 339–355.

11 F.E. Fiedler, "A Rejoinder to Schriesheim and Kerr's Premature Obituary of the Contingency Model." In J.G. Hunt and L.L. Larson (eds.), *Leadership: The Cutting Edge* (Carbondale, IL: Southern Illinois University Press, 1977), 45–50; F.E. Fiedler, "The Contingency Model: A Reply to Ashour," *Organizational Performance and Human Behavior* 9, (1973): 356–368.

12 M.J. Strube and J.E. Garcia, "A Meta-Analytical Investigation of Fiedler's Contingency Model of Leadership Effectiveness," *Psychology Bulletin* 90 (1981): 307–321; L.H. Peters, D.D. Hartke, and J.T. Pohlmann, "Fielder's Contingency Model of Leadership: An Application of the Meta-Analysis Procedure of Schmidt and Hunter," *Psychological Bulletin* 97 (1985): 274–285.

13 F.E. Fiedler and J.E. Garcia, *New Approaches to Effective Leadership: Cognitive Resources and Organizational Performance* (New York: Wiley, 1987).

14 F.E. Fiedler, "Research on Leadership Selection and Training: One View of the Future," *Administrative Science Quarterly* 41 (1996): 241–250; F.E. Fiedler, "Cognitive Resources and Leadership Performance," *Applied Psychology—An International Review* 44 (1995): 5–28.

15 R.P. Vecchio, "Theoretical and Empirical Examination of Cognitive Resource Theory," *Journal of Applied Psychology* 75 (1990): 141–147; P.J. Bettin and J.K. Kennedy, "Leadership Experience and Leader Performance: Some Empirical Support at Last," *Leadership Quarterly* 1 (1990): 219–228.

16 R.J. Hughes, R.C. Ginnett, and G.J. Curphy, *Leadership: Enhancing the Lessons of Experience*, 3rd ed. (Burr Ridge, IL: Irwin/McGraw-Hill, 1999), 70.

17 R. Tannenbaum and W.H. Schmidt, "How to Choose a Leadership Pattern," *Harvard Business Review*, March-April 1958, 95–101.

18 R. Tannenbaum and W.H. Schmidt, "How to Choose a Leadership Pattern," *Harvard Business Review*, May-June 1973, 166.

19 R. Tannenbaum and W.H. Schmidt, excerpts from "How to Choose a Leadership Pattern," *Harvard Business Review*, July-August 1986, p. 129.

20 R.J. House, "A Path-Goal Theory of Leader Effectiveness," *Administrative Science Quarterly* 16 (2), 1971: 321–329; M.G. Evans, "The Effects of Supervisory Behavior on the Path-Goal Relationship," *Organizational Behavior and Human Performance* 5, (1970): 277–298.

21 See note 7, House and Aditya.

22 A.J. DuBrin, *Leadership: Research Finding, Practice, and Skills* (Boston: Houghton Mifflin, 1998), 138.

23 R.J. House and T.R. Mitchell, "Path-Goal Theory of Leadership," *Contemporary Business*, Fall 1974, 81–98.

24 J.C. Wofford and L.Z. Liska, "Path-Goal Theories of Leadership: A Meta Analysis," *Journal of Management* 19 (1993): 858–876; P.M. Podsakoff, S.B. MacKenzie, M. Ahearne, and W.H. Bommer, "Searching for a Needle in a Haystack: Trying to Identify the Illusive Moderators of Leadership Behavior," *Journal of Management* 21 (1995): 423–470.

25 C. Schriesheim and L.L. Nieder, "Path-Goal Leadership Theory: The Long and Winding Road," *Leadership Quarterly* 7(3), 1996: 317–321; see note 7, House and Aditya; J. Beeler, "A Survey Report of Job Satisfaction and Job Involvement among Governmental and Public Auditors," *Government Accountants Journal* 45 (Winter 1997): 26–32.

26 G. Yukl, *Leadership in Organizations* (Upper Saddle River, NJ: Prentice Hall, 1998), 270; R.L. Daft, *Leadership: Theory and Practice* (Fort Worth: The Dryden Press), 107.

27 See note 7, House and Aditya; see note 20, House, pp. 323–352, for a discussion of how the original path-goal theory led to the development of the 1976 Charismatic theory and a description of the 1996 version of path-goal theory.

28 A. Cohen and D. Bradford, "Create a New Mindset," Leaders-Ezzay, MG website **www.mgeneral.com,** 9 June 1999; V.H. Vroom and P.W. Yetton, *Leadership and Decision Making* (Pittsburgh: University of Pittsburgh Press, 1973); V.H. Vroom and A.G. Jago, *The New Leadership: Managing Participation in Organizations* (Englewood Cliffs, NJ: Prentice-Hall, 1988).

29 N.R.F. Maier, *Problem Solving Discussions and Conferences: Leadership Methods and Skills* (New York: McGraw-Hill, 1963).

30 G. Yukl, *Leadership in Organizations* (Upper Saddle River, NJ: Prentice Hall, 1998), 131.

31 R.H.G. Field, P.C. Read, and J.J. Louviere, "The Effect of Situation Attributes on Decision Making Choice in the Vroom-Jago Model of Participation in Decision Making," *Leadership Quarterly* 1 (1990): 165–176; see note 28, Vroom and Jago.

32 R.H.G. Field, "A Critique of the Vroom-Yetton Contingency Model of Leadership Behavior," *Academy of Management Review* 4, (1979): 249–257; J.B. Miner, "The Uncertain Future of the Leadership Concept: An Overview," In *Leadership Frontiers*, eds. J.G. Hunt and L.L. Larson (Kent, OH: Kent State University, 1975).

33 G. Yukl, *Leadership in Organizations* (Upper Saddle River, NJ: Prentice Hall, 1998), p. 132.

34 P. Hersey and K.H. Blanchard, "Life Cycle Theory of Leadership," *Training and Development Journal* 23 (1969): 26–34; P. Hersey and K.H. Blanchard, *Management of Organizational Behavior: Utilizing Human Resources*, 3rd ed. (Englewood Cliffs, NJ: Prentice Hall, 1977); P. Hersey, K.H. Blanchard, and D.E. Johnson, *Management of Organizational Behavior: Utilizing Human Resources*, 7th ed. (Upper Saddle River, NJ: Prentice Hall, 1996).

35 R.P Vecchio, "Situational Leadership Theory: An Examination of a Prescriptive Theory," *Journal of Applied Psychology* 72 (1987): 444–451; C. Graeff, "The Situational Leadership Theory: A Critical Review," *Academy of Management Review* 8 (1983): 285, 296.

36 T.D. Cairns, J. Hollenback, R.C. Preziosi, and W.A. Snow, "Technical Note: A Study of Hersey and Blanchard's Situational Leadership Theory," *Leadership & Organization Development Journal* 19 (March-April 1998): 113–117; J.R. Schermerhon, "Situational Leadership: Conversations with Paul Hersey," *Mid-American Journal of Business* 12 (Fall 1997): 5–11.

37 G. Yukl, *Leadership in Organizations* (Upper Saddle River, NJ: Prentice Hall, 1998), 272; see note 36, Schermerhon; R.J. Hughes, R.C. Ginnett, and G.J. Curphy, *Leadership: Enhancing the Lessons of Experience*, 3rd ed. (Burr Ridge, IL: Irwin/McGraw-Hill, 1999), 61; J. Monoky, "What's Your Management Style?" *Industrial Distribution*, June 1998, 142.

38 See note 37, Yukl.

39 O.M. Irgens, "Situational Leadership: A Modification of Hersey and Blanchard's Model," *Leadership & Organizational Development Journal* 16(2), 1995: 36–40.

40 Statement taken from Tom Brown's review of Russell Ackoff's work. MG website **www.mgeneral.com,** Top 10 Resources, September 1999; R.L. Ackoff, *Re-Creating the Corporation: A Design of Organizations for the 21st Century* (Oxford: Oxford University Press, 1999).

41 J. Pfeffer, "The Ambiguity of Leadership," *Academy of Management Review*, April 1977, 104–112; J. Howell, D.E. Bowen, P.W. Dorfman, S. Kerr, and P. Podaskoff, "Substitutes for

Leadership: Effective Alternatives to Ineffective Leadership," *Organizational Dynamics*, Summer 1990, 23.

42 S. Kerr and J. Jermier, "Substitutes for Leadership: The Meaning and Measurement," *Organizational Behavior and Human Performance* 22 (1978): 375–403.

43 P.M. Podsakoff, S.B. MacKenzie, and W.H. Bommer, "Transformational Leadership Behaviors and Substitutes for Leadership as Determinants of Employee Satisfaction, Commitment, Trust, and Organizational Behaviors," *Journal of Management*, 22(2), 1996; 259–298; see note 41, Howell et al.

44 J.E. Sheridan, D.J. Vredenburgh, and M.A. Abelson, "Contextual Model of Leadership Influence in Hospital Units," *Academy of Management Journal* 27(1), 1984: 57–78; see note 43, Podsakoff et al.; R.E. de Vries, R.A. Roe, and T.C.B. Taillien, "Need for Supervision: Its Impact on Leadership Effectiveness," *Journal of Applied Behavioral Science* 34 (December 1998): 486–487.

45 P.M. Podsakoff, S.B. MacKenzie, and W.H. Bommer, "Meta-analysis of the Relationships between Kerr and Jermier's Substitutes for Leadership and Employee Job Attitudes, Role Perceptions, and Performance," *Journal of Applied Psychology 81*, (August 1996): 380–400; G. Yukl, *Leadership in Organizations* (Upper Saddle River, NJ: Prentice Hall, 1998), 276.

46 MOCON is a successful company. However, Kim Rogers is not the actual name of a manager at MOCON. This character is used to illustrate contingency leadership.

Chapter 6: Dyadic Relationships, Followership, and Delegation

1 G.B. Graen and Mary Uhl-Bien, "Relationship-Based Approach to Leadership: Development of Leader Member Exchange (LMX) Theory of Leadership over 25 Years: Applying a Multi-Level Multi-Domain Approach," *Leadership Quarterly* 6 (2) 1995: 219–247.

2 J.R. Meindl and S.B. Ehrlich, "The Romance of Leadership and the Evaluation of Organizational Performance," *Academy of Management Journal* 30 (1987): 90–109.

3 G. Graen and J.F. Cashman, "A Role-Making Model of Leadership in Formal Organizations: A Developmental Approach." In J.G. Hunt and L.L. Larson (eds.), *Leadership frontiers.* (Kent, OH: Kent State University Press), pp. 143–165.

4 See note 1 above.

5 See note 3 above.

6 T.A. Scandura, G.B. Graen, and M.A. Novak, "When Managers Decide Not to Decide Autocratically: An Investigation of Leader-Member Exchange and Decision Influence," *Journal of Applied Psychology* 71 (1986): 579–584; R.C. Liden, R.T. Sparrowe, & S.J. Wayne, "Leader-Member Exchange Theory: The Past

and Potential for the Future," *Research in Personnel and Human Resource Management* 15 (1997): 47–119.

7 Ferris, T.R., "Role of Leadership in the Employee Withdrawal Process: A Constructive Replication," *Journal of Applied Psychology* 70 (1985): 777–781; S.W. J. Kozlowski and M.L. Doherty, "Integration of Climate and Leadership: Examination of a Neglected Issue," *Journal of Applied Psychology* 74 (1989): 546–553; S.J. Wayne, L.M. Shore, and R.C. Liden, "Leader-Member Exchange Theory: The Past and Potential for the Future," *Research in Personnel and Human Resource Management* 15 (1997): 47–119.

8 Gary Yukl, *Leadership in Organizations,* —ed. (Englewood Cliffs, NJ: Prentice Hall, 1998), 151.

9 See note 8.

10 G.B. Graen and T. Scandura, "Toward a Psychology of Dyadic Organizing," *Research in Organizational Behavior* 9 (1987): 175–208; G.B. Graen and M. Uhl-Bien, "The Transformation of Work Group Professionals into Self-Managing and Partially Self-Designing Contributors: Toward a Theory of Leadership-Making," *Journal of Management Systems* 3(3), 1991: 33–48.

11 S.J. Wayne and M.K. Kacmar, "The Effects of Impression Management on the Performance Appraisal Process," *Organizational Behavior and Human Decision Processes* 48 (1991): 70–88; S.J. Wayne and R.C. Liden, "Effects of Impression Management on Performance Ratings: A Longitudinal Study," *Academy of Management Journal* 38 (1995): 232–260.

12 W.E. McClane, "Implications of Member Role Differentiation: Analysis of a Key Concept in the LMX Model of Leadership," *Group & Organization Studies* 16 (1991): 102–113; G. Yukl, *Leadership in Organizations*, 2nd ed. (Englewood Cliffs, NJ: Prentice Hall, 1989).

13 See note 1; see note 12, Yukl.

14 Richard L. Daft, *Leadership: Theory and Practice* (The Dryden Press: Harcourt Brace College Publishers, 1999), 83.

15 See note 14 above; R.K. House, and R.N. Aditya, "The Social Scientific Study of Leadership: Quo Vadis?" *Journal of Management* 23 (May-June 1997): 409 (65).

16 J.M. Wheatley, "Remembering Human Goodness," *Fourth Annual Worldwide Lessons in Leadership Series*, Workbook, November 17, 1999.

17 E.P. Hollander, *Leadership Dynamics: A Practical Guide to Effective Relationships* (New York: Free Press, 1978); see note 10, Graen and Scandura.

18 See note 15, House and Aditya; R.C. Liden and J.M. Maslyn, "Scale Development for a Multidimensional Measure of Leader-Member Exchange," Paper presented at the *annual meeting of the Academy of Management*, Atlanta, Georgia, 1993.

19 See note 1.

20 R.J. Deluga and T.J. Perry, "The Role of Subordinate Performance and Ingratiation in Leader-Member Exchanges," *Group and Organization Management* 19 (— 1994): 67–86; R.C. Liden, S.J. Wayne, and D. Stilwell, "A Longitudinal Study on the Early Development of Leader-Member Exchanges," *Journal of Applied Psychology* 78 (1993): 662–674; A.S. Philips and A.G. Bedeian, "Leader-Follower Exchange Quality: The Role of Personal and Interpersonal Attributes," *Academy of Management Journal* 37 (1994): 990–1001; R.A. Scandura and C.A. Schriesheim, "Leader-Member Exchange and Supervisor Career Mentoring as Complementary Constructs in Leadership Research," *Academy of Management Journal* 37 (1995): 1588–1602.

21 See note 15, House and Aditya.

22 G.R. Fairhurst, "The Leader-Member Exchange Patterns of Women Leaders in Industry: A Discourse Analysis," *Communication Monographs* 60 (1993): 321–351; M.W. Kramer, "A Longitudinal Study of Superior-Subordinate Communication During Job Transfers," *Human Communications Research* 22 (1995): 39–64; see note 1; see note 6, Liden, Sparrowe, and Wayne.

23 G. Yukl, *Leadership in Organizations*, 4th ed. (Upper Saddle River, NJ; Prentice Hall, 1998).

24 See note 23.

25 See note 18, House and Aditya

26 See note 8; G. Graen, M. Novak, and P. Sommerkamp, "The Effects of Leader-Member Exchange and Job Design on Productivity and Satisfaction: Testing a Dual Attachment Model," *Organizational Behavior and Human Performance* 30 (1982): 109–131; T.A. Scandura and G.B. Graen, "Moderating Effects of Initial Leader-Member Exchange Status on the Effects of Leadership Intervention," *Journal of Applied Psychology* 69 (1984): 428–436.

27 See note 26.

28 J. Cashman, F. Dansereau, Jr., G. Graen, and W.J. Haga, "Organizational Understructure and Leadership: A Longitudinal Investigation of the Managerial Role-Making Process," *Organizational Behavior and Human Performance* 15 (1976): 278–296.

29 See note 1; see note 6, Liden, Sparrowe, and Wayne.

30 See note 6, Scandura, Graen, and Novak.

31 P.M. Podsakoff, S.B. Mackenzie, and C. Hui, "Organizational Citizenship Behaviors and Managerial Evaluations of Employee Performance: A Review and Suggestions for Future Research." In G.R. Ferris (ed.), *Research in Personnel and Human Resources Management*, vol. 11, (Greenwich, CT: JAI Press, 1993), 1–40.

32 P. Manogran and E.J. Conlon, "A Leader-Member Exchange Approach to Explaining Organizational Citizenship Behavior." In *Proceedings of the Annual Meeting of Academy of Management* (Atlanta, GA: Academy of Management, 1993), 249–253; F.J. Yammarino and A.J. Dubinsky, "Superior-Subordinate Relationships: A Multiple Level of Analysis Approach," *Human Relations* 45 (1992): 575–600.

33 See note 7, Ferris; G.B. Graen, R.C. Liden, and W. Hoel, "Role of Leadership in Employee Withdrawal Process," *Journal of Applied Psychology* 67(6), 1982: 868–872; R.P. Vecchio, "Predicting Employee Turnover from Leader-Member Exchange: A Failure to Replicate," *Academy of Management Journal* 28(2) 1985: 478–485; R.P. Vecchio, R.W. Griffeth, and P.W. Horn, "The Predictive Utility of the Vertical Dyad Linkage Approach," *Journal of Social Psychology* 126 (1986): 617–625; R.P. Vecchio and W.R. Norris, "Predicting Employee Turnover from Performance, Satisfaction and Leader-Member Exchange," *Journal of Business and Psychology* 49 (1996): 436–458.

34 N.R. Duarte, J.R. Goodson, and N.R. Klich, "Effects of Dyadic Quality and Duration on Performance Appraisal," *Academy of Management Journal* 37 (1994): 499–521; K.J. Dunegan, D. Duchon and M. Uhl-Bien, "Examining the Link between Leader-Member Exchange and Subordinate Performance—The Role of Task Analyzability and Variety as Moderators," *Journal of Management* 18 (1992): 59–76; see note 26, Graen, Novak, and Sommerkamp.

35 M. Mindell, and W. Gorden, *Employee Values in a Changing Society: An AMA Management Briefing* (New York: American Management Associations, 1981); J. Naisbitt, and P. Aburdene. *Megatrends 2000* (New York: William Morrow, 1990).

36 See note 35; J. Naisbitt, and P. Aburdene, *Reinventing the Corporation* (New York: Warner Books, 1985).

37 Richard L. Daft, *Leadership: Theory and Practice* (The Dryden Press: Harcourt Brace College Publishers, 1999), 80.

38 See note 35, Naisbitt and Aburdene.

39 Richard L. Daft, *Leadership: Theory and Practice* (The Dryden Press: Harcourt Brace College Publishers, 1999).

40 J.B. Rotter, "Generalized Expectancies for Internal versus External Control of Reinforcement," *Psychological Monographs* 80 (1996).

41 R.R. Mitchell, C.M. Smyser, and S.E. Weed, "Locus of Control: Supervision and Work Satisfaction," *Academy of Management Journal* 18 (1975): 623–30; D.E. Durand and W.R. Nord, "Perceived Leader Behavior as a Function of Personality Characteristics of Supervisors and Subordinates," *Academy of Management Journal* 19 (19):427–438.

42 See note 35, Mindell and Gorden.

43 See note 35, Naisbitt and Aburdene.

44 R.L. Hughes, R.C. Ginnett and G.J. Curphy, *Leadership: Enhancing the Lessons of Experience* (Irwin McGraw-Hill, 1999).

45 See note 12, Yukl; D.E. Whiteside, *Command Excellence: What It Takes to Be the Best?* (Department of the Navy, Washington, DC: Leadership Division, Naval Military Personnel Command, 1985).

46 Robert E. Kelley, *The Power of Followership* (New York: Doubleday, 1992).

47 I. Chaleff, *The Courageous Follower: Standing Up to and For Our Leaders.* (San Francisco: Berret-Koehler Publishers, 1995); D.A. Whetton and K.S. Cameron, *Developing Management Skills* (New York: Harper-Collins, 1991).

48 See note 44.

49 "Delegation: It's Often a Problem for Agency Owners," *Agency Sales Magazine*, May 1995, pp. 35–38; Ted Pollock, "Secrets of Successful Delegation," *Production*, December 1994, pp. 10–12; Jack Ninemeier, "10 Tips for Delegating Tasks," *Hotels*, June 1995, pp. 20–21.

50 See note 49; Rebecca Morgan, "Guidelines for Delegating Effectively," *Supervision*, April 1995, pp. 20–22.

51 See note 49.

52 See note 49, Ninemeier.

53 See note 50, Morgan.

Chapter 7: Leading Effective Teams

1 "Cincinnati Milacron Benchmarks Flexible Manufacturing Systems via Computer Modeling," *Industrial Engineering*, March 1991, 24–83; Peter Nulty, "The Soul of An Old Machine," *Fortune*, 21 May 1990, 67–72; Jon Teresko, "Two Builders Look for a New Image," *Industry Week*, 21 January 1991, 42.

2 Peter F. Drucker, "The Coming of the New Organization," *Harvard Business Review*, January–February 1988, 45–53; Richard S. Wellins, William C. Byham, and George R. Dixon, *Inside Teams: How 20 World-Class Organizations Are Winning through Teamwork* (San Francisco: Jossey-Bass, 1994).

3 Jon R. Katzenbach and Douglas K. Smith, "The Discipline of Teams," *Harvard Business Review*, March-April 1993, 112.

4 See note 3 above.

5 Manfred F. De Vries and F. Kets, "High-Performance Teams: Lessons from the Pygmies." *Organizational Dynamics* 27, Winter 1999: 66–77; Neil Merrick, "The Lions Share" (British Lions rugby team's team building and leadership program), *People Management* 3 (June 12, 1997): 34–35.

6 Richard L. Daft, *Leadership, Theory and Practice* (Orlando, FL: The Dryden Press, 1999).

7 See note 6.

8 D.R. Denison, S.L. Hart, and J.A. Kahn, "From Chimneys to Cross-functional Teams: Developing and Validating a Diagnostic Model." *Academy of Management Journal* 39 (4), (August 1996): 1005–1023.

9 "What to Do When You're Asked to Lead a Cross-functional Team," *Getting Results—for the Hands-on Manager* 41 (October 1996) 3.

10 R.C. Ford and W.A. Randolph, "Cross-functional Structures: A Review and Integration of Matrix Organization and Project Management," *Journal of Management* 18 (2), (June 1992): 267–294.

11 See note 6; "Creating Unbeatable Teams: Advice from Three Top Management Gurus (S. Covey, P. Senge, and T. Peters)," *Today's Realtor*, December 1996; 55–56.

12 Eleanor White, "Relying on the Power of People at Saturn," *National Productivity Review* 17 (Winter 1997): 5–10.

13 J.R. Katzenbach and D.K. Smith, *The Wisdom of Teams* (Boston: Harvard Business School Press, 1993).

14 Milan Moravec, Odd Jan Johannessen, and Thor A. Hjelmas, "The Well-Managed SMT," *Management Review* 87 (6), June 1998: 56–58.

15 Dennis Coates and Martha Miller, "Self-Directed Teams: Lessons Learned for Local Government," *Public Management* 77 (December 1995): 16–21; Val Arnold, "Making teams work," *HR Focus* 73 (February 1996) 12–13.

16 Pierre van Amelsvoort and Jos Benders, "Team Time: A Model for Developing Self-Directed Work Teams," *International Journal of Operations and Production Management* 16 (2), 1996: 159–170.

17 See note 11, *Today's Realtor*.

18 Milan Moravec, Odd Jan Johannessen, and Thor A. Hjelmas, "Thumbs Up for Self-Managed Teams," *Management Review* 86 (July-August 1997): 42–47.

19 Richard L. Hughes, Robert C. Ginnett, and Gordon Curphy, *Leadership: Enhancing the Lessons of Experience*, 3rd ed. (Boston: Irwin/McGraw-Hill Publisher, 1999).

20 Dexter Dunphy and Ben Bryant, "Teams: Panaceas or Prescriptions for Improved Performance," *Human Relations* 49 (5), 1996: 677–699; S.G. Cohen, G.E. Ledford, and G.M. Spreitzer, "A Predictive Model of Self-Managing Work Team Effectiveness," *Human Relations* 49 (5), (May 1996): 643.

21 Ted Pollock, "Know What Your People Want," *Supervision*, March 1999; 24–26; see note 6.

22 "Bad Team Decisions?" *Getting Results—for the Hands-on Manager* 42 (September 1997): 3.

23 Gary Yukl, *Leadership in Organizations*, 4th ed. (Englewood Cliffs, NJ: Prentice Hall, 1998).

24 "The Impact of Direct Report Feedback and Follow-up on Leadership Effectiveness," *Human Resource Planning* 21 (4), 1998: 14–15.

25 See note 23.

26 J.A. Cannon-Bowers, E. Salas, and S.A. Converse, "Shared Mental Models in Expert Team Decision Making." In N.J. Castellan, Jr., ed., *Current Issues in Individual and Group Decision Making* (Hillsdale, NJ: Lawrence Erlbaum).

27 See note 23.

28 P.M. Denge, C. Roberts, R. Ross, B. Smith, and A. Kleiner, *The Fifth Discipline Fieldbook* (New York: Doubleday, 1993).

29 Edward Glassman, "Self-Directed Team Building without a Consultant," *Supervisory Management*, March 1992, 6.

30 Robert L. Firestien and Kenneth F. Kumiega, "Using a Formula for Creativity to Yield Organizational Quality Improvement," *National Productivity Review 13* (Autumn 1994): 569–585.

31 Richard W. Woodman, John E. Sawyer, and Ricky W. Griffin, "Toward a Theory of Organizational Creativity," *Academy of Management Review*, April 1993, 293.

32 See note 30.

33 Teresa M. Amabile, "How to Kill Creativity," *Harvard Business Review 76* (5), September/October 1998: 76–87.

34 Shari Caudron, "Strategies for Managing Creative Workers," *Personnel Journal*, December 1994, 104–113.

35 T.M. Amabile, "Motivation and Creativity: Effects of Motivation Orientation on Creative Writers," *Journal of Personal and Social Psychology 48* (2) (February 1985): 393–399; T.M. Amabile and B.A. Hennessey, "The Motivation for Creativity in Children." In *Achievement and Motivation: A Social-Developmental Perspective*, ed. A.K. Boggiano and T. Pittman (New York: Cambridge University Press, 1988).

36 A.G. Robinson and S. Stern, Corporate Creativity: How Innovation and Improvements Actually Happened (San Francisco: Berrett-Koehler Publishers Inc., 1998), 14; Gail Dutton, "Enhancing Creativity," *Management Review*, November 1996, 44–46.

37 See note 33.

38 Robert E. Quinn, Sue R. Faerman, Michael P. Thompson, and Michael R. McGrath, *Becoming a Master Manager: A Competency Framework* (New York: Wiley, 1990), 255.

39 G.M. Prince, "Creative Meetings through Power Sharing," *Harvard Business Review 50* (4), 1972: 47–54.

40 A.C. Filley, "Committee Management: Guidelines from Social Science Research," *California Management Review 13* (1), 1970: 13–21; Michael McGrath, "Ten Steps to Better Decisions," *Electronic Business*, March 1999: 23–24.

41 F.A. Shull, A.L. Delbecq, and L.L. Cummings, *Organizational Decision Making* (New York: McGraw-Hill, 1970).

42 A.V. Carron and K.S. Spink, "The Group Size-Cohesion Relationship in Minimal Groups," *Small Group Research 26* (February 1995): 86–105.

43 S.M. Gulley, D.J. Devine, and D.J. Whitney, "A Meta-Analysis of Cohesion and Performance: Effects of Levels of Analysis and Task Interdependence," *Small Group Research 26* (4), (November 1995): 497–520.

44 W.W. Liddell and J.W. Slocum, Jr., "The Effects of Individual Role Compatability upon Group Performance: An Extension of Shutz's FIRO Theory," *Academy of Management Journal 19*, 413–426.

45 Glenn H. Varney, "Helping a Team Find All the Answers (manager facilitation skills result in better problem solving)," *Training and Development Journal*, February 1991, 15–18; L.P. Bradford, *Making Meetings Work* (La Jolla, CA: University Associates, 1976).

46 See note 45, Bradford.

47 Blanchard Smith, "A Survivor's Guide to Facilitating," *Journal for Quality & Participation*, December 1991, 56–62; Robert Levasseur, "People Skills: What Every Professional Should Know about Designing and Managing Meetings," *Interfaces*, March/April 1992, 11–14; "More Meetings?" *Wall Street Journal*, 30 May 1995, p 1.

48 Patricia Buhler, "Managing in the 90s," *Supervision*, May 1994, 8–10.

Chapter 8: Leading Self-Managed Teams

1 D.E. Yeatts, M. Hipskind, and D. Barnes, "Lessons Learned from Self-Managed Work Teams," *Business Horizons*, July/August 1994, 11–18.

2 M. Moravec, O.J. Johannessen, and T.A. Hjelmas, "The Well-Managed SMT," *Management Review*, June 1998, 56–58.

3 R. Evelyn, M. William, and K. Ira, "Self-Managing Work Teams: Do They Really Work?" *Human Resource Planning 18*(2), 1995, 53–57; J.R. Katzenbach and D.K. Smith, *The Wisdom of Teams* (Boston: Harvard Business School Press, 1993).

4 See note 2 above.

5 J.E. Gloriosus, "TQM and the Team Solution," *Security Management*, October 1994, 33–35.

6 O. Stephanie, "Saturn Teams Working and Profiting," *HR Magazine*, March 1995, 72–74.

7 "The Teaming of America" (corporate training, 1993 annual survey), *Training*, October 1993, 58–59.

8 P.S. Goodman, R. Devadas, and R.G. Hughson, "Groups and Productivity: Analyzing the Effectiveness of Self-Managing Teams." In J.P. Campbell and R.J. Campbell (eds.), *Productivity in Organizations* (San Francisco: Jossey-Bass) 295–327; J.H. Pearce, II, and E.C. Ravlin, "The Design and Activation of Self-Regulating Work Groups," *Human Relations 40* (November 1987): 751–782.

9 J.R. Hackman, *Groups That Work (and Those That Don't)* (San Francisco: Jossey-Bass, 1990).

10 W. Scott and H. Harrison, "Full Team Ahead:" Nationwide Building Society Introduces Self-Managed Team Working; Britain," *People Management*, October 1997, 48–50.

11 G. Yukl, *Leadership in Organizations*, 4th ed. (Englewood Cliffs, NJ: Prentice Hall, 1998).

12 J.L. Cordery, W.S. Mueller, and L.M. Smith, "Attitudinal and Behavioral Effects of Autonomous Group Working: A Longitudinal Field Study," *Academy of Management Journal 34* (2), (June 1991): 464–476.

13 S.G. Cohen and G.W. Ledford, *The Effectiveness of Self-Managed Teams: A Quasi-experiment*, (Los Angeles: Center for Effective Organizations, University of Southern California, 1991).

14 C.A.L. Pearson, "Autonomous Workgroups: An Evaluation at an Industrial Site," *Human Relations 45* (9), (September 1992): 905–936; R.D. Banker, J.M. Field, R.G. Schroeder and K.K. Sinha, "Impact of Work Teams on Manufacturing Performance: A Longitudinal Field Study," *Academy of Management Journal 36*(4), (August 1996): 36 867–890.

15 R.C. Ginnett, "Crews as Groups: Their formation and their leadership." In E. Wiener, B. Banki, and R. Helmreich (eds.), *Cockpit Resource Management* (Orlando, FL: Academic Press, 1993).

16 K. Bettenhausen and J.K. Murnighan, "The Emergence of Norms in Competitive Decision-Making Groups," *Administrative Science Quarterly 30* (3), (September 1985): 350–372.

17 E. Sundstrom, K.P. Demeuse, and D. Futrell, "Work Teams: Applications and Effectiveness," *American Psychologist 75* (3), (June 1990): 120–133.

18 C. Carr, "Managing Self-Managed Workers," *Training and Development*, September 1991, 36–42; M. Moravec, O.J. Johannessen, and T.A. Hjelmas, "Thumbs Up for Teams," *Management Review*, July/August 1997, 42–47.

19 W. Scott and H. Harrison, "Full Team Ahead: Nationwide Building Society Introduces Self-Managed Team Working; Britain," *People Management*, 9 October 1997, 48–50; L. Holpp, "Ways to Sink Self-Managed Teams," *Training*, September 1993, 38–40.

20 L. Stokes, "Moving toward Self-Direction: An Action Plan for Self-Managed Teams," *Information Systems Management 11* (Winter 1994): 40–46; T.E. Benson, "A Brave New World: Managing Self-Directed Work Teams," *Industry Week*, 3 August 1992, 48–49.

21 D. Davidson, "Transforming to a High-Performance Team," *Canadian Business Review 21* (Autumn 1994): 18–19.

22 See notes 9 and 21.

23 G.S. Odiorne, "The New Breed of Supervisors: Leaders in Self-Managed Work Teams," *Supervision*, August 1991, 14–17; H.R. Jessup, "New Roles in Team Leadership," *Training and Development Journal 44* (11), (November 1990): 79–83.

24 See note 23, Jessup; and note 18, Carr.

25 J. Neal and R.N. Lussier, "Redesigning for Empowerment and Effectiveness: Issues of Implementation and Commitment," *Business Journal 13* (1 & 2), 1998: 15–24.

26 E.E. Lawler, *The Ultimate Advantage: Creating the High Involvement Organization* (San Francisco: Jossey-Bass, 1992).

27 D. Barry, "Managing the Bossless Team: Lessons in Distributed Leadership," *Organizational Dynamics* 20 (Summer 1991), 31–47.

28 "Even in Self-Managed Teams There Has to Be a Leader," *Supervisory Management*, December 1994, 7–8.

29 See notes 11 and 28.

30 See note 25.

31 K.G. Koehler, "Effective Team Management," *Small Business Reports*, 19 July 1989, 14–16; C. Gersick, "Time and Transition in Work Teams: Towards a New Model of Group Development," *Academy of Management Journal* 31 (11), (March 1998): 9–41.

32 R.N. Lussier, *Management: Concepts, Applications, and Skill Development* (Cincinnati: South-Western, 1996).

33 B. Carroll, "The Self-Management Pay-Off: Making Ten Years of Improvements in One," *National Productivity Review*, Winter 1998, 21–27.

34 E. White, "Relying on the Power of People at Saturn," *National Productivity Review*, Winter 1997, 5–10; S. Overman, "Saturn Teams Working and Profiting," *HR Magazine*, March 1995, 72–74.

35 R.J. Bowman, "The Lessons of Honeywell," *Distribution*, March 1997, 48.

36 See notes 21 and 35.

37 W.R. Coradetti, "Teamwork Takes Time and a Lot of Energy," *HR Magazine*, June 1994, 74–75.

Chapter 9: Influencing: Power, Politics, and Negotiation

1 Information in the opening case was taken from the websites listed at the end of the case. The information presented throughout the chapter related to Ross Perot is also taken from these sources. The information has also been published in various U.S newspapers.

2 R.N. House and R.J. Aditya, "The Social Scientific Study of Leadership: Quo Vadis?" *Journal of Management* 23, (May-June 1997): 409–474.

3 G. Yukl, *Leadership in Organizations*, 4th ed. (Upper Saddle River, NJ: Prentice Hall, 1998), pp. 175, 207; F.E. Fiedler, "Research on Leadership Selection and Training: One View of the Future," *Administrative Science Quarterly* 41, 1996): 241–250.

4 H.C. Kelman, "Compliance, Identification, and Internalization: Three Processes of Attitude Change," *Journal of Conflict Resolution* 2 (1958): 51–56.

5 See note 3, Yukl.

6 G. Yukl, H. Kim, and C.M. Falbe, "Antecedents of Influence Outcomes," *Journal of Applied Psychology* 81 (3) June 1996: 309–317.

7 R. Mowday, "The Exercise of Upward Influence in Organizations," *Administrative Science Quarterly* 23 (1978): 137–156; C.A. Schriesheim and T.R. Hinkin, "Influence Tactics Used by Subordinates," *Journal of Applied Psychology* 75 (1990): 246–257.

8 G. Yukl and B. Tracey, "Consequences of Influence Tactics Used with Subordinates, Peers, and the Boss," *Journal of Applied Psychology* 77 (1992): 525–535.

9 This section is based on G. Yukl, *Leadership in Organizations*, 4th ed. (Upper Saddle River, NJ: Prentice Hall, 1998), 207–230.

10 M.S. Nesler, H. Aguinis, B.M. Quigley, and J.T. Tedeschi, "The Effect of Credibility on Perceived Power," *Journal of Applied Psychology* 23, (1993): 1407–1425.

11 See note 6.

12 L. Kenneth, "Elite Teams," *Fortune*, 19 February 1996, 90.

13 See note 6.

14 See note 6.

15 S.J. Wayne and G.R. Ferris, "Influence Tactics, Effects, and Exchange Quality in Supervisor-Subordinate Interactions," *Journal of Applied Psychology* 75 (1990): 487–499.

16 See note 6.

17 D. Kipnis and S.M. Schmidt, *Profiles of Organizational Strategies* (San Diego: University Associates, 1982).

18 K.R. Xin and S.A. Tsui, "Different Strokes for Different Folks? Influence Tactics by Asian-American and Caucasian-American Managers," *Leadership Quarterly* 7 (1996): 109–132; G. Yukl and C.M. Falbe, "Influencing Tactics in Upward, Downward, and Laterial Influence Attempts," *Journal of Applied Psychology* 75, (1990): 132–140; G. Yukl, P. Guianan, and D. Sottolano, "Influencing Tactics Used for Different Objectives with Subordinates, Peers, and Superiors," *Group and Organizational Management* 20 (1995): 272–296.

19 G. Yukl, C.M. Falbe, and J.Y. Youn, "Patterns of Influence Behavior for Managers," *Group and Organizational Management* 18 (1993): 5–28.

20 See note 6.

21 D. Kipnis and S.M. Schmidt, "The Language of Persuasion," *Psychology Today*, 1985, 40–46.

22 T. Case, L. Dosier, G. Murkinson, and B. Keys, "How Managers Influence Superiors: A Study of Upward Influence Tactics," *Leadership and Organizational Development Journal* 9 (4), 1988: 25–31; C.M. Falbe and G. Yukl, "Consequences for Managers of Using Single Influence Tactics and Combination of Tactics," *Academy of Management Journal* 35 (1992): 638–653.

23 J.M. Burns, *Leadership* (New York: Harper & Row, 1978); T.R. Hinkin and C.A. Schresheim, "Development and Application of New Scales to Measure the French and Raven Bases of Social Power," *Journal of Applied Psychology* 74 (1989): 561–567; G. Yukl, *Leadership in Organizations*, 4th ed. (Upper Saddle River, NJ: Prentice Hall, 1998), 175.

24 A. Etzioni, *A Comparative Analysis of Complex Organizations* (New York: Free Press, 1961).

25 C. Avery, "All Power to You: Collaborative Leadership Works," *Journal for Quality and Participation* 22 (2), March-April 1999: 36–41.

26 T.O. Jacobs, *Leadership and Exchange in Formal Organizations* (Alexandria, VA: Human Resources Research Organization, 1970).

27 G. Yukl and C.M. Falbe, "The Importance of Different Power Sources in Downward and Lateral Relations," *Journal of Applied Psychology* 76 (1991): 416–423.

28 J. French and B.H. Raven, "The Bases of Social Power." In D. Cartwright (ed.), *Studies of Social Power* (Ann Arbor, MI: Institute for Social Research, 1959), 150–167.

29 R. Weylman, "Building Your Power Base with Insider Information," *National Underwriter*, 3 July 1995, 16.

30 J.G. Marsh and H.A. Simon, *Organizations* (New York: John Wiley, 1958).

31 J. Vancouver and E. Morrison, "Feedback Inquiry: The Effect of Source Attributes and Individual Difference," *Organizational Behavior and Human Decision Processes* 62 (June 1995): 276–285.

32 See note 27.

33 A. Cohen and D. Bradford, "Influence without Authority: The Use of Alliances, Reciprocity, and Exchange to Accomplish Work," *Organizational Dynamics* 17 (1989): 5–17.

34 P.M. Blau, *Bureaucracy in Modern Society* (New York: Random House, 1956); D. Brozik, "The Importance of Money and the Reporting of Salaries," *Journal of Compensation and Benefits* 9 (January-February 1994): 61–64; D. Katz and R.L. Kahn, *The Social Psychology of Organizations*, 2nd ed. (New York: John Wiley, 1978).

35 P. Buhler, "The Evolving Leader of Today," *Supervision*, December 1998, 16–18.

36 Radio Broadcast, *Gallup Poll Report*, "Most Important Point in Retention of Employees," WFCR, 17 May 1999.

37 See note 35.

38 See note 26.

39 A. Pettigrew, "Information Control as a Power Resource," *Sociology* 6 (1972): 187–204.

40 J. Pfeffer, "Power and Resource Allocation in Organizations." In B. Staw and G. Salancik (eds.) *New Directions in Organizational Behavior* (Chicago: St. Clair Press, 1977).

41 C.A. Schriesheim, T.R. Hinkin, and P.M. Podsakoff, "Can Ipsative and Single-Item Measures Produce Erroneous Results in Field Studies of Power?" *Journal of Applied Psychology* 76 (1991): 106–114; H.J. Thambain and G.R. Gemmill, "Influence Styles of Project Managers: Some Project Performance Correlates," *Academy of Management Journal* 17 (1974): 216–224; see note 27; see note 6; J.P. Kotter, *The General Manager* (New York: Free Press, 1982).

42 A Zaleznik, "Power and Politics in Organizational Life," *Harvard Business Review,* May-June 1970, 47–60.

43 E.P Hollander, "Conformity, Status, and Idiosyncrasy Credit," *Psychology Review* 65 (1958): 117–127.

44 W.M. Evans and M. Zelditch, "A Laboratory Experiment on Bureaucratic Authority," *American Sociological Review* 26 (1961): 883–893.

45 D.J. Hickson, C.R. Hinings, C.A. Lee, R.S. Schneck, and J.M. Pennings, "A Strategic Contingencies Theory of Intra-Organizational Power," *Administrative Science Quarterly 16* (1971): 216–229.

46 H. Lancaster, "Managing Your Career," *Wall Street Journal,* 23 March 1999, p. B1; D. Knights, "When 'Life Is A Dream': Obliterating Politics through Business Process Reengineering?" *Human Relations* 51 (6), June 1998: 761–798; see note 2.

47 P. Wilson, "The Effects of Politics and Power on the Organizational Commitment of Federal Executives," *Journal of Management 21* (Spring 1995): 101–118; see note 46, Knights; J. Pfeffer, *Power in Organizations* (Marshfield, MA: Pittman, 1981).

48 H. Lancaster, "Ignore the Psychics and Stick with What You Find Meaningful," *Wall Street Journal,* 25 April 1995, p. B1; J. Byrne, "How to Succeed: Same Game Different Decade," *Business Week,* 17 April 1995, p. 48; Staff, "Executives Point the Finger at Major Time Waster," *Personnel Journal,* August 1994, 16.

49 See note 2.

50 M.L. Randall, R. Cropanizano, C.A. Bormann, and A. Birjulin, "Organizational Politics and Organizational Support as Predictors of Work Attitudes, Job Performance, and Organizational Citizenship Behavior," *Journal of Organizational Behavior 20* (March 1999): 159.

51 S. Robbins and D. De Cenzo, *Fundamentals of Management* (Englewood Cliffs, NJ: Prentice Hall, 1995), 10–11.

52 P. Lowe, "The Keys to Networking Success," *Success Yearbook,* 1998, 47.

53 W.B. Stevenson, J.L. Pearce, and L.W. Porter, "The Concept of Coalition in Organizational Theory and Research," *Academy of Management Review 10* (1985): 258–268.

54 I. Bass, "Politics of a Good Day at the Office," *The Guardian,* 7 March 1998, S28.

55 R. Mason, "Securing: One Man's Quest for the Meaning of Therefore," *Interfaces,* July-August 1994, 67–72.

56 P. Lowe, "How to Effectively Manage Conflict," *SuccessTalk* 57, 1999.

57 See note 50.

58 L.A. Witt, "Enhancing Organizational Goal Congruence: A Solution to Organizational Politics," *Journal of Applied Psychology* 83 (4), August 1998: 666–675.

59 K. Patching and R. Chatham, "Getting a Life at Work: Developing People beyond Role Boundaries," *Journal of Management Development* 17(5-6), May-June 1998: 316–338.

60 D. Ertel, "Turning Negotiation into a Corporate Capability," *Harvard Business Review,* May 1999, p. 55; J. Butler Jr., "Trust Expectations, Information Sharing, Climate of Trust, and Negotiation Effectiveness and Efficiency," *Group & Organizational Management,* June 1999, 217.

61 J. Pouliot, "Eight Steps to Success in Negotiating," *Nation's Business,* April 1999, 40.

62 R. Fisher and W. Ury, *Getting to Yes* (Boston: Houghton Mifflin, 1981).

63 See note 61; P. Lowe, "9 Secrets of Superstar Salespeople," *Success Yearbook* (Tampa, FL: Perter Lowe International, 1998), 38–39.

64 See note 61.

65 See note 60, Ertel.

66 See note 63, Lowe.

67 See note 61.

68 T. Nagle, "Evening the Odds in Price," *Across the Board,* March 1999, 56–58.

69 T. Hank, "Four Sales Objections and How to Handle Them," *Success Yearbook* (Tampa: FL: Perter Lowe International, 1998), 58–59.

70 S. Lorge, "The Best Way to Negotiate," *Sales and Marketing Management,* March 1998, 92–93.

71 See note 70.

72 See note 61.

73 See note 63, Lowe.

74 See note 69.

75 See note 69.

76 See note 61.

77 See note 63, Lowe.

78 This is an actual case situation. However, the names have been changed for confidentiality.

Chapter 10: Leadership and Change

1 Ponchitta Pierce, "Blazing new paths in corporate America: American Express president set to become first black to lead a Fortune 500 company (Kenneth Chenault)," *Ebony,* July 1997.

2 See note 1 above.

3 M. Weber, *The Theory of Social and Economic Organizations,* translated by T. Parsons, (New York: Free Press, 1947).

4 Katherine J. Klein and Robert J. House, "On Fire: Charismatic Leadership and Levels of Analysis," *Leadership Quarterly* 6(2), 183–198.

5 Gary S. Yukl, *Leadership in Organizations,* 3rd ed. (Upper Saddle River, NJ: Prentice Hall), 207.

6 P.M. Blau, "Critical Remarks on Weber's Theory of Authority," *American Political Science Review* 57(2), 1963: 305-315; E. Chinoy, *Society* (New York: Random House, 1961); H. Wolpe, "A Critical Analysis of Some Aspects of Charisma," *Sociological Review* 16(3), (November, 1968):305–318; H.H. Gerth and C.W. Mills, *Max Weber: Essays in Sociology,* New York: Oxford University Press, 1946); R.S. Kanter and D.P. Norton, *The Balanced Scorecard: Translating Strategy into Action* (Boston: Harvard Business School Press, 1996).

7 R.C. Tucker, "The Theory of Charismatic Leadership," *Daedalus* 97(3),1968: 731-56; T.E. Dow, "The Theory of Charisma," *Sociological Quarterly* 10(3), 1969: 306–18.

8 B.M. Bass, *Leadership and Performance Beyond Expectations* (New York: Free Press, 1985); J.A. Conger and R. Kanungo, "Toward a Behavioral Theory of Charismatic Leadership in Organizational Settings," *Academy of Management Review,* 12, (October 1987) 637–647; H.M. Trice and J.M. Beyer, "Charisma and Its Routinization in Two Social Movement Organizations." In L.L. Cummings and B.M. Staw (eds.), *Research in Organization Behavior,* vol. 8 (Greenwich, CT: JAI Press, 1986), 113-164; A.R. Willner, *The Spellbinders: Charismatic Political Leadership* (New Haven: Yale University Press, 1984).

9 Jay A. Conger, Rabindra N. Kanungo et al. (1998). *Charismatic Leadership: The Elusive Factor in Organizational Effectiveness* (San Francisco: Jossey-Bass, 1998); Robert J. House and Jane M. Howell, "Personality and Charismatic Leadership," *Leadership Quarterly* 3(2), 1992: 81–108; see note 4.

10 Andrew J. DuBrin, *Leadership: Research Findings, Practice, and Skills,* (Boston, MA: Houghton Mifflin Company, 1998), 62.

11 J.A. Conger, *The Charismatic Leader* (San Francisco: Jossey-Bass, 1994); B. Shamir, M.B. Arthur, and R.J. House, "The Rhetoric of Charismatic Leadership: A Theoretical Extension, A Case Study, and Implications for Research," *Leadership Quarterly* 5(1), (Spring 1994): 25–42.

12 See note 11.

13 Andrew DuBrin,. *Leadership: Research Findings, Practice, and Skills,* (Boston, MA: Houghton Mifflin Company, 1998) 60.

14 D.N. Den Hartog and R.M. Verburg, "Charisma and Rhetoric: Communicative Techniques of International Business Leaders," *Leadership Quarterly* 8(1),1997: 51–68.

15 J.M.Howell and P.Grost "A Laboratory Study of Charismatic Leadership," *Organizational Behavior and Human Decision Processes* 43 (1998):, 243–69.

16 B.M. Bass, "Evolving Perspectives of Charismatic Leadership," In J.A. Conger and R.N. Kanungo (eds.), *Charismatic Leadership: The Elusive Factor in Organizational Effectiveness* (San Francisco: Jossey-Bass, 1988); B.M. Bass, "Does the Transactional-Transformational Leadership Paradigm Transcend Organizational and National Boundaries?" *American Psychologist* 52(3), 1997: 130–39; B.M. Bass and B.J. Avolio (eds.), *Increasing Organizational Effectiveness through Transformational Leadership* (Thousand Oaks, CA: Sage, 1994); G.J. Curphy, "An Empirical Study of Bass' (1985) Theory of Transformational and Transactional Leadership." Ph.D. dissertation University of

Minnesota, 1991; G.A. Yukl, *Leadership in Organizations.* 2nd ed. (Englewood Cliffs, NJ: Prentice Hall, 1989).

17 S.J. Musser, *The Determination of Positive and Negative Charismatic Leadership.* Working paper (Grantham, PA: Messiah College, 1987).

18 R.J. House and J.M. Sowell, "Personality and Charismatic Leadership," *Leadership Quarterly,* 3(2), 1992: 81–108; J.M. Howell, "Two Faces of Charisma: Socialized and Personalized Leadership in Organizations. In J.A. Conger and R.N. Kanungo (eds.), *Charismatic Leadership: The Elusive Factor in Organizational Effectiveness* (San Francisco: Jossey-Bass, 1998), 213–236.

19 J.A. Conger, The *Charismatic Leader: Behind the Mystique of Exceptional Leadership* (San Francisco: Jossey-Bass, 1989); B. Shamir, R.J. House, and M.B. Arthur, "The Motivational Effects of Charismatic Leadership: A Self-Concept Based Theory," *Organization Science 4* (November 1993): 1–17; J.R. Meindl, "On Leadership: An Alternative to the Conventional Wisdom." In B.M. Staw and L.L. Cummings (eds.), *Research in Organizational Behavior,* vol. 12 (Greenwich, CT: JAI Press, 1990), 159–203.

20 See note 19, Shamir et al. and Meindl.

21 See note 8, Bass.

22 See note 5.

23 See note 8, Bass.

24 Bernard M. Bass, "Theory of Transformational Leadership Redux," *Leadership Quarterly* 6(4), Winter 1995: 463–478 and "From Transactional to Transformational Leadership: Learning to Share the Vision," *Organizational Dynamics* 19(3), Winter 1990: 19–31; Francis J. Yammarino, William D. Spangler, and Bernard M. Bass, "Transformational Leadership and Performance: A Longitudinal Investigation," *Leadership Quarterly* 4(1), Spring 1993: 81–102.

25 N.M. Tichy and M.A. Devanna, *The Transformational Leader* (New York: John Wiley & Sons, 1986).

26 Ray Maghroori and Eric Rolland, "Strategic Leadership: The Art of Balancing Organizational Mission with Policy, Procedures, and External Environment," *Journal of Leadership Studies* (2), 1997: 62–81.

27 John E. Prescott, "Environments as Moderators of the Relationship between Strategy and Performance," *Academy of Management Journal 29,* 1986: 329–346.

28 P.M. Ginter and W.J. Duncan, "Macro-environmental Analysis for Strategic Management," *Long Range Planning 23,* 1990: 91–100.

29 See note 28.

30 Gary Hamel and C.K. Prahalad, "Competing for the Future," *Harvard Business Review,* July-August 1994, 127–128.

31 Richard L. Daft,(1999). *Leadership: Theory and Practice* (Dryden Press, 1999), 126.

32 W.G. Bennis and B. Nanus, *Leaders: The Strategies for Taking Charge* (New York: Harper & Row, 1985).

33 James Collins, "It's Not What You Make, It's What You Stand For," *Inc.,* October 1997, 42–45.

34 Richard L. Daft, *Leadership: Theory and Practice* (Dryden Press, 1999), 136.

35 C.C. Miller and L.B. Cardinal, "Strategic Planning and Firm Performance: A Synthesis of More than Two Decades of Research," *Academy of Management Journal 37*(6), 1994: 1649–1655.

36 See note 31.

37 Robert K. Greenleaf, *Servant Leadership: A Journey into the Nature of Legitimate Power and Greatness* (Mahwah, NJ: Paulist Press, 1997), 7.

38 LaRue Tone Hosmer, "Trust: The Connecting Link between Organizational Theory and Philosophical Ethics," *Academy of Management Review 20* (April 1995): 379–403.

39 See note 37.

40 L.J. Bourgeois, III. and David R. Brodwin, "Strategic Implementation: Five Approaches to an Elusive Phenomenon," *Strategic Management Journal 5* (1984): 241–264; Anil K. Gupta and V. Govindarajan "Business Unit Strategy, Managerial Characteristics, and Business Unit Effectiveness at Strategy Implementation," *Academy of Management Journal* (1984): 25–41.

41 Daniel C. Kielson, "Leadership: Creating a New Reality," *Journal of Leadership Studies* 3(4), 1996: 104–116.

42 John P. Kotter, *The New Rules: How to Succeed in Today's Post-Corporate World.* Copyright 1995 by John P. Kotter. Adapted with permission from The Free Press, New York.

43 K. Lewin, *Field Theory in Social Science* (New York: Harper & Row, 1951).

44 John P. Kotter, *Leading Change* (Boston: Harvard Business School Press, 1996), 20–25; R. Maurer. *Beyond the Wall of Resistance: Unconventional Strategies That Build Support for Change* (Austin, TX: Bard Books, 1996); John P. Kotter and Leonard A. Schlesinger, "Choosing Strategies for Change," *Harvard Business Review,* March-April 1979, 106–114; D.R. Connor, *Managing at the Speed of Change: How Resilient Managers Succeed and Prosper Where Others Fail* (New York: Villard Books, 1995).

45 See note 44, Connor; John P. Kotter, *Leading Change* (Boston: Harvard Business School Press, 1996).

46 See note 44, Connor and Kotter; D.A. Nadler et al. (1995). D.R. Connor, *Managing at the Speed of Change: How Resilient Mangers Succeed and Prosper Where Others Fail* (New York: Villard Books, 1995); J.P. Kotter, *Leading Change* (Boston: Harvard Business School Press, 1996): 20–25; D.A. Nadler, R.B. Shaw, E.A. Walter & Associates, *Discontinuous Change: Leading Organizational Transformation* (San Francisco, CA: Jossey-Bass, 1995): 66–83.

Chapter 11: Leadership of Culture, Diversity, and the Learning Organization

1 Frances J. Milliken and Luis I. Martins, "Searching for Common Threads: Understanding the Multiple Effects of Diversity in Organizational Groups," *Academy of Management Review 21* (2), 1996: 402–433.

2 W. Jack Duncan, "Organizational Culture: Getting a 'Fix' on an Elusive Concept," *Academy of Management Executive 3* (1989): 229–236; Linda Smircich, "Concepts of Culture and Organizational Analysis," *Administrative Science Quarterly 28* (1983): 339–358; Andrew D. Brown and Ken Starkey, "The Effect of Organizational Culture on Communication and Information," *Journal of Management Studies 31* (6), (November 1994): 807–828.

3 E.H. Schein, *Organizational Culture and Leadership,* 2nd ed. (San Francisco: Jossey-Bass, 1992).

4 John Alexander and Meena S. Wilson, "Leading Across Cultures: Five Vital Capabilities." In Frances Hesselbein, Marshall Godsmith, and Richard Beckard, *The Organization of the Future* (San Francisco: Jossey-Bass, 1997), 291–292.

5 John J. Sherwood, "Creating Work Cultures with Competitive Advantage," *Organizational Dynamics,* Winter 1988, 5–27.

6 John P. Kotter and James L. Heskett, *Corporate Culture and Performance* (New York: The Free Press, 1992), 6.

7 Bernard Arogyaswamy and Charles M. Byles, "Organizational Culture: Internal and External Fits," *Journal of Management 13* (4), (Winter 1987): 647–659.

8 Terrence E. Deal and Allen A. Kennedy, *Corporate Cultures* (Reading, MA: Addison-Wesley, 1982): 22.

9 See note 6.

10 Justin Martin, "The Man Who Boogied Away a Billion," *Fortune,* 23 December 1996, 89–100.

11 Vijay Sathe, *Culture and Related Corporate Realities* (Homewood, IL: Richard D. Irwin, 1985).

12 W.B. Johnson and A.H. Packer, *Workforce 2000: Work and Workers in the 21st Century* (Indianapolis: Hudson Institute, 1987); M. Galen and A.T. Palmer, "White, Male and Worried," *Newsweek,* 31 January 1994, 50–55; H.W. Fullerton, Jr., "New Labor Force Projections Spanning 1988–2000," *Monthly Labor Review,* November 1998, 3–12.

13 See note 11.

14 Deanne N. Den Hartog, Jaap J. Van Muijen, and Paul L. Koopman, "Linking Transformational Leadershp and Organizational Culture," *Journal of Leadership Studies 3* (4), 1996: 68–83; see note 3.

15 Harrison M. Trice and Janice M. Beyer, "Studying Organizational Culture through Rites and Ceremonials," *Academy of Management Review 9* (October 1984): 653–669.

16 A.A. Thompson and A.J. Strickland, *Strategic Management,* 11th ed. (Boston: Irwin McGraw Hill, 1999).

17 Thomas J. Peters and Robert H. Waterman, Jr., *In Search of Excellence* (New York: Harper and Row, 1982), xviii, 240, and 269; Thomas J. Peters and Nancy Austin, *A Passion for Excellence* (New York: Random House, 1985), 304–307.

18 Benjamin Schneider, Sarah K. Gunnarson, and Kathryn Niles-Jolly, "Creating the Climate and Culture of Success," *Organizational Dynamics*, Summer 1994, 17–29.

19 See note 3.

20 See note 15.

21 Alan Farnham, "Mary Kay's Lessons in Leadership," *Fortune*, 20 September 1993, 68–77

22 See note 17, Peters and Waterman.

23 H.M. Trice and J.M. Beyer, "Cultural Leadership in Organizations," *Organization Science 2* (1991): 149–169.

24 John Humble, David Jackson, and Alan Thomson, "The Strategic Power of Corporate Values," *Long-Range Planning*, December 1994, 28–42.

25 Jennifer A. Chatman and Karen A. Jehn, "Assessing the Relationship between Industry Characteristics and Organizational Culture: How Different Can You Be?" *Academy of Management Journal 37* (3), 1994: 522–553.

26 L.V. Gordon, *Measurement of Interpersonal Values* (Chicago: Science Research Associates, 1975).

27 Paul McDonald and Jeffrey Gandz, "Getting Value from Shared Values," *Organizational Dynamics*, Winter 1992, 64–76; Daniel R. Denison and Aneil K. Mishra, "Toward a Theory of Organizational Culture and Effectiveness," *Organization Science 6* (March-April 1995): 204–223.

28 Jennifer Reese, "Starbucks: Inside the Coffee Cult," *Fortune*, 9 December 1996, 193.

29 Thomas A. Steward "3M Fights Back," *Fortune*, 5 February 1996, 94–99.

30 Brian Dumaine, "Those High-Flying PepsiCo Managers," *Fortune*, 10 April 1989, 78–86; L. Zinn, J. Berry, and G. Burns, "Will the Pepsi Brass Be Drinking Hemlock?" *Business Week*, 15 July 1994, 31; S. Lubove, "We Have a Big Pond to Play In," *Forbes*, 12 September 1993, 216–224.

31 See note 26.

32 See note 26.

33 Linda Klebe Trevino, "Ethical Decision Making in Organizations: A Person-Situation Interactionist Model," *Academy of Management Review 11* (3), (1986): 601–617.

34 Carolyn Wiley, "The ABCs of Business Ethics: Definitions, Philosophies, and Implementation," *IM*, January–February 1995, 2–27.

35 Jennifer Reese, "Starbucks: Inside the Coffee Cult," *Fortune*, 9 December 1996, 190–200.

36 Lawrence Kohlberg, "Moral Stages and Moralization: The Cognitive-Developmental Approach." In *Moral Development and Behavior: Theory, Research, and Social Issues*, T. Likona, ed. (New York: Holt, Rinehart, and Winston, 1976), 31–53; Jill W. Graham, "Leadership, Moral Development, and Citizenship Behavior," *Business Ethics Quarterly 5*(1), January 1995: 43–54.

37 Geert Hofstede, *Culture's Consequences: International Differences in Work-Related Values* (Beverly Hills, CA: Sage, 1980); "A Conversation with Geert Hofstede" (interview by Richard Hodgetts), *Organizational Dynamics*, Spring 1993, 53–61.

38 Cresencio Torres and Mary Bruxelles, "Capitalizing on Global Diversity," *HR Magazine*, December 1992, 32.

39 W.B. Johnson and A.H. Packer, *Workforce 2000: Work and Workers in the 21st Century* (Indianapolis: Hudson Institute, 1987); M. Galen and A.T. Palmer, "White, Male and Worried," *Newsweek*, 31 January 1994, 50–55.

40 See note 12.

41 General Mills, Inc., *Annual Report* (1998).

42 Taylor H. Cox, *Cultural Diversity in Organizations* (San Francisco: Berrett-Koehler, 1994).

43 Frances J. Milliken and Luis L. Martins, "Searching for Common Threads: Understanding the Multiple Effects of Diversity in Organizational Groups" *Academy of Management Review 21* (2), (April 1996): 403.

44 Ann M. Morrison, *The New Leaders: Guidelines on Leadership Diversity in America* (San Francisco: Jossey-Bass, 1992), 29–56.

45 Michele Galen with Ann Therese Palmer, "Diversity: Beyond the Numbers Game," *Business Week*, 14 August 1995, 60–61.

46 Taylor H. Cox and Stacy Blake, "Managing Cultural Diversity: Implications for Organizational Competitiveness," *Academy of Management Executive*, August 1991, 45–56.

47 C. Hall, "Hoechst Celanese Diversifying Its Ranks," *Dallas Morning News*, 27 September 1992, pp. 1H, 7H.

48 F. Rice, "How to Make Diversity Pay," *Fortune*, 8 August 1994, 78–86.

49 David A. Garven, "Building a Learning Organization," *Harvard Business Review*, July-August 1993, 80.

50 Tom Burns and G.M. Stalker, *The Management of Innovation* (London: Tavistock, 1961).

51 Peter M. Senge, "The Leader's New Work: Building Learning Organizations," *Sloan Management Review*, Fall 1990, 7–22.

52 P. Senge, *The Fifth Discipline: The Art and Practice of the Learning Organization* (New York: Doubleday Currency).

53 Mary Anne DeVanna and Noel Tichy, "Creating the Competitive Organization of the Twenty-First Century: The Boundaryless Corporation," *Human Resource Management 29* (Winter 1990): 455–471; Fred Kofman and Peter M. Senge, "Communities of Commitment: The Heart of Learning Organizations," *Organizational Dynamics 22* (2), Autumn 1993: 4–23.

54 Lee G. Bolman and Terrence E. Deal, "Leadership and Management Effectiveness: A Multi-Sector Analysis," *Human Resource Management 30* (4), Winter 1991: 509–534.

Appendix A: Leadership and Spirituality in the Workplace

1 K.T. Scott, "Leadership and Spirituality: A Quest for Reconciliation, in Spirit at Work." In Jay Conger (ed.), *Discovering the Spirituality in Leadership* (San Francisco: Jossey-Bass, 1994), 63–99.

2 G. Fairholm, *Capturing the Heart of Leadership: Spirituality and Community in the New American Workplace* (Westport, CT: Praeger), 1997.

3 C. Barks *The Essential Rumi* (San Francisco: Harper, 1996).

4 J. Autry, *Love and Profit: The Art of Caring Leadership* (New York: Avon Books, 1991).

5 J. Neal, "Employees Seek Jobs that Nourish Their Souls," *Hartford Courant*, 8 August 1995, p. A12; J. Neal, B. Lichtenstein, and D. Banner, "Spiritual Perspectives on Individual, Organizational, and Societal Transformation," *Journal of Organizational Change Management 12*, (3), 1999: 175–185.

6 C. Schaefer and J. Darling, "Does Spirit Matter? A Look at Contemplative Practice in the Workplace," *Spirit at Work* newsletter, July 1997. Available at Spirit at Work website (http://www.spiritatwork.com).

Appendix C: How to Research Case Material Using the Internet

1 J. Pask, "It's on the Web, But Is It Right?" *Wall Street Journal*, 4 November 1999, p. 1.

Applying the Concept Answers

Chapter 1

Applying the Concept 1-1

1. H
2. E
3. C
4. B
5. A
6. F
7. I
8. J
9. A
10. D
11. J
12. B
13. D
14. H
15. G

Applying the Concept 1-2

1. C
2. E
3. B
4. D
5. A

Chapter 2

Applying the Concept 2-1

1. A
2. D
3. B
4. E
5. C
6. A
7. B

Applying the Concept 2-2

1. G
2. C
3. E
4. I
5. B
6. D
7. F
8. H

Applying the Concept 2-3

1. B
2. C
3. A
4. B
5. C

Chapter 3

Applying the Concept 3-1

1. A
2. A
3. B
4. A
5. B

Applying the Concept 3-2

1. B
2. D
3. A
4. C
5. E

Applying the Concept 3-3

1. B
2. D
3. C
4. G
5. F
6. A
7. G
8. B
9. E
10. C

Chapter 4

Applying the Concept 4-1

1. D
2. I
3. B
4. A
5. G
6. H
7. E
8. C
9. J
10. F

Applying the Concept 4-2

1. A
2. A
3. B
4. A
5. A

Applying the Concept 4-3

1. B
2. D
3. E
4. A
5. C

Chapter 5

Applying the Concept 5-1

1. E/B
2. H/A
3. B/A
4. G/B
5. D/B

Applying the Concept 5-2

1. D
2. A
3. C
4. F
5. E

Applying the Concept 5-3

1. C
2. A
3. C
4. D
5. A

Applying the Concept 5-4

1. C
2. A
3. B
4. D
5. C

Chapter 6

Applying the Concept 6-1

1. A
2. A
3. B
4. B
5. B

Applying the Concept 6-2

1. D
2. B
3. C
4. A

Applying the Concept 6-3

1. A
2. C
3. B

Applying the Concept 6-4

1. F
2. C
3. H
4. D
5. E
6. G
7. B
8. I

Chapter 7

Applying the Concept 7-1

1. A
2. A
3. B
4. B
5. A

Applying the Concept 7-2

1. B
2. C
3. A
4. C
5. A

Applying the Concept 7-3

1. B

2. A
3. C
4. D
5. C

Applying the Concept 7-4

1. B
2. D
3. C
4. A
5. E

Chapter 8

Applying the Concept 8-1

1. A
2. D
3. B
4. C
5. D

Applying the Concept 8-2

1. C
2. D
3. B
4. A
5. C

Applying the Concept 8-3

1. B
2. F
3. D
4. G
5. A

Applying the Concept 8-4

1. C
2. E
3. A
4. B
5. D

Chapter 9

Applying the Concept 9-1

1. E
2. B
3. H
4. D
5. F
6. A
7. G
8. I
9. C
10. F

Applying the Concept 9-2

1. D
2. B
3. E
4. A
5. C

Applying the Concept 9-3

1. A
2. B
3. B
4. A
5. A

Chapter 10

Applying the Concept 10-1

1. F
2. J
3. E
4. C
5. G

Applying the Concept 10-2

1. B
2. A
3. B
4. B
5. A

Applying the Concept 10-3

1. A
2. B
3. B
4. A
5. B

Applying the Concept 10-4

1. C
2. A
3. G
4. B
5. D

Chapter 11

Applying the Concept 11-1

1. B
2. A
3. B
4. B
5. A

Applying the Concept 11-2

1. A
2. B
3. B

4. A
5. B

Applying the Concept 11-3

1. C
2. A
3. D
4. B

Applying the Concept 11-4

1. B
2. A
3. C

Applying the Concept 11-5

1. A
2. B
3. A

Subject Index